Ibadan

Wole Soyinka was born
was educated at Government College, Ibadan and
then at England's Leeds University, and worked
in British theatre before returning to Nigeria in
1960. His earlier prose works include *The
Interpreters*, which was awarded the Jock
Campbell Prize for Commonwealth Literature.
Wole Soyinka received a New Statesman John
Whiting Award for 1966–67 and was Overseas
Fellow at Churchill College, Cambridge in
1973–74, where he wrote the widely acclaimed
Death and the King's Horseman. He has been
awarded the George Benson Medal of the Royal
Society of Literature and the Unesco Medal for
the Arts. In 1986 he became the first African
writer to win the Nobel Prize for Literature.

Wole Soyinka

IBADAN
The Penkelemes Years
A Memoir: 1946–1965

Minerva

A Minerva Paperback
IBADAN

First published in Great Britain 1994
by Methuen London
This Minerva edition published 1995
by Mandarin Paperbacks
an imprint of Reed Consumer Books Ltd
Michelin House, 81 Fulham Road, London SW3 6RB
and Auckland, Melbourne, Singapore and Toronto

Copyright © 1994 by Wole Soyinka
The author has asserted his moral rights

A CIP catalogue record for this title
is available from the British Library
ISBN 0 7493 9590 7

Printed and bound in Great Britain
by Cox & Wyman Ltd, Reading, Berkshire

Dedicated to
Madam Olabisi, Ayinke Akindele ('Alhaja')
and other unsung volunteers who gave silently,
spontaneously and with unflagging commitment

Contents

Foreword

IBADAN does not pretend to be anything but faction, that much abused genre which attempts to fictionalise facts and events, the proportion of fact to fiction being totally at the *discretion* of the author. My adoption of the genre stops short of the actual *invention* of facts or events, however, or the deliberate distortion of the history or character of any known figure. It has become one of the hazards of having a public name, when this licentious principle is not only put into practice, but is defended by some writers and critics, perhaps in the belief that public figures – especially if they are unfortunate enough to have died recently – have no further right to their authentic existence. In recent times, in the United States most notoriously, it would appear that such writers cannot even wait for the blissful translation of the victim to the limbo of indifference. And sometimes, of course, such practitioners are not even of the breed who profess the vocation of fiction, or faction, or indeed literature of any kind: their mission is anything but the establishment of truth or the elevation of the imagination.

That last observation only partly explains why I succumbed, in the end, to the incitement (no less) to embark on a 'Son of *Aké*', (and in the future, alas, on a 'Son of *Ibadan*' – now a must!) After I had written *Aké* I was quite confident of having successfully 'perished the thought' by simply retreating into a pre-*Aké* narrative – *Ìsarà* – and was embarking on plans to write one or two biographies of certain Nigerian characters whose personalities have consistently intrigued me.

The principal general cause of my change of mind (and temporary suspension of those other projects) came from the politics, the unfinished business, of that political entity, Nigeria, into which I happen to have been born, its sociology and political pathology, especially as the last relates to my primary constituency – the university – with which I still retain a love-hate relationship. The immediate, triggering event was the Nigerian 1993 democratic venture and its aftermath.

Underlying it all is also the agonising, truly lamentable brief memory span that appears to bedevil my society. Well, perhaps it is not so much a matter of mental retention as the seeming inability to extend meaningfully the *affective* span of memory. It was not by chance that I selected – for a volume of Nigerian essays that was meant for publication over two years ago (and may yet emerge this year) – the title *Continuity and Amnesia*.

We have been through this before; we appear never to have left this groove! That, in effect, is what finally provoked this 'autobiography' into being. For fear of being hauled up for breach of the Trade Descriptions Act, let me rush to say that *Ibadan* tries very hard *not* to be about politics, but does concede that its author was a by-product of the *penkelemes* of Nigerian politics, and, indeed, sociology. *Penkelemes*? In a moment.

Let me be a little more forthcoming. As the current president of the Association of Nigerian Authors, the poet Odia Oleimun – and other *agents provocateurs* – will confirm, I had indeed resisted all their efforts to provoke me into any autobiographical account beyond the age of eleven – the age of innocence for most, certainly somewhat earlier or later for others. Any testament after the 'age of innocence' is a lie, or half-truth, doctored truth, selective truth or annotated truth, or – in simple diction – a confection of sorts. I was content to let others do the lying or fantasizing – at least, until some time between the dates of 12 June and 27 August 1993, Nigerian datelines. The first, 12 June, was the date on which Nigerians triumphed over every act of sabotage by the incumbent military dictator, Ibrahim Babangida, aided by his civilian accomplices, such as the Minister of Injustice, Clement Akpango; the Minister of Disinformation, 'Comrade' Chukwumerije, known variously as 'Lord Haw-Haw' and 'Joseph Goebbels'; and the arch-villain, Arthur Nzeribe, a notorious arms dealer and ponce of power, self-declared leader of a mythical group that called itself Association for Better Nigeria, with a ghost list of twenty-seven million members – out of a total population of ninety million Nigerians! The all-powerful Controller, financier and hit man was General Halilu Akilu, head of the nation's combined security forces, a Uriah Heep in military attire. More of him in another place. On that day, 12 June, however, democratic elections were held SUCCESSFULLY, without any dissent from within or from various groups of international observers.

27 August was the date on which ten years of continuous military rule would terminate, a stretch which came after a brief four-year civilian intervention in nearly thirty years of rule by guns, boots, loot, whip, whims, decrees and prison bars. To forestall this handing-over date, seeing that the elections had not proceeded the way he had planned, General Babangida nudged his errand boy, Arthur Nzeribe, to file a phony legal action to stop the continuation of the formal broadcasting of the election results – over one-half being already announced and all results already posted in the various states. A handpicked rookie judge, duly briefed, obliged. The opposition filed five counter suits to compel the Electoral Commission to release all remaining results: all five appeals, in courts of both equal and higher jurisdiction, were granted. Babangida then annulled the entire elections in order to 'save the judiciary from being thrown into disrepute'! It is doubtful whether the entirety of Nigerian history can match such a coldly calculating expression of provocation, disdain and cynicism.

The most violent day of the first wave of protest riots was the second one, on 27 June. I was in the bloodstained midst of it all between Badagry and Lagos, crossing over a hundred roadblocks, manned by truly angry and determined citizens – civil servants, businessmen and women, professionals, artisans, students – and a number also by plain cut-throats, extortionists and opportunists, the so-called 'area boys'. I was compelled to address the crowd on four occasions, and was eventually responsible for dispersing thousands of them that same night in the Agege-Ipaja sector. Two hundred people died, mostly shot by the Police and the Army; several more were blinded or crippled for life. Shortly after, I left Nigeria to reinforce the President-Elect's worldwide campaign for recognition. I was still in Washington when I received frantic messages that I should remain outside the country. In short, I found myself once again in undeclared exile.

During this period, in a Japanese restaurant in Swiss Cottage, London, at a birthday dinner to honour the Nigerian President Elect, Basorun M. K. O. Abiola, I found myself suddenly overwhelmed by a disorientating feeling, a combination perhaps of unreality and of *déja vu*. It was an eerie echo of a 'last supper' – a lunch it was, in fact – that I had partaken of nearly thirty years before with my late friend, the insurance broker and actor, Femi Johnson, just before I embarked on a course of action that could only lead to a fugitive existence.

This time (in July 1993), our birthday celebrant, Abiola, had himself been compelled to flee Nigeria, soon after my own departure, for reasons of life and death. The civilian controller of the conspirators against Abiola's safety, the same insolvent Government lickspittle, Arthur Nzeribe, would later boast in the public media of his role. Among those present at the dinner, I recall some half dozen faces – two of Abiola's children; the West-Indian-born parliamentarian, Bernie Grant; Patrick Wilmot, bundled out of Nigeria some years before like a sack of potatoes; Lord Avebury, a passionate but tersely discriminating Africa-phile from the House of Lords; and a former President of the Nigerian Bar Association, Aka-Bashorun, who had himself fled Nigeria two years before. The celebrant himself arrived, as usual, panting late.

I had long given up the President-Elect as a stubborn, irredeemable disciple of the philosophy of non-violence and, early that morning, had been in a totally different kind of gathering. This also involved several fugitives from the mailed fists of the Nigerian military, including an ex-soldier who was introduced as having been involved in the attempted *putsch* of 22 April 1990 against Babangida. At the Swiss Cottage get-together, however, I was struck by the contrast between the moods of the two gatherings – both resolute and committed, yes, but one upbeat, while the other was sombre. At the end of the earlier meeting, I knew that I was about to set off on a long journey, had no idea how long it would be, or how it would end, but I found that I had come round yet again to an acceptance of a less pacific principle of response as being justifiable in the cause of terminating the *penkelemes* of Babangida's eight-year military despotism. I suppose it is at such moments that one tends to look back on one's existence, and begin to accept the necessity of setting something down. Certainly, I began to think seriously of hoarding some exile time for the project.

Ah yes, *penkelemes*! Starched khaki or civilian variety, there cannot be many of the generation of 'Maren' – the name (also occasionally Akínkòyí) under which the author has chosen to masquerade in this narrative – who can boast of having heard the expression. The inventor and embodiment of this deliberate, populist corruption of 'peculiar mess' was, appropriately, a certain Ibadan *shon of de shoil**** by the name of Adelabu. If the calculations of this political maverick had been as certain as his charisma, Adelabu would have become the first Premier of the Western Region of Nigeria, in 1958. Such was his hold on his followers that when, as a then regional Minister, he was accused of financial wrongdoings, he drove his newly acquired motorcar into Dugbe market and invited the throng to ride in it and treat it as their own, protesting: 'This is what I bought with the money I am alleged to have stolen. It belongs to you all. Treat it as your very own property.'

If they could have done so, the ecstatic crowd would have lifted the car, with him in it, and danced round the town. It was, however, one of those long, gaudy American limousines so beloved of the first-generation politicians, so they settled for carrying him shoulder-high all the way from Dugbe to Mapo Hall, taking up the song that a voice from the crowd had spontaneously composed:

> *Owo o wa ni, saa maa na b'o ti fe.*
> *Owo o wa ni'saa maa na b'o ti fe*
> *Se bi 'gunnu lo ni Tapa*
> *Tapa lo ni 'gunnu.*
> *Owo o wa ni, saa maa na b'o ti fe!†*

The excitement mounted. They proceeded to the living quarters of his main detractor, summoned him out, stripped him naked and ransacked his residence.

I missed the Adelabu phenomenon in its entirety as I was then still a 'student abroad' in those days of partial Independence, and

---

*Son of the soil
†Isn't the money ours? Go ahead, spend it as you please.
 The *igunnu* mask belongs to the *Tapa*
 The *Tapa* owns the *igunnu*. So?
 The money is ours – go on, spend it as you please!

the 'stormy petrel' of Ibadan was dead before my return. Nevertheless, politics in the early sixties was still very much of the Adelabu type, at once fascinating and repulsive, with figures as charismatic as they were unconscionable, sometimes downright evil. Invariably, they proved rallying points for the basest instincts, as much of the 'many-headed multitude' as of the individual or cabal operators, cynical, calculating, sophisticated and opportunistic. In short, *plus ça change . . .* ?

I have kept some real names in this book, quite a number, in fact, unavoidably. Even total faction must be anchored in some recognisable historical reference points. Because the originator of '*Penkelemes*' was from our own Government College, Ibadan, let me use the example of the light-hearted secondary-school section in this narrative to make a special appeal to the 'old boys' who read it to excuse any lapses of memory in my account but, more generally, to illustrate that aspect of faction that I have tended mostly to employ – the deliberate dislocation of some actual names and events from their physical moorings and, occasionally, actual time.

The character of Komi, for instance, is a three-in-one composite: 'P.O.' from the class of '46; Oso, an engineer who never even attended G.C.I. and now lives in Bodija, Ibadan – he was the one who nearly lost an ear; plus a fair amount of input from yet a third individual who has implored me to leave him out of anything I write!

With whom did I have that acid fight? I am no longer certain, so I have logged it among 'Major Kakiika's' seeming attempts to terminate my existence – it seems fair enough, since he did throw me through a glass pane in the library door. And *please* don't write to correct me about the episode of the lightning bolt, which I have hoisted from its place of occurrence – the uncompleted building near the school farm, where three of us had taken refuge during a thunderstorm – and transposed it onto the occasion when a snake decided to take shelter from the rain in the prep room, selecting the space beneath my feet – perhaps because they didn't touch the ground. (There was yet another that we found coiled under my pillow when I transferred to the new (Field) House.) It will be obvious that I had to save up the appearance of the snake for its more interesting cohabitation scenario in Agodi. No reader would believe the actual persistence of snakes in their recurring, strange and dramatic attachment to this now fictionalised person of Maren, continuing all the way from *Aké*. Even to me, it sometimes appears abnormal.

And so on and so forth: never really more – I have tried to ensure – than the most mundane literary opportunism.

For the rest, I have indemnified my publishers against any charge of libel.

Wole Soyinka
Abeokuta, 13 February, 1994

1 Homecomer

Homecoming was, at the time, so ordinary, so uneventful that even he felt dissatisfied. Something was missing. This end to a five-year absence, a fifth, nearly, of his entire life, lacked some form of rounding-off, a ritual resonance that would echo, even as it reversed, the excited yet unformed longings that surrounded his departure. Yet the secretive approach was, after all, what he had determined and plotted, a quiet return, known only to a trusted few. And he had waited until after the familial claims of christmas and the New Year, exchanging the bleak, weepy skies of London on the first day of the year, for a Harmattan mist and spiral wisps from invisible bushfires, distant from the airport, he hoped. A dawn landing. The picture-postcard skyline of egrets that the plane had displaced from the tarmac, etched on his instantly dehydrating skin the once familiar patterns of seasonal responses. Excepting the hard noon heat that would come later, the Harmattan, he acknowledged, was a good season for blurring absences and separations; it had this disposition, one that came back to him in a nostalgic flash, that just as it muted the hard edges of walls and roofs, limbs and faces, it also dissolved the past and time, and his mind leapt the intervening years to yet another Harmattan, and a time, for him, of momentous change. Already he could predict the same negotiation of the ties of blood, love and/or possessiveness.

It would come no easier, he knew, simply because this was familiar territory. The first skirmish was after secondary school but that was one contest that he had easily lost, the odds were too heavily weighted against a sixteen-year-old, sixteen and a half to be exact. His armoury then was of the purely speculative kind that made him buy a shaving set with his very first salary – earned as a Stores Assistant in the Government Medical Department. It had seemed so obvious at the time, to him at least, if to no one else. One left school; therefore one became an adult, and this meant that facial hair followed as a matter of course. The seal on the plastic case of the shaving set remained unbroken for nearly three years, no matter how hard he gazed in the mirror, day after day, then weekly and month after month, drew a finger over the upper lip or rubbed his chin in impatience. The elusive hair waited until he had given the set away as a christmas present to a cousin in shared exile. Then, perhaps in defence against that first assault of winter in northern England, the first timid tufts emerged, much too late to join in the battle against familial attrition on his self-determined, adult status. Leeds and a scholarship were, he felt, a divine intervention on his side, cleaving the battleground to win a five-year respite. He did not deceive himself, it was only a welcome respite and he knew that a resumption of the contest only awaited his return. Returning now, it was best to signal, from the beginning, his unyielding stance.

He struggled through crowds of jubilant relations towards the figure of Komi, his main conspirator, glad to see that he had entered into the spirit of the game and isolated himself from the delirious throng. So far, the return was perfect, this much at least had been achieved – avoiding the fate which awaited most of his fellow passengers: they would be whisked off straight to a thanksgiving service, then rounds of family reunions, grand receptions, speeches and toasts and the endless chain of blood claimants. . . no, none of that for him. Still, something was missing. Was it perhaps a sensation, something he ought to feel, and did not? As if responsive to his thoughts, Komi hugged him yet again, staring at him with wonder in his eyes.

'So-o-be! Na your face this?'

'What?' For a brief moment he was blank, then Maren gasped as he recalled the near-disaster that had earned him the nickname.

'Oh my god!'

'So-be!'

'Oh, you! Are you ever going to let me live that down?'

Komi fingered the junction of his right ear and head, and grinned. 'Not while this hidden scar is still alive and kicking.'

The homecomer sighed, shook his head. 'Ah well. The partitions between rooms are solid concrete these days anyway.'

'I still prefer the old site. I never got used to that new campus, you know. All glitter and no soul.'

'Your soul is simply conservative, full stop!'

Komi shook his head, suddenly morose. 'It's like this Independence,' he complained. 'They're tearing up everything, and wait till you see the replacements . . .'

'What have they torn up now?'

'Wait. You'll see for yourself. And I'm not talking simply about buildings. Oh, look at me welcoming you back with my grouse routine. I've been boring everyone to death with it. Actually some things are not so bad. And there are still nine months before October first.' They moved towards the uncompleted car park, picking their way through the workmen's rubble. 'So how was the flight? Are you glad to be back?'

The homecomer looked around the hazy surrounding. 'I wouldn't know yet, would I? But I'll tell you something. I must have been damned eager to get back, so eager I was afraid deep down that something might happen to prevent it at the last moment. You'll see what I mean when you receive an unusual present in your mail.'

Did you have to sneak home like a thief in the night?

The insurance policy machine gave him away – to himself, that is. At London airport, he encountered the instant policy dispenser for the first time, and simply lost control, spending like a long-unemployed pools winner let loose in a shopping arcade. It was a compulsion; within minutes he had purchased half a dozen, five shillings premium apiece for a windfall of five thousand pounds. Now he began to suspect why his return had appeared so uneventful. The beneficiaries were firstly his parents, then the mother of the son he was leaving behind, next his siblings. So far the consideration could be deemed rational. So was the policy mailed to the Head of the University Department to which he would be attached in Ibadan; he owed her some money. A short while later, however, he had bought and mailed her yet another policy, adding a letter that named her, in effect, executor for an unwritten Last Will and Testament!

Then the bug truly bit him and he began to think of anyone he knew – I know I shall never live rich, he announced to his fellow travellers returning, like him, from their study stint in the colonial stronghold, but this is my only chance to boast I shall die rich! Others spent their spare money on gifts of a different kind, bewildered at the abandon with which he filled out one form after the other, assailed by such a prodigal generosity that he even asked them to volunteer names of deserving beneficiaries from their own families. They moved away from him, superstitious. A few wondered if they should abandon their flight; this fellow was acting not merely as if he was afraid the plane would crash, but as if he actually wanted it to crash!

But he continued purchasing more policies from the automated machine, filling out the forms and popping them in the special post box. Then he settled down to writing to the one who had attracted the double policy: 'Thank you once again for that rescue remittance to me in Paris, and here is an insurance cover for repayment, just in case: the surplus is so you can help establish the kind of theatre company we discussed.' He could not avoid feeling that there was something a little abnormal about the proceedings or at least, that a virtual stranger – they had met only once – might find it weird, so he tried to reassure her: 'I intend to make it home, of course, but I am rather enjoying this sudden idea for which the automated insurance machines should, in any case, be held responsible. I hope you don't imagine that I am being morbid; on the contrary, I am suddenly over-anxious at the thought of returning home after five years. I can't imagine why anything should stop me but, after all, planes do crash, which is why someone thought of installing the machines here in the first place. I mean, I do not expect this one to crash, but it would be such a mindless shame if one did fail to make it home after all, and then, to add insult to injury, lost the one opportunity of making things happen much faster than they ever would relying on one's lifetime's savings or on fledgling governments which believe that the Arts come last in a newly independent state, etc, etc . . .' Ah well, to hell with it – he crossed out most of what he had written and then decided that it was simpler to take out the middle page altogether – let her think me touched in the head by snowstroke; he posted the truncated letter with the policies.

No, he continued to assure himself, as he noted the wary distance the others maintained from him, it was neither morbidity nor fatalism, just plain common sense. But also something beyond it, this orgy of distributing largesse as he took the definitive step towards homecoming. He became drunk on the idea. Impecunious, yet, at least for the duration of the flight, he was the unseen god of plenty showering plenitude on unsuspecting recipients miles below. The conceit remained with him throughout, and perhaps prompted his sense of deflation when the plane made its final landing and all his policies were voided. But the contradiction was apparent to his co-passengers, who eyed him triumphantly after the plane had taxied to a stop, part convinced that the flight had signified a contest of wills. Hang your head in shame, their looks said, all your psychopathic hopes have come to nought. No use insisting any further that he was nowhere close to wishing, much less willing the plane to crash. If the slightest shred of such a destructive thought had nudged his mind – and his grandfather had warned him against invoking the power of the god of metals even in a moment of levity – he would not have moved near the insurance machine. No, the opposite was the case; he was simply delirious with anticipation, and apprehensive, all within the same impulse.

A definite lightheadedness, yes, the euphoric feeling of terminating yet another phase of his existence, but again, he recognised something else. Deep down, as the moment approached for boarding and his meagre savings finally approached depletion, he began to suspect that all this was the surfacing of things forgotten, like the making of *saara*.* The urge had risen without effort, and he had submitted to it in a mood akin to embracing a foretaste of what was yet to come. Home had reached out to him in London, in tantalising fragments; in reality he was acting no differently from what awaited the others on landing – the thanksgiving services, the rounds of celebration feasts, the rituals of reintegrating the long-absent spirit. He had stolen a march on the others, that was all it was, a sudden upsurge of long-suppressed observances, and he had begun to

*A communal sacrificial feast.

improvise, scattering his minted *akara** and *ekuru*† to the winds, to be carried into the rafters of the gods' abode.

The road through Ikorodu was the shorter route from Lagos to Ibadan, even in its uncompleted state, and Komi turned his car in that direction, but the homecomer said, 'No, let's take the other route.'

'You mean, go through Abeokuta?'

'Hn-hn.'

'But I thought you said you wanted to avoid . . .'

'We won't stop. Just drive straight through.'

Komi gave his companion a strange look, but turned the car in the desired direction, shaking his head dubiously. 'Before I forget, congratulations.'

Receiving only a puzzled look in reply, he smiled. 'Your reputation preceded you. Two of your plays were staged at Ibadan University, remember?'

'Oh, yeah.'

He mimicked him. ' "Oh, yeah." Just like that? How many indigenous plays do you see performed in the country? You had two, and they were very successful. And then you had the London performance you mentioned in your last letter . . .'

The passenger squirmed. 'Don't remind me of that. Terrible night.'

'Yeah, I bet you would say that. Nothing would satisfy you unless you landed on Broadway.'

'Broadway! Oh, you ignorant stay-at-home. You think Broadway is theatre?'

'Isn't it? Well, Broadway is the place we hear most about. And Hollywood. Anyway, as far as everyone here is concerned, you are already famous. And all those short stories and talks over the BBC? I used to send word to Abeokuta any time there was notice of something by you.'

'Oh. Well, I'm sure they appreciated it.'

---

*Bean cake.
†Baked bean granules.

'Of course they did.' He eyed him warily, waited some moments. 'Are you quite sure you don't want to stop at Aké?'

'Later. When I've settled down.'

So it became a triple betrayal. It was bad enough that he arrived without notice; he had chosen to head straight for Ibadan and, most unforgivable of all, this involved sneaking through Abeokuta without stopping.

'I may tell them later that I had just enough time to make an interview for a position.'

Komi slid him a dissatisfied glance. 'I am glad your conscience is at least troubling you. But that excuse simply won't wash.'

The homecomer shrugged. 'It will have to do. After all, they can't go checking on me at the University.' He chuckled. 'Please, Mr Registrar or Professor Head of Department, when did our son actually return? And why have you kept him away from his loving family all this while?'

Komi shook his head in mock despair. 'You are a ba-a-a-d son.'

For a while, they drove in silence, then Komi decided it was time to raise the one subject that still made him nervous. 'Oh, er . . . talking about bad sons and so on, how did they take it?'

'Take what?'

'Your marriage, of course. Oh, I take it you did go through with it.'

'Of course. I had decided, or I wouldn't have written you. But I didn't inform them.'

Komi nearly lost control of the car. 'You did not – what?'

'Hey, steady! What's the matter with you?'

'You did not inform them? Oh my God, how am I ever going to face them? There is no way I'll ever persuade them I knew nothing about it.'

'But you did.' And the homecomer was laughing. 'You're implicated.'

Komi cut a doleful image, sinking deeper in exaggerated misery. 'This really puts me in their soup. They'll never trust me after this.'

'You are not the one who got married – why should they take it out on you?'

'He married a white woman, he married a white woman and you didn't tell us! You rush to inform us when he's going to tell his stories on the BBC but not when he's making a story of his own life, and a dangerous story at that. You're supposed to be his friend; you're like a son in this house and yet you keep this from us. Ah, Sobe, how can I ever face Mamma after this?'

'I wrote them about the child . . .'

He screamed at him. 'You know that's different! To them the two things are separate, at least when it's between us and *them*.' Then he became curious. 'By the way, why? You've always said you were the non-marrying type. What made you change your mind? You didn't explain. Just the one throwaway sentence in the midst of – weightier – matters.'

Maren looked grimly ahead. Across his mind flashed several scenes: the slights; the condescensions; the subterfuges; the crude rejections and the subtle, smarmy type that made you want to push his jutting nose into the slab of pale flesh; the obvious excuses that would not fool a child, nor were meant to; the flat refusals; the dual-function glance, seeing and unseeing in a single motion; the self-conscious retreats; the unhumanising retraction within the touch that could not be avoided; the fierce showdowns with landlords and landladies, even involving the police, unapologetic in their racist conditioning, indeed glorying in their moment of unmediated power, since their accuser had less than human standing . . .

'You do remember my *Telephone Conversation*, don't you?'

'Oh yes, god, I've read and re-read it, I don't know how many times.'

'It's a very racist country still, Komi. And also damned puritani-cal, you know, sanctimonious. Oh, there are circles in which you can move, protected from it all. But you had to go home in the end; you had always to bear that in mind. You had to go back to that bed-sitter and pass the racist bitches on the landing, wheeling in their lily-white, inside-wedlock brats and looking down on the woman beside you, with the tanned baby. And of course the first thing they always found out – don't ask me how – was the non-marital situation. *Oh, the shameless girl, she's not even married, you know, the nerve of her to walk about with that baby!* You had to go to the shops, enter buses, walk in the park or go to the cinema. Even apply for jobs, no matter how temporary. I could cope, you see. As long as I was around, I knew damned well how to deal with them.

But then it was time for me to leave. By then we were already living apart and I saw what was going on when she was on her own. I had to reduce the boy's handicap some way. Nothing I could do about the milk chocolate but at least I could provide some protection on the other front. Look, you'll be amazed how much of a stigma attaches to it in that country . . .'

'Is it any different here?'

'Very, very different, believe me. Of course there are exceptions. In certain circles . . .'

'Precisely. That's the point I'm making.'

'Well, I've never considered myself part of such circles. And I intend to make damned sure I never stray into them.'

'All right. Good luck. But you still haven't said how, if or when you'll break the news at home.'

The homecomer shrugged. 'All in good time. Who knows? We may decide we want to give it a try out here – living together that is. Anything may happen. My outlook on life may change, or hers. The two may suddenly coincide: it would take a miracle, I know, but – bingo – you'll find yourself a best man at the second edition of the wedding, with all the traditional trimmings. Haven't you heard the expression: "Never say never?" '

'You'll break their hearts,' he sing-songed.

'Don't waste your sympathy on those two. They're tough. But soft, too, in places. I know them. They cannot even wait to see their grandson.'

'Yes, but without the mother, as long as she's white.'

'Komi, better get your shoulder ready for them to weep on, because one thing I am dead certain about, who I live with is strictly between me and the who. Just as who I sleep with is strictly an issue of consenting adults. My embrace of "tradition" is very selective – look, we've thrashed all this out in our letters . . .'

'This is not correspondence, this is the real thing. Real people. Real families. Real expectations.'

'Then why are you conspiring to drive me through Abeokuta without stopping and doing the rounds of expectations?'

'This is your show. I'm doing a brother a favour. Even the law accepts the plea of "Guilty, with extenuating circumstances".'

'No, no, no,' warned the homecomer. 'That won't help you one bit. The verdict will still read: Warri boy banned from further access to complainant's famous vegetable palm-oil stew with dried fish and smoked crayfish and *temperead*** snails and locust, bean and smoked pork and aromatic peppers in quadruplicate and . . . oh really, Komi, you deserve every punishment that comes to you! Couldn't you at least have developed a flat tyre in front of Aké church?'

Did you have to sneak home like a thief in the night?

Suddenly it all seemed so remote, even a little unreal, and this included the immediate past of a bare week or two, three weeks, or a year – or a mere yesterday. The transition from alien winter to Harmattan was sudden, and he had preferred it that way, foregoing the choice of a ten-day journey by boat. But he found himself intrigued by the negative images that clung with such tenacity to his mind. The moors of Yorkshire, their fluid slopes of green and snow pocked with furry anguish, dead and dying rabbit victims of myxomatosis, a viral warfare that was launched, it was claimed, from Australia. Now why that, of all the receding images? It had, after all, happened years before, the very year that followed his arrival in Leeds. Perhaps it was the Harmattan mist, evoking the moorland fog that shredded in patches beneath a tepid sun – those weekend hikes that tried to substitute for rambling through the tropical-bush surround of Government College and later, Oshodi. And the car had just slowed down at the railway crossing after Odeda, and into the smoky line of venison on charcoal grills, a few rodent grasscutters and antelopes, fresh from the hunters' guns, suspended from stakes. Myxomatosis had blighted much of the Yorkshire Moors' delight, as did the cold slush that seeped through supposedly waterproofed boots and the several layers of woollen socks. No, there was far too much padding required, and too-soon frozen fingertips and ears – always the most vulnerable – to sustain for long the eagerness which the moors had, at first, evoked in him.

It all receded further and further into alien time, and this within a flight of fourteen hours – stops in Tripoli, Kano . . . the companion textures, faces, voices and sanitised smells and colours of five years

*Fabulously seasoned.

beginning to fade in the spotty light of Harmattan. He clung to a handful of kindred sensations. Autumn in Europe was closest to this season, but the Harmattan lacked its chromatic rave that slowly, with such tenacious protest, weakened in stages and fell to earth, curling inwards to brown deaths to be swept into brief mounds by wind or broom. Harmattan fell to earth in one sere, crinkly swoop; one moment proud tassels, defiant leaves and lethargic pods, the next, nothing but skeletal stalks and inward curling blades awaiting the stray flicker from bush fires. When the hardy, drought-resistant flowers came into their own, lording it over denuded boughs, saturating the air with pollen dust, there would be clouds of dark butterflies, while the earth became riddled by spiked caterpillars that left persistent itches on bare feet. Within its dust-speckled air, it was only a matter of time before he began to feel disembodied, a favourite escape sensation whenever he was crowded by approaching changes – spaces, seasons, human ties . . . decisions of some weight, of risk, confrontations, or uncertain consequences, but always the overwhelming certitude of change. The Harmattan was the more-than-willing agent of transition.

> *Where hast tha been since I saw thee?*
> *On Ilkley Moor baht'at.*
> *Where hast tha been since I saw thee?*
> *Where hast tha been since I saw thee?*
> *On Ilkley Moor baht'at,*
> *On Ilkley Moor baht'at,*
> *On Ilkley Moor baht'at.*
>
> *I've been a-courting Mary Jane*
> *On Ilkley Moor baht'at . . .*
>
> *There thou shalt catch thy death of cold*
> *On Ilkley Moor baht'at . . .*
>
> *Then we shall have to bury thee*
> *On Ilkley Moor baht'at . . .*
>
> *Then worms will come and et thee up*
> *On Ilkley Moor baht'at . . .*
>
> *Then ducks will come and et up worms*
> *On Ilkley Moor baht'at . . .*

Then we shall come and et up ducks
On Ilkley Moor baht'at . . .

Then we shall all have eten thee
On Ilkley Moor baht'at . . .

Ilkley Moor had long since yielded to the lure of London theatres; and the lowlands of Holland where he built houses; and the Isle of Man, where he served drunken Scots and Irish; and other waystops, where he simply did as others or did not; . . . but the letter from Ibadan finally caught up with him in Paris: did he have any immediate to future plans to return home? Oh yes indeed, he had long fled the North anyway, never had any intention of remaining long enough to be eten up with Yorkshire pudding on Ilkley Moor baht'at – he never did discover the meaning of that refrain.

Did he think that he might be interested in a place in the English Department? The writer, the Head of Department, had hoped to meet him in London, but learnt that he was in Paris. She could meet him there if he wished: she had business in Paris and would gladly time her visit for their mutual convenience. One of her staff, on leave at his home in England, had heard of a Nigerian who had staged a play at a students' drama festival in London. He tracked him down, obtained copies of his two scripts and took them back to be staged at the University theatre in Ibadan. The new Arts Theatre was under construction when Maren had left Ibadan five years earlier; he could hardly wait to see the completed structure and sample its spatial offerings. The signs were propitious – at least within the hallowed walls of academia; it was clearly time to return. Negotiating the conditions of his return was easy enough; all that remained was to negotiate the manner of homecoming, to create space around himself, large enough to insulate himself from, or confront, the menace of an incipient disorder, one that an apprehensive few had begun to suspect from the bearing and language of rival claimants to the midwifery of a new society; it was a disorder he preferred to diagnose as a common lust for power.

Did you have to sneak in like a thief in the night?

'It would serve you right if someone who knew you caught a glimpse of you.'

'They would think it was a ghost; or they wouldn't believe their eyes.'

'Later they would. When you finally decide to reveal your presence, that person would put two and two together. And if it were someone with any curiosity, a simple check at the airport . . .'

'Nobody is that idle.'

'Talking of ghosts,' Komi persisted, 'that very word spells your greatest danger. You know our people. If they are really convinced that they saw someone who is supposed to be miles away, they assume it is his ghost come to announce his death. If you hear that the household has been thrown into premature mourning, you'll never forgive yourself.'

'All right, all right, I'll go through Abeokuta crouching down. As a matter of fact, you have no idea how right you are. My sister had a very warm welcome home on that account.'

Teniola had also 'sneaked' in, although she had not really intended to do so. Her nursing course completed, she had booked herself on the *M. V. Apapa* and duly informed the home front. However, the boat had docked early, taking ten instead of twelve days. Impatient to be home, Teni cleared her luggage, obtained a lift from a cousin and appeared in Aké at dusk. Neither parent was home, they had gone to spend the night in Lagos so as to meet the boat as it docked the following morning. Mayode, the baby of the family, was in the dining room, about to begin his supper of *eba* and vegetable stew. He was only seven but apparently had a good recollection of his elder sister whom he had not seen for three years. The rest of the household were busy with various chores in the backyard.

Teniola entered the front room, calling out but receiving no response. She proceeded through the parlour, the darkest unit of the house at any time of day but particularly grey and silent at dusk. She probably lingered in the familiar room, savouring the familiar smells, glancing at the framed homilies that hung on the walls before emerging through the open doorway into the dining room like a soft shadow that had detached itself from the twilight gloom. She extended her arms, expecting Mayode to leap into her embrace. Instead, the gloom was pierced by his scream.

'It's me, Mayode. Teni. Don't you recognise me?'

'Go away! Get away from me.'

Teni moved forward, her smile broadening. Mayode leapt from his bench, clutching his plate of *eba*-and-stew and extending it forward like a defensive shield.

'But it's me. Don't you remember me?'

Mayode remembered her only too well, and knew she was not supposed to be in Aké in the flesh. Nobody had told him his sister was on her way back, nor that his parents had gone to Lagos to meet the boat. So, as Teni advanced, he retreated. Through the door, into the backyard, Mayode backwards, a smiling Teni gently forwards. Then came the moment when Mayode grew desperate at this apparition that refused to vanish even in the clearer light of the open courtyard. He flung his plate of *eba*, stew and all, at Teni, then turned and fled, screaming all the way through the gate into the parsonage proper, heading towards the catechist's house next door.

'You know,' as Maren recounted the story to Komi, 'my father wrote me about it. He was particularly gleeful about the flying *eba* welcome. He said it served her right, and let that be a lesson to me, he added.'

'But it wasn't really her fault.'

'For both parents, and for the clan of friends and relations that had proceeded to the port to receiver her, it was a capital offence. She should have slept the night in her cabin, like most others, and waited to be properly welcomed.'

The long drive, he knew, would more than ease him home, internally that is, and he was right. It began appropriately when the car drove over Lafenwa bridge into his maternal town of Abeokuta, where he slid onto the car floor, only the overhead arches of the bridge and some distant rocks visible from his cramped position, and continued as they drove through Abeokuta; through the Aké of his infancy, whose church spire still stood as he remembered it, framed against the immense boulders of the parsonage; then the palace of Oba Alake, with the two now slightly chipped cement-sculpted elephants with whitewashed tusks still seated on top of the gate pillars; then the stolid Centenary Hall, and on to Adatan; after which he regained his seat in good time for the car to be swallowed by the arcade of rain trees, evenly spaced on either side; then on to

Odeda, the village whose name uniquely acknowledged its founding hunters. The passage was part of the restoration, mainly sight and odours for now, the tactile resumptions would follow in due course, a resorption on his own long-suspended but still unyielding terms, not on the terms of his blood relations and friends, warm and secure though that might be.

The aroma of roasting game gave way to the heady mix of oranges, pineapples, tangerines and bananas at the junction from Olokemeji, where he stopped to buy a basket of fruits for Molly Mahood, the Head of Department, who had wired him the money to return to London after his débâcle with the Parisian Levantine, a seedy impresario who had lured him to Paris for singing engagements and abandoned him without a centime. The memory of that final encounter still rankled; it would soon dissipate – but not altogether, no, he did not seek to forget – some day he intended to return to Paris and, better prepared, confront the villain once more. Assault, was it? Or was it mere threat his wife accused him of? No matter, he had made all kinds of friends in Paris. He could count on three or four at least who would gladly accompany him on a return encounter, and this time it would be from a position of strength.

But it was to Apataganga that he looked for the deepest restoration of his long-absent self, in a far more complete sense than Aké. Apata was where he first knew freedom, it was there, in the woods of Government College, though he had not given it much thought, or defined it thus at the time, that he had commenced a spiritual questioning and attained even some kind of resolution, still tenuous, yes, but that was where it all began, in the orchard traversed by a path with the strange name of Unter den Linden. Apataganga had, he felt, defined him in some unchangeable way and the major craving he now had was to walk through the grounds of that school again while it was empty, definitely while it was empty, which it would be at this time of the year. Apataganga was where he had first *understood* conflict. True, he had begun his induction even at Aké and Igbehin, where his aunt, Beere, Mrs Ransome-Kuti, led the women to war and routed the paramount king the Alake of Abeokuta; where the same Beere faced off the British District Officer and denounced the use of the 'yellow' Japs as guinea-pigs for the atomic bomb, rather than their fellow white Germans, whose crimes were definitely more deserving of the atomic solution. But even the war against the Alake was not concluded by the time that he left Igbehin for Government College. It had erupted all over again twice when he returned to Abeokuta on holidays, causing Beere to remark that if she were the District Officer she would banish him from Abeokuta, since his return always coincided with a resumption of the unrest.

He no longer took messages between the various women's commands, but had become involved in the women's plight on a very different level, seeing it now as part and parcel of the perennial struggle among peoples for a quality of existence that was often intangible, but was regarded by them as the *equal* of existence. It was in Government College that he became compulsively ruminant, regurgitating all the passionate debates of his father's argumentative circle, chewing them at leisure and flinging their partially acquired insights into other disputes with staff and fellow pupils alike – and failing to relate this to why he came to be regarded as a pestilence. The blatant acts of racial discrimination, in colonial Lagos especially, filtered through the woods of Government College into their classrooms, common rooms and dormitories, and the women's riots became just another facet of an overall human tableau of wrongs, like the shooting down of unarmed miners in Enugu's Iva Valley.

Then the iconic names of nationalism – Azikiwe, Imoudu, Herbert Macaulay, Mbonu Ojike, Tony Enahoro – all came alive in Government College, Ibadan, bolder than the boulders of Apataganga. It was from Apata that he had played truant and travelled to Mushin in Lagos to listen to Imoudu's fiery oratory after the massacre of Iva Valley miners, and later to watch Hubert Ogunde's musical drama on the events, *Bread and Bullets*, and be no longer surprised that the colonial Government would ban the play and imprison Hubert Ogunde for his daring. And then, of course, his own bloodying in numerous petty battles with bullies and the trivial and not-so-trivial causes, but all passionate, of life-and-death magnitude on a secondary school scale: from the very first entry through those gates he had guessed that the place would mark him for life. There was something about Ibadan itself, a definite feeling, both restraining and exciting, that he had taken away with him after his final year in school, a year earlier than more than half the class, since he was one of those not selected to participate in the post School Certificate year, newly introduced.

This feeling was that it would not be Lagos, where he had first earned a living and which might therefore claim to have turned him into an adult; and that it would not be Abeokuta where, after all, he had been born; nor Ìsarà, his second home and birthplace of his truculent grandfather; nor indeed any place that he had yet to visit, but Ibadan itself, with its rusted arteries, its ancient warrens and passions and intrigues, that would confirm what he had begun to be apprehensive about, in himself. Others might give it different names, but he was inclined to see it as having a preternatural affinity to a lightning rod. Was it not during the very first rains of that first year in Apataganga that lightning had struck the prep room, travelling down the surface wiring and exploding the switch next to his head? Even tough, clowning Ezeoba, who supervised studies that evening, had fainted; he was sitting at the opposite end of the room and, unable to utter a word, watched in terrified stupefaction as the ball of light struck directly at a junction box, and a searing ball of fire sheered downwards to detonate the light switch. When Ezeoba was revived, and had recollected his bearings, his first words were: 'Did he survive?'

He had joined the others in blubbering about what they had seen, robbed, for once, of his usual bombast. His written report to the Housemaster was, that teacher said, the most lucid exposition of the phenomenon of lightning he had ever read. For the rest of the term the scorched line in the wood became a tourist attraction for several who heard about the event but, by then, a few of the senior boys and two at least in his class had begun to regret that he had not been sitting directly in front of the switch. Once they had all recovered from the initial shock and uttered fervent thanksgiving prayers, nasty second thoughts began to creep into some minds. Considering their owners' long-suffering, the bolt of lightning had missed a good chance of ridding the school of a cantankerous, argumentative pest, whose size and early demeanour belied – typical of his slyness! – his capacity for disruptiveness. The headache that kept the victim in bed throughout the following day was by then considered inadequate punishment. Indeed, was the lightning visitation itself not yet another proof of the boy's tendency to create devastation totally out of proportion to his size?

Faithful to the secret promise he had made to his grandfather, he reported the event to him by letter. The old man shrugged with smug satisfaction. 'I named you Maren,' he wrote back, through his letter-writer. 'You will not walk when the gods are angry.' And he killed a ram and shared its meat among all the occupants of Ile Ligun, sending Aké's own portion, smoked, to his son, the Headmaster. The morsel to be eaten by the celebrant was preserved by the old man until he could feed it to the boy with his own hands; he would not trust his son to carry out all the motions that should accompany this re-fortification of his grandson's psychic shield.

And then the drama of the broken key! So, the key broke in his hand. Why should the entire House hold him responsible? It was the key to the food store; Ezeoba had assigned him and two other junior boys to help the cook. Dinner was two hours late and, as they searched for a duplicate key, then gave up and began to break down the door, he had this feeling that they were all looking at him as if he should be cooked in place of the imprisoned dinner.

'Swanston House,' moaned Ezeoba, 'was built before you were born. This door, Master 'Koyi, or Maren, or whatever you call yourself, this massive door, made of the stout iroko tree, was in place before you were born. The lock, you tiny disseminator of gargantuan misery, was forged in the furnace of the blacksmiths of *oyinbo** ancestors. It has withstood the bombardments of the Great War. Adolf Hitler tried, he could not force this door to rob Swanston House of its supplies to feed his men, that is why he had to surrender last year. His men were starving to death, because he could not break down this door. But you sir, you invisible gnat, you speck of dust, you . . . you . . . tiny filament on the head of a grasshopper, you not only draw down lightning on innocent heads, nearly setting our prep room on fire, you have broken a key that is ten times your size, and imprisoned its effective component in the lock. What do you say to that, Mr Ironhand? What shall we say to these poor, innocent, starving pupils who merely wish to get on

*White man.

with their evening prep, as praiseworthy followers of that time-honoured saying: *mens sana in corpore sano?* Where, tonight, shall we provide them the commodities of sound nourishment that guarantee the *corpore sano*, within which the *mens sana* must find its habitation?'

'When we get to Apata, can we turn off at Government College?'

'Sure. You want to see one of the staff?'

'No. Let's just drive through the compound. I want to see if it has changed much.'

'I know it has expanded, but there are still only the four boarding Houses?'

'Expanded? How?'

'The Education Department planted another school next to it, then removed it, so the College expanded into the vacated land. Then the College was pushed further inwards to make room for some other project, I forget what. Then a decision was taken to plant a sister school right inside or turn it into a mixed school and the parents association or somebody protested . . . look, the truth is, I don't even know what it's like on the inside at present.'

'Would that have to do with the Western Region programme for free education?'

'It's a Federal College. It's just difficult to get people to accept that some things deserve to be left precisely as they are.'

'Change is supposed to go with Independence, and partial change – that is, trial and error – with partial Independence.'

'Yeah, keep playing the devil's advocate. You'll never change.'

'On second thoughts, maybe it's best we just drive past the College for now.'

'No, no problem. We can take a look.'

'No, go straight ahead. I'll visit it over the weekend, when I can meander through at my own pace.'

'As you please. It's vacation now so you'll have the place to yourself.'

He nodded. 'Precisely what I wanted.'

'All right. You can borrow my car whenever you wish.'

'You couldn't find me a bicycle somewhere?'

'A bicycle? What for?'

'What do you mean, what for? What does one do with a bicycle?'

'Come on. You don't mean you're going to ride all the way from the University campus to Apata? We're talking of the new campus you know, halfway to Oyo.'

'Stop exaggerating. Anyway I was riding all over London for more than a year, day and night, snow or rain, from one end of outer London to the other. I got used to it. And anyway, how do you expect me to go round the compound itself? There are all those footpaths, I'd just like to go through them again.'

Komi chuckled. 'Nostalgia, enh? I wouldn't have thought it of you.'

'No-o-o, just part of homecoming. Apataganga was also home, you know.'

'Yes, yes, so is Aké . . .'

'Blood last, because it lasts . . . doesn't that sound good?'

'Does it? Well, let me tell you one that I think speaks better to your lopsided programme. I've been thinking about it quite a bit since I picked you up, and I think I know what your problem is.'

'Well, go on. I'm listening.'

'The name your godmother stuck you with. I think you've been too long away and have forgotten the right intonation, which means of course, you've lost the correct meaning. She called you Akínkòyí, remember? Although to me you will be Sobe till my dying day, or yours, whichever comes first. But Akínkòyí she said, not Akínkoyì, which was, on her part, and so early in your life, a most perspicacious observation on your stiff-necked nature . . .'

Chuckling, he remarked, 'You sound just like Ezeoba. I wonder where he is, what he is doing.'

'Ezeoba does not have a monopoly of orotund expressions, I haven't heard of him since he left school after failing his second attempt at the School Cert, and please don't interrupt me.'

'You know, I thought of him often.'

'He was a terror to every new boy, though a heart of gold did beat, as they say, beneath all that bombast. Anyway, I was saying to you, I know your secret. Mr Kòyí-Kòyèn. Your godmother's astute observation of character is different from the other meaning of the same word which – in case you have become tone-deaf – means

Akin refuses praise, or glory. You see, I know what you're running from. You don't fool me.'

'Oh, you'll have a hard time arguing that with my godmother, because she never tired of renaming me. Once, I was Lagilagi, because I took on the chore of splitting firewood in the house. Then she changed it to Ajilagi, because I took to waking up before everyone else, splitting more than enough firewood for the day, so I could go off on my own and wander around or read. Then she decided that this sneaking off on my own was the key to every other nickname – Okunrin Jeje, Omoruyide, etc, etc – the last one being the one she coined when I won two prizes in the Arts Festival – but, to get back to her, then, very latest invention, she decided finally that she had hit on the missing theme. She turned to my mother one day and said, "You know what name you forgot to give this 'husband' of mine? It is – Otolorin*." My view, therefore, is that each one of them cancels out the others and I can get down to the business of re-naming myself.'

'Why all the names? She has only created confusion.'

'She was my "wife".'

'Oh, that childish infatuation of yours.'

'Now who is the alien here? I am not referring to my silly crush. I was born before she married into the family, so she could not call me by my own name. But she was creative. She enjoyed being inventive.'

'Oh yes. And talking of being inventive, you said you would be re-naming yourself. What improvement have you thought up on your godmother's? Or grandfather's? There can be no improvement on mine, of course.'

'Plenty, but I'm still trying them for size. If you don't beat me to the draw, you may be able to read it on my tombstone.'

And suddenly they were in the heart of Ibadan, passing by the railway station at Dugbe, the entry point to his secondary-school-days' adventure. He tried to recollect how many times he had climbed and descended those steps, leaving on vacation or returning to school, but it was the second entry that remained firmly etched on his mind. That was the beginning of the road that was yet to

*The one who walks apart.

have an end. As if in a conscious replay of that past, Ibadan had yet again denuded herself in a lean rite of induction and welcome. Gone were the spongy leaves that would normally shade the frontage of the railway station. No heavy mangoes with their train of fat blue-bottles, no scent in the air of their thick, treacly juice. Only the skeletal boughs remained, and a few brittle leaves. Ibadan was all rust, but a few petals of the frangipani had survived, the tree trunks ringed, as usual, by the regulation whitewashed stones. Not nearly so white, he reflected, except on special days. It was either the mud in the rainy season, which was when he first stood on that spot, full of trepidation for the selection interview that had brought him then to Ibadan, or else the brown dust of Harmattan, when he returned to begin his first year at the boarding school. He remarked how the dry season always seemed to visit Ibadan earlier than Abeokuta, which they had just left behind, and with such severity. So that much at least had not changed in the five years of absence, or indeed the six and a half years since he left the boarding school, or in any of those first five years that he sheltered under the mango trees outside the station, waiting for a likely motor vehicle, each year increasing both anxiety and self-assurance since that first entry into the school as one of the chosen few.

Did you have to sneak home like a thief in the night?

The return had quickly ceased to be a speculative event in some indefinite future, once he had received that letter of invitation. The prospect of returning to teach remained an unfavoured one, undoubtedly much to be preferred to entering the Civil Service where office and desk already awaited him, but still remote from the gradual induction into the now distanced environment that he instinctively craved. It was a contradiction that he accepted; on the one hand, the eagerness to be whisked home with the sudden, propulsive force of *ofe*;* on the other, a need to insinuate himself gradually into what had become, after all, a space of estrangement. Even the stay-at-homes, he knew, would have to adjust to a new

*A magic wind.

community; the one that would come into being after full Independence.

Now he counted himself lucky; he had nine months to blend into the old, emerge with it from its cocoon into a new order, or sensibility, or responsibility of being. The offer of a Research Fellowship, with its loose, itinerant association with the University, had settled all his qualms when he received it the previous year. Teaching could come later, and welcome – and his nerve-ends had become taut with the eagerness of return. But not before an orgy of leave-taking, even of places he had never been before. Have rucksack, will travel, be it within the isles of Britain or the extended European family. It had been only a matter of time before he found himself well and truly 'down and out in Paris'.

II Down and Out in . . . ! !

That had not been planned. George Orwell was more than welcome to all the resilience demanded by such experiences; likewise Arthur Koestler, who enjoyed a more harrowing immersion in the predicament of starvation all over Europe. Maren had not sought to share the crown of thorns with any starving artist. But a small-time impresario from Paris had been sitting among the audience at a Sunday night show at the Royal Court Theatre, London, an evening of half drama, half poetry and music, where he had made his début on an English stage in 1959 – if one ignored the earlier contribution to a students' theatre festival, sponsored by the *Sunday Times*, and wet-nursed by that journal's resident critic, Harold Hobson. Mr Hobson was a man of hyperbolic hates and loves and, unlike his rival Kenneth Tynan of the *Observer*, of distinctly limited intellect. Throughout Maren's stay in England, he remained unpersuaded by this critic's claim to any artistic sensibility or theatrical instinct, despite his often treacly declamations of adoration for the actress Sarah Bernhardt, against whose immortal genius all British actresses – and theatre – would periodically be measured, with mind-boggling irrelevance . . . *It reminded me of the immortal moment at the Comédie Française, when the inimitable Sarah Bernhardt fluttered her eyelashes, raised her arm with such limpidity that a frisson was discharged from her very armpits and crackled through the length and breadth of the stalls; this was imperious theatre at its most sublime.* But Harold Hobson's instinct was right in one respect; he had gauged the insularity of British theatre at the time, and would simply browbeat his readership – and theatre managements – with continental name-dropping. He was an embarrassing loyalist of the Royal Court Theatre, a view that Maren was relieved to find was shared by a number of other young playwrights and would-be directors of the fifties, who were gathered around the vision of a unique theatre manager and director, George Devine. Devine, the English quintessence of the strong, silent worker, brought promising talents under his wing and then left them severely alone to develop in their own unique way – John Osborne, Edward Bond, Anne Jellicoe, Ian Johnstone, John Arden, Harold Pinter, Arnold Wesker among others. Where he could not immediately produce their plays, George Devine offered them acting roles or other part-time work in the English Stage Company. Others he made script-readers, ten shillings a script. His young collaborators, William Gaskill and Mariam Brickman, shared out the scripts as equitably as possible.

Then there was the Sunday night innovation, where new plays would be tried out for one night only, freed of commercial pressures and expectations. But best of all treats was to sneak quietly into the back stalls and watch George Devine rehearsing, consulting quietly with the playwright – N. F. Simpson, Samuel Beckett, Arthur Miller, Sean O'Casey . . . patiently coaxing the performance of a lifetime from an alcoholic actor in *Krapp's Last Tape*, *Cockle-a-Doodle-Dandy* . . .

Weekends and some evenings, the Pipers – the husband John, an art critic – offered the warmth and space of their homes for reading one another's scripts, acting out scenes and indulging in all kinds of improvisational creative lunacies. Tea, coffee and other more inspirational kinds of drinks, hefty sandwiches, buns and scones – they surely guessed the gnawing innards of their wards, despite their professional *insouciance* – knitted mind and body together, created a rarefied camaraderie and a cosseting, creative indifference to the exterior setting of the gilded rat-race and hypocrisies of that genteel Britain that would be excoriated with such rhetorical and passionate vigour by John Osborne in *Look Back in Anger*. Such lacerating outrage touched a chord of response in himself, whose terms of revolt were much more straightforwardly racial. This host country was a racist battleground that he skirted with progressive skill, but he could never totally evade the anti-personnel mines that littered the landscape, from working-men's pubs and public transport, to the restaurants and hotels of Chelsea or Belgravia.

And so, Sloane Square became a special tribal community over

which the benevolent chief, George Devine, presided, a theatre
that broke the taboos of the Establishment, reached into forbidden
language, forms, and themes, defying the censorship of the Lord
Chamberlain by turning its territory when necessary into a private
theatre club, where the ticket became an instant membership card.
The Making of Moo by Nigel Dennis unleashed an outcry of blasphemy, but for Maren, it was instant rapport: the not-so-subtly
archiepiscopal figure in a 'primitive' setting, presiding over the birth
of the new god Moo, and the unforgettable moment that he guessed
he would never stop relishing – *à la* Harold Hobson – even into
senility. That was the gesture of sheer hyperbolic theatre, after the
ritual sacrifice. The incredibly long forefinger of the 'bishop' – at
least nine inches long, illusion or not – dipped into the bucket of
blood; it was raised and a red tongue slowly extended itself, gave it
a long, lingering and noisy lick from the root of the finger to its
dripping nail, and smacked its lips. The actor was John Osborne.
When his *Look Back in Anger* eventually seared the English stage,
that cannibal image of Osborne's bloody snack would become fused
in Maren's mind with a notion of the angry spokesman of a new
generation, as a regenerative young Dracula with its fangs fastened
on the jugular vein of a bloated British bourgeoisie.

Sloane Square, home also to exiled artistes, especially from South
Africa. Diminutive but feisty Bloke Modisane, fresh from the col-
umns of the racy South African journal, *Drum* – yes, it would be
Bloke who would embarrass him so intensely on another Sunday
night's offering, an indictment of British policies in Kenya, then
embroiled in the Mau Mau uprising. *Eleven Men Dead at Hola*
dramatised the beating to death of eleven detainees, though the
official report claimed that they died from drinking water from a
poisoned hole. Keith Johnstone at the lectern, reading the report
dispassionately as the actors enacted a gruesome reality in slow
motion, the beating to death of eleven human beings by black
guards, and the white camp commandants giving the orders. But
there was a moment in which the Nigerian felt that he could not
participate. It had to do with a feeling of the cheapening of senti-
ment, a well-meant device that, however, robbed the scene of its
edge of rage. Someone had proposed it in rehearsals, it was tried
out and, argue and fulminate as he pleased, it ended up in the final

version. 'Well, I shall not take part,' he warned. 'When the moment comes, I shall slip into the wings and return after that scene is over.' Director and performers all agreed. Then along came Bloke and proceeded to drag him out, in full view of the audience. A most untidy struggle which covered him in embarrassment as the first tug, totally unexpected, had already catapulted him into the spotlight . . . each time the scene returned to his mind, he squirmed, his one sour note against Devine, whose spirit of indulging the unexpected would sometimes suffer such crude manifestations.

It was home of a kind, and the Pipers made it even more so, but this stranger among them remained, at least within himself, a stranger. He took to the children, all daughters. They ran in and out of rehearsals and were sometimes commandeered into taking on roles or managing props. Their artlessness was such a contrast, an oasis of spontaneity and lack of guile, even of the creative kind that went into the theatrical improvisations. He wrote them a poem, needing to thank them for what he felt he and the others had lost and were seeking to recover. The paradox continued to plague him, this constant standing apart from them all, standing apart even from himself and watching his other being in a circle that he found at once congenial and alien, one whose offered selves he shared so positively and enjoyed without any reservation, but from which he felt quite comfortably distanced. It had been no different, thinking back now, from life in Leeds; indeed, he would fall to wondering if there was really any time that he did not stand apart and watch his other self in some situations, idiotic or inspirational. Not all the time, no, but certainly in many circumstances. No matter, he cycled from the remote ends of London to these sessions, his guitar tied to his back, threw himself into the exchanges with as much ardour as any of the others. But constantly he located himself at the outer edge of their concerns, their themes, even their search for techniques and styles. Soon he ceased to permit any of this to surprise or disturb him, simply letting go and enjoying the luxury of absorbing it all and withdrawing, inwardly detached, saying to himself: it doesn't matter anyway; this is not my world.

Finally, it was his turn for the Sunday night début, and it needed none of the reviewers, from the most painfully considerate to the grossly abusive or condescending, to tell him it was a disaster.

What surprised him, on reflection, was that he was not in the least downcast, and the brief anger with himself quickly dissipated in the smoke, booze and dancing at the cast party in the Notting Hill basement flat of the West Indian actor Lloyd Reckord, and his Australian painter companion, Colin Garland. The mother of his son watched Maren with some astonishment as he argued over the faults of the production; she could never do that, she said. She was certain she couldn't bear to speak of a production she had just concluded, failure or success it did not matter which. 'Neither can I,' he replied truthfully, wincing inside.

She smiled knowingly as she put it down as one of the paradoxical statements he liked to indulge in when he was ill at ease, confused, on the losing end of an argument, or simply wanted to be anywhere but where he was. He saw the Stage Manager standing forlornly apart and went over to him. His special effects had failed to function at the crucial moment and he remained inconsolable. The laboratory of the South African scientists should have shuddered to a resounding explosion as they experimented with chemicals to attain a final solution to the race problem. But there was no bang, only a whimper of despair as the actors waited in vain for their cue, before the SM threw off his paralysis, then threw himself into a frenzy of creating mayhem backstage to simulate some distant relation of an explosion . . . The rest of the one-act merely fizzled away but of course the problem had begun much earlier. It lay in his direction, he concluded easily, watching from the wings. Too bad, it was only a one-night stand, so there was no re-inventing *The Invention*. He dragged off the self-exiled white South African dancer to sample her expertise on Lord Kitchener's calypso beat.

Bonamy Dobree, his professor from Leeds, lived in Blackheath, and came into London to see the show. Afterwards he said to him, 'I came expecting to suffer in the first half, the poetry section, and enjoy the play in the second. The opposite proved to be the case.'

The visiting impresario, a bulbous-nosed Parisian of Levantine extraction, was indifferent to both play and poetry; it was the songs in the first half of the programme that held his interest. Would Mr Playwright care to try out the cafés and *caves* of Paris? He controlled an impressive agency network that could guarantee him a season of lucrative engagements. The offer was puzzling. It could not have been his guitar playing, which never did exceed the basic chord sequence – tonic, dominant and sub-dominant, plus the odd concession to a seventh, and the very occasional diminished or augmented chord, very sparingly and uncertainly applied. As for the singing, at his outing during the Student Rag Concert at Leeds, the Mayor had come backstage to congratulate the cast. Shaking Maren's hand, he had smiled wickedly and said, 'Of course, you are no Paul Robeson', a remark which Barry Cryer, the producer and comic compère, ensured that everyone out of earshot eventually heard.

Still, he did not bother to ask the Frenchman why he considered his stage performance – two songs only, a contemporary blues and a Yoruba folk song – marketable stuff. Or was it the politics that attracted him? Paris was a hotbed of numerous leftist tendencies, from madcap to solemn and activist. And the music-poetry half had indicted France for exploding the atom bomb over the Sahara, and denounced Britain for the death of Kelso Cochrane, a West Indian victim of racial psychopathy. There was his own personal favourite, the blues number into which he had poured his share of the trans-Atlantic racial despair, an empathy that became truly palpable only after his departure from home and his contacts with his kin in the diaspora. Deliberate or not, some form of censorship had made this expression in literature and music inaccessible in his colonial Nigeria. Where, at home, could he have encountered as harrowing an account of a judicial lynching as in *Scottsborough Boy*? The public libraries did not stock it.

Reinforcing this mood was the emotive, *j'accuse* white American Ralph Schoenemann, a haunted figure who would end up after two years in London, as private secretary to Bertrand Russell, coordinating for the philosopher and anti-nuclear campaigner, the later marches from Aldermaston. Ralph had fled the United States, and before then the state of Mississippi, only a few steps ahead of the murdering sheriff of Little Mo. He had found himself a target for taking up the cause of an orphaned boy, so he fled north, one step ahead of the sheriff's posse, clutching in his head both the account of the murder and the handful of lyrics of the young survivor, just in case the sheriff's spies did catch up with him and seize his jottings. America, land of the free? Weekend after weekend, Ralph stood in his favourite spot of Hyde Park Corner and retold the story of Little Mo, working up to the colossal immorality of a nation in whose hands such a powerful weapon of destruction as the atomic bomb was nested. As he finished each declamation, he began all over again, almost precise to the comma, fending off hecklers with the dare – go into Little Mo, into the hundred Little Mos all over the United States and look into the eyes of their sheriffs: theirs are the trigger-happy fingers on the atom bomb, keeping the world safe from communism! You ask the boy from Little Mo – if he's still alive!

> *Sometime I feel*
> *I could kill a man*
> *Just for being good Lordy*
> *Just for being good*
>
> *So be my man*
> *Be my man O Lord*
> *So be my man Lordy*
> *Before the day is done*

For the stranger from colonial Nigeria, this was no longer an anonymous voice from Little Mo, Mississippi, any more than Billie Holiday or Leadbelly. Ralph Schoenemann, wiry, obsessed exile from injustice, had ingested the story at the very height of his dissident idealism; it had become the mission of his viscera. The black boy had seen his father lynched, his crime was talking back and standing up to a white supremacist. Then his home was burnt out, and the rest of the family run out of town. No more than thirteen, he had begun to compose the dirges of his traumatised existence whose lyrics Ralph had memorised, but being tone deaf and impervious to the rhythms of the blues, he had only a ragged recollection of the boy's original melodies. So the playwright created new tunes, added the story of Little Mo to the musical fare of the Sunday night at the Royal Court.

> *Got to rise with the sun*
> *Got to work with it too*
> *The sun's been gone a long, long time*
> *But I still ain't gone to rest.*

Little black mother heavy with my child
Take that child out of here
Take the child out and leave it there
Before he find out he black.

The budding folk singer had no idea what French audiences knew, or cared of Little Mo, Mississippi, or indeed of the land of Ambrose Campbell, Denge or the tortured life of Njemanze, and other Nigerian minstrels, but, if Mr Impresario thought they would pay for an evening of such fare, even from an amateur's rendition, he was more than willing to stress their sensibilities.

His only visit to France before then had been to Lyon to build houses, on a programme run by an Albert Schweitzer lookalike (even to his passion for music), a fanatic whose mission was to cater for the *sans abri*. The year before, it had been Holland, in Zeedyke Zee where the dykes had burst and the seawater flattened an already featureless land. Dr Inebnit, he was sure, would travel to Mars with volunteer students and build shelters for Martians if he heard that there had been a cosmic disaster that left one inhabitant homeless. No disaster had overtaken the Lyonnais that anyone knew of, but perhaps the grape-pickers needed shelters so, off went Inebnit, to be joined by his international volunteers, all students but with a sprinkling of professional volunteers who supplied the precision ends of construction. When it was all over, the wanderer hitch-hiked to Paris before returning to London where his re-entry gift was from a customs officer who actually proposed to charge him duty on the extra half of an opened bottle of wine.

'You are permitted only one bottle duty free, so I have to tax you on this half.'

He could not believe his ears but the man was in dead earnest. So he put the bottle to his mouth and – glug-glug-glug – denied British Revenue its Shylock claims. 'I may get drunk, but later I shall become sober,' he said to the customs officer, 'while you, sir, will always be a racist.' It felt good to be able to paraphrase Winston Churchill.

To return to Paris, with a singing stint on the professional stage, sounded too good to be true. Certainly it was a class up on the profession of bricklayer or indeed the barman-cum-bouncer stint at the Douglas Bay Hotel, Isle of Man, where you learnt to dodge chairs and bottles especially at weekends when the boats came in simultaneously from Scotland and Ireland with the one ritualistic mandate, and none other – to break the heads of the rival tribe and uproot Douglas Bay Hotel, an ancient manorial establishment, and hurl it into the bay. The head barman was the calmest individual he ever encountered in a mêlée, and he quickly learnt from him the technique of seizing a man by the belted-trouser-end, yanking his neck back by his shirt collar and rushing him through the swing-doors while dodging flailing arms, chairs and bottles. There was not much dimension to him anyway, so the missiles generally found more substantial targets, such as the head barman whom he never saw flinch, not even once, or Peter, another of the group of four from Leeds, a lanky, six-plus-footer whose gangling limbs occupied so much space that the missiles did not have to be aimed at him to find him. The head barman would eye the direction from which the offending missile had emerged, so casually that the culprit never noticed, complete the task in hand, then re-enter the bar through another door and calmly bounce the felons, sometimes two at a time. When the going got really rough, the student amateurs simply left him on his own, plunging into the turbulence from time to time only when an easy prey had been spotted, preferably one who was so plastered that he yodelled an Irish or Scottish aria as he was propelled into the salty air of Douglas Bay.

The bar was, of course, called Texas Bar, all complete with a platform, honky-tonk piano and a rent-a-cowboy Cockney Texan with a guitar, who warbled the same three- or four-piece Wild West repertoire, with the odd negro spiritual, rounding off with a medley that was intended to encourage participation but appeared to be the signal for the fights to commence, night after night. He was a sight in his artificial tan, complete with a rakish stetson, red polka-dot bandana, high-heeled boots with gleaming spurs. On slack nights, the budding Nigerian songbird took over the platform and tried out his own repertoire, sometimes in the afternoons also, which was when the girls dared invade Texas Bar, coming in twos or threes. In the evenings they drank only in the genteel saloon of the hotel, though they could hear the raucous goings-on next door and would sometimes peep in when the action really began. There was a raven-haired big-bosomed one that stood out from the rest, the way her eyes sought his and never left off; she took to returning in the evenings but sat close to the bar for safety. Welsh, so he named her Welsh Rarebit. She stayed to help with the cleaning up afterwards, then they went for night walks up the path that went past some kind of religious grotto, combing out the island wilds for discreet spaces in the ferns and brambles.

'I hope there are no snakes on the isle,' he said.

'No, just Manx cats, the ones without tails.'

'But what happened to the tails? Suppose they dropped off in previous lives and reincarnated into snakes?'

'You're trying to scare me,' she said. 'You should worry more about getting your head knocked off by those wild men from Scotland and Ireland.'

'Oh, we tame them, we get out our lyres and we tame them like Orpheus did the hounds of hell.'

The days ran off fast, hauling the crates of empties down into the cellar in the mornings, and hauling up full cases, then twice a week offloading from supply lorries into the cellars – quite a back-breaking job, he would remind her, just to get her to take it easy, but no, that did not impress the Welsh Rarebit. Sometimes, after really heavy nights, he and his three student companions collapsed into bed one after the other, fully clothed, too tired to eat or wash. Then suddenly it was time to sign off and return to University, and they would sign off in grand style – for this was the end of summer and Texas Bar was closing down till the following year. So, together with his daredevil colleagues, when the time came to bid ol' Texas adieu, and even the Manx lawmen shut their eyes to regulation closing time, they took to the stage with songs he had written specially for the clientèle, ending with the ritual number, and a favourite in which everyone joined, drunk or sober, swaying to the rhythm and crying in their beer:

> How we loved them in ol' Tex
> Female, male and neuter sex
> Oh, the brotherhood of guzzlers we shall miss
> And we hope they know we loved them
> The way we smiled and served them
> And cursed and muttered:
> 'Hope it chokes you, Turd!'

A trade being a trade and a skill a skill, be it bricklaying, bartending or bouncing, he soon found himself at Orly Airport, headed for a professional début as a folk singer, where he became stuck at Immigration, and all though no fault of his. He had made enquiries at the British Council in London and was assured that he required no visa to enter Paris. The official was ignorant of the fine distinction between a passport that pronounced you a British Colonial, and the other kind that labelled you merely British-Protected. Only citizens of Lagos were 'colonials', which entitled them to British Government scholarships and so on, and exempted them from visa requirements for several countries in Europe. All other Nigerians belonged to the 'protectorate', a fact which made them feel inordinately superior to the 'colonials' until they came up against the implacable figure of the French immigration police, armed to the teeth on account of the Algerian war, which had begun to come home to roost in the French metropolis.

'No visa?' and he tossed his passport back with sadistic relish. 'You return to London.'

Return to London on the next plane? The man must be joking. The agent had been quite adamant over the procedure for this new career – the new star in the folksong firmament must find his own way to Paris; once there, all other things shall be added for his wellbeing. So there he was, with a large slice of his money invested in the cut price air fare, which was actually air and bus fare since they were bussed to some extreme point of the British Isles, a no-name staging point from the last war, with a single runway that sheered off into the sea, probably rented to the charter company for one penny a year and a pledge to keep the grass down. No matter what, it had cost him money, and now he was to return to London without even one audition?

'The next flight is in three hours, *Monsieur*, and you will be on it.'

Monsieur yourself, he muttered to himself. We'll see about that!

He telephoned the agent, who was very ho-hummy and stolidly unhelpful. Visas were visas and immigration laws often inflexible. Then it was the turn of the British Embassy; after all, its London agency, the British Council – the formal induction centre for overseas students which even organised classes on the correct use of fork and knife – had created the mess, so its Paris office should feel an obligation to come to the rescue. The man at the end of the telephone was all kindness and courtesy. Yes, Nigeria had a fledgling desk at the British mission and the representative would be urged to make enquiries. He asked for the number of the public telephone and promised to call back. Sure enough, the telephone rang after half an hour. Again, most friendly, most concerned. The new speaker appeared to take it personally – a fellow countryman stranded for want of a visa? Still, it was all regrets. He was himself in Paris accompanying the Prime Minister. The message had been transmitted to him in the PM's presence and that personage had instructed him to enquire about what could be done to ease his plight etc, etc – at least, so understood the stranded voyager. It was a rather rushed period for him, the voice further explained, but perhaps if the wanderer did find his way to Paris while the delegation was still there, he should not hesitate to give the mission a call. For now, nothing could be done. Only course of action was to return to London, obtain a visa and try again.

As if the agents of Air France had been listening, one of them then approached and invited him to their desk. Would *Monsieur* now like to pay for his return ticket? Pay for . . . ! *Monsieur*, your mother! Listen, I am not the one requesting a flight to London. I am not the one deporting my innocent self, so don't you dare pull that one on me. And let me tell you, we are now an independent nation – well, not quite, but we have an embassy here already tucked inside the British Embassy, so don't think you can trample on my rights, anyhow. In any case, even if I wanted to pay, I have no money. I was coming here to fulfil an engagement, yes, a singing engagement, and all you have done is deprive me of my rightful earnings, so don't try to *Monsieur* any change out of me.

He stormed off, headed for the lavatory, emptied his pockets and stuffed his few currency notes in his socks. There was no knowing how far these desperate *faranse** might go. Then he returned to the lounge and tried to make himself as inconspicuous as possible. Another flight took off and the lounge emptied. There was a change of shift at the airline desk, then a change of the police guards. He

*The French.

sauntered across to the airport shops, noting again how thoroughly the lounge emptied itself of personnel and attention between flights, then strolled downstairs to the lavatories. This time he entered the female part of the lavatory – even the *pourboire* Amazonian lavatory attendants took a longish break in between planes – locked himself in one of the cubicles, pulled out a book and settled down to read.

An hour later, a short while before the plane was due to leave, he heard his name on the public address system. For a moment, he hesitated, then carried on with his reading. Several announcements followed, quickening his pulse, but he remained hidden. Footsteps came down into the toilets, turned off towards the male lavatories. He heard the cubicle doors being flung open and wondered how well he would manage a female voice if there came a knock on his door. But the boots merely raced up again and he breathed more easily. He guessed rightly when his plane took off and settled down to sweat it out for the next two hours.

There was no one to pay him any attention when he emerged; as usual, the lounge was empty between planes. Walking with as casual a briskness as he could muster, he moved towards the first set of barriers, crossed it without incident, then moved towards the second and last. Already he could hear himself twanging his guitar and warbling some Yoruba dirge in some *cave* in the Latin Quarter; what came over the airport lounge, however, was a female screech, which sounded to his ears as: '*Arrêtez, Nigérian!*'

He had made it abundantly clear to the airport personnel that he neither spoke nor understood a word of French, so he continued past the barrier. The sounds which he heard next, however, cut across all linguistic boundaries. Even without the experience of his brief training stint with the cadet corps at the University, he easily recognised the rapid but assured cocking mechanism of several guns, and he knew at whose now-petrified Nigerian back they were aimed. He spun round even before the sounds had died down and the next incomprehensible order given, slowly retraced his steps and confronted the airline agent who had sounded the alarm.

She screamed at him: 'Where have you be-e-en? We have been loo-ooking for you everywhere! Your flight has departed for London and you have gee-eeven us all trouble!'

But he was not even given a chance to reply. The guitar was

yanked off his shoulder, unseen hands snatched his bag while others virtually lifted him off his feet and bundled him into an office. The door was slammed behind him. Two nervous gendarmes fingered their guns and eyed him like a cornered quarry.

At the desk was a calmer figure, into whose hands the female ground staff now thrust the captive's passport, and what he assumed was the ticket already issued for him. She glared at him with ill-contained fury, so intense that it made him feel protected, no longer menaced by the guns. The man examined the passport carefully, then looked up at the prisoner, and down again at the passport.

'*Mais*,' and he turned to the prisoner, 'you are not Algerian?'

'No. I am a Nigerian.'

A rapid babble followed, with quantities of gesticulations, arms flailing in all directions at once. Amidst it all, the alien gathered that the woman's screech of '*Arrêtez le Nigérian!*' or whatever, had been heard and interpreted as 'Stop that Algerian desperado!' or worse, which instantly set the airport on maximum alert, flushed out the anti-terrorist squad from their ambush points, ready to deal with the guitar-toting illegal immigrant whose guitar-case, in any case, probably contained a machine-gun ready to spatter the FLN message on the murals of Orly.

'You could have been shot, *Monsieur*,' the official remarked, and he was smiling!

At a quarter to six p.m. on the fateful day, a thoroughly exhausted and starved folk singer *manqué*, looking nothing like any known Algerian terrorist, could be seen floating across the floor of Orly departure lounge between two burly gendarmes who had not taken their eyes off him for the prior hour and a half. They carried him up the gangway into the plane and plonked him into a seat. Looking through the porthole, he could see them still standing guard, keeping their eyes on the gangway until it was moved, the doors closed and the plane sealed up, lost to sight only when the plane taxied away and carried a most unwilling passenger back to the protective bosom of his imperial hosts.

'Ah, but it is now *vacances*; there is nobody in Paris during *vacances*, only tourists. The *caves* are closed, the *petits* nightclubs or café-théâtres that would be interested in your kind of music, they are all closed. Only the revue-type clubs do any business now, and they only cater for tourists. I am sorry, but you have missed the season.'

Could this man be serious? After taking all the trouble to obtain a visa, strip the girlfriend of her savings to make up a new air fare and confront the Algeria-fixated immigration guards all over again, the oily accent that oozed over the telephone line, accompanied no doubt with Gallic shrugs and other dismissive gestures, was not one of excited welcome but plain indifference. Not a shred of sympathy did the agent permit to humanise his own involvement in the predicament of his invited guest.

With some difficulty, he taught his voice to affect the same indifference, as if this was not a matter of wine and starvation. 'I see. Bad timing, enh? So when does the season resume?'

'Soon after the *rentrée*, of course . . .'

'The what?'

'The *rentrée*. After the summer. That is when the real Paris comes back to life. I'm afraid I have to hurry now, we were just setting off ourselves for the south, you were most fortunate to catch me. Get in touch with me before you return to Paris, then I'll begin to work on your bookings.'

'Oh, sure. Of course. Well, have a nice *vacances*.'

'*Merci. Au 'voir*'.

Stranded! He was trying to come to terms with the sensation, but there was no other word for it – he was stranded. Never was a reversal of expectations more complete – from the moment he announced his arrival, the agent would take him over, body and soul. A modest hotel room on the Left Bank – he would insist on that location; a reasonable cash advance, surely he had a right to take that for granted, and then it was up to him to fulfil his own professional part of the bargain. What could be simpler? Damn it! He had, after all, been invited. The impresario had sought him out, not the other way round. All he was doing was minding his own business at the Royal Court Sunday-night theatre!

He knew, to the last centime, just how much he had in his pockets. The notion of returning to London, which the agent had so blithely assumed, was not even to be considered. He had come to Paris to sing, and sing he would, and he did not buy the notion that Paris simply died in summer and would only resurrect after the *rentrée*.

True, his only incursion into that city had taken place after summer, since that slave-driver Inebnit had kept them raising low-cost houses all summer on the suburban slopes of Lyon. What wouldn't he give to be back among the volunteers for Inebnit's *sans abri*, where the labouring horde would plead with him to unsling his guitar after work and strum his half-dozen chords to an international medley of songs. Thinking of the days ahead, he savoured with nostalgia the crusty, jam-plastered French bread and mugs of sugary *café au lait* that began the day, summoning the fat drones and wine-flies to join in the breakfast. Lunch was a working-man's platter of meat and rice or buttered potatoes, real edible potatoes that belonged to a different family from the anaemic British breed, almost yam-textured, and again un-British vegetables that were anything but overboiled sludge for convalescents; sometimes it was *ratatouille*, prepared by the Algerian or Tunisian women volunteers. And there would be the periodic, unexpected treats. Obviously this impresario had never learnt from people like Inebnit or he would understand that a labourer deserved his hire and a would-be folk singer knew how to live it up as well as an amateur bricklayer. But Inebnit picked a different country every year for his projects, so he could be in Australia at that moment for all he knew. Still, he knew where the Paris office was located and he recalled that all Inebnit's volunteers were welcome at his various *sans abri* hostels if the situation became truly intolerable, but that bridge would be crossed when he got there, the idea of such a mendicant descent filling him with horror for now.

Rapidly, he performed some mental calculations, then headed for the Left Bank, thanking his stars that he had previously under-taken the hitch-hike to Paris after the hard but quite enjoyable labour in Lyon. He still kept some addresses and telephone numbers, knew the locations of all the subsidised student eateries, the cheap Chinese eating shacks located somewhere near the Gare du Nord and patronised by beefy workers, students and revolutionaries, where a large bowl of noodles cost next to nothing, and there were ways of getting into hostels at the Cité Universitaire and camping down for a few days before being detected . . . but before that slide into the world of the romanticised *clochard*, he would establish residence for a day or two in that same cheap hotel in Rue St-André des Arts where he had lodged before. The advantage of that was that he could leave his luggage with the *concierge* for a day or two after leaving the hotel, and that could extend into weeks and months afterwards, and of course he would also continue to use the toilet and showers simply by walking in with the assurance of a resident and plunging into the narrow corridors as of right. In any case, those hostels spun webs of mutual assistance that radiated from the permanent student residents and he might even encounter familiar faces in the hotel to whom he could frankly confess his plight. In that earlier visit he had done no more than take the measure of the Left Bank, amused by its pretensions but caught up nonetheless in its singular vitality, unmatched by nothing in the character of its nearest London equivalent, Soho, or Chelsea. Even the smells and the sounds were replicated in no other city of his knowledge. But one virtue above all stuck in his mind: students and pavement artists, wandering minstrels, café philosophers, refugees from real and imaginary tyrannies, black francophones from the French *'départements'* (that typical French quibbling to disguise the reality of colonies), out-of-work actors and dancers, would-be-poets and struggling writers, etc, all appeared to share one talent in common – the art of survival in the cafés and streets of Paris.

'You do not speak French, that is a pity.'

'Of course it is a pity. I would like to speak all the world languages. It would be marvellous to find oneself anywhere in the world and converse like a native.'

'No, you do not understand. French, it is different. If you do not speak French, the French looks at you to say, *Quel sauvage*. To be accepted as civilised, you must speak French.'

'In that case, I shall remain uncivilised and *sauvage*. I take it that means savage, not so?'

'Aha, already you speak French, *mon vieux*. I help you to register in Alliance Française, is okay? In three months . . .'

'Listen, firstly, I have no money to spend on your Alliance, and if I had it, I would spend it on better things. You know, you blacks are worse than the French people who own the language. What is it to you, anyway?'

'But French is *civilisation*. Even the rest of Europe know it eez a fact. To be French eez to be cultured. Believe me, if you don't speak French, the Frenchman will not see you as cultured.'

'Does the Frenchman speak Yoruba?'

'*Comment?*'

'Yo-ru-ba! Ever heard of it? Does your Frenchman speak my language? Does he speak yours?'

'But really, you cannot be serious. Why should the Frenchman speak my language?'

'For the same reason as you expect me to speak his language. Listen, you study here, you have to study their language, but what has that to do with me? I am a mere bird of passage. Three months at the most, and I am off home. I shall pick up the odd phrase or two I need to get along but just don't give me that rubbish about French being the same as culture. Just what do you know of Yoruba culture?'

'You have the wrong attitude, my friend.'

'No, you have the wrong attitude. You won't find any black student or worker in England carrying on about the superiority of British culture. Impossible! These French have actually done something to you French colonials.'

'The British know that French culture is the only culture, that is why they cannot teach you, their colonials, anything different. It would be false teaching.'

'Shall I tell you where the French, at least the Parisian, is superior to any other being?'

'Aha, you admit . . .'

'Greed. Plain avarice. Sheer, cold-blooded, bloody-minded, pitiless, inhuman avarice. And you know something else? You are wrong. Your average Frenchman perfectly understands Yoruba.'

'*Comment?*'

'This afternoon, I looked in my pockets, and all I could afford was a glass of wine or milk. No, to be more accurate, two glasses of wine or one of milk, milk being dearer in France than wine, to which I normally say Hurrah. So, I went into a bar and bought that glass of milk. Believe it or not, the barman wanted to keep the few cents change.'

'For tip, yes?'

'For greed, yes. Just greed. How could anyone take a look at me

– just look at my *espadrilles*, they've given up since that night trek I told you about, all the way from Champs Elysées to Cité Universitaire, no fibre-and-canvas slip-ons survive that kind of forced march, I tell you. The damned cheapies are meant strictly for ambling between cafés on the Left Bank, keeping strictly off the early-morning swab teams with their reckless run of water . . .'

'Only in Paris you see that. Only in Paris even the streets are given every morning bath. It is such a beautiful city.'

'All right, I'll concede that point to you. Mind you, the streets of London can hardly be called dirty, but the English bathe less frequently than Parisian streets. We Africans had a problem there. Many landlords simply could not understand that there are human beings who are accustomed to bathing every day, sometimes twice. They thought we were sick, or trying to scrub ourselves white. Your average Englishman's body never tasted water more than once a week.'

'Ah, the French too, no. But we have such perfumes in France. And the women are chic. You know, I think the French woman, she bathe very much like African, but the men, well, I don't think so. For him, it is *comme ci, comme ça*.'

'Now you've made me lose the thread of my story . . .'

'Your *espadrilles* – you know, you really will speak good French. Just give it some attention and your French will become respectful . . .'

'I suppose you mean respectable. See? You can't even speak decent English and you used to be from the British Cameroons. Shame on you. Anyway, back to my story and why I am in such a good mood that I can tolerate your imbecile notions. Look at you, for instance. No, take a serious look at you. That is, look at me and you'll agree neither of us is in a particularly impressive shape, right?'

'Well, yes, I suppose the time is difficult for us.'

'Good. Now, let us say you walk into a bar. Imagine that I am behind the bar and I see you come in. I will say to myself, now here is a human being who maybe cannot afford his next meal. Would you agree with that?'

'*Alors, oui.*'

'So now, you enter the café, and you order a glass of milk. Yes, milk. I hate milk. But I have no choice because I have not eaten for two days and I must have something, and milk is more nutritious than wine, though I am ready to dispute that any day, but, a desperate man does not argue with primitive medical claims. So, I fish out my last coin in the world, and order a glass of milk. Where my next nutrition will come from, I leave in the hands of the gods. I pay the barman. He takes my last coin on this earth, punches the cash register, throws in this precious coin, takes out my few centimes change and throws that into that voracious jar they all keep under the counter for tips.'

'So?'

'So? I don't think you've got it yet. I never said, "Keep the change." In any case, I don't know the French for "Keep the change." And even if I did, I wouldn't have said such a stupid thing. And if I had been stupid enough to say it, any being with the slightest humane feeling would have taken one look at me and given me back, not even my change, but the entire coin. But we shall not argue over that. What really matters is, I never asked him to keep the change.'

'But, *mon vieux*, a little change like that, it is *automatiquement* for the waiter.'

'I demanded it back. He looked at me as if he hadn't understood. I repeated, "My change. I want my change. Give it back, quick." He ignored me. So I began to curse him – in Yoruba. I began with his ancestors, then moved on to his wife. When I set upon his evil progeny, including the ones he is yet to father, he suddenly lost all that superior look of ignorance, snatched up the jar and plonked it down on the counter in front of me. I assumed that whatever he muttered was an invitation for me to pick out my change, which I proceeded to do.'

'Be careful, *mon ami*. He could have called for the police.'

'What for? I was within my rights.'

'The gendarmes are racist. They do not care, they will arrest you for being nuisance. And believe me, especially when you cannot speak French . . .'

'No, I do not speak French, and I have sworn never to learn that language, given the pretentious arrogance of its owners. And greed. Let me tell you something, apart from my specific reaction to this particular waiter, I hate the entire culture of tipping. It is most uncivilised and demeaning. It is uncultured. I tell you, I shall never get used to it.'

He laughed. 'Wait until you have monee and you feel beeg. You will dispense the *argent* like water to make yourself superior.'

'That is the point, it dehumanises. When I won the annual oratory contest in my University, my topic was tipping. I knew I would win because my passion was not faked; it was genuine. All the other contestants were beaten hollow. They were being technical and abstruse all over the place but I just went in for an indictment of the entire rotten society which is split into the two disgusting classes – the tippers and the tipped. I still have that speech in my head, and if the police had come for me, that is what they would have received, full text. In good old English, no French version.'

'You would have failed to impress the gendarmes, believe me. You are lucky he did not send for them.'

'Well, I did give him a good reason for summoning the gendarmes, only he didn't see it.'

'What again you do?'

'He was so busy doing that arrogant stuff, you know, he simply plonked the glass in front of me and turned his back. Giving me the old gesture of contempt and all that. Or maybe he thought that the other customers would police his jarful of tips for him . . .'

'*Impossible*! You did not . . .'

'I bloody well did. There were some notes sticking out prominently. I think they do that to challenge their victims – see what the last person tipped, so try and do better. I took my time digging out a coin – and not even my worthless change by the way, something more substantial – and then also palmed a note *en route*. So, if you will kindly cut out your French cultural nonsense, let us stroll in the direction of the Gare du Nord, and ease a three-day pang of hunger. Have you noticed, by the way, that those Chinese noodle cooks don't speak any French . . . ?'

'*Mon vieux*, I think Paris is not good for you. I fear for you. Believe me, French police are very brutal, their cells are not nice.'

'Shut up and let's go eat. Now at least we'll have some energy for tomorrow.'

'Tomorrow?'

'If you're interested. That German student is taking me to Les

Halles tomorrow morning. You have to be there very early, no later than five a.m. That's when the meat vans arrive and they engage porters on a first-come-first-served basis. I don't ever want to have to drink milk again in a Parisian bar, least of all on an empty stomach.'

Did you have to sneak home like a thief in the night?

The long, empty streets of Paris late at night and in the early dawn, pocked by bundles of rags over the Métro vents, so still that only by staring hard and long, or when the occasional mound was racked by some inner torment, or a sudden alcohol-induced writhing, did one recognise that they hid the living body of a *clochard*; the concrete pill-boxes in front of the police stations, at strategic junctions and buildings, manned by anti-terrorist squads with their machine-guns trained permanently on passers-by, especially late-nightlifers, for Paris was kept definitely alive by valiant bars and a few bistros that opened only at night and remained open till dawn, home to the insomniac, the hard-working ladies of the night and the clientèle that sought them out; home also to tourists to whom Paris was either Paris by night or nothing, and the grey world of lesbian and homosexual loves that would sometimes turn ugly and violent in a mode of jealousy that remained incomprehensible to onlookers; each night, a different measure of sadness and hurt, of laughter and tenderness, and conspiracies. Fugitives, especially from the dictatorships of Latin America, and their sudden switches of mood. One moment, a table filled with fierce denunciations of the forces that flung them out of their homeland, combative declamations about return and the historic *coup de grâce* for the impostors; the next moment, lachrymose nostalgia, each body clinging to the next for courage and solidarity.

'Sing something, please.'

'What do you want me to sing?'

'Anything. Just sing. But what a pity, you do not know Guatemala. You do not know what the United States have done to us. No, you cannot understand what the capitalist monster has done to the cream of our writers and artists, to the youth of our nations. If you knew how we escaped . . . ask Pablo. Ask José. You do not know

what forms of torture the CIA taught our police, how they used
their inhuman techniques to break our comrades. Play something.
You are so lucky. Africa is a young continent. You have hope. All
over the continent your countries are throwing out their colonial
masters. You plan your own future. You control your destiny. Our
continent is old and dying. You cannot imagine the torment. We
are young but they have made us old, the bastards, dictators and
traitors. The fascist lackeys of Uncle Sam. Look what they did to
us in Panamá. You see José, he has just escaped from Nicaragua.
José, tell him what those goons of Somoza did to your family.'

'No, let him play. I want to sing. Will you accompany me, *amigo*?'

'I don't really know Latin American music.'

'It is not Latin American music, it is the music of the world, the
music of change. You will understand it as I sing. Just strike a chord
from time to time, that's all.'

> *No pasarán? No pasarán?*
> *Pero los muertos han pasado*
> *Y el tiempo, ahora pasando . . .*

'I composed it myself, so you mustn't mind if the music is not as
good as yours, *camarade*. Actually, I try to be a poet, try to be, you
see. I did not really have time to find out if I was one before it was
time to take up the gun. You know where the "*no pasarán*" comes
from, don't you? The Spanish Civil War – they shall not pass! Well,
that was also our motto. We adopted it, but they passed us just the
same, you know. The enemy overwhelmed us and passed on their
way, so did the dead among us.'

He raised his eyes and looked round the interior of the café. 'They
are here, you know. They follow us about. In the streets of Paris, I
encounter them all the time. When I sit down to eat in a bistro,
they take their places opposite me, drink wine from my glass. They
stand in my bedroom and watch me go to sleep . . . hey, your glass
is empty. Barman, why is this? Fill his glass, please. The *camarade*
has been singing all night.'

The choice of Maren's rebellious stomach, empty since morning,
screamed out *sandwich*, and the barman would have been only too
glad to substitute one for the drink. But here – it was something he
could not explain – among the fugitives of La Méthode, he could

never admit that he was hungry. It was different in the other bars, where he would gladly accept a drink from the clientèle but announce quite clearly, 'Make that drink a sandwich. Or a *croque-monsieur*. Or anything to eat.' Not at La Méthode, which thus complicated his strategy for feeding, since that night bar remained his favourite haunt. Not even the repellent presence of Tomás, who had attached himself to the Guatemala group, succeeded in turning his feet away from La Méthode at the approach of midnight, not even after he nearly got them shot dead by the nervous gendarme manning one of the pill-boxes in the early hours of the morning.

Somehow, Tomás had taken possession of his guitar-case as they left the bar, as usual, on not-so-steady feet. They kept their usual respectable distance from the pill-box at the entrance to the Mairie near the Panthéon, José, Almeida and himself, each floundering in his own wine-soaked thoughts. That was the moment Tomás picked to raise the guitar-case, swivel it like a third-rate Errol Flynn in the direction of the guard and, trilling his tongue in a reasonable imitation of a machine-gun, went: '*Krrr-ke-ke-ke-ke-krrrr-krrrr-krrrr* . . .'

Never, Maren would later admit, had his reflexes worked with such perfect coordination. Only Tomás was left standing, still going *krrr-ke-ke-ke*, seemingly oblivious to the rapidity with which the gendarme had readied his gun and was now pointing it directly at him. José's head reappeared a fraction above ground level, his frantic lungs imploring: '*Es loco, Señor, muy loco*. Madman. *Fou, il est fou.* Don't shoot.'

'Why not?'

'Ho, Tomás, you hear our African friend. He says why not? And me too, I now ask myself, why not indeed?'

'If I had a gun I would shoot him myself.'

The gendarme still looked uncertain, so José raised himself up very slowly, his hands well above his head. 'Believe me, it is only a guitar, *Monsieur*. The fool is drunk. Mad. *Idiota! Imbécile!*' He touched his head. 'You understand, *Monsieur*.'

Almeida got up next, rescued the guitar-case from Tomás, then gave him a punch that was meant to be a mild rebuke but sent him into the opposite end of the gutter. Their singing companion waited. A song had sprung involuntarily to his head, a song for all voyagers by his musician compatriot, Ambrose Campbell, an exile of many years in England. He found that he had begun to hum it, his face turned to the Paris night sky:

> Irin ajo l'awa yi oo
> Irin ajo l'awa yi o
> Oyi gbe wa d'ele . . .*

Resisting the urge to stamp Tomás deeper in the gutter into which he had fallen, he took back his guitar-case, dusted himself, and bade good morning to both madmen and revolutionaries. He had just made up his mind to return to portering at Les Halles, at least until his nerves were restored and he could face the Latin boys without wanting to smash in Tomás' head with a litre bottle of Côtes du Rhône.

The routine continued. Night belonged to the all-night bars and cafés. Barring rainy spells, sleep was a strictly daylight affair; the soft lawns of the Luxembourg or some other gardens. He took them in rotation, exercising care not to appear an habitué with no alternative – cultivating a sun-worshipper posture that suggested that falling asleep was a mere accident, not the real purpose of spreading out on the bench or lawn. And there were the occasional studios that came with an affair, offering its welcome even after the relationship was over. The male approaches were the more problematic; men tended to be far more desperate, unwilling to accept that he had no inclination whatever for such relationships: not even the evident sexuality of his exchanges with the women around deterred them.

The pathos of some, the delicacy of their often unspoken pleas, of furtive signals among the exclusive tribe, diffident, unpredictably lachrymose and aggressive, led to their definition in his own mind as twilight beings, incomplete existences that vied with the tenuous psyche of the *abiku*.† They were different from the homosexuals he had met in London, those who had indeed incurred his wrath by proposing that homosexuality was a sign of genius, especially of the

---

*This is a journey on which we are bound
 This is a journey
 May the gods bear us home . . .
†The mythical 'incomplete child' that must die and return again and again to the womb.

creative kind – at the Royal Court Theatre the proof settled often on Diaghilev and Nijinsky. The handful that he had come to identify among his co-students in Leeds were either simply timid or exhibitionist. At first he assumed that the difference had to do with Latin American culture, or the withdrawal symptoms of a violent, revolutionary past, but he settled eventually for the simple fact of exile, a double kind of exile, of physical and emotional alienation.

The thought of exile frightened him suddenly, bringing with it a feeling of being trapped in an alien land, penniless, *sans abri*, and a tenure whose control appeared to slip daily from his hands. It was then he recalled the earlier telephone contact with his surrogate home in the British Embassy. The earlier delegation would have departed but it was possible that someone else was passing through, it would be pleasant to receive direct news from home and, who knows, there might even be a reception for the visitors, to which he would certainly scrounge an invitation, or simply gatecrash.

He could not believe his luck. It was the same voice that answered his call; yes, the delegation had indeed left Paris, but it was an extensive tour and the same Excellency was now back in the French capital, on the way home. Certainly, it would be no problem to arrange a meeting, though he would recommend that he contact the August Visitor directly at his hotel . . .

From the moment the door opened to his ring at the suite in Claridges Hotel on the Champs Elysées, he knew he had committed some kind of error. The young man who opened the door was no more than thirty-five. He was dressed in what at home they would call a 'Palm Beach' suit, speckless and ironed with a precision edge that reeked of protocol. His appearance was a study in contrast to himself, the visitor ruefully admitted, though he had done his best to spruce up and present his most respectful appearance to the venerable leader of the delegation of a nation that was already exercising self-rule, and was only one more phase away from the club of independent nations. The young man confronted him with a cold bureaucratic hostility, but it was the sight that he glimpsed in the gap between the official and the open door that intrigued him. In a multiple-star hotel whose name exuded the staid weight of British tradition and was planted in the chic heart of Paris, an oasis of discretion along the glitzy, broad boulevard he had just traversed on a brilliant Sunday morning, this was a surreal flash straight from the cinematic vision of the Arabian Nights.

'Yes?'

The visitor introduced himself, adding, 'I have an appointment.'

Making no effort to disguise his scepticism, Mr Protocol opened the door wide enough to let him pass. Disposed all over the floor of the lounge were some twenty-odd boys and youngish men, certainly none of them older than eighteen or twenty, the youngest perhaps eight. Outfitted in their traditional attires, they looked out of place only if one recalled the outer environment. Within the plush furnishings of a hotel lounge, whose interior world took on independent life once the heavy oak door appeared to swing shut of its own weight, they seemed perfectly at home and in place, composed in a variety of postures on the carpet. Languid stares assailed him, then returned to the reading material that had occupied them until his entrance – mostly picture comics.

'Wait here. I shall tell his Excellency.' Close by the door to an inner room, he stopped abruptly and turned. 'You did say you have an appointment?'

'I called the Embassy on Friday and it was there I learnt where the Prime Minister was staying. I called this morning to make an appointment and was told I could come any time this morning.'

There were chairs in the room but none of them was occupied. The young court retainers – as he concluded they were – appeared to have been installed with the carpeting, so studiously did they complement the wood panelling, oriental rugs and other exotic furnishings of the room. Every gesture was fluid, giving off the impression of a life study whose oils had not quite dried on the canvas, a spell that remained unbroken even by the subdued giggles from an irrepressible group of three who appeared to be the youngest of the train. From time to time he felt more limpid eyelids raised to question his presence in that place, not with any great curiosity but simply as a distraction on an idle Sunday morning in a strange land. He could sympathise.

The door opened and Protocol returned. 'His Excellency will be with you shortly.'

Protocol remained standing and did not offer him a chair. The visitor felt a trifle annoyed but concluded that courtesy required that he do the same until the arrival of the Excellency.

He was puzzled by the appearance of the Excellency, and could not reconcile his figure with the pictures he had seen of his nation's Prime Minister. Those pictures were nothing like this heavy-set individual swathed in layers of billowing gowns, a rotund face loosely framed in turban folds and a Bhudda smile that complemented his Bhudda figure once he was seated. The image he had received of his Prime Minister was of a taller and sparser frame, more likely to be seen in a plain kaftan than in the elaborate *alkimba** that sat like a tent over the panoply of power that the presence before him sought, he guessed, to radiate. His Excellency took his place in a chair that had obviously been set to dominate every seat in the room, none of which he was still invited to occupy, not even by an imperious nod of the head in the direction of the seats or a studied wave of the hand. He turned to the young official, hoping that this simple act of courtesy belonged to his department, but the man's voice put paid to such expectations.

'Yes? Why did you want to see His Excellency?'

O-oh, so that's the way it's going to be. The visitor carefully picked his way through the sprawling bodies and made for a seat, responding *en route*:

'But I did explain all of that to the official.' He reached a chair and turned to the Presence. 'May I take a seat, sir?' He was rewarded with a generous smile and a series of gasps from the young courtiers. Suddenly they lost all interest in their comics, most heads being turned in the direction of their master. 'Thank you, sir. I learnt you were in Paris and, as a Nigerian, I thought I ought to pay a courtesy call on one of our pioneer leaders.'

The Presence beamed slightly and nodded. Some form of silent communication took place, a fraction of which Maren caught and interpreted rightly as permission from the Presence to his aide to follow the visitor's clearly resented example. Protocol bowed in one direction, scowled in another, but took a seat below the raised section on which His Excellency's throne was placed.

'A courtesy call? Do you study in Paris?'

*Cape.

'No, I have just graduated in the UK. As a matter of fact, I ran into some slight trouble with French immigration on my last visit, and the mission here was very sympathetic and helpful. I was very impressed by His Excellency's personal interest in my predicament.'

The official glanced rapidly at his boss, then turned a vicious smirk on his guest. 'And when exactly was this?'

'About a month ago. I called the mission simply to express my gratitude. That was when I learnt that His er . . . Excellency was again passing through.'

Protocol swooped down on him in triumph. 'His Excellency was not in Europe a month ago. So he could not have taken any interest in your problems.'

'Oh?' He was a little shaken, not so much by this revelation but by the importance it appeared to hold for this aide. 'Well, obviously some misunderstanding then. Someone telephoned me back at the airport, and I was given the impression that it was the Prime Minister himself. Maybe it was just a Minister who was passing through . . .'

Every response appeared to aggravate the young aide, as if it went to prove some prior theory of this visitation by someone he had never met. In the few minutes of the exchange, and despite the efficient air-conditioning of the lounge, sweat had broken out on his forehead and his Palm Beach suit was becoming drenched beneath the armpits.

'And what are you, exactly?'

'I've told you. I have just completed my studies and I am on my way home.'

'Through Paris?' he sneered.

'Through anywhere,' – accepting reluctantly that the gloves were off. 'I understand His Excellency is also on his way home, through Paris.' He could not understand where he had gone wrong, what had bred the hostility – except perhaps that the crime was in his sitting down without an invitation. He continued, blithely, 'I am sure His Excellency is here on important business. I came here to earn a few francs before going home. One's scholarship doesn't accompany one home, you know.' And he smiled in the direction of his silent host, willing him to intervene in this unnecessary warfare. But the man remained stolidly silent, permitting only the avuncular smile on his face. And by now Protocol was nearly screaming.

'Yes, just who are you? I mean, what is your background? Why should you think that His Excellency would take time off his busy schedule to take an interest in your problems with immigration . . . ?'

'Well, I must confess that I found it unexpected, but, I was impressed. It made me very optimistic about the leadership of our nation . . .'

'His Excellency did not, and could not possibly have intervened.'

'So now I know, thank you.'

But Protocol refused to let go. Some preposterous crime seemed to be embedded in this plausible error, an affront of presumptuousness, no less, and he was determined to ferret out the motives behind it. 'You say you telephoned our mission at the British Embassy and someone phoned you back?'

'Yes.'

'And you were told it was His Excellency?'

'I believe that was what I heard. A British voice said, "As a matter of fact the Prime Minister is here right now and I'm sure he would have liked a word with you," something like that. Maybe all he said was Minister – the airport is a noisy place. There could even have been a word after Minister – like Minister's assistant – or flunkey, you know. Something like that.' And he looked up and down to ensure that the point was not missed.

'Even if it was just a Minister, why should he concern himself with you? That is what I am asking you. You imagine that a Minister who travels out on national business would leave his busy schedule and . . .'

'Listen, I don't know what you would do as a Minister, but if I were one and I found myself in a strange country and one of my nationals was in trouble, I would take an interest, one way or the other. Especially if we had no proper mission yet in that country.' Turning to the Presence, he tried yet again to draw him into the exchange. 'I am sure His Excellency does not find it in the slightest bit abnormal, and anyway, all this misunderstanding has given me the chance of meeting him . . .'

But the Excellency only continued to beam on the assemblage, saying nothing. Twenty pairs of eyes rolled on and off the beleaguered visitor, and the atmosphere grew eerie, as if in anticipation of some sinister conclusion towards which this exchange was a mere prelude. Damn it, this is Paris, he reminded himself. Soundproofed as the suite was, and despite the lightness of the Sunday morning traffic, he could hear the dull rumble of vehicles several floors below. He could not escape the feeling that he had somehow been transported as a common felon into the court of a feudal potentate but surely, even before summary judgement was effected, there would be rescue in the form of a liveried French waiter or whatever. His eyes roved the walls to locate the button for room service . . .

'And now that you have met His Excellency?' The sneer was palpable.

'It is a privilege, and I am grateful for the opportunity. If there is anything I can do for His Excellency in return while he is in Paris . . .'

'And just what do you think you can do for His Excellency?'

'I beg your pardon?' He had heard, of course, but had not expected what he had intended as a routine extension of a 'Thank you' to become yet another cause for interrogation.

'His Excellency is on an official visit to France and is being looked after by the British Embassy. He is not here as a tourist, and even if he were, there would still be officials to take care of his visit. So what makes you think there is anything you can do for His Excellency?'

The visitor now decided that any further reply would be to the Presence. He wanted to have nothing more to do with this over-heated individual, so he turned his head fully to the Silent One. 'Nothing much I can think of, to tell the truth, Your Excellency. I don't even speak any French. But er . . .' and he began not only to improvise but to enjoy himself: 'I take it that you need to promote the nation in your travels. My field happens to be cultural, maybe I could assist you with some ideas in that direction. And if you decided to throw a party, you know, a touch of Nigerian music would not be out of place – I accompany myself on the guitar, in fact, that's the business that brought me to Paris. So, please consider me entirely at your service . . .'

Blood vessels on Protocol's throat throbbed and threatened to burst and his voice rose to a scream. 'Do you think His Excellency has travelled abroad just to give parties? Do you think he has time for such frivolities?'

The visitor's eyes swept the entourage that littered the carpet, looked into Protocol's eyes and smiled.

By now the young official was nearly beyond control. 'You burst in on His Excellency without an appointment . . .'

'I did make an appointment.'

'I looked in the appointment book. Your name is not there.'

'I spoke to someone here, in this suite, this morning. He told me I could come over any time after half past nine when His Excellency would have finished his breakfast.'

'Who? Who did you speak with?'

'How do I know? Ask your own staff.'

His eyes raked the carpet in subdued fury. 'Did any of you take a call from this man?'

One of the more mature specimens of the gilded layabouts replied with studied casualness. 'Someone telephoned. He said he wanted to come and greet His Excellency.'

' "Meet", I said.'

'Oh, so that was you. Yes, I was told. And what I was told was that you wanted to come and greet His Excellency.'

'No, not "greet",' the intruder persisted, feeling that even though the difference was not a matter of life and death, it did matter to the court, and he was not about to bargain away his lifeline. 'I did want to meet His Excellency. In London, we students try to seize every opportunity to meet our leaders. We like to discuss the nation with them, to see what lies in store for us when we get back. We don't go out of our way simply to go and "greet" them.'

Protocol half rose. 'Well, now that you've . . .'

'Yes, now that I am here, I do have a question for His Excellency.'

'His Excellency has a busy day ahead of him.' But he resumed his seat.

'Just one question. You see, it is essential for us to know the thinking of our leaders, and you'll find that many of us are very concerned about issues of ideology. So, my question is, Your Excellency, what is your view of communism?'

The result was total silence, a deathly stillness, except for the disappearance of the fixed benevolent smile on the face of the

Presence. Then Protocol rose in a towering, stuttering rage. 'What is all this about? Who are you to come here and ask His Excellency his views on communism? Who sent you here?'

His voice tinged with some astonishment at the extent of the reaction, the visitor repeated yet again that he was just a student, then explained further: 'I am a nephew of Mrs Ransome-Kuti, whom you prevented from visiting the Republic of China for a conference. You seized her passport. But I hope you do understand, I am not asking this because she happens to be my aunt, I want to know because I am a Nigerian and a student.'

'You have no business coming here to ask His Excellency that kind of question. Are you a reporter?'

'I have every right. I am not a reporter. The papers reported, Your Excellency, that you said, and I'll try and use the exact quote – you were reported as saying, "Personally, I think that communism is an evil thing." Your Excellency, I would like to explore some ideas with you about communism. And freedom of movement, even to communist countries.'

'Are you a communist?' snapped Protocol.

'No, I am not. I am probably less of a communist than you are. But I would like to understand what our self-rule Government knows about communism that makes it condemn it as evil and confiscates the passports of citizens who wish to travel to communist countries, even if it is purely out of curiosity. Your Excellency, what do you know of communism?'

Protocol was already halfway to the door. 'His Excellency is not here to answer such questions, and he has a busy schedule.'

The visitor rose, gratefully, even with relief. He was not, after all, about to be flayed in the secrecy of a Claridges suite, packaged in a diplomatic bag and dumped in the Seine. He acknowledged the moment when he had decided that the visit had been a mistake, a waste of time and a probable handicap in his eventual homecoming. He blamed the conduct of Mr Protocol for his sudden abandonment of discretion, and a deliberate change of course to one of provocation. He knew precisely when he had become so nettled by the BIG SILENCE that he decided to needle the figure of pomp and circumstance with his secret weapon. Until that moment, he had entered the suite with no motive but to make contact, however tenuous, with home in a hostile environment. It was, after all, something to do on an idle Sunday morning. The genuineness of concern in the voices from the Nigerian desk of the British mission had left him curious. It was such a marked contrast to the self-centred, exhibitionist train of the politicians that he had encountered in London, making him wonder if he had not been too sweeping in his judgement of the class. Flamboyant, egotistical and extravagant, they turned up with or without reason, with baggage and entourage far in excess of their mission, cultivated students who would bring them girls to sleep with, whom they would reward extravagantly – one was actually paid with a cheque, signed by a famous national leader. She was a strange, brilliant London University student from an upper-class family, who provided paid sexual services to VIPs but slept free with any student she liked. She kept the cheque, flaunting it at Nigerians in the students' cafeteria – see how stupid your leader is; if I chose to blackmail him with this cheque, how would he explain it? Those politicians wooed student leaders with material gifts and promises, exhorted them to return, not so much for service as to ensure that they were first in line for the vacated positions of colonial officers. Their children were spoilt, élitist brats who infested the British public schools with their loutish manners, imitation accents and a moneyed condescension towards the talented children of less privileged families.

After a few encounters with this new breed of leaders and their scions, he had come to view the prospect of return as acceptance of engagement in a different kind of concern, one that lacked the clarity, or aura of nobility, of the battle for the liberation of southern Africa. That obsession, which formerly represented the summation of all his commitment to a continent, had led to more than one unsatisfactory play and several short stories, before *The Invention*. Somehow, in the humane accents of the 'Minister' who had taken the trouble to call him at the airport, he had interpreted traits of what genuine leadership should be and had looked forward with sincerity at the opportunity to say a simple 'Thank you'. Instead, he had run headlong against a cult of leadership that was not embarrassed to express outrage that any citizen should dare mistake its mission as one that could possibly, even as a quixotic gesture, as mere form without substance, even as an empty populist gesture, involve a moment of concern for a fellow citizen, however lowly or faceless . . .

'It was most considerate of you to receive me, Your Excellency. I hope it has not proved too tedious a morning.'

The Presence beamed. The inwardly seething figure meandered carefully through the lolling seraglio, passed through the door held open for him by Protocol whose Palm Beach suit was now devoid of one dry spot. Out in the soft sunshine that bathed the Champs Elysées that Sunday morning, he cast a look up at the windows that appeared to belong to the suite of his inhospitable hosts. Protocol's face was at one of the windows and, as his gaze moved downwards again, it encountered the figure of the young man who claimed to have taken his call. At the junction with Avenue George V, he turned round to face the Arc de Triomphe, fully expecting to find that the young man had been instructed to follow him. There was no sign of him, however, no trace of the encounter that had taken place in the luxury suite in the Champs Elysées. He began to wonder if the entire event had been imagined, if he had begun to hallucinate from the effects of too much coarse wine and too little nourishment.

They called it the *rentrée*, which meant that the lemmings were rushing home from the coast. This was a nation that claimed to represent the soul of European culture, the seat of her intellect, yet they all chose the same month for their annual vacation, set off in a bunch as if a gun had been fired for the start of a mammoth marathon amphibian race, for the cars that clogged the traffic nearly all dragged or carried on their roofs yachts, sailing boats, catamarans and other floating craft, and that was the way they re-entered Paris – fathers, mothers, grandparents and the latest generation all squeezed into one vehicle with beach spades and buckets, swim-suits and picnic baskets, paddles and poodles – setting off as if by arrangement so that they arrived at the same time in Paris, honking, cursing and gesticulating more from ritual instinct than from pur-pose or realistic expectation of any change in the snail's pace of their repossession of a city they had abandoned to a much despised but lucrative season of tourism.

Maren had posted a letter to the impresario to await his return. It was an exaggeratedly cheerful letter, designed to let him know that he had been usefully though not gainfully occupied. He thought the agent would be encouraged to learn that he had gained some experience with Parisian and tourist audiences, had obtained a taste of the ambiance and imbibed something of their moods and likely responses. He left the phone numbers of La Méthode and another occasional but friendly haunt in Montmartre, asking that the agent contact him before his newly acquired tan wore off, as he would like to fulfil at least a full month of engagements before returning to London and then – home.

The call came, as expected, hard on the heels of the official date of the *rentrée*. Into his ears poured a torrent of hot lava, blistering and implacable.

'Your conduct is unforgiveable. Unprofessional. I have spent much time and expense – yes, at my own expense – making contacts for you, professional contacts. I have presented to them a definite picture of a professional, who would be coming over for engagements for a limited period, the beginning of many great things for you. You said you were returning to London but what do you do? You go about singing in seedy cafés and making yourself seen publicly as an unserious artist, disgracing the image I have been so carefully cultivating at great expense, yes at my own expense. And you expect me to continue with your career? Ah no, but you have ruined a career which I have built up so carefully at great expense, at my own expense, going around with all sorts of unrespectable types and consorting with sleazy characters in no-good joints and let me tell you that there is nothing more I can do for you and I wash my hands of you completely.'

He was stunned. 'You are abandoning me?'

'It is not I who have abandoned you, *Monsieur*; it is you who have abandoned your career. You are unserious, unprofessional.'

'What was I supposed to do while you were away on vacation?'

'Is it my fault if you came at the wrong time? That is not my business, *Monsieur*. And I told you to go back and return when the season has resumed. Instead you choose to remain in Paris where you ruined . . .'

Slowly, he replaced the phone. Shortly after, unaware of any conscious decision, he found himself on the way to the Métro, clutching the agent's address. After several minutes scrutinising a

Métro map, he found the location of the street and plunged into
the Parisian underbelly. He had no idea what he would say to the
agent when he confronted this man, all he was aware of was a need
to come face to face with this new symbol of Parisian heartlessness,
first cousin to the barman specimen who would try to wrest a few
centimes' change from a starving vagrant. He needed to see this
well-vacationed impresario in his luxurious environment and ask
him, at the very least, how he expected him to find his way back to
that same London from which he had dislodged him, without so
much as offering him one drink or a meal, or even negotiating his
air fare or a night's performance fee. It was the inhumanity of it all
that drove him. No human being behaved like this to another, least
of all to a stranger brought into one's own environment, no matter
what errors of judgement such a stranger committed. And he did
not acknowledge any such errors. Mr Impresario was the professional and he was his responsibility. It was his responsibility to
instruct him about the dos and don'ts of the profession, he knew
bloody well that he never claimed to be a Pete Seeger. And Pete
Seeger never looked down on him when they met in that singer's
apartment and went out afterwards for a drink; he even offered him
some tips on folk music and performance.

Frankly, he did not see the big deal between the friendly ambiance
of La Méthode and the coy, chichi pretentiousness of L'Abbaye
where the audience was not even allowed to clap their hands but
must snap their fingers, which was what one did at home to ward
off evil. (You snapped your thumb and middle finger around your
head and hoped you had exorcised a curse.) But L'Abbaye, where
the big strapping negro held court, seated in a high chair framed
against a shrine with candles and icons, yes, exactly like a shrine,
with his male Eurydice at his feet, a demure, diffident voice cultivated to contrast with the big black buck Orpheus of a six-foot-six
basso profundo American exile with earrings like a roving pirate –
was that the 'professional' image this impresario claimed he had
ruined by singing for his drink among Guatemalan exiles and not
so preciously mannered lesbians and homosexuals who clapped or
did not clap their hands and cried and danced on the tables as the
mood took them?

And anyway, was this pasty-faced heartless Parisian Levantine about to tell him that no singing star in the firmament ever sang for pennies thrown into tins and hats on the pavements of cities at some time in their career, which he, to his credit at least, had scrupulously avoided doing – purely from inhibition, temperament, not professional propriety – because if the sated vacationer claimed that, he would confront him with a long list that need not even stretch across the Atlantic to include the great twelve-string blues saint Leadbelly – not that he would dare commit the sacrilege of comparing himself with that genius, god forbid – but if the liar called himself an agent worth his salt he must know of the Little Sparrow Edith Piaf and they certainly didn't come more Parisian than that! If only he knew some choice French expletives to utter when the moment came, although that really did not matter since the crook spoke and understood perfect English and probably a dozen other conning languages. Perhaps it was all for the best, anyway, this kind of agent probably brought him to Paris to work him, starve him, rob him of his earnings and abandon him, so it was just as well it had all happened before he had earned a cent for the slave master . . .

It was a dingy neighbourhood in the seventeenth *arrondisement*, not at all what he had imagined, and the address at which he now stopped fitted neatly into the distressed neighbourhood. He climbed up the narrow, mouldy stairways along worn carpets, past peeling doors and walls that would have been better off left grimy than ineffectively disguised by a veneer of cheap paint that let the damp through. The agent lived at the very top, the sixth floor. He checked the address for the tenth time, just to be certain. It was impossible to associate the torrent of rebuke to which he had been subjected, which centred around his unprofessional slumming, with anyone who actually resided in such a *bâtiment* of ungenteel decay. But it was the right address, and he eventually stood before the man's apartment and knocked. It was opened by the agent himself, and he went visibly white despite his impressive tan.

'You! What are you doing here? Who asked you to come here?'

Maren took in the interior at a glance, a tiny cubicle of an apartment; he had seen bigger even in the heart of Paris. From its shallow labyrinth a husky female voice called out to enquire who was the caller. The agent responded in a French torrent, of which Maren understood only the word *chérie*.

'May I come in?'

Reluctantly, the agent stood aside. Almost at once, a busty replica of the agent crashed through a blown flowery curtain hanging in front of the door that separated the living room from the rest of the apartment. Maren could only think that she was not his idea of anything *chérie*, but his attention shifted even quicker to the heavy four-poster bed that he glimpsed through the door, and then the woman slammed the door angrily, but not before he had observed that the bed took up nearly the entire bedroom. The sight completed the destruction of the professional class that the agent had fraudulently claimed for himself in London. Everything about the apartment was tawdry, right down to the apron on which the woman wiped her hands as she stood with both hands on her hips and stared at him like a *tricoteuse* willing the fall of the guillotine.

'Is that he? What does he want here?'

Her husband shrugged, shut the outer door and proceeded to occupy an armchair. In a motion that was expressive of a resolve to protect him if need be, or form a common front, the woman pulled out a chair and sat next to him. The man gestured to a chair opposite.

'What can I do for you? Didn't you understand all I said to you on the phone?'

Maren sighed. This marked the fruitless end of the journey that began from Sloane Square, London, and he reconciled himself to the futility of his visit. 'You brought me over from London; at the very least, you should help me return there.'

'You did not fulfil the conditions of your visit.'

'I do not know of any conditions of my visit. All I am saying is that you have a moral obligation towards me. You have done absolutely nothing to help me out.'

The woman rose, raging. 'My husband has done everything possible for you, but you ruined it all through your irresponsible conduct. You have finished several months of careful preparation.'

'Madam, I have not seen any evidence of any preparation.'

'You are ungrateful, *Monsieur*, very ungrateful and crude.'

'Crude?'

'Yes, crude, very crude. Or else you would not sing in those places, those places which are so opposite to what my husband has prepared for you.'

'Can I have just one address of these other kinds of places so I can try my luck without his help?'

'Why should I provide such an address after what you've done?' the man snarled.

'Because I don't believe you, sir. One moment you tell me there is no "season" in summer. Nobody that is anybody is supposed to remain in Paris. The next moment you tell me that I have been seen in undesirable places. So who are these genteel nightclub owners and agents and clientèle before whom my professional image has been compromised? Do they ever visit places like La Méthode even in season?'

'You are insulting, *Monsieur*,' came the scream from the woman. 'You lack appreciation of the work my husband has done and then you have the nerve to barge into his residence and insult him. You have no claims on his concerns and you are irresponsible . . .'

'Yes, yes, I've heard that over a hundred times, but not once have you tried to apply the word to your husband's conduct. I think it's time to take my leave.'

'Yes, you had better. Or I'll call the police. You cannot come here to threaten my husband.'

'Threaten your husband!' Maren looked the two of them over; even the woman looked capable of flinging him down the stairwell without any assistance from the husband, who was himself a decent imitation of a Mafia enforcer. 'I think I understand, madam. Don't bother to get up, I'm on my way.'

He gathered around him all the dignity he could muster and walked briskly from the apartment. It could have been worse, he reflected. What would he have done if the couple had assaulted him: yelled for help and summoned the police? 'SAVAGE SINGER SAVAGES AGENT AND WIFE IN THEIR APARTMENT!' There was no doubt in his mind whose story the police would believe, and he without one decent French phrase worth a shred of innocence. At the Métro, he hesitated. Then he began to study the map, this time not for the train connections but for the shortest way into Paris on his two feet.

Did you have to sneak home like a thief in the night?

III *Avanti*, Evanti!

His exit was not without pomp, and gravity, though he would himself have preferred, in his familiar style, the expression *'gravitas'*. Accomplished orator that he was, as Independence approached, the great 'Zik' of Africa, Dr Nnamdi Azikiwe, was bowing out of partisan strife in a biblical flourish that moved many but left many more dissatisfied. The 'fight well fought', the 'race well run' read well, and his hypnotic lilt, so familiar and beloved, endowed his leave-taking with a serenity that promised to establish a model for emulation. It accepted and dignified the acrimony of the past, the suspicions and divisions, as if they were all necessary preludes to this great symphony of destination, of finally attaining at once a sovereign goal and the hearth of one great family. The divisions, resentments, humiliations, even hatreds of the past years, from partial self-government to full Independence, were forgotten. The humiliation of the cream of the North, led by the stolid Sardauna of Sokoto, whose party had insisted on the safety net of 'Independence as soon as practicable', in opposition to the militant South, whose spokesman, the quietly intense Anthony Enahoro, had launched the SGNN catchphrase – Self-Government for Nigeria Now – all this appeared to be forgiven. Emerging from the pristine chambers of the National House of Assembly only five years before, the northern delegates had been jeered, their turbans and *babanriga*** tugged, their persons manhandled by the southern radical mobs, indifferent to future consequences.

Nnamdi Azikiwe's valedictory passage had sealed that past, anointed his erstwhile enemy, to whom he now publicly ceded power, a

---

*A huge, billowing gown, much favoured among the Hausa.

humble teacher and latecomer to the nationalist struggle, Alhaji Tafawa Balewa, whose party, the Northern People's Congress, had emerged victorious at the political centre. Azikiwe was not yet sixty years of age, but he had chosen to retire from the slings and arrows of outrageous politics, becoming the Governor-General of the Nigerian nation, a ceremonial office that still owed allegiance to Queen Elizabeth of England. Many preferred the old Zik, wished that he would remain in the turbulent centre of nation-building, that he would lead his NCNC, the National Council of Nigeria and the Cameroons, in 'loyal opposition' to a Federal Government that was meticulously modelled on the Westminster parliament. The ancient warrior, however, chose to become an elder statesman, arbitrating the inevitable contentions that would follow Independence, superintending the pomp and circumstance that were surely the modest deserts of the most populous black nation on the African continent, and indeed the wide world over.

His installation was separate from the Independence celebrations. These had not only been opulent and magnificent, they had narrowly escaped sabotage in the form of a play entitled *A Dance of the Forests*, which had been thoughtlessly selected by a jury as befitting a nation's rites of passage. Very few people in Nigeria, even among those – white or black – charged with the awesome responsibility of organising splendiferous spectacles that would celebrate the end of colonial rule, were aware of the disgrace that nearly befell the nation. Certainly the Governor-General-to-be was himself a victim of the awesome veil of secrecy thrown around the non-event; how else would he have agreed that this spoilsport playwright of whose media contributions he had heard only flittingly, might be permitted near his own installation festivities, much less be the Master of Ceremonies at the culminating concert at the Federal Palace Hotel, Victoria Island, Lagos? This event was the marzipan on the Independence cake. In addition to established Ambassadors and High Commissioners, quite a handful of his former college mates, friends, mistresses, fellow pan-Africanists, front-line nationalists, independent militants . . . plus the inevitable clutch of cronies and hangers-on, had been invited from all corners of the world.

Thousands of birds-of-paradise, ostrich and cockatoo headdresses; clean-shaven heads with the single red feather sprouting from an adhesive lump of pitch; then mask upon mask; beads and bangles, drums, *kakaki**, wooden xylophones; riverine and coastal regattas; ex-servicemen beribboned and bemedalled, uniforms starched and ironed into glossy leather, buckles and belts and puttees; human blobs from fattening houses, weighed down even further with tons of ivory and bronze limb casings, yet humanised by their impossibly sweet and forlorn smiles and stately steps of transitional being, their agemates from other cultures on display with far more rational fleshing, firm buttocks and truculent breasts; feathered warriors and leather shields and silver-ringed spears, timber thighs and calves – and not a few spindly and arthritic legs – for there was no leaving out the aged, the undernourished or simply ill; hunters' guilds in fortified breastplates – cowries, amulets, gourds – and the massed discharges of dane guns and muskets; women's guilds in measured dance steps, their pneumatic bottoms nonetheless lascivious in infinite gyrations, the pubescent acrobatic marvels, balancing for a hypnotic micro-second on the gleaming tips of butcher's knives; masquerades of mundane orders and of cultic secrecies, huge as huts, lean as lentils, their superstructures brushing tree branches and the hanging eaves of dung-smeared buildings . . . all emerged from open village compounds, from hidden recesses forbidden to the uninitiated, to startle, confound and transform the regional capitals and major cities of the nation – Ibadan, Kaduna, Enugu, Kano, Jos, Port Harcourt, Calabar, Makurdi and, of course, the federal capital itself, Lagos – flaunting the exuberant cultures that forgave anthropologists their obsession and challenged a new generation of creators with an embarrassment of riches.

The competition for a national flag was nationwide, resulting in a green-white-green doctrine of the virtues of simple-mindedness, a three-piece quilt in a land of pregnant motifs, of colours, contours, fauna and flora, one that was needlessly explained even to the most moronic citizen as symbolising: green for agriculture, the country's staple product, white for peace, and once again, green for agriculture. It was, however, a testament to the ingenuity of a serious-minded, pragmatic people, for who else could dream up a colour scheme that would be equally at home as a football jersey, a dish-

*A long bugle, associated with royalty.

cloth or a bathroom towel? Even flowerpots and driveway markings, palm trunks and roundabouts, uniforms and office paperweights, official diaries, office furniture and interior decoration . . . nothing appeared immune to the rampaging lure of the flag motif. What, a few stubborn heads wondered, would the country resemble if a more ornate design had been chosen, such as the Stars and Stripes?

The national anthem had itself been thrown open to the entire world of the British Commonwealth, the victorious entry – both lyrics and music – being the brainchild of a British housewife, composed, it was suggested by unpatriotic elements, naturally, in between changing the baby's nappy and boiling cabbage and potatoes. This of course could have been a pure invention of the critics who lacked the forthrightness to state what they really thought of an insipid, brain-damaged anthem. The Durbar of the Northern Horsemen was, as always, a triumph of the strange rhythmic rapport between man and this graceful beast, coordinated in a massed charge of a hundred riders, an animated canvas that rendered wind, colours, and the roar of hooves almost tactile, a thunderous control at breathtaking speed, always the *pièce de résistance* of any festive occasion in the country. There were art exhibitions galore, even special commissions for decors and public designs that introduced to the world the natural inheritors of the acknowledged genius of traditional artists. And the organising committees did ensure, at least, that the great talent hunt that ended in British suburbia did not prevent composers from the Nigerian musical firmament from adding their own flowering to the patriotic garden of the Arts on an occasion that was, after all, designed to project the nation at her most procreative.

The play, *A Dance of the Forests*, was, therefore, frankly not missed by anyone, dignitary or ordinary. On the contrary, a spontaneous drinks party was held by the committee to celebrate the narrow escape that the nation had had, thanks to a member who had discovered that the work struck a discordant note in the Independence suite – subversive, cynical, iconoclastic, that it mocked the glories of the past and was pessimistic about the future. The writer 'had been too long away', lacked the patriotic spirit of hope and confidence that was needed for a nation that was taking the first step into a rose-tinted future.

The playwright remained unaware as to why suddenly there was no official venue for his play in the capital city, but was left in no doubt of something gone wrong when the play, which had won a competition sponsored for the very purpose of the Independence celebrations, failed even to appear on the official programme, which included events that were taking place in the regions. He soon settled for the University theatre in Ibadan as being more than adequate, assembled a semi-professional team of performers and designers under the name Nineteen-Sixty Masks, and produced the taxing, over-ambitious play that just managed to hold together for a handful of performances.

If his purpose was to 'break in' both himself and the company that he had put together, the choice could not have been more suitable. A large cast of over thirty, it incorporated an already estab-lished group of Igbo *atilogwu* dancers that was, however, based in Lagos. So also was half the rest of the company, some of them civil servants, teachers, company workers, a few students and some unemployed. The other half, of roughly the same occupational com-position, lived in Ibadan, a distance of one hundred and forty kilo-metres. Full rehearsals could therefore take place only at weekends, alternating between the two towns, while the playwright-director worked on individuals during the week, even conducting rehearsals, mostly on the finer points of interpretation, in the canvas-topped Land Rover in which he transported his artistes from one town to the other. The weekend rehearsals took place anywhere – in school halls, in the homes of the members, who took it in turns to feed the mob, and sometimes overfed them, rendering them virtual somnam-bulists for the afternoon half of the rehearsals. Then there was the halfway stop at Sagamu Arms Hotel, where peppered snails and cold beer interfered with line rehearsals, or hot *suya** from the dust-flavoured Hausa grills at the motor garage – this was usually on the way home after weekend rehearsals. If no one else missed the Nineteen-Sixty Masks after it gradually dissolved in the seventies and gave way to Orisun Theatre, the *suya* vendors of Sagamu surely did, for Orisun Theatre, tighter, younger and less experienced than the Masks but full-time, more flexible and more (politically) adventurous, was to stay in one place, Ibadan, basing most of its

*Skewered meat.

activities on the Mbari Arts Club, right in the teeming heart of Gbagi market and the surrounding streets that were only an extension of the market.

It was exhilarating, and it did mean for him the long-dreamt-of homecoming – what more could a theatre-obsessed mind desire? The ingredients were all present – a creative reunion, experimentation and innovation. The creative energy around him appeared inexhaustible; not even the already evident profligacy of the politicians could deplete *that* – it was mercifully beyond their reach. The complexity and physical demands of *A Dance* extracted from the participants resources that most admitted they had never suspected in themselves, being long accustomed to a standard fare of J. B. Priestley, Galsworthy or Sheridan, the occasional Bernard Shaw, the operettas of Gilbert and Sullivan, and the genteel volunteerism of amateur productions.

The blessing and support of Independence officialdom had long been jettisoned and so they had no master to please but themselves, no other goal but the masochistic relish of immersing themselves in a demanding experience that robbed them of nearly every weekend with their families. Even the sense of liberation that came with the disappearance of all official intervention was tempered by the somewhat draconian regimen imposed by a driven 'returnee'. They forged a tight-knit clan of diverse origins, temperaments, and normal preoccupations, adapting to circumstances as they came – from sleeping on the carpet and cushions in a small living room to acting as emergency chauffeurs, props-and-costume scavengers, to wading through torrential downpours to rehearsals – rain and storm having been declared natural events of tropical climes which could not be permitted to interfere with man-made concerns, such as theatre rehearsals.

Patrick Ozieh, a petroleum engineer; Olga Adeniyi-Jones, of a long-indigenised 'expatriate' line, and an accomplished contralto; Ralph Opara, Yemi Lijadu, Segun Olusola, all broadcasters; Funmi Asekun, of ample proportions, who soon abandoned stage appearances but continued to effectively 'mother' the company; Francesca Pereira, of an old Brazilian stock, a melifluous soprano – I knew it, the mother screamed, after her motor accident on a Sunday morning as she rushed to rehearsals with the playwright – that young man will not rest until he has killed you all, see what he's done now, you who never had a motor accident in your life! No, his kind never has an accident, it is others who have the accidents for him; Gaius Anoka, a schoolteacher, as was Dapo Adelugba . . . Then the fledglings, Tunji Oyelana, Femi Fatoba, Sola Rhodes, Yewande Akinbo, Segun Sofowote, Femi Euba, Wale Ogunyemi, Jimi Solanke, Yomi Obileye, Bimbo Bolarinwa, Betty Okotie, Nike Sote, Femi Ogunbanjo, Taiye Ayorinde and Deli Oti, who would form the core of the new Orisun Theatre, less the ones that got away, the parents barring the gates against their wards – yes, we've heard about that upstart and you are having nothing to do with him; you will study medicine and that's flat; that no-good is up to no good, just trying to distract you from a respectable course, so don't let me catch you even taking a phone call from him, and that goes for your mother whom I know has been abetting you in such frivolities. Drama – ptueh! – just what is that? Are you now going to join the Ogunde chorus girls, all those prostitutes? Just remember in what sort of a home you were raised and stop trying to hobnob with those types with no background and I don't want to hear anything about him and his bohemian types, that's all they are, dirty bohemians, no background to speak of. They are dissolute, no morals. I know all about him, they've even named him after one of the characters in his plays – Baroka – that's the dirty old man who seduces young girls, so don't think I don't know what I'm talking about. And tell your mother if I see you near any of them she will pack out of this house and take you with her . . .

No matter, Orisun Theatre continued to draw nourishment from the teats of the Nineteen-Sixty Masks, whose individual and collective pedigrees and backgrounds were every bit as prominent as the claims of the 'colonial aristocrats', as variegated as those of the nation itself, the company's internal fusion and generous bond of fellowship seemed to reflect the nation's ambition to weld together such apparent incompatibles. Alas, in that regard, there was no question about which had the greater success.

Not even the participation of such 'responsible citizens' of impeccable social pedigrees in this venture permitted second thoughts to the officials – would they really lend themselves to an enterprise to undermine the new nation? And of course, even if the first generation of politicians had been compelled to see the completed work, and had it analysed to them, shorn of all symbolism and ambiguities, it would not have made the slightest difference to the future of a nation, the kernel of which was already implanted in the machinations of the departing colonial power. The farewell smile on the British face was broken razor, the hand outstretched for a genteel handshake, or snapped up in a farewell salute, cunning crab claws whose sidewise sleight of motion hid the toxification of the passage it traversed, and the sowing of tares – such as falsification of the nation's population figures. The parting gift of the British to themselves was thus a solid base in a region that the colonial power had rendered pliable to her will, one that would guarantee continuing control over the vast nation for decades to come – at least until the centennial anniversary of the Treaty of Berlin – and maybe even until the third millennium – why not? All the signatories would meet and compare notes, crow over who had completely lost out, and who were still in business.

If at any time then, or afterwards, the British felt a twinge of guilt, it was easily rendered superfluous. The first-generation leaders, irrespective of region, and with pathetically few exceptions, were already serving up the bounty of inheritance on the festive board of all-comers, but of course the British had ensured the lion's share for themselves. All they acknowledged as owing in return was in the manner of their departing, a programme of celebrations that encouraged all manner of extravagant shows and catered for the fun-loving and pomp-besotted 'natives', one also that would remind them always of the unmatchable majesty and pageantry of the British monarchy.

The message caught up with him in Benin, his latest stop in the research that was taking him all over the nation, worrying out dramatic forms from the mould of rituals, festivals and seasonal ceremonials. Would he return urgently, produce and compère the gala evening that would round off the festivities at the installation of Zik of Africa as Governor-General of the nation? Nothing more was required of him, no dramatic sketches of his own, no excerpts from *A Dance of the Forests*, no song, no poetry reading: it seemed safe enough, and, of course, he was flattered. He shared the unease of many about this self-transformation of the nationalist into a

ceremonial surrogate for the Queen of England but, honour to
whom honour was due. If the great Zik was determined to lock
himself in a gilded cage, let it at least be done with style and, if
possible, with a professional resolve.

So, back to Lagos in the tireless Land Rover, to the Federal Palace
Hotel, where the shortlist of would-be artistes had been arrayed for
final selection and the beginning of rehearsals. Most were familiar,
even fellow criminals from *A Dance* were on the team, another
reassuring sign. There were the mandatory troupes from traditional
music and dance repertory. Proficiency and variety had to contend
with regional representation, but this was no real problem, the
standard being predictably high. It was only a question of soothing
ruffled egos and assuaging natural disappointments.

There was one region, however, that was not within Nigeria's
natural boundaries: her name was Madame Evanti. And this region
was barred to any selection process. She was the special guest of
the Governor-General, flown over from the United States at his
own personal and official invitation. A former operatic and concert
performer, her presence generated genuine excitement among the
more Western-acculturated company, the Show Director-cum-
Master of Ceremonies not excepted. He could not wait to hear her
burst into song.

Mentally, he allocated Madame Evanti all of fifteen minutes, a
disproportionate time compared to other artistes. However, she was
not only a foreign guest, she was also the guest of the celebrant, the
official Head of State. It was his occasion. And in plain honesty,
the young compère was not averse to European opera, and was
more than willing to devote the entire evening to a different form
of art from what had dominated the Independence proceedings
until then. Francesca Pereira's operatic voice, performing special
arrangements of Yoruba traditional songs by Akin Euba, and
accompanied by him on the piano, promised an exciting contrast to
the experienced performance of this international professional.

Madame Evanti looked a little blown, even blowsy, used far too
much make-up and tended towards annoyingly exaggerated gestures. She was obviously one of the great believers in the grand
entrance, and this did not matter whether the 'entrance' was being
made from her seat in the hall onto the stage during rehearsals, or

just to call someone's attention for a glass of water. Her Italian accent sounded somewhat Brooklynese, or whatever accent was used in *Guys and Dolls* – the compère had never been to the United States, and all accents that did not sound Deepest Alabama South or Eugene O'Neill theatre had to be Brooklynese. Her neck was heavily powdered and seemed eternally poised (even when she was seated) to charge the ceiling on a high C; neither powder nor interrogatory head lift, however, could disguise the wrinkles on her neck.

None of these affectations diminished the anticipation of the gathered company as she walked onto the stage for her first number, an aria from *Madame Butterfly*. The sparsely populated hall, filled with only the artistes, the protocol and other functionaries from the office of the Governor-General, plus dawdling cleaners and other hotel staff, listened to her rendition with rapt attention. They remained equally silent after her second number, a negro spiritual.

Then she announced, with great pride, that she had composed a special song for the celebrant. It was a long, treacly song, whose every second line was a long-drawn refrain, packed, she was evidently convinced, with all the emotions of love, fervour, homage and veneration. It went *A-zee-kee-e-we* on a rising note, then again *A-zee-kee-e-we*, on a drowning note that expired in a heart-rending sigh, a massive fluttering of her mascara-ed false eyelashes, and a demure contraction of her buoyant *décolletage*. The tribute to the Governor-General had one impeccable advantage over the other two offerings: since no one was familiar with the tune, it was possible to argue that it was her accompanist, Akin Euba, who continually struck the wrong notes. With *Madame Butterfly* and the negro spiritual, however, there was no question that Madame Evanti was tone deaf, that her vocal chords were pumiced beyond salvage, and her sense of tempo in permanent dislocation.

She, of course, misread the silence. 'You find eet mooving, yes?'

In his walk up to the stage, the compère eyed Akin Euba, asking silently, Why have you done this to us? Akin shrugged his shoulders to indicate that the matter was never in his hands. As an employee of the Broadcasting Service, he had been summoned to duty, and his not to reason why; his instructions were to rehearse with and to accompany Madame Evanti on the piano. The compère felt all alone as he climbed the makeshift stage to confront the radiant figure and still-heaving breasts of the diva. He had already decided how to approach the problem.

'Madame Evanti, thank you, thank you so much. But now you see, we have a problem: time. Your three songs took twenty-five minutes.' He waved his hand around the hall, full of waiting performers. 'You see for yourself how many groups and individuals have to share one and a half hours.'

Her wrinkles sagged. 'But, but what can we dooo? The Governor-General himself specially eenvited me to seeeng for him.'

'I know, I know, and I wish we could give you one whole hour to yourself.' The idea then took hold of him and he proceeded more confidently. 'That's it! What we must do is arrange a recital, all to yourself. We could hold it on the lawns of Government House . . .'

'But I must return to Europe next week. I have engagements. The concerts are already booked.'

Yeah, in an institution for the deaf, no doubt. But he only smiled with increased confidence. 'That is no problem. We'll do it by this weekend, either Saturday or Sunday. I know His Excellency's programme and we can fit it in, believe me. Akin will start rehearsing with you beginning from tomorrow morning.'

She still wouldn't give up. 'Are you sure? Perhaps if I came last, to round up the evening . . . I am sure His Excellency then will not mind if we run over the time . . .'

'His Excellency gave firm orders that the concert must last exactly one hour and a half – you know he is giving a dinner afterwards . . .'

'Yes, yes, that ees true.'

'It's too bad but, Protocol, you know. They are rather strict about these things. Now, my suggestion is this. Obviously you must sing the special composition for Zik, that goes without saying.'

'Oh yes, of course.'

'I suggest, however, that you cut out two of the stanzas. If you can do that, we gain several minutes. Then you can choose one of the other two numbers, the negro spiritual or the aria – one, but not both.'

'But that eez eemposseebeelay. The tribute weell be ruined. It ees one seengle piece. The speerit will be destroyed eef I remove one verse.'

'The chorus then, Madame Evanti, the refrain. Can you reduce that by half? It takes up almost the entire song.'

Akin Euba left his piano and came to the rescue. 'Er, look, why don't I try to work this out with Madame Evanti? I am sure we can both think of a way of going about this.'

'All right. I leave it to you. And you will also decide which of the two songs is going in before the run-through this afternoon, agreed?'

Euba nodded. The woman looked querulous, no longer pleading but truculent. The compère smelt trouble and braced himself for it.

Madame Evanti did not appear for the run-through. But for the performance itself she came in the entourage of the celebrant, dressed in glittering rejuvenation of faded glory, flicking open a tortoiseshell fan at the slightest excuse, swishing the train of her evening dress, primping and giggling among the gilded moths that surrounded the acknowledged candle of the night, a sorry coquette that would not admit the toll of years, neither on her person nor on her talent. As the guests moved to take their seats, she went straight to the piano, sinking onto the stool that was placed for the assistant who would turn over the sheets of the pianist's score. The compère was backstage, checking the final details when Akin Euba approached him.

'I'd better warn you. Madame is determined to sing all three songs.'

'Then you do not accompany the third.'

'I've seen to that. I made the excuse that the special tribute is too complicated for me to accompany. I reminded her of this morning's rehearsals, told her there simply wasn't enough time to rehearse so as to do justice to it. So she agreed we should rehearse the first two. She is to let me know tonight which one of the two will share place of honour with the tribute. But I could tell. She is going to announce both numbers, then continue with the third, unaccompanied.'

'No she is not.'

'How are you going to stop her?'

'I'm going to warn her now.'

He sent one of the staff to bring her backstage. She swept in and tilted her face in irritation, a great artist interrupted in her moment of intense mental rehearsal.

'Good evening, Madame Evanti. We missed you at the run-through.'

'I could not come. His Excellency insisted that I join the tea party for some Heads of States.'

'I understand. Well, I thought I would ask which of the two numbers you have decided upon. Akin doesn't seem to know.'

'I do not know myself. When the moment comes, I shall be guided by inspiration. That is the way of we arteests. I have rehearsed both, but I shall choose when ze moment comes.'

'Of course. By all means, do play it by ear. That means, I take it, that at the end of *two* songs, whatever they are, I shall come on stage with my assistant. Since you were not here this afternoon, I had better explain the sequence. We come on stage, I say nice things about your performance and formally thank you. I then proceed immediately to announce the next performers as my assistant escorts you off-stage. We have reserved a seat for you in the auditorium – it is just behind His Excellency and you will be accompanied there during the brief intermission. You can then enjoy the rest of the show with the other guests. Is that arrangement all right with you, *Madame?*'

Curtly she said, 'Thank you,' and turned towards her place by the piano.

'Not that way, please. You must have noticed that all our artistes remain backstage – that is the convention I prefer on occasions like this. After the intermission you will of course be free to become just another of His Excellency's guests. We have provided you with a comfortable armchair in our improvised Green Room – it's all make-shift backstage I'm afraid, but the chair is certainly more comfortable than that stool . . .'

Again she snapped, 'Thank you,' turned and consented to be led backstage. The MC hoped that the rest of the evening would be as easy.

It was not. If the morning rehearsal had been torture of an unusual kind, Madame Evanti, in full performance flight, proved that there were still several turns left in the screw. The audience was well trained, however, and only a few heads turned to exchange pained or puzzled looks or squirm in their seats in disbelief, and in obvious discomfort. She began with *Madame Butterfly*, milked the polite applause for several bows, and then composed herself for the negro spiritual. The compère shrugged, exchanged last-minute instructions with his team backstage, leapt onstage before the last note of the spiritual had died down and was himself leading the applause lustily, bowing to Madame Evanti as she took her fifth bow, then taking her gallantly by the elbow to turn her over to his deputy compère for a well-deserved recuperation in the emergency Green Room.

'Thank you, Madame Evanti, thank you very much,' he repeated over and over again, giving her a final bow and swivelling round immediately so he would not notice whatever drama might take place behind him. There was none, however, no untidy proceeding that involved his deputy. One glare from the diva's basilisk eyes had given the assistant such stage fright that he simply continued his walk across the stage as if he had no business whatever with Madame. He tidied a corner of the curtain as if that was his only purpose for invading the stage and vanished from sight, disappeared into the wings where he was found later, shaking his head and muttering, '*Aje!** That woman na *aje*! Nobody fit go near am.'

Oblivious to the failure of his deputy's assignment, the compère carried on his duty of announcing the next contribution. A few seconds later, he was rudely alerted to the continuing presence of Madame but betrayed no sign whatever, neither missing a beat in his introduction nor flicking a glance in the direction of the interruption. Only he in the entire hall appeared to be unaware of the woman who had come up to his shoulder and was sweetly insisting, as if it was all a misunderstanding, 'I have steell one song for His Excellency. I have steell one song. My special tribute.'

'. . . and the next item is a dance by the famous Obitun dancers from Ado Ekiti who . . .'

'. . . I have steell one song . . .'

Drumming had erupted from the wings: the Obitun dancers were following strict instructions – 'On pain of losing your slot, start the drumming the moment you hear the word Obitun and dance onto the platform as soon as I turn in your direction.'

'. . . I have steel one song.'

*Witch.

Ignoring the panic on the faces of the dignitaries – diplomats, ministers, society cream, rustling headties and tinkling jewellery, ignoring VIP heads turning to one another in hurried consultation . . .

'. . . the long Obitun tradition of elegant discipline, under the leadership of . . .'

'. . . I have steell one song . . .'

Come on, Obitun, come on!

Until it became impossible not to notice or hear T. O. S. Benson, Minister of Information, who was seated next to His Excellency, his trunk bent urgently forward, 'MC! MC!', his finger jabbing in the direction of the determined figure at the compère's back. So he turned round and – Surprise, Surprise! – someone had been trying to gain his attention all this time. He fooled no one. Now he leant with excessive attentiveness towards her, cupping his ear as if to overcome the drumming. Then, a wide-eyed 'O-oh', and a beatific smile as he returned to the audience with good tidings.

'Your Excellency, ladies and gentlemen, but Your Excellency especially, it would appear that we have an unexpected treat for you. Madame Evanti has composed an original song in honour of the occasion which she will now render, unaccompanied,' glaring towards Akin Euba at the piano in case he had a change of heart and decided to accompany her with a chord or two. The lady warbled her way through the masterpiece, milked her refrain of every lachrymose drop, awarded herself several curtain calls – the audience was ecstatic, that could not be denied; they had heard the name of their beloved Zik at least three dozen times – and finally, reluctantly, conceded the stage to lesser mortals.

The long, weary night drew at last to a close, the compère fleeing to the comfort of his favourite Lagos nightclub, the Caban Bamboo, owned by Bobby Benson, the brother of the same Minister of Information who had salvaged the situation at the concert. The others would later join him to cool stretched nerves in cold beer and Bobby's high-life music. It was well that he fully savoured those hours of recuperation late into the night because, unknown to him, the final applause had hardly ended before the baying for blood began and the gleeful face of *penkelemes* looked in. Who was that Master of Ceremonies, the Master of Impertinence more accurately, who had humiliated the special guest of His Excellency? Word went out that he must be sacked from his post, prohibited from holding any public office for life, hanged, quartered and his remains displayed in Tinubu Square to serve as a lesson to all others. Tried to prevent an international operatic star from singing, an icon of the music stage that had condescended to grace the travelling show of Nigerian Independence? Action was to be taken at once and reported to the office of the Attorney-General in case there were also grounds for public prosecution. The Secretary to the Prime Minister was to be informed, Interpol to be alerted in case he tried to leave the country.

Then was it discovered that sacking the villain presented a problem. He was not, as had been imagined – thanks to the heavy involvement of the Government Broadcasting Service in the concert – an employee of that institution. But he must be in the employment of one institution or another! Oh yes, it was revealed, he had some kind of attachment to the University of Ibadan, but no one tells the University what to do with its erring staff. Even so there must be a way to discipline him, to punish him for this deed of *lèse majesté*. This was a crime committed against the Governor-General of the giant of Africa, this was a sabotage of his inauguration event!

Wait! Wait a minute now. Yes, there was something, a connection. How could anyone have missed it? Of course, it was the same man. Mr *Dance of the Forests* – who else would have dared such a thing! First he tried to slip this work of subversion past our noses. Thanks to the vigilance of the committee, he fails, so he must take it out on the Governor-General's inauguration! This writer, or whatever he calls himself, is clearly dangerous, somebody to be watched. What will he attempt next? Where? And when? How does one protect decent citizens against his type? How does one know what he is planning at this very moment?

In any case, where was this man? Where was he hiding?

In his Land Rover in fact, three hundred miles north, on the way to Bida, back on the trail of less dangerous forms of drama. Mysteriously – probably owing to a combined dragnet of the Broadcasting Service, which was desperate, as all the blame was being laid on that innocent office, and the police – a message did catch up with him, urging him to return to Lagos at once, in the name of every god and especially the new god of Independence, and soothe ruffled nerves. T. O. S. Benson, the Minister, was most anxious to put the matter to rest. So the Wanted Man turned his Land Rover southwards and sought him out. Tos Benson, debonair as always, tried to make light of the episode. Still, would the young man consider writing a letter to the great Zik, assuring him that no harm was meant, no slight intended? Azikiwe, he assured him, was not in the slightest bit put out by the events, which he assumed must have been due to some misunderstanding backstage. He had enjoyed the concert immensely and was especially delighted to see the young man, about whom he had heard favourable things. It was the lackeys, the sycophants and favour-seeking officials who kept the pot on the boil, and he, Benson, could put an end to their manipulations by informing them all that the culprit had himself been in touch with His Excellency and all was settled. So would he please write a letter? Of course, the criminal assured him, the letter would be written, and if an appointment could be arranged, he would gladly apologise in person. Anything at all, as long as it did not involve embracing Madame Evanti or listening to one single note from her sandpaper vocal chords. A letter would suffice, Tos Benson decided. It was written and the ill-starred Master of Ceremonies swore to himself that he had seen the last of any such occasion, even as a mere spectator.

Desperately in need of a rest, he returned to his small apartment in Ibadan. Even before he opened the door, he had a feeling of foreboding. Entering, he found them seated in the living room. The glumness on their faces had overcome the little cheer in the sparsely furnished room, making it close, oppressive.

'What is the matter?'

'Sit down. We came to see you.'

'What has happened? Why didn't you simply send for me?'

'Sit down,' the father repeated. 'What brought us is very serious.'

He sat down slowly, bracing himself for the worst. This was the manner of breaking news of death, but there was the unusual fact that it was his parents who had chosen to convey such news, whatever it was. It could only mean a close friend, someone of his age group, perhaps a childhood friend to whom his own parents were more or less also parents. His mind raced through a short list from which such a loss might have emerged.

'We have been to Lagos,' the father said. 'We went to see Uncle Segun. He took us to Pa Doherty . . .'

'Dr Daddi?'

The mother nodded. 'Yes. You know he is close to these politicians.'

So no one was dead, that much had become clear. Now he felt only irritation with the ponderous proceedings. 'Are you going to tell me just what you went to see these people about?'

The two parents exchanged looks of surprise. 'But surely you know what would have brought us.'

'No, I do not. At first I thought someone was dead.'

'The trouble with the Governor-General,' the father snapped. 'Surely you must realise we could not sit at home quietly and let matters become . . .'

The young man let out a long, low whistle, got up and paced the room.

'These are very powerful people,' the mother persisted. 'You have to be very careful.'

Come, gentle language, the beleaguered one conjured silently, the gentle language of perfect adjustment that must yet be firm, loving but firm, a language that gently, lovingly forbids any repetition, any interposing of their selves between him and the world. Just that gentle, knife-edge balance of filial diplomacy, loving but forbidding. But his anger was reserved for the yet-unknown individual who had involved them in the first place. He managed a deceptive smile.

'By the way, how did you find out about this?'

Almost in concert, they shook their heads. It was the father who spoke. 'That is not of any importance. We learnt about it, that is what matters. Listen to me. You have barely returned. You don't know what changes are taking place. These people you are dealing with, they are not the old colonial officers . . .'

'Why, why, why, why, why? Who has come to you blowing up this trivial incident?'

'Trivial? You call it trivial?'

'Trivial. And the man you are worrying about, Zik, you think he is such a small-minded person?'

'That's exactly what Uncle Segun warned against. It is not the people at the top you have to worry about, it is those around them, *awon alagbejoro*,* the lackeys who only live to spoil the career of others, to pour petrol on the fire . . .'

'I know, I know. Tos Benson said the same thing. And what do you propose to do about them? Seek every such potential busybody out and plead with them? Or maybe you want me to do that?'

'You have seen Tos Benson?'

'I just handed him a letter for Zik. In Lagos. I have just driven here directly from his office.'

Eagerly, the mother asked, 'What did he say? Did he promise that everything would be all right?'

Laughing now, he teased. 'You tell me who brought you the news and I will tell you what Tos Benson said.'

A pained look in his face, the father spoke tersely. 'I really don't see how the two things are connected. Your mother wants to know how the Minister reacted and all you do is keep harping on who brought us into the worrying business.'

Maren resumed his seat. 'I want to find him because I want to tell him off, that's why. If you have a right to worry about my well-being, I have a right to worry about your health.'

Smiling at their look of bafflement, he continued. 'You see, if you start worrying about little things like this, when the big ones come, what are you going to do? A pure accident, and you are tossing yourselves all over the place. I came in here, and I thought the family had suffered a bereavement. Now, I don't want to be bereaved of you. It will happen eventually, but I don't want it to happen for a long, long time. If either of you collapses from hypertension, I cannot give you a decent burial. I am not earning any salary, I am just a Research Fellow on a modest grant . . .'

'You are just trying to make light of a serious matter!'

'Of course it's a serious matter. Bringing you into this is a serious matter. That's why I want to find who the busybody is so I can wring his neck.'

She began to gather up the head-tie she had laid aside on the chair. 'Dear, let's go. This one is not serious.'

*Unsolicited advocates.

'This one is very serious,' he laughed. 'I forbid you to court high blood pressure on my behalf. Look, I promise you, honestly-honestly, if I need help, I'll come to you. But please, keep the Uncle Seguns and Dr Daddis – whom I love dearly, by the way; his appetite for women makes me feel celibate, but that's neither here nor there. But I want the heavyweight extended family out of my life. I appreciate that they care, but no, I do not want them close.'

'Uncle Segun is the very person you should see. You know he and Sir Francis Ibiam are very close friends. Sir Francis will talk to Zik.'

His voice rose. 'About what? Did Zik tell anyone he was looking for an intermediary?'

'Both Uncle Segun and Dr Daddi agreed that Sir Francis be contacted.'

Between his teeth, he swore. The pattern was expected, but that made it no more bearable. Finding that gentle language of distancing – not exactly a rebuff but a firm distancing – establishing the safety gulf that would protect his private space, once and for all, without the need to recreate the no-entry zone over and over again: he had long engaged himself in that very search, but of course, only the actual situation could mould the needed language. His mother's voice broke in on his frustration.

'Anyway, he's expecting you.'

'Who?'

'Who have we been talking about? Uncle Segun. He's expecting you in Lagos.'

'That's just too bad. I'm off to Bida tomorrow. You can tell him you didn't find me here, can't you? That way you'll spare his feelings.'

The mother swung her handbag at him; he caught it as she snapped, 'Who do you think is going to tell your lies for you? Go and tell your own lies.'

'That reminds me,' and he began to rummage in the capacious bag, 'I'm broke. Let's see what you have in here.'

'Give that back! Is that what they taught you in England, to look inside a lady's handbag?'

'And what will I find in there that I don't know already?' He shook his head in mock amazement. 'When will you stop loading all the *wosi-wosi** of Itoku market inside an innocent-looking handbag?'

'Mind your own business and leave my bag alone. That's how I was loading it before you were born. That's how I kept carrying it with you strapped to my back.'

'Aha, kola nut. And *orogbo*,† of course. What, no *ataare*?'‡

Impatiently, the father snapped, 'Are you sure the Minister can take care of this matter?'

The cause of all the anxiety stopped what he was doing, turned serious in turn. 'You still insist on placing your faith in those Ministers? I wrote you from England. I described to you how our Ministers conducted themselves all over the place.'

'Ye-es, but . . .'

'Do you really think that crop of leaders can take care of anything in this country?'

'You are trying to change the subject.'

'No, I am not. There is trouble ahead, father; that's all I am trying to tell you.'

'And if there is, what business of yours is it? Stay out of its way, that's all. And keep out of the way of all these politicians.'

Suddenly he was laughing. They stared at him in offended amazement and he waved his hands in an attempt to prevent an outburst. 'No, I just remembered something that happened to me in Paris. I had a run-in with someone I thought was the Prime Minister himself, and I only discovered later that it was the Premier of the North, Ahmadu Bello.'

They both gasped, but it was the father who said, 'Ahmadu Bello? The Sardauna of Sokoto? In Paris. What on earth brought you and the Sardauna together?'

'Fate,' he replied. 'Just fate. I thought he looked a little on the plump side at the time; I only discovered who it was I actually encountered when I got back home. Not a very friendly meeting, I must confess.'

'But the Sardauna!' the father repeated.

'We met, and the audience was not on the most amicable terms,

---

*Bric-a-brac.
†A local nut, a mild stimulant.
‡Alligator pepper, sometimes used medicinally.

though to look at his silent, smiling face, you would never have guessed it. So, tell me, what would you have done if you had known about it? Flown to Paris to intercede for me?'

Genuinely puzzled, the father asked, 'Do you go out of your way to cross these powerful people? Is that what you've come back to do?'

He shook his head intensely. 'I have far more productive ambitions. But I must confess, these incidents form quite a coincidence. If I were superstitious, it would give me some sleepless nights. Those two constitute two-thirds of the power nucleus of the nation – Tafawa Balewa is just a figurehead – and I have to go bumping into them and rubbing them up the wrong way. I wonder when and how I intend to clash with the remaining third.'

'Can't you just keep off the politicians?' It was a passionate plea from the mother.

'I intend to. I don't go looking for them, I'm telling you. Isn't that why I opted for the University? My desk is still unoccupied in the Civil Service but I will sooner pay back their scholarship than take up that offer.' He waved his arms about expansively. 'This whole territory is off-limits to the politicians. Not like the Civil Service which they can dominate and manipulate at will. Well, try to anyway. In our own West, Heads of Service like S. O. Adebo don't make it that easy for them. And – oh yes, take Uncle Segun, Pa Doherty and Co. Those are the very backbone of the politicians you keep warning me about . . .'

She rose to the defence of her uncle. 'Uncle Segun is no politician!'

'Oh yes he is. He's still a Civil Servant, so he can't come out in the open. But he is right within the caucus of the Action Group. Worships the very ground Awolowo treads upon and discusses party business with Chief Akintola every spare moment – the Akintola family house is just at the back of his, you know – they visit each other across their backyards, and all I ever heard the two of them talk about is how to put paid to the ambitions of the NCNC and chase them across the River Niger.'

'How do you know, when you don't even visit them?' she accused. 'Mama Yemisi complains that she's hardly ever set eyes on you since you returned. It's not right, you know. They are family, and after all you lived with them after you left school, all the time you were in Lagos, before you left for England.'

He wagged his finger playfully. 'Oh no, no, no, you don't use that one against me. You know I stayed there only for the sake of peace. You were afraid of me being let loose in Lagos all on my own. I had already packed in with my friend, T. B. Thomas – you remember him?'

'That wild Lagos devil? We rescued you just in time.'

Laughing, he conceded, 'Who knows, you may have been right there. T. B. T. was strong stuff for a young school leaver.' He shook his head suddenly. 'Look, we are getting away from the real issue. All I am saying is – try, try, try not to draw me into this family network business. And I don't want to have to worry about you worrying about me all the time, you'll only get high blood pressure. Believe me, what happened in Lagos was pure accident – some silly woman who lacked simple decorum, nothing more. I am back on my academic beat where politicians do not interfere with us. All right? Now tell me about home. How is grandfather? And the Odemo?' He broke off abruptly, grinning. 'See? We can't seem to avoid them. If you think of all unapologetic loyalists of Awolowo and the Action Group, they don't come any fiercer than your royal cousin, the Odemo.'

The father spoke defensively. 'The Odemo knows what he's doing. And anyway, you are not the Odemo. At least he always has Ìsarà to return to. If these people undermine your career here, do you think they will stop at that? No! They will pursue you everywhere you go.'

The tiny sitting room was filled with a silence that was tinged with a sad reality of distancing, broken only by the crunch of the pilfered *orogbo* as he bit into it, his mind momentarily clouded by the thought of how often this scene might yet recur, and how difficult it was proving to find the right language after all. Finally, he found that he could only say to them: 'The University is more secure than the throne of Ìsarà. You really must stop thinking that it's a secondary school. It is not Abeokuta Grammar School, and it isn't Government College, Ibadan. And please, let me say this to you as gently as possible – neither is this nineteen hundred and forty-six.'

IV Apataganga

With his travelling companion, he stood outside the Ibadan railway station, surveying a new world that was no longer on trial, but firmly belonged to him. The *boum-boum* shrub had also survived the drought, as it did at home. He watched a ragged boy, roughly his own age, pull down a branch and tug at the pods. He placed one on the ground and stamped on it, just the way they all did at the parsonage. The explosion was startling in the thin air. It occurred to him that these were childish games that he would be expected to abandon, and wondered what other habits he must leave at that railway frontier, not even wait until he passed through the school gates. Waiting for transport, he let his mind drift over the changes that would be expected in him at this boarding school, even as a new boy.

The motor vehicles appeared in long-spaced-out relays, headed anywhere but in the direction they desired – Apataganga. He drifted off into the khaki mist, tinted a deeper brown by the wheels of the various transports – the occasional government truck, usually a station wagon, then the passenger lorries, and the rare private saloon cars. They came in from seeming crevices in the hastily welded scrap-iron hive that Ibadan appeared to be, save for those obvious official buildings, a few of which dotted the lumpy terrain of Dugbe, where they kept the railway station some meagre kind of company – the Native Administration block, the modest Electricity building – and of course the Post Office. As each vehicle appeared and dissolved in a cloud of dust, leaving in its wake moments of drowsy silence, he felt increasingly drawn along their own passages into the distance, becoming alienated from all that was familiar. He recognised the sensation instantly – it was the effect of the Harmattan, but he had never experienced the Harmattan under these troubling conditions – not while propelled towards a drastic, though feverishly anticipated change. Nibbling at the edges of his mind was a feeling he simply refused to acknowledge – homesickness. How could that be, so early? Perhaps it was only a warning of what to expect. He began to relish the sensation of floating. Floating free of Aké, floating free of Igbehin, floating free even of valued attachments, of others that were mere habits, floating free of the iron discipline of his father, the Headmaster, and the pious hoops by which his mother had sought so hard to bind him. Yes, there was a word that summed it up so simply: Freedom!

Nathaniel shuffled his feet, looking guilty. Finally he said, 'I have to see an uncle in Oke Bola. I have a message for him.'

He found it strange. Here was Nathaniel, admittedly bigger and older, but they were both new intakes, new boys, as the seniors in the school would label them, with studied condescension. Yet his own parents, dispensing with all pretence at subtlety, had virtually handed him over to Nathaniel, all but saying, Now here is your chaperon. Once on the train, however, the imposition had been mutually dissolved. It had served its purpose and there was no sense in prolonging the pretence. He acknowledged that, but for the older boy, his parents would probably have followed him to Ibadan, or sent Joseph, one of the eldest among the acquired strays and wards of the household, to cushion his separation from home by accompanying him on the train. Still, there was Nathaniel now, wondering what to do with his charge while he made his way to Oke Bola. Anyone would think that their relationship had not been corrected on the train.

'I expect to get my pocket money from him,' he explained. 'Do you want to come?'

'Is your uncle expecting me?'

'No, but . . .'

'Then you go. I shall settle in before you. Do you want me to collect your supplies for you?'

'All right.' But he still wouldn't leave. 'Are you sure you can manage by yourself? Maybe we should keep together . . .'

But the smaller boy was already out of hearing, his wooden box firmly planted on his head, bare feet scuffling the dust on the way to Apataganga.

It had worked out much better than he dared hope; he would walk through the portals of that boarding school on his own, resume his exploration of the grounds that had been restricted the previous year, as every moment was devoted to last-minute revisions of possible General Knowledge questions, that unchartable territory that could sometimes seal the fate even of the best tutored. But he had savoured enough of it to want desperately to be among the lucky and, there he was, actually on his way to paradise.

Excepting the rocks, Apataganga overwhelmed Aké without a struggle. The new Garden of Eden, no less, of a NEW AGE, boldly inscribed on the mental slate of a freshly uncooped chicken. With every step he took, the foretaste of the previous year was being translated into a five-, maybe six-year odyssey, a seemingly endless prospect of unfettered freedom amid exotic growth, and far from family demands, strictures, impositions. There would be rules and regulations, of course, but they would be spelt out in advance, not arbitrarily evoked through the envious tell-tale cousins, strays and other household wards, who saw no reason why he should spend an entire afternoon lounging among the casuarina simply because it was well past the lunchtime that should have been, had visitors not disrupted the household routine. Well, he had abandoned the house to them, hadn't he? What more could they demand of him . . . ?

The wooden box contained the sparse requirements that had been listed in the letter of admission. A sum of one shilling and sixpence was secured in a piece of paper, folded over and over again to muffle the feel of its contents – had he not been warned repeatedly about the thieving propensities of those who would be his fellow boarders? As for the token fees required by the school – he was on a scholarship, not the highest grade where the Colonial Government paid everything, but an enviable one just the same – that sum, the father flatly pronounced, could not be entrusted to him. Joseph was detailed to bring that on Monday when the office would open for the formal registration. He admitted that he would be glad to see a familiar face again, Joseph's especially. They were practised conspirators and Joseph would report anything that was agreed between them how he found him in excellent health, already in the prep room with his head stolidly stuck in his books, and all the religious literature – bible, the weekly catechism, tracts, hymn book, etc – neatly stacked on the desk.

His levitating session ended abruptly and he winced at the unpleasant thought: suppose they choose to come in person? It would be like them, the mother especially, to seize the chance for a scouting mission. Check up on his welfare. The humiliation! He could see them already, seeking out a friendly face among the staff, or among the senior boys, to commend their son to his special care. The boy groaned. From this likely tribulation, may the good lord deliver me! A spy on the spot, keeping watch on every move, noting down any infractions, probably a religious maniac who would stuff him full of biblical injunctions and even – horror of horrors! – ensure that he said his prayers first thing in the morning and last thing at night. Perhaps even take it on himself to test him on the weekly homily from that prized tract that his father had handed him as his best considered gift. Week One, Week Two, Week Three . . . a story, a moral lesson, a prayer for the avoidance of related temptations. There were even pictures in the tract, scenes from biblical events with pasty white faces, bloodless, with long-haired men and house-trained sheep that were nothing like the scrofulous goats that declared a permanent war on his father's prized crotons and rose petals . . .

Komi! Komi would have to prove more than a friend; he must become an ally. Nathaniel was pleasant and friendly, but he was too much in awe of his parents to be a reliable ally, much less a conspirator. Now Komi – right from the selection interview, he had uncovered in Komi a kindred spirit. It went beyond Komi's ready embrace of the lure of the woods, which well near matched his own. Lucky Komi. He had the background that Maren sometimes wished he had. His parents lived in far-off Warri, so he was placed under the lax supervision of a relation in Lagos. Not for those parents any undue concerns with the scholastic and spiritual health of their son. Despite this immune existence, however, Komi intuitively under-stood his friend's problems and would collaborate in any plans to thwart all unwanted, surrogate intervention in his life. Perhaps they would recruit others of similar inclinations and set up an early-warning system against parental incursions . . . the future began to regain its lustre. He walked with a carefree step. There were still two and a half miles to go. He was by no means tired but he decided to pause and savour his surroundings, mostly dessicated, though the railway embankment appeared to have been carefully maintained, even watered. No doubt some ardent station master lived in that neighbourhood.

Moor Plantation was the other name for the location of Government College, but the plantation itself was further down the road, a quarter of a mile in the direction of Ibadan. A perfect grid of dwarf oil palms was its most conspicuous feature, visible from the road that linked Ibadan and Apataganga. Tucked further inland, however, were acreages of subsistence crops and citrus trees and exotic hybrids colonised by the black bat, stealthily silent by day, ignored by the monogamous brown pigeons and furtive squirrels. Larger game sneaked into the preserve occasionally, the odd antelope and the sluggish rodent grasscutter, which was, however, capable of unbelievable bursts of speed in time of danger. They were all lured, no doubt, by the irrigation pools, because their real forage grounds were deeper still into the plantation, like the cassava farm, where the grasscutter dug down into the tubers from dusk to dawn and the antelope chewed on the greener shoots of the cassava. But the antelope's real treat was the *okro*, leaves, pods and all, which drove the young farmers to distraction. So did the brown bush fowl. These flew against the corn stalks, bringing them violently down, then proceeded to rip the corn cobs with powerful claws, ignoring the strategic scarecrows erected to deter them. Moor Plantation was the training field for the colony's would-be farming professionals, but after his quick 'ramble' of the previous year, in the company of Komi – they had actually come upon an *egbin*, the most elegant of the deer family, the metaphor for beauty that defied description! – he simply registered this preserve as his private recourse, a considerately cultivated outpost of the Garden of Eden that was Government College, Apataganga.

Apataganga! What a name. And how pretentious when he compared its display of rocks to those of Abeokuta. This was clearly a case of no contest. As he rested his sweat-soaked body against the railway embankment, he began to consider dozens of ways in which such a presumptuous, but compelling, name could be translated. In the end, he felt reasonably satisfied with the sound of 'Gangling Rocks'. Perhaps Komi would think up a better one; after all, he had done watercolour postcards of the main outcrops after their interviews, and sent him one as a christmas card. That was the other thing he envied about Komi – he had a talent for painting.

Enough of this laziness, he decided with some reluctance, hoisting his box back onto his head and stepping back on the road. He covered half a mile, then, unbelieving his luck, watched a motorcar pull up. It was shaped very much like a box, hardly different from the one he was carrying on his head, except that this was canvas-topped, and it really was not much bigger. He recognised the driver from the selection interview, a conspicuously mannered white man on whose face he and his fellow candidates registered the feature of lips, only because the heavily nasal sounds did seem to emanate from beneath a precision moustache. By keeping careful watch, a few had affirmed the existence of an articulating slit. Yet even those privileged few could not boast that they ever saw it open. Flutter at the edges, yes, but only a little. They had passed four days in periodic encounters with the moustache, but all the candidates agreed that they never did see him open his lips.

Still, he had no difficulty in translating the sounds that came from the white face as an invitation to enter the contraption, which he did gratefully, placing his box in the back and squeezing without difficulty through the narrow gap between the front seat and the open door. A morose dog stared at him without much curiosity. The other occupant of the car was a lady, also white, seated in front. She turned, smiled some form of encouragement to him and muttered something to her companion. The boy guessed what it was because he succeeded in making out the word 'young'. The man nodded and responded with more nasal rumbling.

The boy now fell to wondering how many weeks, even months, it would take to be able to follow lessons in school, since a fair proportion of the teachers were white and would speak mostly in variations of this nasal dialect. He decided not to allow that prospect to occupy him long, shrugging it off with the proverb: So the heavens are falling; is that the burden of one man alone? Other pupils would encounter the same problem.

But the heavens did fall – and very soon after – and the boy found that it was his burden and his alone. In the long-hoped for Garden idyll, a serpent reared its head, and his youth found itself unprepared, outmanoeuvred. There was no question of his becoming an adult in that instant, far from it, but he took that moment as his formal entry into the treacherous world of adults, and alien ones at that. Innocence ended at least a mile before the gates of paradise.

And yet the tone was all friendly innocence as the driver twisted in his seat and enquired, somewhat more articulately than hitherto: 'By the way, just how old are you?'

'Eleven years, sir.'

Now what was the meaning of that strange look that this man exchanged with his companion? A rather knowing look, filled with secretive, triumphant amusement. Prickles of unease danced all over the boy's skin. He felt suddenly hot. Again the man was twisting in his seat.

'But you also claimed last year you were eleven.'

Hotly, without pausing to think, the young passenger denied it. 'No, sir, at the interview I was ten. I said I was ten.'

Curiously, he chose that moment to recall the man's name – Brown, of course. Mr Brown. It was he who had supervised their mathematics test, but he certainly had his figures wrong. This being the first week of 1946, the boy knew that he was definitely eleven, so he could only have been ten the previous year, and would have claimed nothing else. He had no reason to lie about his age. Why had Mr Brown tried to prove him a liar?

Watching the two adults lapse into silence, the boy felt his insides begin to knot. So it was true after all; to these Europeans, all Africans were liars. He had heard it said, heard this prejudice discussed in resentful circles, but his few and brief encounters with those white aliens had never brought him into direct experience with such attitudes. Of course, he lied himself, as often and as stoutly as was needed, usually to escape punishment. At home and in school, lying was an art of survival, deplored and doubly punished at home, but certainly expected, even admired in school, especially when ingenious and persuasive. The Reverend I. O. Ransome-Kuti, or Daodu to all of Abeokuta, who presided over an assortment of pupils from every Nigerian background in his grammar school, himself relished a well-embellished improvisation around facts, half-truths or downright fantasy. The more outrageous the tale, the faster his eyes twinkled. At the end, the culprit's punishment might be reduced as a gesture of respect for the imaginative mind – take Iku's misapplication of the phlogiston theory of spontaneous combustion to explain away why he was caught, at the bottom of the field, roasting one of the Principal's prize cockerels! Now, that was a piece of sublime impertinence. But Daodu, unsmiling though he was throughout the narrative, had clearly enjoyed every moment of it. His dancing eyes always gave him away.

And of course others lied for far more serious causes; it was clear which of these was on the minds of his two companions, especially that of Mr Brown, who had posed a question to which he had already supplied an answer in his own mind. The quest for education was often desperate. The life-and-death struggle for admittance into schools, especially Government-funded schools with their strict age limit, simply forced prospective pupils to lie about their age. Their circumstances demanded that they work on farms or assist with the family petty business until sufficient savings were put together. Then came the moment of fulfilment. Prayers, ritual dedication, practical gifts from different branches of the extended family, admonitions, tears and the commencement of a five-, ten-, sometimes over thirty-mile trek since the motor fare must be saved for more essential needs, and the village protagonist, almost old enough to start his own family, entered the magic world of learning. It was easier, of course, if he won a scholarship; then he would travel on a government warrant. No matter how, the well-matured adventurer found his way into the promised land. He would return with the precious certificate, find a job immediately and proceed to put his siblings through the same process.

This pattern, the youngster was certain, formed the sole fabric of falsehood with which the likes of Brown would be familiar, one in which he so superciliously, and undiscriminatingly, sought to cloak him. Knowing himself fortunate in this respect, the ploy of lying about his age was so inappropriate that Maren could only grasp it as proof of all he had heard about this breed of people. His aunt, Beere, the principal's wife, was right. Now he had something to contribute to her race tirades. In fact he was beginning to wonder if this entire adventure had not been a mistake after all, if he should not have remained within the secure belonging of Abeokuta, instead of being welcomed with such humiliation in the tin-box of this villain with the hidden lips. He glared at the dog, which merely stared back of him.

And then he gasped, audibly enough to make the two teachers turn in their seat. He ignored them, turning self-pitying eyes at the dried-up vegetation along the dirt road. You lied after all, he accused himself, and he felt miserable. Not in his first reply to Mr Brown's question, but in his attempt to contradict the teacher. Idiot! Of course you *did* claim you were eleven at the interview because you were eleven. Four months ago, you were eleven, and so you still are. A new calendar year doesn't make you one year older, you dullard! Now see what you've got yourself into. See the first impression you have made on your future teachers? Perhaps it was not too late to put the matter right; the explanation was so simple, and of course an apology to begin with.

'I . . . er . . . sir . . .'

'Yes, what is it this time?'

That tone again! And at that moment his mind was made up. Tricked! Nothing but a dirty trick. You, Mr Thin Moustache and Thinner Lips, you tricked me. After all, you are the mathematics teacher and you know very well that twelve months do not necessarily begin with the calendar and end with it. And anyway you collected all our papers, my baptismal certificate among mine, and you knew very well how old I was and am, but you asked anyway and the question is – why? Why did you pick on me? Why use that tone except to get me confused and fall into your trap – *but you claimed you were eleven last year*. Of course I did claim I was eleven last year, you boiled coco-yam face! But you trapped me into deny-ing it without thinking. And as for you, Master New Boy, that serves you right, how often were you told to *think* before opening your mouth, twin warning to looking before you leap! Now can you already hear what story will go round the staff when Moustache opens his mouth in their staff room? No one will be there to defend you, and you won't be asked to come forward and explain how you came to contest a plain truth with a lie when no one was threatening you with any kind of punishment. So what conclusion does it merit? Yes, they all lie, even when they don't need to!

As for you in front, don't bother to continue to wait expectantly on me; and you can stop glancing back at me because I would sooner talk to your dog than exchange another word with you, and anyway I find the dwarf palms of Moor Plantation more pleasant to look at than either of you – or your dog for that matter. I ignore you. I owe you no explanation because you played me a low-down trick unworthy of an adult, and one who is supposed to take charge of my education. Let me tell you, back in Abeokuta, adults do not play such tricks on children. They do not deal with eleven-year-olds with that kind of tone which traps them into saying things they think are true but which aren't. If we need to lie we choose our own lies and we make a good job of it, let me tell you. And you'll find out soon enough, Mr Brown. Beere had warned me about people like you, and you won't find it so easy putting one over on me in the future, I promise you. From now on, anything you and your kind say to me, I shall sift it with a sieve finer than the one my mother uses on her cornflour, which you seem to have rubbed all over your face and body. I don't know what I am doing in your tin-box of a car anyway; I've ridden in better, let me tell you, Mr Clever White Man. I didn't even need your ride, I was doing very well on my own; I have trekked greater distances – go and ask them at home – with a pile of firewood on my head heavier than that box, or a basket of yams or oranges. You should see how fast I move when I am sent on an errand between Aké and Igbehin – all the grownups remark on it – I am sure I move faster than your noisy tin-box.

I said don't bother to look at me, you and your companion – I suppose you were trying to impress her, to show how smart you are but you should try that nonsense on people your own size. My Uncle Ransome-Kuti would make mincemeat of you. As for Essay himself – that's my father, you ghost, and I didn't name him Essay for nothing – you, you'll run ten miles before you get in an argument with him because when he's finished with you, he will hand you over to Osibo, the pharmacist, or even Orija, the organist, to scrub the floor with. Come to think of it, why should any of them condescend to exchange a sentence with you? If you hadn't played foul and caught me unprepared, I would have taught you a lesson myself. No wonder my aunt keeps denouncing all you colonial imposters and what a pity Hitler didn't get you before you threw that atom bomb over the Japanese and you did it only because they were brown, not white. Aha, because they were brown, Brown, what do you say to that? White Brown who picks on children, probably eats them like a cannibal, no wonder you keep your lips hidden, heaven knows why you pretend you have no lips, obviously so we won't know how many Government College new boys have disappeared behind them . . .

Oh I know, you are trying to get your own back, that's all it is. The *West African Pilot* and the *Daily Times* did for you, and all those nationalists who descended on your backs when you humiliated Ivor Cummings . . . yes? . . . Ivor Cummings, that's who it was. Denying him his right of accommodation at the Bristol Hotel because he was black. And this was not just anybody. He was a high official in the Colonial Welfare Department but that was not good enough for you; you showed him the door and told him to find lodgings where his kind belonged. But we were having none of that, were we? Daodu and Beere flew into a rage and Essay's debating circle nearly marched on Government House all the way from Aké to lodge a personal protest. Public rallies all over Lagos; Imoudu, the fiery labour leader, threatened to lead his workers to burn down the hotel. You lost, didn't you? The Governor had no choice but to pass a law to ban all forms of discrimination in public places. Ha, that's what hurts, isn't it? That's why you had to trick me into your car so you can write to the Governor that Africans mustn't be allowed in European places because they are all liars, and they start young, I have proof of it. Imagine what this young pupil will become in ten years when he is old enough to be admitted into our exclusive European clubs, and that would just be typical of you because Mr Cummings was not trying to enter your stupid clubs, he just wanted to lodge in a public hotel but that would be just the kind of twist you'd put on it, twisting things round to make me say I was ten when I was eleven and said I was eleven until you started confusing me . . .

'What House are you in?' The question twanged ineffectually over the boy and Brown repeated it with some impatience, having turned into the school compound and approached the clutch of buildings nearest to the school gates, Greer House.

'Swanston House, sir.' Just leave me anywhere you please, you sly ghost, before this matchbox catches fire from my righteous rage.

Another hundred to two hundred yards, and the car slowed to a stop. The boy recognised the ranch-style bungalows, squeezed himself out and pulled the box after him. As he muttered his thanks, he saw the woman turn round for a last look at him; it was not unfriendly, but Brown said something which made her chuckle, so he hoped she would share by telepathy every opprobrious syllable he continued to launch in the general direction of Mr Brown. He felt somewhat depressed; this was not the triumphant entry into this hallowed community that he had dreamt of. You have not even registered and you have already made yourself a mortal enemy, and even picked him among the staff! Ah well, cheer up, no Garden of Eden can claim to be complete without a serpent.

The senior boy who met him in front of the common room was obviously in charge. He eyed the new boy disdainfully, cast a super-cilious eye over his box and stabbed it repeatedly with a thick finger.

'What apprentice carpenter fabricated this arboreal eyesore?'

Perplexed, the boy merely stood and stared at his questioner.

'You have problems with your auricular faculties? A perforation in your tympanic membrane that interferes with your hearing, perhaps?'

'I don't understand you.'

'Please!' the larger boy barked suddenly. 'When you address a senior boy, you say Please!'

'Please.'

'And the name is Ezeoba. And I am in charge of your dormitory. I shall allocate you your facilities and monitor your conduct. So if you are one of these bush new boys from a village . . .'

'I am not from a village. Please.'

'I am not from a village, Ezeoba, please!'

'I am not from a village, Ezeoba, please.'

'The proof of the pudding is in the eating. When you get to the dining hall, we shall see with what hand you pick up your fork and knife – that always gives you rough boys away. We can tell when you dig your spoon in your beans like a shovel, ha ha ha! So you say you are not a village boy.'

'No, Ezeoba, please.'

'Then that wooden receptacle for what I presume must be your private paraphernalia strikes my judgement as being incompatible with your protestation, which I am inclined to accept, since your phonetical articulation of the English language is passable, intelligible, and you may not require remedial coaching to save the House public embarrassment. But that decision is, of course, the prerogative of the Housemaster.'

'Do you mean my box?'

'Oh. You understood me?' The senior boy sounded disappointed. 'Yes, the box, young sir. For the status of Government College, a portmanteau would have been more appropriate.'

The boy was hurt. The box had been specially commissioned, built to careful specifications and supervised by his mother in every detail. On completion, the household had gathered to admire the product, viewing it from every angle, caressing the varnished wood. And the carpenter was his friend, anyway; from the moment he received his letter of admission, with the list of items that must accompany the new entrant to school, he had assured Rafiu that the making of the box was reserved for him. And now this masterpiece was being accused of being incompatible. What 'status'? In any case, the list distinctly read 'box', with specified dimensions.

The senior boy misread the puzzlement on the newcomer's face, and leant forward, hopefully. 'Or perhaps you do not quite understand? Your physiognomy has taken on the appearance of bewilderment.'

Physiognomy! Now that floored him. He ran his mind over the words that had commenced the barrage, wondering if this was a special Government College language, or, as he began to suspect, a deliberate attempt to intimidate him. Or make a fool of him. He had read all the books in his father's library but rack his brains as he might, he could not recollect the word physiognomy, not even in the volumes of Charles Dickens. He had no intention of asking him for an explanation, however, especially as he had a fair idea what it had to mean. The senior boy waited expectantly but the other said nothing, so he turned away abruptly and barked: 'Follow me.'

Conducted to the dormitory, he took possession of a bed made of two trestles and three planks. Four upright poles, cut square, fitted into holes at the extreme ends of the trestles. Their top ends had nails onto which four thin slats of wood, flat, two long and two short, with holes at their ends, were clearly intended to fit, forming a rectangle, creating a frame for a mosquito net. Left to his own devices by his mentor, who had spied another victim, he quickly unlocked his box and laid the blankets on the planks. Out came the pillowcase, with embroidered words which reminded him that 'The Lord is my Shepherd'. A rose filled up one corner, while the other corner bore the name, encased in brackets: MAREN, his grandfather's shorthand compromise on the shepherding christian lord. It was not St Peter's crook whose protection he desired for his grandson, however, but that of another demiurge altogether. And his invocation for blessing from that direction, his mind filled with the perils of the road that his grandson would traverse over and over again, not to mention the strange lands his diviner had prophesied that the boy would visit, and the alien beings with whom he was destined to cohabit, was: *We nu ren n'ojo ebi n'pona**, which he shortened to: *We nu ren*. But he knew that his daughter-in-law would decipher it too easily, so he contracted it further to the imperious injunction: *Ma ren*. There! Paint it on his school box where it is open to human and other, invisible eyes. But what did it mean, the mother asked?

'The same as "The Lord is my Shepherd",' he said, looking her straight in the eye. 'That is deep Ijebu dialect, which you cannot understand. Nor your husband for that matter,' he threw casually at her, knowing full well that she would enquire from him. 'He's been too long away from home.'

'Well, in that case,' she said, 'we shall simply embroider it on the pillow.'

He shrugged. 'That will do just as well.'

So she had it embroidered in a corner, in small letters, and placed

---

*May you not walk when the road waits, famished.

it also in brackets, where its potency would be subordinate to 'The Lord is my Shepherd'.

On the other side of this tattooed pillowcase was his godmother's contribution to the naming process or, more accurately, the one she had chosen out of her many coinages: Akínkòyí. This choice was surrounded by embroidered forms that could have been canna lilies or the white hibiscus – it was difficult to tell. Since the pillowcase itself was a present from her anyway, she was able to claim one entire side to herself, and a most intricate riot of needlework was the result. Now his matter-of-fact decision, and not so many years ago, that this was the wife for him whenever he was ready, brought an embarrassed wince to his face. Was it really possible for him to have been that much of a child? Well, this was growing-up time, and growing-up place. He was all braced up for any manhood test the boarding school could throw at him.

Next to emerge was the mosquito net, also specially sewn, not bought from the store. He wondered if Mr Ezeoba, please, would also have some caustic comments on the sewing. He did not have to be told, after he and his mother saw the price tag on the ready-made net in John Holt's, that they would settle for some yards of netting and the services of a tailor. And the entire tent was not made of the netting; the wide rectangle at the top was made of baft cloth, again to save money. So was the border, over a foot wide, at the bottom. Having seen the genuine, ready-made net, he was frankly nervous about the product. He had the nagging fear that it would compare poorly with what the others had – probably ordered straight from Europe, with the maker's label ostentatiously displayed on them. Some of the boys who had attended the selection interview came from wealthy families. They brought provisions with them that made him salivate, and some wore shoes that were surely ordered through Lennard's Overseas Catalogue. Still, that would not do them much good in Government College. Shoes were out, except in the evenings when sandals or tennis shoes were permitted. And it was khaki shirts and shorts for everyone, evenings again excepted. Then they were free to show off their private clothes. Laying out his *dansiki*, *buba*, *soro*, a wrapper and two shirts, he was satisfied that there, at least, he did not feel deprived. Assuming that the locker next to the bed was for his use, he proceeded to arrange in its small space his cutlery, mug, packet of sugar, Ovaltine . . .

The booming voice nearly sent him through the window. 'What do you think you are doing?'

Standing next to Ezeoba was another boy, loose-limbed, glazed eyes, obviously lost and intimidated beyond recall, but the question was directed to him, not to the newcomer. 'Have I taken an inventory of your worldy possessions? No. Have you been given permission to take possession of those items? No. Until those conditions are fulfilled, those items are not yours and you cannot touch them. Now, does that fit into your impoverished comprehension?'

'Yes, please.'

'What's that?' His eyes had alighted on a packet of biscuits, still sitting on the planks. 'Yes, that packet there.'

'Biscuits, please.'

'Ants, please. Ants. You wish to invite ants into the dormitory?' He held out his hand. The boy placed the packet of biscuits in it. 'Confiscated!' snapped Ezeoba. 'No ants in this dormitory. Ah . . .' He walked slowly forward. 'Now, that is a very nice pillowcase. "The Lord is my Shepherd." A christian home, very nice.' He turned it over in his hands. 'What is this?'

The boy waited. Please or not please, if he was thinking of also 'confiscating' his pillowcase . . .

'Is this yours?'

'It is, please.'

'Then whose name is this?'

'It's mine, please. A nickname. That is a present from my godmother.'

'A nickname, enh? And how, may one enquire, did you acquire it? What did you do to deserve it? And last but not the least, what means the cognomen?'

He savoured the exchange of helpless looks between the two boys, a clear concession of defeat. Looking immensely pleased at this triumph, he smirked, 'The meaning, new boy. The meaning. What does "Akínkòyí" mean?' He pronounced it with a tonality that came with unfamiliarity, not merely with the name, but with the language.

'It means . . . it means . . . er . . . Akin rejects this. Akin says No to this. Something like that, please.'

The senior boy eyed him in silence for a long while. 'No. You know what I think it means?'

'No, please.'

'It means "Trouble". Double, double, toil and trouble – that is Shakespeare.'

'Yes, please, *Macbeth*.'

'Oh. You know Mr William Shakespeare?'

'My father had some of his books in his library.'

'I see. A new boy not totally devoid of elementary erudition. Well, Mr Akínkòyí, I want you to know that William Shakespeare knew your type, and he named you "Trouble". I smell it. So you used to reject this and that? Like what?'

'Food sometimes, please. I did not like some kinds of food. And once I refused to prostrate myself to some grownups in Ìsarà, because we did not do that in Aké, and she heard about it.'

Ezeoba's ever-widening grin spoke days and days of future diversion with this new boy.

'Well, well, well, I can see that your young life is already bursting with a plenitude of anecdotal repertoire. You will therefore be interested in the following information, to wit: all new boys are obliged to introduce themselves to the House after supper tomorrow night. In the prep room. That is when you will also receive your general introduction to the House history, House rules, the House emblem, the House colours and so on. You will be taught the House song and will be privileged to participate in your first singsong. Later, you will be assigned a teacher from the senior class, and it will be his responsibility to teach you everything else you have to know. A date for your House test will be announced, when you will have a chance to prove that you are properly schooled in your House history and traditions. To fail that test is to bring eternal disgrace to yourself and your teacher. And you will have to wait until the following year to retake the test – with the new boys. Oh, what a humiliation, what a devastation, what a disgrace and degradation!' And then he paused, looking confused. 'Now where was I? I was about to . . . come on, you whippersnappers, what was I saying before I was rudely interrupted?'

Persuaded that he must have interrupted him somehow, according to the yet-to-be-learnt House rules, the boy suggested helpfully, 'The House test, please. You were telling us about the House test.'

'No, I remember now. Introductions. You will introduce your-selves to the House tomorrow night. And the tradition is that each boy must tell an interesting story about himself. If the story is not interesting you will go on, night after night until your seniors are all satisfied. Now you, I shall expect you to tell us the story of how you earned your cognomen – or nickname if you like. I want to hear what a gnat like you is doing with the name of a stormy petrel.'

'A stormy petrel, please?'

'A troublemaker. A walking catastrophe. A *palava* head . . .'

'I am not a troublemaker, please.'

'We had one before you. I know my House history, new boy. Anyone called Akínkòyí means trouble.'

'No, please, she also used to call me "Okunrin Jeje".'

'Another one! And meaning how much more trouble?'

'No please, it means someone who is gentle. My junior brother was the troublesome one, so she called me . . .'

Ezeoba held up his hand. 'No, young sir, the name on your pillow says it all.' Turning over the pillowcase, he jabbed at the inscription with a stubby finger. 'This, sir, confirms it. Knowing you for what you are, your people have inscribed here an antidote – The Lord is my Shepherd – but, wait a minute, what is this I also espy in brackets? "Ma-ren". What does it mean?'

'My grandfather says it means the same thing as "The Lord is my Shepherd",' glad that this was a half-truth that he could tell with a straight face. The old man had taken him into his confidence, and he was not about to betray any of their secrets to this stranger.

'A double antidote,' pronounced Ezeoba. 'A double antidote against the bane, the affliction and calamity of Akínkòyí.'

'Ezeoba, please, Akínkòyí is only my godmother's nickname for me. It does not mean trouble.'

'And I say it does, new boy, most certainly it does. I believe the evidence of my eyes since seeing is believing. Those who embroid-ered your pillowcase with that cognomen, with such capital bold-ness, with central prominence across this pillowcase, and in red silk thread, the sign for danger, knew what they were doing. From the remote city of Abeokuta, they were sending us a warning. And respond we shall, and begin to take all necessary precautions. To be forewarned is to be forearmed. I shall leave you to the pestilential company of each other while I betake myself to a place of safety. Another Akínkòyí! What have we done to deserve this, O Lord?' He rolled his eyes towards the ceiling, then jerked his head downwards and, almost splitting the head of the newcomer, bellowed: 'Introduce yourself, you miserable specimen of humanity from Ondo savage interior!'

'My name is Yanju, please.'

Ezeoba gave a melodramatic sigh. 'I knew we would have trouble with this one. This . . . Master Akínkòyí here – or Maren for short and for safety – is your classmate, a new boy like you. You do not say "please" to your own class. Now do a correct introduction so I can go about my father's business.'

'My name is Yanju.'

'That's better. Now get cracking. You'll take this bed next to his. I shall be back in fifteen minutes and by that time I want to see your planks laid out neatly over the trestles – just as this Master Akínkòyí has done – he thinks he is clever but we shall see. Then lay out all the items you brought from home for inspection. We don't want ants here and we don't want parasites and other bugs you have imported from the interior bush to contaminate our sanitised environment and infect innocent people with all sorts of diseases and pestilences. Fifteen minutes! When you have passed your inspection, I shall condescend to introduce you to your dormitory duties.'

By unspoken mutual consent, neither breathed until he was out of the dormitory and safely out of hearing. Then the boy called Yanju sank onto the cement floor, squatting from habit. He held his head in his hand and rocked it from side to side.

'What is it? You have a headache?'

'I should never have left my village. 'Kínkòyí, I don't think I can . . .'

'Ah please, don't call me that, I just hope Ezeoba forgets it. I prefer Maren, anyway. It's the name my grandfather began to use for me once he came to accept that I was leaving home . . . hey, are you feeling sick?'

'I couldn't understand one word he was saying to me. I should never have left my village. I think I want to go back to my village.'

'You don't understand. He thinks he's in his village. That must be the way he talks to the people in his village. Come on. I'll show you how to set up the trestles . . .'

Although the exchange had taken place in Yoruba, the boy admitted to himself that he understood Yanju's words only with great difficulty. It was his first encounter with the Ondo dialect. Now he wondered how many mental dictionaries one would have to employ in this place to cope with Brown's nasal dialect, Ezeoba's bombast, Yanju's outlandish accents and how many others yet to be encountered!

It began, as always, as an idle argument, developed into a dare. There was not much to do, after all, during half-term holidays, taken earlier in the first term than in the rest of the year. It enabled the new boys to travel home if they wished, so as to make up the gaps in their boarding requirements, or simply to ease the wrench of being torn away from familiar terrain. Several of them had rushed home, mostly the ones from well-to-do families. For Maren, it was the first chance to explore the school grounds thoroughly, as well as the city of Ibadan itself. For the former, Komi was his eager accomplice; for the city, he had Nathaniel, Chris and Muyi, all three of whom had relations living there. So did Maren. He knew of his father's friends and a cousin around Oke Ado, but he was not anxious to visit them and introduce himself; they might take to visiting him in turn and attempting to take a parental interest in his welfare. Ibadan had to be discovered in her own right, which meant, as one stranger encountering another.

That encounter had commenced the night before; he was still savouring the walk back in total darkness, pierced only by the occasional lights of a passing vehicle. They sang loudly to keep up their courage, although none of them could really tell what they were afraid of. Just the eeriness, perhaps, the fusion of silence and a darkness so thick that they could not even discern the forms of one another. That was nearly three miles of walking through the unknown, an infinity when he compared it to those short spells of darkness, very few and far between at home, when he was sent on an errand after dark. And anyway, in Aké or Ìsarà, there were always those pinpricks of light in the distance, the lone night hawker or an isolated home, beacons of reassurance between one pool of menace and the next. Between the final lights of Ibadan and the first of Apataganga, however, there was only an expanse of fear.

Perhaps the relief and the euphoria of the following morning had something to do with it. Komi lived in Greer House but, to simplify catering and discipline during half-term, everyone had been moved to Swanston. It was only a matter of time before rivalry between the Houses came to dominate all their discussion. Then came the turn of the House emblem. Greer's was a fleur-de-lys, Swanston had been allotted the literal crest of a swan.

No amount of House loyalty could parry Komi's barbs. All he had to do was shout 'Up Swans', the rallying cry for Swanston House on the sports field, and the 'swans' were left feeling foolish and inadequate. Normally Maren had no problem in accepting the House emblem; the shield itself was a pretty piece of painting, and he had nothing against the exotic water bird with the snaky neck which, he had been told, was deceptively willowy but could break a man's arm. He had tried that argument too, the spirit of Swanston boys being strength disguised as supple grace, but not even that could withstand the jeer of 'Up Swans'. It was something he had also sensed as being disastrously 'incompatible' – Ezeoba, the original Senior Incompatible was the furthest thing from a swan; so were all the athletes from either House, hurtling around the race tracks or smashing one another's legs on the football field in preference to securing the ball.

Muyi was a remarkable case; in the swimming pool he certainly developed the grace of a swan, on land, however, when his unmatchable knock-kneed pair of K-legs rose in their natural habitat, his lower trunk simply splayed itself all over the compound while the upper half pursued its own single-minded vocation. Somehow the House prefect had picked up the news that the Principal was making enquiries at the new Orthopaedic Hospital in Lagos, to see if something could be done for him. The treatment was that the legs would be broken deliberately, then put together again in a more coordinated manner. He would have to be in hospital for six months, but the earlier it was done, while the bones were still young, the better. The thought of breaking someone's bones deliberately, then hoping that they would be restored to normal, struck Maren as fiendish; trying to imagine it happening gave him goose pimples.

No matter, there it was. Apart from the swimming pool, there was simply no other time when the cheer 'Up Swans' did not rankle, and even then, it was only by making a deliberate, visual transposition. The blunt truth was that neither the Swanston House boys, nor indeed Greer nor any pupil from former schools – in short, no youth or adult of his acquaintance – bore the slightest resemblance to swans, and here was Komi rubbing it in, brushing aside all their defence by inflicting the cry on them. The conquest of fear of the previous night was undoubtedly at work, for, without announcing his intention to anyone, he suddenly took off, merely remarking that he had a solution to the argument.

'There he goes again. What solution?'

'You'll see.'

'He's running away from the argument.'

'I'll be back. And then you'll see. We'll leave you nothing to make fun of, that's the answer.'

'And how do you propose to do that?'

He walked away from them, filled with confidence. His short legs took him straight to the Housemaster's office. When he came past the window, he was surprised to glimpse, not the Housemaster, but Mr Kaye, the English teacher. Kaye had struck him from their first encounter as a likely counterpoise to the offensive Brown. He had a way of looking at objects and people as if they had taken him by surprise – probably the effect of his rimless glasses. The boy knocked and was invited to enter. He walked up to the desk, the top of which came nearly level with his head. He began to shuffle his feet.

'Yes? And what can I do for you, young sir?'

The boy's roving eyes now settled on a replica of the House shield on the wall above Mr Kaye's head. His tongue also recovered its use.

'Are you our new Housemaster, sir?'

'No-o-o. I am standing in for the half-term. Your Housemaster needed to travel, so I am here to see that discipline does not break down in his absence – fair enough?'

Maren, preoccupied with finding a sound introduction for his concerns, ignored the final query that was Mr Kaye's well-known trademark. He braced himself squarely on both feet and took the plunge.

'It's the swan, sir.'

'The swan?'

Maren nodded, relieved that the subject had been broached at last.

'And what about the swan, Master . . . er . . . Maren?'

'We were discussing it, sir, in the dormitory. It was an argument. We felt that the House emblem should be changed. It's when we're on the sports field, sir, when we have to shout "Up Swans". We think, sir, perhaps if we could have something else, sir . . .' He let his voice trail off.

For what seemed hours, the startled man stared over his rimless glasses at the diminutive object before him, sighed and enquired: 'And what do you propose in place of this time-tested, tradition-hallowed symbol of the House, young Maren?'

Maren had not actually thought of an alternative, and he admitted it. 'There you are,' chortled Mr Kaye. 'It's not quite so easy to be innovative as we think, is it now?'

Nettled and feeling challenged, Maren blurted out the name of the first bird that flew across his memory. 'What about the parrot, sir?'

'Parrot, Maren? Did I hear you say parrot?'

'Or pigeon, sir. What about the pigeon? Or hawk, I mean kestrel. Yes, kestrel, sir.' And the young advocate of change felt a surge of confidence that this was an inspired choice. In his head he listened to the rallying cry, 'Up Kestrels', and it sounded unbeatable. It left him wondering why it had taken him so long to recommend the hawk-like bird that nested in the turrets of Aké's St Peter's Church.

Kaye snorted in derision. 'Up Parrots! Up Pigeons! Up Kestrels! Now, young Maren, tell us truthfully, how does any of that sound to you?'

Maren felt obliged to be honest, and he admitted that 'Up Parrots' and 'Up Pigeons' did not sound quite so inspiring. But 'Up Kestrels' did make quite an aural impression. The boy became increasingly convinced, and he was prepared to stand his ground on that choice. Indeed, the more he thought about it, the more committed he became to the change of name. Levitating on the wings of the kestrel, he flew around the sports field, swooping down on the opponent's goalposts as the ball approached and putting the goalkeeper off an easy save. Below him, all around the field, the erstwhile swans turned cartwheels of triumph, screaming, 'Up Kestrels!' Without a doubt, this was it. If Kaye remained unconvinced, he would suggest the topic to the House prefect for the next House debate: 'Why the Kestrel is a superior emblem to the Swan'. Or maybe move directly to the goal – wasn't that what Daodu himself would have advised? When you have a goal, don't beat about the bush. Lead your people directly there, but marshal your arguments in advance and be firm in your own conviction. That was how he had persuaded the National Union of Teachers to pass a resolution on introducing traditional music into the school music curriculum, wasn't it? Come to think of it, music was another issue to be tackled – but that could come later. He was already very fond of Government College Ibadan, wouldn't dream of going back to Abeokuta Grammar School. It was just in one or two areas that he felt that GCI could borrow a lead from Daodu's Grammar School. Olumo Rock was the symbol of AGS, not swans or whatever else they had in the land of the Kayes. So, back to the House debate. A harmless straightforward debate, no need to alarm the Housemaster as yet, even while planting the seed: 'That this House believes that the Kestrel is a superior bird to the Swan'. He would go to the library first thing the following morning and find out everything about the two birds . . .

From a distance he heard Kaye's voice calling out his name, and suddenly his face loomed up aggressively from the pages of the encyclopaedia, bird section, the encyclopaedia vanished and it was Kaye's normally benign face thrust against his across the table, his normally bloodless voice irritated beyond measure, startling him back into the present: 'Are you paying attention, Master Maren?'

'Sir?'

'Kindly pay attention and avoid day-dreaming so early in the morning.'

'Yes, sir.'

'My question was – what do we do about the House name?'

'The house name, sir? We don't need to touch that.'

'Well, I must say that is most generous of you, Master Maren. Most generous. You are quite sure about this? You wouldn't like us to change to, er, perhaps Apataganga House?'

'Oh no, sir. I know my House history, sir. Swanston House is all right.'

Mr Kaye, enunciating with deliberate exaggeration, 'SWAN-STON . . . SWAN-STON. And if I may just anticipate you, Master Maren – STON, not STONE. So we can't really have you shouting "Up Stones", fair enough?'

'I wasn't going to suggest that, sir.'

'You would, you would. I have that feeling, young Maren, that you certainly would.'

A gasp interrupted further conversation, followed by a rap on the door. In stormed the intimidating figure of Ezeoba, the nearly six feet of him quivering with astonishment and outrage.

'How did you get . . . what is he doing . . . oh sorry, sir, good morning, sir.'

'Good morning, Ezeoba.'

'I was looking for him, Mr Kaye. I didn't know you had sent for him yourself.'

'Sent for him, Ezeoba? No, I did not send for him. He walked in of his own volition.'

Ezeoba treated Maren to a long look of withering contempt. 'Is that so, Maren? I suppose you thought that by running to the Acting Housemaster, you would save yourself from a fate worse than death.'

'Good gracious, Ezeoba, what has young Maren done?'

'He broke bounds, Mr Kaye. In company with some other felons of like criminal inclination, he broke bounds last night and engaged in a nocturnal excursion to the Odeon cinema.'

Kaye, suppressing a smile behind his luxuriant but ragged moustache, a study in contrast with Mr Brown's military clip, said, 'Did he now? And what do you have to say for yourself, young Maren?'

'We have explained it, sir. We didn't realise that we needed an exeat, since it is half-term holidays. We didn't know, sir.'

'Have you not been told that ignorance is no defence in law, you young delinquent?' Ezeoba turned to Mr Kaye, holding out a folded sheet of paper. 'I was actually coming in to present a report which I had prepared on the nocturnal episode, Mr Kaye. And to find him here trying to take preventive action in anticipation of the dire consequences . . .'

Holding out his hand for the document, Mr Kaye explained, 'No, Ezeoba. As a matter of fact Master Maren only came to discuss birds. Or, to be more accurate, the species known as the swan.'

Confused, Ezeoba looked from one to the other. 'He came to discuss swans, sir?'

'Yes, Ezeoba, the swan. Perhaps he had better explain the nature of the problem himself. Come on, Maren. This is the gentleman with whom, to adhere strictly to protocol, you should first have broached the ornithological conundrum.' And, preoccupying himself with the report just handed him by Ezeoba, Kaye left them to it, his moustache twitching from time to time as he tried to control an outbreak of mirth.

'Well, go on, what is troubling your head, Maren, that you should come and bother the master instead of reporting first to me? I suppose you were not aware of the correct procedure, as well? You wish to claim ignorance of the law again as mitigating circumstances? Go on, I'm listening.'

Sighing in full knowledge that he had well and truly launched himself into his first term on the wrong foot, Maren had no choice but to proceed along the route of self-damnation. Ezeoba listened, and his expressive features left no doubt in the new boy's mind of the woes that the rest of the term, even the year, had in store for him. Ezeoba took a deep breath and settled into his favourite pastime, oblivious of what, in the boy's view, should have been the restraining presence of the master. Or was it the very presence of Mr Kaye, as English teacher, that spurred him to attain such heights of intimidating absurdity? All Maren could tell was that Kaye was accustomed to such scenes from Ezeoba, and found them, as did Daodu with a different kind of rhetorical self-indulgence, diverting.

'You infinitesimal mote of the human species. Did I not say it? Did your name not forewarn us and put us on our guard? You problematic, disruptive factor of inverse proportion to your physical mass, so you want to tamper with the traditional emblem of Swanston House which your predecessors, of infinite wisdom and cumulative maturity, have thought fit to retain and maintain all through their turbulent scholastic passage through the courtyards of this institution! Now tell me, do you know the story of the ugly duckling?'

Maren shook his head. He knew the story but sensed somehow that it was no time to admit knowledge of anything, even of the identity of his tormentor.

'Yes, ignorance is bliss, which explains why the earth has not opened to swallow you, young Akínkòyí – or maybe Maren after all. I think, for our own protection, and insulation from dire predictions, we shall restrict your name to Maren. Discretion, after all, is the better part of valour. The ugly duckling, which, compared to you, Master Maren, was a paragon of beauty, was turned into a beautiful swan. And that is what, despite all evidence to the contrary, and in valiant defiance of the law of probability, this noble House of unparalleled cultivation intends to do to you. From the ugly duckling of ignorance, you shall be turned into a swan of intelligence and scholastic stature. Do you realise how envious our sister house, Greer House is, when we rend the air with our battle-cry, 'Up Swans'? Compare this to their pitiful response, 'Up Greer', and even a deaf man can tell the difference. And you want to create disaffection, dissatisfaction and rebellion against this time-honoured emblem of many victories, beloved of old boys of the house who have become beacons and pillars of the outside society . . .'

Mercifully, Kaye coughed, cleared his throat and called a halt. 'I think, Ezeoba, that Master Maren has now grasped the general idea. Haven't you, Maren?'

The battered object nodded gratefully. 'Oh yes, Mr Kaye. It was just an argument. I wasn't trying to . . . I mean, we were just er . . .'

'That's all right. And, er Ezeoba, do you think we could also consider the matter of the, er, nocturnal excursion closed? Fair enough?'

'But sir . . .'

'Now, Ezeoba, I am sure that Master Maren has had an earful that would take care of the other felony, maybe half a dozen more, wouldn't you say? I really would suggest giving him, and his fellow sinners, the benefit of the doubt. Fair enough?'

Ezeoba made no attempt to disguise the ill grace with which he accepted the verdict. He pinned Maren to earth with his famous crossed eyes and the newcomer braced himself for what he knew would be exceedingly stormy weeks ahead. Mr Kaye's 'You may go now' was hardly out of his mouth before Maren was out of the office and into the approach to Unter den Linden, covered in perspiration, his head buzzing with the inordinate riot of the hornets he had unwittingly aroused. Unlike his normal practice, he did not wait to make a choice of trees; at the first avocado tree that opened its branches securely, he stopped, swung his tiny frame up and climbed to the topmost branch. Never in his life had he felt so devastated. The only consolation, perhaps, was Mr Kaye who appeared to have taken none of it too seriously. There was no question of that glint of mischief in his eye. But he did not have to live with Mr Kaye. Ezeoba was his Nemesis. Now he would watch him night and day, ready to pounce on him for the slightest infringement of rules, or whatever. He had behaved as if his lifelong heritage had been assaulted. One did not have to be told to realise that such a thing had never happened in all his four years at Government College. This was his fifth. He had graduated to become Head of a dormitory... oh yes, that was the other thing. The would-be reformer had forgotten the very dimension that triggered off the argument. Swanston House had two dormitories – Swan, and Ston. Those who stayed back were all billeted in Swan, Ezeoba's very own constituency, his sphere of authority. The year marked the beginning of his term of office, hardly begun, and a mere new boy had tried to undermine his treasured symbol of authority. Unless, of course, he was also playing a role, a role he believed was expected of him? No one really talked like that if they were in earnest. Or did they? Well, Maren was on the way to finding out, and the prospect appeared to offer nothing but unpleasantness.

Unter den Linden. Thus the Germans had named the path through the lush orchard that linked Greer with Swanston House. Even in the Harmattan, the orchard remained green. When war broke out, the unlucky Germans, caught in this British territory, were interned. The spartan Nissen huts that served as their billets, refurbished, had now become the boarding House dormitories. Unter den Linden was more than the link path, it lent its name to that entire environment on which the Germans had landscaped their nostalgia. They planted citrus and avocado, tricked it out with shrubs, moulded artificial hillocks that were soon grassed over, enlarged the lean trickle of a stream into a noisy brook that turned in places to miniature waterfalls, sunk into marshy spaces and resurfaced in sparkling, pebbled rivulets. Where the earth turned to hard, gravelly clay, they had succeeded in creating gorges four to five feet deep, so that the stream ran over ochre hollows, a distant world below surface level. Unter den Linden was made to pass over such a gorge; a plank had been placed over it for easy crossing, though it was so narrow that it made the plank superfluous. And so, among avocado pears, cashew trees and shea-butter pod clusters, they must have wandered and dreamt of home.

Wandering along their path, the boy felt their presences. These were surely not compatriots of the monster Hitler, who had sent people scurrying home before dark in Abeokuta, compelled to place dark shades over their lamps at night so as to offer no tempting target for his marauding planes. Unter den Linden reeked of their loss; their presences haunted the trees, as piteous as they must have been when they endured the confines of the school compound.

Like a tree rodent to a new found hole, he adopted Unter den Linden for his own. The vaster, more densely tree-populated orchards between the boarding Houses and the school compound were reserved for lengthier forays; Unter den Linden was the quick respite, within easy call of Swanston House. As it also served as the route to the sports field, it was a simple routine to peel off from the sports enthusiasts, then rejoin them on their way home. When one's absence was noticed, there was, of course, the penalty to be paid. The German's pastoral made any penalty trivial, but a succession of such penalties built up towards severer sanctions. And worst of all it earned the delinquent a reputation that went into the school report.

Hostilities may have ceased in faraway Europe; it would appear, however, that the armistice was never heard of in the orchards of Unter den Linden. Perched above it all among the avocado branches, he watched the scrappers square up to one another, cheered on by partisans on both sides. Only rarely was it a structured, regulated affair, with a senior boy acting as referee, calling the rounds and making the gladiators shake hands at the end. Then gloves were employed. At other times it was wrestling, and it went on until the loser was firmly pinned to the ground. Most often, however, the contestants came hotfoot on each other's heels, threw off their shirts and threw aside any consideration of rules. For some reason he did not resent this abuse of his appropriated sanctuary; after all, it was mostly entertaining and somehow the combatants stopped short of inflicting any permanent damage on each other. More troubling, however, were the growing indications that it was only a matter of time before he found himself on the receiving end of one pair of these flailing arms, locked in unequal combat.

It did not take long for the race for a pecking order to commence. An offence strangely taken, a flurry of blows, a harmless exchange, turned into a declaration of war . . . any excuse to magnify a slight, real or contrived, and he soon found himself a bewildered participant in sudden, impromptu bouts. They took place on the way to the farm or sports fields, in daytime or evening, in between changing classrooms, or in the classrooms themselves before the teacher entered and took charge. A swift blow, parried, taken full force, but always returned, however feebly. He had identified the bullies, and gradually built up a passionate hatred for each one, in a personalised response. Two at least he knew as natural bullies. It was their nature. They would bully their own baby sisters at home and hit their crippled grandmothers. The others were mimics. They observed the swagger of the naturals and proceeded to establish their private systems of domination. He despised these especially, countered their terror with inventive verbal abuse. The attacks multiplied. He took to loading his pockets with stones, with the small paint jars from the art class, recognised with unfailing precision the glint of impending attack in the sidelong glance of the bully, even when that predator feigned indifference to the midget pestilence that was passing within his reach, or was isolated in the reading room.

Yanju was their favourite target. Sickly, inoffensive, simply studious, he clung to the walls like a gecko and only desired to be left alone. Odali would bait him, cruelly, pointlessly. The helplessness of Yanju appeared to provoke him. Maren found it difficult to accept, and the club of bullies decided that the boy was mad. Here was this runt, who had enough problems just maintaining a whole skin, but did he thank his stars that the club had found a substitute butt? No, he had to tell Odali off for picking on the pathetic Yanju!

Odali stalked him until he found him alone in a classroom. His face broke out in a grin of self-satisfaction.

'Ah, good. Repeat what you said in the classroom this morning.'

'What did I say?'

'What did you say? Are you asking me what you said?'

'Well, you asked me to repeat it. What did you ask me to repeat?'

'Don't play your funny games with me, understand. I am not Ashie and all those people who take that nonsense from you. Just repeat it if you dare.'

'I'm reading. You're disturbing me.'

'Disturbing you! Disturbing you! I said, repeat what you said this morning.'

'But I don't remember what I said.'

'You're reading on me. I am talking to you and you're reading on me. Take your eyes from that book when I'm talking to you.'

Working himself up, he knew, working himself up. The attack would come any time now. But still the boy hoped he could avoid it. Someone might come in, even a teacher might pass by, then all he had to do was get up, gather his books and stroll out to safety – with a final verbal taunt or aggravating gesture – he never could resist that. He hated these fights, but he hated the antics of Odali even more. He carefully closed the book he was reading, slid his hand under the desk and closed his fingers on a paint jar. 'Right. I'm listening.'

'Look at him. You think so much of yourself, don't you? A pagan like you.'

'I am not a pagan.'

'Don't talk back at me. I said you are a pagan. What is your christian name? You don't even have one, you Abeokuta pagan.'

'I have told you, Odali. You don't need a foreign name to be a christian. And having a foreign name doesn't mean you are a christian. Your conduct decides that.'

'Be quiet! You are all pagans in your family.'

Odali knew what he was doing. For reasons of his own, he wanted the smaller boy to make the first move. Casting a slur on the opponent's family could always be guaranteed to unleash the aggressive beast in the mildest pupil.

Maren's knuckles were already taut with his grip on the bottle, but he knew he must not be the first to attack. He never was. 'Keep your mouth away from my family,' he warned.

'I said your family is all pagan. Pagan. Bush. Primitive pagans.'

The boy would recall what had worked before in a similar situation. He shrugged, re-opened his book, and appeared to resume his reading. It never failed. Odali leapt forward to snatch the book away from him, encountered a fist wrapped around a jar. With that initial advantage, the fight proceeded on reasonably equal terms. All the younger boy had to do now was engage the desks and chairs in the contest as noisily as possible, hoping that someone would look in to investigate the fracas. In the meantime he defended himself as best he could, using his teeth in close clinches when the going got really tough. Odali, he knew, would never use his teeth, he had peculiar notions of fair play, which, however, did not include picking a fight in the first place with someone of far lesser height and weight.

And then, after the welcome interruption: 'I'll see you later in the orchard. You meet me there if you dare.'

'Why should I?'

'If you are your father's son, you meet me there.'

'I'm always there. If you are your father's son, try and find me.'

'Good. Expect me this afternoon. After siesta.'

And he was always as good as his word. From his vantage perch, the younger boy watched him. He would walk up and down, drop into a sudden low crouch, shadow box, spar with invisible partners and work up a solid lather of sweat. His hero was Randolph Turpin. Time and time again, the boy hoped he would pass under his perch so he could drop on him and bear him down, pound him thoroughly before he recovered his breath, then take to his heels. But Odali never did, and he never spotted him. After giving up all hope of his adversary's appearance, he sprinted back to his dormitory in the other House, flung himself on his bed and reviewed his battle-plans for the next encounter.

v Frogs, Toads
and the Facts of Life

One cold wave of the Harmattan merged into the next, yet the school did not even consider varying the morning routine. It was up even before it was properly dawn, into special shorts for Physical Training or some form of sports, then the cold shower, or, more accurately, the cold jet from overhead pipes that had long abandoned their perforated caps. Lips, palms, skin, soles of feet were all chapped. Mugs of tea froze as they were passed down the table at breakfast. The first classes of the day, before the sun fought its way through a stubborn haze, were torture, especially when the wind vented its spleen on the school compound. Vests were rigorously forbidden except for the sick, and they had to be so certified by the clinic. Jars of vaseline and the scented pomade favoured by some emptied rapidly, but the most agonising experience of all was simply quitting the warmth of the bed in the mornings. Ezeoba was the only one who appeared to enjoy it all, yanking the covers off the shivering bodies of sluggards and ringing the bell next to their ears as if determined to deafen them. Even the library ceased to be a favourite haunting ground for Maren, especially during the morning class breaks. With Komi, he sought out sun-spots on the rocks and let the little heat the rocks had then absorbed seep through his shorts. With a dedication that was not shared by the rest of the class, the two had already catalogued every feature of the compound, and could almost walk blindfolded from any selected spot to the next.

That sun-favoured rock also had an attraction that went beyond its comparative warmth in Harmattan – it overlooked the wall directly onto the bustling village of Apataganga. Unobserved, they could watch the goings-on in the village, and what they found astonishing was the presence of certain senior boys who seemed to be very much at home, and at different times of the day, in a place that was supposed to be out of bounds. Out of their school uniforms, they merged easily with the locals.

There was one house especially, a two-storey building, the upper floor of which appeared to be inhabited by two women. They were to be seen lounging against the wooden railing with nothing more than a wrapper knotted above their breasts, their shoulders bare. Their callers were mostly male, and they never appeared to stay long. Sometimes they joined the customers in the bar downstairs, where a gramophone played selections that ranged from Denge to the latest songs of Bing Crosby or the Andrews Sisters. At such times, they might leave the bar and return to their place upstairs, only to be followed later by someone with whom they had been drinking in the bar.

'Oh, imagine that,' Komi remarked one day. 'I would never have thought a place like Apata would have one of those.'

'One of what?'

'That place, upstairs.'

'Where the women live?'

'Where the women work,' corrected Komi.

'They don't do any work. All I've seen them do is drink with customers downstairs, then go back to their rooms.'

Komi chuckled. 'Ah, look at this missionary boy. Don't you know anything?'

'Like what?'

'Like what the women do. Why do you think the men are always going upstairs to visit them? You think they're just friends going for a chat?'

'Komi! Look. Quickly. Do you see who's just coming out of the upstairs room?'

Komi stared hard, let out a long whistle, then muttered, '*Et tu, Brute?*'

'Why do you say that?'

Komi began to clamber down the rock, shaking his head and chuckling. Maren ran after him, questioning him with increasing impatience. But Komi would only continue his chuckling, loping forward in the favourite half-crouch he engaged in when he found something wildly amusing, which was not often. Komi subscribed to a journal called *Popular Psychology*, which advised that a self-possessed man should never yield to inordinate laughter. That afternoon, however, Komi had clearly forgotten all his character-forming instructions. He bounced all over the grass like a stranded fish.

'Bombastic Ezeoba! Bombastic Ezeoba! Who would ever have imagined that he was one of them.'

As if on cue, one revelation followed fast upon the last, most of it due to his obsessive hunt for secretive spaces. There was an abandoned school hall, almost at one edge of the southern limits of the compound. Since the new assembly hall had been opened, the hall had retained the sole loyalty of the school dramatic society, and a few lizards and snakes. The latter had taught him caution, so he never entered the hall without first peering into areas where they might be lurking.

That afternoon, he had sneaked off from the sports field. Behind the heavy curtain in front of the platform which served for a stage, he knew that there was a pile of drapes which came into use only when the dramatic society was rehearsing, or close to performance. He had once watched a long, black snake emerge angrily from its disturbed peace among the drapes. It did not matter that the squatter had taken off in the opposite direction from where he stood, while he fled back through the door, the experience had unnerved him, and, thereafter, he found that he could not settle down to his reading until he had poked into the pile with one of the long poles lying around the platform. That day, however, even as he approached a suitable pole for the vetting routine, he heard sounds of thrashing that could only belong to two or more reptiles locked in deadly combat. They had to be pythons at least, or boa constrictors.

In a flash, he was out through the door which he always left open in any case until he was satisfied that the hall was reptile-clean. Some calm returned, as usual, after he had regained the security of open space, and he began to listen more carefully to the sounds, but these had changed so rapidly, so confusedly, that he was momentarily at a loss whether to stay where he was or continue running. The sound became distinct as that of a door being flung open, and there was heavy scampering that could by no means be attributed to any snake, of whatever size. Burglars, was his next thought. The thought of burglars, sufficiently desperate as to raid even a part-time school hall in broad daylight, was the remaining spur required to make him head in full flight towards Swanston, in the sudden realisation that the school compound was deserted, everybody was on the sports field, staff, students, even the non-teaching staff. At five in the afternoon on sports day, the school compound was ghostland. Any living being was either sick in the dormitories or in staff quarters enjoying the peace of absent pupils.

It was strange. The burglars, he confidently expected, would head away from the school compound, vanishing quickly into the surrounding bush. Not these ones. They must have gone round the back of the hall and emerged onto the path leading towards the main compound, where they came face to face with him. Two of them, a man and a woman. He recognised both instantly: Esuri, the popular cricketer in Class Four and – the gardener's daughter. Esuri was still buttoning up his shirt as he ran, while the girl was holding up her wrapper with one hand.

For several moments, the two parties stood still, Esuri and his companion breathing heavily while Maren pondered into what new trouble he had now plunged himself.

Finally: 'You! It's you! Why are you not on the sports field?'

'Sorry, Esuri, please, I just came to read.'

Esuri was from Greer House. He held his head and groaned. 'Oh yes, it's you all right. I've heard about you. Yes, I've heard about you. And you don't know how lucky you are not to be in Greer House. They say you're a nuisance, now I see why. You're always where you are not supposed to be. You're argumentative. You're noisy. And nosey. Yes, one sees quite clearly that you are also a nosey-poker.'

'But I only came to read . . .'

'And what of the library! Isn't that where you're supposed to read?'

'But it's closed at this time.'

'Because everyone is supposed to be at the sports field, you nosey-poking troublemaker. Why are you not at the sports? Do you see anyone here except your tiny, troublemaking self?'

Maren thought he did, but sensed that it was hardly the time to point out that fact to him. In any case, the girl had begun to tug at his shirt, telling him that it was best to be off. Esuri appeared to agree, regaining something of self-control. He drew himself up and became a Senior Boy.

'I shall decide what to do with you later. Now, I'll tell you what.' His voice took on a mixture of authority and wheedling. 'I may decide to forget this whole episode. You are out of bounds, I hope you know that?'

The boy nodded; he did not need reminding. Unless there was a function designated for this part of the compound, it was out of bounds outside teaching hours.

'Well, we shall just have to wait and see whether or not you know what is in your best interest. You know I've caught you breaking the rules but, as I said, I may just decide to give you another chance. That depends on whether or not you do not invite an official report by giving yourself away.'

Gratefully, Maren assured him that he had no intention of doing any such thing.

'Good. In that case, I shall forget that I ever saw you here. Now, I shall proceed to close my eyes. When I open them, I want you to have disappeared.'

Maren did not bother to see the shutting of Esuri's eyes before he took off.

That very evening, he narrated the events to Yanju who listened attentively, fascinated by every detail.

'But what I don't understand is why you went back,' Yanju remarked.

'I just wanted to be sure.'

'Sure of what?'

'Sure of what I guessed they were doing before I entered the hall and they ran.'

'But what? Are you saying they went to burgle the place?'

'No-o.'

'But you said you thought they were burglars.'

'Don't you understand? They were not burglars!'

'Then why did you bother to go back?'

'Because I wasn't fooled. When he shut his eyes and told me to run, I knew they were just trying to get rid of me.'

'But what for? You said they didn't steal anything. The gardener's daughter wouldn't do a thing like that.'

Maren sighed. 'Tell me something, Yanju. Seriously now, were you ever brought up in a parsonage?'

'No, I told you. My father is a farmer. We're all christians in the family, mind you.'

'And you are – fourteen years old, not so?'

Yanju became irritated. 'Why are you asking me what you know already? So you went back. You haven't told me what happened.'

'I saw what I saw, that's all. I returned through the back, I stood by that door leading onto the stage.'

'Yes?'

'I saw everything, I tell you.'

'We're back where we started. What did you see?'

Maren shook his head. 'If you don't know, I can't tell you. You talk to Komi. He wouldn't be asking questions like you. When I tell him about it tomorrow, you'll see, he won't need to ask any questions.'

It should have been a normal raid like several others before. The Principal's routine had been carefully scouted and it never failed. This was his siesta hour; lunch was over and he had no visitors. The short, fat History teacher should have been in bed.

And then he suddenly appeared from behind the house. He was shirtless, dressed only in a pair of baggy shorts. In his hand was a short-handled garden fork. There were a few cheerful-faced plaster figures in the garden and, but for their smiling features and their comic headgear, the History teacher could easily pass for an animated version of one of this tribe of imported garden gnomes. He moved about slowly, conscious of the heat, relaxedly, as if he had come to settle in the garden plot at the back of the house for a long while. The garden was next to the orchard among whose trees Maren now found himself stuck, unable to move.

Some ancient predecessor among the staff of Government College was surely born with a grapefruit seed for a navel: it was difficult to understand why those trees should outnumber every other fruit tree in the compound at least two to one. Tangerines came next, while oranges and avocado pears shared the third place. The grapefruit came in several dozen varieties of size, colouring and taste, and these included the colour of the interior flesh, which varied from off-white to a blazing red. Of these seemingly limitless varieties, however, there did grow one exceptional tree whose fruits, a unique, exotic breed, were duplicated nowhere else in the entire school compound, and it was located in the Principal's private orchard. Komi, Chris, Muyi, Shida, Dipo . . . everyone had warned him that that tree would prove his undoing, but there was nothing he could do to resist its call. The most vulnerable period was the school siesta when he prematurely exhausted the single novel that was permitted each boy during the rest hour. Then he grew restless. His mind went to the orchard whose sole proprietor would, by then, be preparing for his own siesta. Sports, or farm, followed the school siesta hour. If he sneaked out of the dormitory minutes before the bell rang, he had a full half hour to race to the orchard, snatch a half dozen or so of the grapefruits, hide them and join the others at the appointed field.

It was not the apple that tempted Eve, but this grapefruit; thus did Maren revise the tale of paradise lost, and even Chris, shocked as he was at such blasphemy, confessed himself tempted to agree whenever Maren returned from raiding the Principal's compound, with a shirtful of the booty to share, especially on a hot afternoon. This fruit combined the flavour of tangerines, the chunky bittersweet grapefruit flesh itself and, most remarkable of all, the pomegranates of Aké. Its fragrance, even from a hundred yards, was overpowering, the aromatic lemon grass blended with the tangy pink fruit loosely called the apple berry. But Maren admitted to himself that he was driven by more than a passionate craving. He had a score to settle with Mr Jefferies, who was now the Acting Principal. Raiding his special tree was the only way he had of settling that score, while he indulged his insatiable palate at the same time.

Komi had been satisfied with the initial raid, and even the tempestuous Kehinde, later to find more exciting game with the club of class bullies, had wearied of the risky game after the former Principal had nearly surprised them by flinging a window open unexpectedly and staring in their direction for what seemed an eternity. It was so fixed a stare, locked on the tree with such cold, implacable certainty, that it seemed impossible that he could have missed them both – the raider among the trees and the catcher below. Later, they found that Mr Padell was woefully short-sighted, and that afternoon he was without his glasses. The discovery had restored Maren's confidence and he was soon back on his periodic visits. However, he took the precaution of selecting only branches that provided sufficient foliage to hide him in an emergency, which was not much for his small frame.

Jefferies was standing in for the Biology teacher, Miss Bradlow or 'Bottomless B.' No one knew why she had suddenly disappeared but her absence, which coincided with the annual leave of Padell, the Principal, generated much speculation, especially among the more knowing boys. Maren refused to countenance any such stories; no man in his senses, with eyes in his head, could be attracted to a woman whose rear must have been sliced off in a surgical operation, then the residue left in its skirt for ironing by a professional washer-man. No pretence at the sheerest ghost of a contour, nothing but a wide, smooth expanse, flat as the bottom of a frying-pan. Still, there was no knowing with these people. Kaye, after all, was nearly as featureless in that area of his anatomy.

History was Mr Jefferies' field. He knew nothing of formaldehydes and dissecting plates and specimen jars, and appeared not to have the slightest interest in them. After the first lesson, he shifted his meetings with the class to any spare room in the main classroom block, away from the biology laboratory. That was his first offence. For Maren and at least half a dozen others in the class, the direct classroom instructions were far less important than fieldwork, roam-ing the fields for butterfly and other insect specimens, scooping up frogs and toads and their slimy eggs. Even the earthworm, repulsive as he found it, affirmed the very life and justification of biology lessons, as long as he had it under the scalpel and could tease out its minuscule details under the microscope. Biology was life revealed in ways that he had never suspected.

Then there were the Latinate and proprietary names accorded the simplest, most ordinary crops. *Cola acuminata* for the simple Kola nut. The pawpaw was transformed into *Carica papaya*, the commonplace mango into *Mangifera indica*. In a voice as flat and uninspiring as her flat-iron bottom, Miss Bradlow had at least imbued the commonplace, much taken for granted, with an explora- tory, experimental world of nature's variegation. Even the much contemned *agunmaniye*, that-which-grows-tall-without-sense, had been christened with the euphonious name of *Lucinea Splendifera*. For nearly three weeks of Miss Bradlow's absence, Mr Jefferies had proved himself a hater of the open air, of Latinate biological terms, and indeed of any inclination towards a collector's passion for fauna or flora, rare or commonplace. Beyond his inherited gnome-haunted garden, Jefferies deplored or was simply indifferent to nature. The Killjoy of Biology, the class soon named him; it vied with his other title, Stumpy Jefferies.

He fooled no one with his seeming indifference: he was squeamish about toads' interiors. After making the mistake the first time of inviting the class to carry on where Bottomless B. had left off, then watching the monsters dive into their lockers, drag out their dissecting dishes filled with spread-eagled toads, cockroaches, earth- worms and dung-beetles, the air suddenly clogged with the stench of formaldehyde, Stumpy stared open-mouthed as two dozen pairs of arms dug into their prostrate victims like long-deprived cannibals. Then he dashed quickly into the corridor and leant over the railing for fresh air. After that, he never again took on the biology class in its natural habitat.

Jefferies' next, and mortal, offence was committed in his history classroom, and Maren, as sole victim, sentenced his golden tree to perpetual raids.

The Acting Principal always tried to touch some aspect of biology instruction when he took these classes, so it was not as if he left the boys absolutely to their own devices. His sessions were mostly information exchanges, and he appeared not to notice if even half the class were engrossed in non-biological studies. Not surprisingly, only one or two hands were ever raised when he asked his questions; the class considered them generally beneath notice.

'What is the difference between a frog and a toad?'

It produced yawns and exchanges of knowing looks from most, but one hand did shoot up, mostly to register its owner's attentive- ness as early as possible, leaving him free to his real pursuits for the rest of the period.

'Yes, Maren?'

'The frog is edible, sir, the toad is not.'

Jefferies' cry of horror woke up the class. 'What . . . what did you say?'

'Unlike the toad, sir, the frog is edible.'

Jefferies' jaws worked, soundlessly. Moments later, he rushed out of the classroom. Wondering what could have got into him, Maren turned to the rest of the class only to find them staring at him, their faces contorted in a variety of expressions that were unmistakable as hatred, pity, contempt, and a Jefferies-type horror. Prolonged hisses issued from nearly every sector of the classroom, and anger – raw, raging anger – surged towards him. In a flash, Maren saw the entire world as one phalanx of *egungun** masks bearing down on him, united in a supernatural, consuming conspiracy for his destruction. Because of its suddenness, its arbitrary, inexplicable eruption, the boy was terrified.

Komi, seated next to him in the twosome bench-and-desk combination, stared into his books when he turned to him for some kind of assurance, or explanation. Muyi appeared stolidly determined not to become involved; so did Dipo, from whom he thought he had a right to expect some support. After all, they had made up their recent quarrel after the Head of House had arranged a boxing match between them behind Ston dormitory, a two-rounder that Dipo, with his long, impenetrable arms, easily won. They had shaken hands after the bout and the least Maren expected from him, in return for bloodying his nose, was to come to his aid at such moments. Chris, his musical *alter ego*, was seemingly preoccupied with some mental piano exercise. As he scanned one face after the other, it seemed that, apart from his own small circle, no more than three or four had remained so engrossed in their own work that they could be counted out of the violence in which he was now enveloped. It was Ashie who gave expression to what was still, to him, a profound mystery.

'For someone to come and disgrace his own people before the white man, just like that!' Adeyelu, the origin of whose nickname, Major Kakiika, no one really recalled, could hardly get out his

*Ancestral masquerade.

words. A powerful emotion choked him, but he struggled to spit in the boy's direction: 'Even an illiterate would never do that to his own people.'

'Edible frogs!' another voice added. 'Even if they are so primitive in your village, do you have to come and expose them like that here?'

'Bush boy!'

'Beast of no nation!'

'Have they put frogs in your diet here, you bastard of the black race?'

In a low voice, beside him, he heard Komi say, 'You really shouldn't have said that.'

At that moment, the world fell apart. Komi too? Because by now, he of course understood. For some reason, eating frogs was normal, as long as it was not acknowledged before the white man. But this intensity of hate! Was this also because the white man in question had shown himself shocked, disapproving?

But he himself had never eaten the wretched things, only watched others catch them, clean them out, roast them over wood fires and eat them. *Akere*. Since the earliest childhood he had known *akere* as a delicacy among schoolchildren and even grownups. And of the masks of vicious glares that now confronted him, at least a third of them had converted captured frogs to ends other than the dissection bowls in the biology class, stuffed their pockets with the slender meat and nibbled to their hearts' content at all hours of the day. He had never even been tempted to join them; neither did he disapprove.

Another voice exploded close to his ear: 'You are going to pay for this for a long time, you too-know idiot! Trying to curry favour with the white staff by shaming your own people!'

This, he could not understand. Why should frog-eating be considered a matter for shame? And if it was . . . he tried to recall his answer. Nothing in it suggested that he had attempted to exempt himself from the shame, if indeed shame it was. Yes, frogs are edible, that was what I said. The logic of their attribution, and of their reaction, escaped him. For one thing, he never even said which peoples considered frogs edible, although anyone was free to draw an inference. As for trying to curry favour! For stating a commonplace fact? In any case, what had this to do with one set of people rather than another? Then the teacher himself, Jefferies, what a hypocrite! Why, in the library, he could show them . . .

'That's right. Gi'am!'

A blow had landed on the side of his head, far less painful than the internal turmoil he was then undergoing.

'And that's only the beginning. From now on, you'll see, Mr Too-Clever! We've tolerated all your nonsense far too long. If we'd dealt with you the way you deserved, you wouldn't have disgraced the class like you have!'

Had the world gone mad? What was all this talk of shame and disgrace? Was this some long-brewing conspiracy now brought to a head by mere chance? His eyes raced from one member of the Club of Bullies to the next. They were all enjoying this. The horror had vanished, now it was simple anticipation. He could almost see them salivate at the prospect of venting on his head some kind of righteous indignation. They cursed and insulted him now with the authority of the entire body – at least, that difference now manifested itself very clearly. Their tirade no longer emerged from 'I' and 'me', and 'myself' and 'do you realise who you're talking to?' and so on. They were assuming the role of defenders of the class, and the race, against the treacherous brat in their midst. The prospect was at once terrifying and unreal. Just what had he done?

The bell signalled the end of class; it proved a deceptive respite. The block of classrooms was built on a slope, and while one end of it ran almost flush into the ground, the other end of the long block plunged nearly six feet, and that ground was sheer rock. Jefferies' classroom was the fifth, that is, second to the last before the drop. A wide corridor surrounded the block, one length facing inwards onto a quadrangle, the science laboratories and the staffroom. The end with the long drop overlooked the wooded section through which ran paths to the mechanical workshop, the swimming pool, and Swanston House, while the other length opened on to the chapel, the Principal's office, then, further on still, the Principal's house and its orchard with the Golden Tree. From the short drop, one faced the library, an exhibition gallery or museum, and the clinic.

The boy's desk was at the rear corner of the classroom, furthest from the two doors at the front. In a flash, he saw that Ashie and

Kehinde had positioned themselves at the door to the safe corridor, the one that overlooked the interior quadrangle where the staffroom was also situated. They made no pretence of the fact that they were there to bar his way, to force him onto the exterior corridor. The rest of the Club, he knew, awaited him there.

These people want to kill me, he thought. They cannot even wait, they want to kill me before I can make them admit they are wrong, that they are fabricating this injury. They want to push me over the long drop and kill me.

The various classes were changing rooms. No other class was coming to occupy Mr Jefferies' for the next period; they all knew that. All they had to do was hang around until the rest of the school had settled down; they didn't mind being late to their next class. The boy considered his choices . . . If I come out, they will push me over the edge . . . if I wait, they will come in and give me a rapid beating; even one minute would satisfy them, at least for now.

He settled for the quadrangle corridor. There were only two assailants guarding the door, and early help was likelier, even though the staff would, by then, be mostly in the classrooms. They watched him approach and left their position by the door to close in on him. Kehinde let out a whistle to the others and the boy heard them racing towards the room. He lowered his head and butted blindly. In another moment he was out in the corridor, his books flying in every direction, his arms bruised from the desperate attempt to hold him back.

The penalty for missing a class, without good reason, was serious but Maren had decided that he had no choice but to miss the next, which was the last for the day and would therefore provide his persecutors all the time they required to satisfy their blood lust. Moreover, there was a weapon which he had to obtain, before he was mangled to bits by a frenzy he could not understand. To wait until the end of school was to expose himself to the sightless peril, so he leapt down from the corridor, crossed the quadrangle and maintained a casual walk until he was past the open doors of the classrooms on the abandoned side. Then he sped towards the dispensary, dodged behind the school museum, round the chapel, and into the library. He watched through the window, curious to see if he was pursued, not really fearful that any of them would dare attack him in the library. He settled down to a feverish search: where had he seen it? The page was vivid before his eyes – the picture, in colour, a freckled brown amphibian with bulging eyes and, beneath it, the picture title: THE EDIBLE FRENCH FROG.

His mind raced rapidly through the library titles he had read in the past year; now which one of them contained pictures? And what text on earth had involved a frog, edible or not? Or a toad if need be? He was certain it was a book from the school library, not one borrowed from the senior boys, or from the House library. The French Edible Frog, or The Edible French Frog – one or the other . . . Of course: the encyclopaedia! Now he remembered flicking past that page in a search for something or the other. He had not made any special note of it at the time, but, yes, it had remained lodged in his mind.

Relieved, he shifted to the Reference cupboard and lifted out the book. Within seconds he had found the page – there it was, staring him in the face, a full-blown poised-to-leap frog of identical lineage – to all appearances – with the marshland and grassland African edible *akere*. Library rules forebade the removal of reference books from the library but this was one exception that was more than justified. Moreover, classes were in session, and the hypocritical Jefferies was sitting unsuspecting in his office, the main cause of Maren's mistreatment, as far as he could see. This was the moment to confront him with the book and ask him what was the meaning of that performance he had given before the class.

He looked up triumphantly, only to encounter the gloating face of Adeyelu.

'I knew it. The others thought you had headed for the House, but I knew better. I knew you would take refuge in the library; that's where you get all these stupid ideas from. You think you're better than everyone, don't you? You always know better.'

Maren knew that all he had to do was thrust the open encyclopaedia in his face. Adeyelu would first attempt to bluster his way out, then become gradually crestfallen and join him in cursing the History teacher for the hypocrite he was or, less likely, for an ignoramus. As often happened, however, he became enraged instead by the injustice of it all. They had all turned against him, unleashed an aggression against a simple truth. Why should it matter whether or not Jefferies' kinsmen also ate frogs? Why should that remove the disgrace, if indeed it was a disgrace? From the feeling of triumph, he now felt only contempt for his opponents and most of it now fell on the brute face that had actually followed him into the library, panting for his blood instead of going to class to improve his mind.

'The trouble with you, Major Kakiika . . .'

'How dare you call me by that name?'

'You like the name, don't pretend with me. You preen yourself when others call you . . .'

'You are not others, and can never be. I am not your rank in age, so you do not have my permission to use my nickname.'

'All right. If you're not ashamed to admit that we are in the same class when you're already old enough to father children . . .'

'Good. You are always asking for it. I keep warning you that that mouth of yours will surely land you in trouble. Now come outside where I can teach you a lesson.'

Confident in the sanctuary of the library, Maren laughed. 'Teach me a lesson, you? It is I should teach you. You need teaching 'Deyelu, your mind needs improving.'

His face now contorted with rage, Adeyelu grabbed him and proceeded to drag him out. Maren was alarmed. This was a totally unexpected development. Nobody fought in the library. Next to the chapel, the library was the most sacred place on the compound. The coarse, set face of Adeyelu, however, expressed a different reading of the library code and, to make matters worse, they were alone. Perhaps it was that very fact that spurred him on. Now Adeyelu was attempting to lift him bodily, while he clung to the table. He had no weapons, not even a paint jar, not even a pencil in his pocket. From one table to the next, they grappled, Maren shifting his life-and-death hold to the next as he was dragged off the last. Then suddenly, it was as if Adeyelu was filled with superhuman strength; one moment, Maren was thinking that he had little choice left but to go for the last resort – attack his opponent at his most vulnerable part – the genitals (he had in fact released one hand for that purpose, determined to give it a really violent tug, then leap through the window and head for the Principal's office); the next, he felt himself flying through the air. He crashed through the glass door and landed outside.

From Adeyelu's horror-stricken face, he glanced down, having felt a wet stickiness on one foot. Blood was gushing out of a gash across the sole of his left foot. It was a deep cut and it covered the entire width of the foot. He groaned and lay back, convinced that his fate had been decided; nothing short of amputation could result from this.

Adeyelu's face loomed over him; it was the first time he would see him scared. 'I'll get the nurse,' he managed to gasp, and ran off.

There was no pain, but he felt himself floating away . . . there was something familiar about it all, another Akínkòyí lying somewhere, blood gushing from his body, two of them in fact . . . but surrounded by anxious faces, shouts, hands . . . yes, two bleeding forms of himself soaking the soil of Aké. Once it was his head that was split open – he flew again over a see-saw, over his partner at the other end, looking down above the one whose weight had sent him soaring towards heaven . . . then there was the long knife that nearly took out his right eye – he fingered the spot as he lay there, the scar still deep enough to be felt by his finger. Waiting for help to arrive, his mind raced through the past two years in the school. So it had all come to this. All the way from Aké to Apataganga, only to end up with one foot, and all because of wretched frogs and the peculiar tastes of Africans and Europeans alike. And Jefferies, the lumpy *sigidi** with leaky breasts, yes, Mr Stumpy Jefferies, just come and see what disaster you have caused. This all started because of you, white hypocrite . . .

The nurse came at a fast walk, with the culprit trotting beside him. He made a brief examination of the foot, glared at Adeyelu, then picked up the prostrate figure like a piece of rag. 'You will have to be sewn up,' he announced.

'What, please?'

'I must sew you up at once. Twelve stitches, if not more. As for you,' and he withered Adeyelu with another savage glare, 'twelve strokes from the Principal is what you deserve. But these white people don't cane young criminals the way it should be done. They never go beyond six and even that I don't call caning. I wish sometimes they would let me help out.'

*A figure of an incubus, usually made of clay.

The wound was washed. Maren watched the nurse tear up a wad of cotton wool, soak it liberally with iodine and, holding the foot firmly with one hand, clamp the soaked wad over the wound. He let out a yelp as loud as Jefferies' when confronted with the edibility of frogs. When the stitching began, however, without any anaesthetic, what he experienced above the pain was – again, the sense of floating. Looking down, he saw the nurse fused somehow with his grandfather, overseeing the incisions being made into his ankles only a few years back, the blade sliding in and down while the assistant covered the raw wound in a dark brown unguent. He was aware of the nurse giving him a peculiar look, and he guessed that it was because the elderly man could not understand why he was not crying out in pain. When it was all over, the nurse shook his head and applied a bandage.

'I shall have to send a note to your Housemaster. And the Principal. Because you must stay in bed for at least a week. I don't want that would re-opened, you understand?'

'Yes, sir.'

He snorted. 'Yessah, yessah. I know your type. You will say you're not feeling any pain so you can go and play cricket and ping-pong. Don't think I've been looking after boys for these twenty years for nothing. I am coming to see your dormitory head this evening and I'll give him strict instructions.'

'Ezeoba?'

'Oh, is Ezeoba your dormitory head? Good. I know I can rely on him.' And only then did the foot begin to throb and he felt excruciating pains all the way up to his knee. He sighed. For the first time since he had picked him up from the ground, the nurse actually looked relieved.

'Komi, did you know that Europeans have witches?'

'Well, they did burn witches, didn't they? So they must have had them to burn.'

'Who's talking about those Walter Scott witches? I mean real witches. Proper ones. And we have one right here, among the staff. In fact, not just a witch. A *sigidi*.'

'All right. Which of them? And what, now, is *sigidi*?'

'Mr Jefferies.'

'Is *sigidi* a kind of male witch? Like wizard?'

'Witch. I said, witches.'

'Mr Jefferies is a man, so he cannot be a witch.'

'Suppose he has breasts, what then?'

'Come on, 'Koyi, we know he is fat . . .'

'. . . Squat and blubbery, yes, but that's not what I'm talking about. The man has breasts, proper . . . no, not really proper breasts, but a bit pendulous. They wobble . . .'

'Nothing new. We agree they wobble. One can see that when he walks.'

'Let me finish. I have seen them. They not only wobble, they produce milk.'

'Wait-wait-wait, you saw Jefferies' chest? Bare?'

'He had no shirt on, just shorts. And his breasts were oozing milk, all the way down to his stomach.'

'A-kín-kò-yí!'

'There you go again. You don't believe me.'

'How do you expect me to believe a thing like that? Men do not have mammary glands.'

'Yes, we all have. But males ones do not produce milk. No unless one is a witch.'

'All right, tell me the story. Was he swimming or what?'

'That's the other thing. It occurred to me after what happened. Have you ever seen him use our swimming pool?'

'He doesn't have to. The Principal's house has its own pool.'

'Yes, that tiny thing. That's why even the former Principal preferred to use the common school pool. Have you ever seen Jefferies use our pool?'

'Are you going to tell me what happened or aren't you?'

'I saw him in his garden, yesterday. He was wearing only shorts. By the way, I nearly got into trouble. His gardener saved me.'

'You went poaching?'

Maren nodded. 'I didn't know he was outside, on the other side of the house. I went at his usual siesta time, so he should not have been outside. But he was. And I was right up in the branches, no escape.'

'So, what happened?'

'He stood there, looking up at me, waiting for me to come down.

And I kept looking at his breasts, and all that milk streaming down . . .'

'You mean it was flowing, actually flowing?'

'Call it what you like. A trickle, if you prefer. But the milk was there, and it ran all the way down to his fat stomach. And I was staring at it. He was telling me to come down but I don't think I heard him at first. I was scared, scared I tell you. I wasn't thinking of punishment. I just didn't know what to do, whether to get down and run or scream for help.'

'Why scream for help? He wasn't going to eat you!'

'It's all very well for you. You weren't the one trapped in a tree, with this white *sigidi* waiting for you to descend He didn't say a thing at first, he kept squinting up at me as if deciding what to do with me.'

'All right. Now tell me, what exactly is this *sigidi*?'

'You don't know about *sigidi*? You've never seen one in front of someone's house?'

'We don't have such things in our area.'

'How do you know? You've spent most of your life with your uncles in Lagos, and Lagosians don't encounter things like that. Look, if you wake up in the morning and you find a *sigidi* on your doorstep, don't attempt to pass through that door. Use the window, or send for a *babalawo** to come and remove it. You know someone who always reminds me of a *sigidi* in our class?'

'Adeyelu?'

'How did you know? I thought you said you hadn't . . .'

'He is the nearest shape to Jefferies, isn't he?'

'Actually, 'Deyelu is much closer to a *sigidi*. Jefferies is too blubbery to make a real one, except when you are up a tree and looking down on him. He became even more squat, his head was about ten times larger than usual, it looked as if someone had taken a huge hammer and hammered him into the ground, you know, you saw just that huge head looking up, then the stomach, and the two trickles of milk on all that pink flesh. I tell you, it was as if he was transformed, he was changing right before my eyes. I was clinging to the branches for dear life. Komi, I nearly came tumbling down,

*Diviner.

I felt dizzy. At one time, I thought the man was growing up towards me, with his head nearly touching me, exactly how the *sigidi* does when it is sent after someone . . .'

'There you are. Hallucinations! You see, your mind has been affected by all those *sigidi* stories you've been listening to at home.'

'I am telling you what I saw.'

'I must lend you a special issue of my *Psychology* journal. There is an article in it just for someone like you, with your vivid imagination. That, with the guilt you were feeling at the time, and your fear of punishment. All that combined to turn poor Jefferies into a witch, or a *sigidi*. From there, it was a short step to mistaking trickles of sweat for a flow of milk . . .'

'Komi, that man oozed milk. I know the difference between sweat and milk. This was milk, pure milk, the colour of the fluid from any woman's breast. It was milk, which means the man is a witch.'

'Or else you had sunstroke. You were clinging to that tree and the sun was hot. Just after siesta, you said. That means three thirty or so. You were suffering from sunstroke. Look, you yourself admitted that you felt dizzy. When you feel dizzy, the earth spins around you, not so? See, that also explains why you thought the man was growing up towards you, it was because everything was spinning . . .'

'Milk, Komi, milk!'

'All right, all right. What happened when you came down?'

'I said, "Good afternoon sir," but he just kept on staring at me. So I said, "I hope you don't mind, sir, but I came to ask permission to take the encyclopaedia out of the library." . . . You know, I really hadn't thought of what to say; it came to me like that. Just like that! He looked up at the branch to which I had been clinging and asked if I thought he was an African pygmy, or why did I imagine that he had his sitting room up in the trees? Imagine that!'

'He really said that?'

'I'm telling you. That's exactly what he said. So I said, no sir, but that we do have African tree frogs, and when I was approaching his house, I thought I saw one in the tree, and I wanted to catch it and show him in case it was the edible type. His eyes popped out of his head. "You thought you saw a tree frog and you wanted to catch it and show me in case it was edible?" "Yes sir," I said to him. "It looked very much like the one whose picture is in the encyclopaedia, which was why I wanted permission to take the encyclopaedia from the reference shelf and show it to my classmates. And then you." I said, "You see, sir, I was very disturbed by the fact that you disagreed with the encyclopaedia because it says there, clearly, that there are edible frogs, and one – at least it looked like one – one edible-looking frog was very definitely up your tree, and I wondered if the African tree frog was the same as the French edible frog and there was only one way to find out, which was to try and catch it and at the same time bring out the encyclopaedia" . . .'

'Are you saying he just kept listening to you talking all that nonsense?'

'With the milk running down his chest I tell you. I couldn't even look directly at him because of the milk, though why it should be bothering me when he didn't even seem to notice or care – I mean he must be used to it! Anyway, all he did was keep staring at me. I went on and on until I had nothing further to say and so I stopped. And we both stood there, he staring at me, me looking somewhere over his shoulder so as not to see the milk any more. Then the cook steward came out of the house to tell him his bath was ready.'

'That's the one who saved you?'

'Ngn-hn. If he hadn't come just then, I might have decided to run away, which would have meant trouble later. My feet were itching. Look, Komi, he stood there saying nothing. He was staring at me, not a word, just staring. He wasn't saying anything and I had run out of anything more to say. The way he kept staring, he could have been trying to cast a spell on me. Just imagine, all that time, after his one sentence about African pygmies, which I thought was a deliberate insult . . .'

'But some tribes live in trees.'

'He just wanted to insult Africans, that's the point I am making. Like all that drama about edible frogs. I'm going to find a way of making him repeat what he said before the class, and then I'll see which of those donkeys will have the courage to attack him the way they came after me.'

'Come on. Everybody has forgotten that.'

'I haven't. It's taught me something I'll never forget.'

Unter den Linden survived the violence of the combatants; it even survived Adeyelu's chemical barrage. That compact *sigidi*, whom he often wished he could turn into a frog, edible or not, had become addicted to extra-curricular experimentations, which often took place in a small clearing, well hidden by bushes, not far from the playing fields. It was not enough that, even with the chemistry laboratory, he reversed every instruction that was provided both by tutor and textbook, mixing up just the acids that both warned seriously against; he also ensconced jars of chemicals under his shirt and retired with them into the sanctuary of the bush, which he proceeded to pollute with the most noxious fumes. His favourite mixtures were those which the textbook expressly warned might result in an explosion. And yet Major Kakiika's ambition was to be an airline pilot!

It was just a Harmattan like this one, when Adeyelu finally attained his ambition, and the results were spectacular. Cricket season, and the school was taking on its sister college from Ughelli. Adeyelu would later become a demon bowler – as he then liked to be styled – but in those early years his favourite battleground was the football field, where he played fullback, his mission, as he understood it, being to smash the shins of the opposition and ignore the ball altogether. Freed of any obligations on that cricket afternoon, he had sneaked off to his bush laboratory and, armed with a text that was not in the school curriculum nor in the library – no one knew where he obtained these works but he returned each term with a new one – he began, as he privately confessed afterwards – to unearth the formula that would turn simple saline solution into a combustible fuel such as petroleum.

Everyone on the field heard the explosion but thought nothing of it. Occasionally a rock face in the school compound had to be blasted, and the sports hour was an obvious time to do it, when that part of the school was emptied of pupils. This time, however, a pall of smoke became discernible from the direction of the explosion. It drifted above the elephant grass and coiled around tree trunks and through denuded branches in the distance. Then came the unmistakable crackle of burning twigs and the all-too-ready *ekan* grass, moving steadily towards the sports pavilion. A few rodents had begun to make their escape; and it was only a matter of time before a teacher shouted 'Fire' and the cricket game stopped and the fire drill commenced. Over a hundred pairs of arms were lined up, ready to pass buckets of water from hand to hand, but of course this was Harmattan and the taps were dry, so the drill changed to cutting a swathe around the pavilion and beating down the flames with twigs that were so dry that they soon caught fire in turn, and very soon there were no twigs left within reach and there was nothing to do but watch a vast stretch of bush and farms burn to ashes. The pavilion was saved, but only because the wind mercifully turned and the flames changed direction.

Still, it had to be an ill wind that blew no one any good, and those more knowledgeable in the ways of the bush, and lacking any inhibition, waited a while for the earth to cool down, then began to forage. There were rabbits, grasscutters, *emo*, that failed to escape and were either suffocated or burnt, and bushfowl eggs grilled through the shell. A few yam tubers and sweet potatoes were dug up from the parched farms and, after the formal dull, predictable supper, illegal feasting commenced in odd corners of the compound, to which the boys from Ughelli were invited as privileged guests. The handful of Lagos snoots, scions of the colonial aristocrats, passed the festive lairs with an air of contempt – how could a Government Collegian descend to such a barbaric meal? Maren watched Adeyelu as he tore into a grasscutter's thigh and filled his cheeks with roasted yam. Was it really possible? How could anyone remain unconcerned at so much damage? As he watched this creature gorge himself on the spoils, it seemed the ultimate in studied callousness.

Finally, unable to stomach the sight a moment longer, beckoning Adeyelu out of hearing of the others: 'You caused that fire, didn't you?'

His face smudged with the dripping fat of the bush meat, Adeyelu's insolent grin: 'Prove it.'

'I know where you conduct your mad experiments. I saw you go off in that direction.'

'E-enh, prove it now.'

'You know where I sit as the scorer. From my desk I can see everything, not just on the field, but around the pavilion. I pointed you out to my partner from Ughelli. So it's not just me. We both saw you sneaking off, and you were carrying a bag.'

That stopped him chewing, but not for long. He laughed. 'So what? You can't do anything. Are you going to report me or what?'

'Do you realise that the fire spread to the orchard?'

'Which orchard?'

'*My* orchard! The one in Unter den Linden.'

The arsonist found this so hilarious that he had to share it with the others. 'Hey, you people, come and hear this *o*. Akínkòyí's family now has land in Government College.'

The boy's face grew hard. 'Keep your mouth from my family, I keep warning you. Anyway, you are very lucky, only a small part was burnt. If you had really damaged the grove I would have reported you.'

His face twisted with contempt. 'You? I dare you.'

'Just make sure you keep your madness from that orchard, that's all.'

He turned violent. 'So I am mad? You are calling me mad? Are you calling me mad?'

The others intervened. 'What is wrong with you two? You want the seniors to hear you fighting and then discover us here?'

That checked Adeyelu in his stride. He stopped and grabbed another chunk of yam. 'It's all right. I can deal with him later. You just look out for me in the orchard because that's where I am transferring to, next.'

On those grounds, Maren felt unnaturally calm, very self-assured. He knew the most minuscule detail of that terrain and knew he could handle any hostile intrusion, from whatever direction. 'That is where you will meet your Waterloo, I promise. From the moment I catch a whiff of any of your noxious potions, you are finished!'

The fire-raiser waved him off. 'Just hear him. Me, finished! Me, finished! This runt says he will finish me. We shall see about that.'

Short, stocky, black as coal and quick as a wildcat, Adeyelu's instincts were also good. He knew that, tiny as Maren was, the orchard was not the place to meet him, so he became anxious to force the issue in a more advantageous setting, which was virtually anywhere in the open where Maren's speed was no match for his. In the bush, all sorts of natural obstacles could compensate for Kakiika's brute, charging force. Over the next few days Adeyelu strutted around, more and more like the Major Kakiika of his

imagining, confident in his immunity from exposure. Whatever it
was that had caused the explosion in the bush, it marked him out
as a daring chemist who risked everything the textbook prohibited
to attain his single-minded result. He acquired a timid, tentative
following.

Adeyelu acknowledged only one problem, but this was only to
himself, and that problem was Maren. There was a meanness in the
way in which the younger boy eyed him, the way he made it a point
of duty to pass by whenever the maniac began to expound his
latest discoveries in the field of combinations between sulphides,
hydrochloric acids and the common Epsom salts. There were several
others in the class who remained unimpressed by, or at least indifferent to his inane experiments; they all knew him to be a dunce in
literally every subject, including the very chemistry whose laws he
so desperately assaulted, but they did not show it. Only this insub-
stantial Akínkòyí had the knack of making him know that he,
Akínkòyí, knew that all the explosive obsession was a bluff, his way
of taking revenge on a subject whose subtleties eluded him. This
was easy; the smaller boy hated the subject himself and only barely
coped with the intricate calculations that were involved; it was easy
for him to identify a fellow sufferer. Instinct informed him that
this consuming passion for the trial-and-error practical approach,
carried out for the sole object of noise, one that evaded mathematical
calculations, was mere camouflage and self-compensation. The
worst crime, of course, was that the boy showed it.

Before long the euphoria of the impromptu feast began to wear
off, even Adeyelu's followers began to weary of listening to his
endless plans for ever more lethal explosions. For fear that Maren
would reveal his criminality to the chemistry master if he invaded
Unter den Linden with his poisons, he kept off those grounds.
Moreover, he had some irrational feeling that Maren had the means
to neutralise his acids within that atmosphere, vapourise his crystals,
and probably invoke some supernatural forces from the woods to
blind or cripple him permanently, if not render him sexually impotent. It became clear to him that Maren must be neutralised somehow, and on his choice of battleground.

Adeyelu could hardly believe his luck when the opportunity came.
The British had built up armies in their colonies, several units of

which had seen action on many war fronts – Burma, Egypt, Ethiopia and even France. Schoolboy nationalist activists had been seduced into joining the army and sent off to the front. The sister school in Lagos, King's College, suddenly embarked on a strike, fired by the rising nationalism whose message the senior boys encountered daily on the pages of the newspapers, in public speeches and pamphleteering. There were violent demonstrations. Senior boys were arrested and their ringleaders thrown into gaol. There they were given the option: join up voluntarily or be tried and sentenced for sedition. Adventurous, and not unwilling to acquire some military experience for a liberation struggle that they were convinced had become inevitable, many joined up; quite a few did not return.

An active programme of recruitment was extended to all the schools and it did not end when hostilities ended. On the contrary, it became a yearly ritual in which films were toured in the name of career exposure; but these were mostly films of military training – the Army, Navy and Air Force. They were films that spoke directly to impressionable youth – oil-stained aero-engineers tuning machines, adjusting sophisticated instruments; goggled Icaruses clambering in and out of cockpits and soaring into the clouds; then navy films of spruced-up naval cadets climbing up rigging, sending and receiving telegraph signals in Morse, loading torpedoes, and lining up on deck to set course for paradise islands. The age range was precisely that of the secondary-school student, and Dartmouth Naval College was, it appeared, only too ready to take on eager students of the British Empire, where, they were assured, their formal education would also continue.

Adeyelu was all for the Air Force; indeed he could hardly wait for the forms to be screened in Lagos, following which the applicant would be invited to travel to the capital for a formal test and a personal interview. He dive-bombed with both arms and his grinding-stone head, the superman gladiator of the airwaves, confident that the Royal Air Force of the United Kingdom could not wait to secure his talents before its rivals in Germany, America or Canada did. He was certain to be admitted to the Research Department where he would not only invent new bombs but personally test them from one of those Spitfires they had watched in the film.

'That fool thinks all it takes to get in the Air Force is setting off a few stink-bombs,' Maren muttered under his breath, to Komi. 'He knows he can't pass the technical tests. Why is he deceiving himself?'

It was chemistry class. The laboratory assistant was in charge, the experiments for the morning having been set by the master, who then retired to the staffroom to enjoy his tea while the pupils proceeded to enjoy themselves. The chemistry laboratory was easily the merriest room in the school, so many sounds – hisses, tinkling glasses, frothings, and of course the smells, not all pleasant admittedly, and the numerous coloured chemicals and crystals in display jars – the atmosphere was almost festive, despite the concentration of two dozen heads bent over rows of bubbling beakers bestriding Bunsen burners, transferring multi-coloured fluids into fuming test tubes, held at arm's length in curved tongs. With the master absent, even the most sober students could not resist indulging in competitions for the most malodorous fumes, the base solution of which would sometimes burst through unexpectedly, spluttering down to discolour more patches on the long desks which were pitted and gutted by generations of pupils. Whoever built the workbenches had truly anticipated the tendency of young pupil chemists: the top was made up of a single slab of timber, three inches thick. Water taps and sinks were strategically spaced down the middle of the desk, and the gas terminals came up from underneath, fed by a belltower-like structure some distance from the laboratory itself. Nobody ever explained how the weighted pulleys converted the fuel at the base into gas; it remained one of those scientific mysteries that the staff, for whatever reason, chose to leave unexplained. One turned on the tap, placed a lighted match to the mouth of the burner, and out sprang a blue flame which was itself a subject of several lectures and diagnoses – the yellow core, the blue flame, and the near-transparent sheath of lively gas. Even for Maren, whose mind resisted the logic of HC_1 and F_2S marriages that gave birth to H_2S and allied monstrosities, the actual experimentations were bliss.

The film show of the previous night occupied their non-chemical conversation, and choices and opinions flew from one end of the laboratory to the other.

'Me, I'm for the Navy,' Maren contributed, this time somewhat more loudly. 'I am tempted by the Air Force, all right, but, the company may prove unpalatable.'

Komi frowned. 'Why are you trying to provoke him?'

'He's a nuisance. And I know he's out to get me.'

'The more reason to leave him alone.'

'He nearly burnt down the orchard. And he had the nerve to join in the eating after we went round gathering up the game. He wasn't part of us. He had fled. He didn't show up until supper time.'

'Well, just leave him alone. Anyway, you're not serious about going into the Navy, are you?'

'The only trouble will be my parents. I am filling in the forms, but they have to give permission. You see, if you join young enough, one may get to be an Admineral.'

'A what?'

'An Admineral.'

An explosion of laughter came from nearby Chris who had overheard. 'Admi-what, did you say?'

'Admineral. That's the very highest rank.'

More and more bursts of laughter from around the laboratory as the word was passed round. 'Admineral. Admineral. 'Kínkòyí wants to become an admineral.' It brought out the laboratory assistant who had retreated into his inner sanctum, as always, once he had set the Bunsen burners going and was satisfied that the beakers, test tubes and glass plates contained the right chemicals. He scowled and the class fell silent, but the whispers and glances of derision in Maren's direction continued after he had retreated.

Maren was baffled. It was Brown of the clipped moustache who had taken charge of the film projection. Afterwards, he went to ask him what was the highest position a cadet could aspire to in the Navy, and he could have sworn the man had said 'Admineral'. Obviously he had got it all wrong, how wrong, he had no idea; certainly it must be very wrong to have produced such a spontaneous outburst of derision. Maren sighed. He had provided the class with a powerful weapon and he braced himself for weeks and weeks of being put down, no matter what he did or said. English and Literature were subjects that every one conceded were his special province, even Mr Kaye the English teacher appeared to recognise that. And now, to fall down in the matter of pronunciation? For the first time, he felt defenceless, even doomed.

'Hey, Lemonade!'

'No, he looks more like soda water, all fizz and no taste.'

'Ice poki-poki!'

'Ice cream soda!'

In desperation, he sidled up to Chris. 'But Chris, that was how the man pronounced it.'

'Which man?'

'Brown, who else? I went to him after the film.'

Christopher laughed. 'You must be the only one in the class who still thinks he can understand Brown's English. The word is Admiral. Admiral. How it sounds through Brown's nostrils is a different matter. Anyway, I don't know why you bother. You don't like mathematics anyway.'

'But that's the point. I need to pay attention in his classes, otherwise I will fail maths. And that means no Matriculation.'

Christopher shrugged. 'You will just have to rely more on the textbooks, that's all. You can join me when I do my homework – my House teacher has been helping me . . .'

'Hey, why are you wasting time talking to this mineral water?'

Maren turned. Ah yes, it would be like Kakiika to try and cash in on his present discomfiture with the class. There was a big smirk on his face, he looked so strangely confident on his bow legs, and something incongruous struck Maren at that moment: his two unfavourite bullies, Odali and Adeyelu, shared the same physical trait with himself. He shook off the observation as ill-timed, concentrating on every gesture of the Major, whose arms were crossed behind his back as he stood against the opposite workbench. At that moment, a strange trill of alarm coursed through him. He could not explain it, but he had a flash, so brief that he doubted its passage. For one infinitesimal moment, he was convinced that he saw his grandfather's face superimposed on Adeyelu's. The briefest flash ever, and it was gone.

He shook his head, blinked and retorted: 'Why don't you go back to mixing your poisons, Kakiika? Nobody is talking to you.'

Adeyelu's face congealed in an instant. 'I have warned you, do not call me by that name.'

'Then don't invite yourself to our conversation. Nobody invited you here. Go back to your own desk.'

'Oh, is the laboratory your father's house?'

'Is it your mother's?' came the prompt retort.

'Again! You have taken to abusing my mother again?' His voice rose, and with it came that warning trill again, so strong that he leapt backwards even before Adeyelu shrieked aloud a repeat of his accusation: 'Chris, you heard him. He abused my mother,' and his arm flashed forward at the same instant, the contents of the test tube, which had been hidden behind his back, streaming straight at Maren's face. As if of its own volition, his head jerked sideways.

The potion hit his shirt front and splashed onto the wooden floor, a portion falling on his left foot. Even before he registered the first sensation of burning, Maren's hand went instinctively to the rack of liquids that lined the middle of the workdesks, snatched up a jar, pulled out the stopper and flung the jar and contents at his assailant. Then the howls of pain and alarm from both the injured and the onlookers rent the laboratory.

Maren leapt on the desk and swung his foot into the sink embedded in the workbench, his hand on the tap, but Komi was running towards him, a jar in hand, shouting, 'No, not the water. Use alkaline solution. Here, here . . . Oh my god, acid at ten paces. Acid at ten paces.' Komi had recently read *The Three Musketeers*.

It was pandemonium as Adeyelu rushed to his own station to look for some antidote, screaming, 'What did he throw at me? What did he throw at me?' But the jar had rolled under the desk and no one could retrieve it, though acrid vapour issued from the wood where the various liquids had fallen. Near Maren, the wood was already being eaten into. Adeyelu also jumped onto the workdesk and thrust his arm, which had received the full blow, under a jet of water. The laboratory attendant had rushed out and was tearing through the milling bodies to find out just who had been injured. He rushed back into his room again and emerged with a first-aid box while a babble of voices attempted to explain to him what had been done, what chemicals had been used, what remedies were applied and how it all began with minerals. The poor lab assistant became thoroughly confused and ran to the mineral display box but found it had not been tampered with, so he came back and was shown Maren's foot which had turned a parchment patchwork of all the colours of the rainbow, with pieces of skin lifting off at will, curling in dehydration and threatening to drop off. From next door, the Biology master, Tebite, heard the commotion. A slow, deliberate man who led with a stomach that rolled slightly from side to side, he ambled querulously into the laboratory, and the pupils stood aside while he examined the injured.

Adeyelu had received no injury beyond the bruise inflicted by the heavy jar, whose narrow neck had prevented a more lethal discharge. An arm sleeve was smoking, however, and Tebite tore it off. His screams of anguish had been caused, it transpired, by the conviction that the sulphuric acid had found its mark and was eating deeply into his flesh, a sensation reinforced by the normal discolouration of his shirt from former experiments, which was now dissolving as a result of the water in which he had soaked himself. Tebite hummed and proceeded to the next patient, who was now seated on the edge of the workdesk, his foot dangling and his mind fuddled by fears that, this time, there was really no escaping the amputation treatment. He picked up the injured foot, examined it with clinical interest.

'It strikes me,' he pronounced at the same lumbering pace with which he walked or conducted his classes, 'yes, it does strike me, young Maren, that your foot is undergoing an advanced stage of ecdysis.' His heavy-lidded eyes rolled round the laboratory. 'What a pity! What a pity! If this were a different school, every bottom in this class would equally undergo the extreme stages of ecdysis, innocent and guilty alike. This system of European education is ruining Africa, I tell you.'

Maren had other concerns, however. He pointed to his assaulted limb, still continuing its colourful self-transformations. 'My foot, sir. Do I take it to the dispensary?'

'Am I your class tutor, Master Maren? I am a biologist, not a specialist in skin diseases. My advice, young man, is that you have it cut off as soon as possible, before this disease spreads to the rest of the body. Ah, here comes your master now. I shall return to my class from where your indiscipline aroused me.'

And, taking up the foot delicately between his thumb and forefinger, he gave it one more inspection, shook his head dolefully, and ambled off. Maren felt better almost at once. Tebite was the most motherly of the entire staff, and if he chose to ignore an injury, it could only be because he had concluded that it was not critical. Sure enough, he turned at the door and drawled over his shoulder: 'A soak in saline solution, twice a day. Then coat it in boric acid ointment. Tell the nurse I said so.'

On the front lawn of Mr Kaye's house were scattered a few old gramophone records, 78 rpm, some old shoes, household bric-a-brac, utensils and cutlery, but mostly, discarded journals and books. The stewards were already quarrelling among themselves over the spoils, mostly the wearing apparel, plates and drinking glasses. Mr Kaye, due for a long leave of absence, was house cleaning. In class, he had casually mentioned that he might have some old books that his pupils might like to acquire, if they cared to pass by his house that afternoon, after siesta. Maren and Komi had exchanged looks; a silent agreement was sealed – arrive before anyone else, and share their spoils together. Swanston House was nearer to Mr Kaye's and Maren was first to arrive.

His attention was first caught by the attractive cover of a slim book, rather the worse for wear thanks to the activities of cockroaches. The title was, however, still legible: *Poems*, by William Blake. The drawings fascinated him as he flicked through the pages; he stood in the shade of a cashew tree, arrested by one poem that he had encountered in the classroom, wedged between explicatory texts, other poems and pages of questions and answers. In this volume, however, the poems existed for themselves alone, enhanced only by weird drawings that ranged between animals and seemingly divine personages, forests and heavens and other entities that he could not really identify.

Tiger, tiger, burning bright . . .

He had listened to Mr Kaye's exposition of the poem with rapt interest and a little bafflement. As he read its companions in the volume, however, he felt somewhat more at home with the strange world of this possessed stranger, who appeared to share some of the theology of Aké, yet partook of the fantasy world of Fagunwa's *Ogboju Oke Ninu Igbo Irunmale*, or indeed *Ireke Onibudo*. It was again an echo of the sensations he obtained when he stared at the stained-glass window of St Peter's Church at Aké where the haloed pictures of saints and founding missionaries of the church fused with the masked figures of *egungun*.

He browsed through volume after volume, spending a little more time on yet another slim but broad cover with parchment-thick sheets, each page bordered, and with a larger print than one would normally encounter. *Two Famous Speeches in World History*, read the title page, twined all over in leafy spirals. Oliver Cromwell dissolved a British parliament in one half of the volume. The other half began, 'Four Score and Twenty Years Ago . . .' He was still absorbed in America's Declaration of Independence when Komi arrived.

'I am going to memorise these,' he said, offering him the volume.

'What is it?'

'Recitation. Just wait until the next entertainment evening. And I mean both speeches, so don't get any ideas.'

'I thought we were doing a sketch together for the next one.'

'Sure. But I still want to recite these. I'll do one per term. Just take a look at the speeches, enh; when you hear me dramatise them . . .'

'All right, all right. What else have you found?'

On the cockroach-eaten cover of the next volume that he picked up, the word appeared as 'Merediti', and Merediti would have remained the translator of the volume of Greek plays for weeks or months but for Mr Kaye's intervention. *Medea*! He recalled the story of Medea from other sources, mostly narratives of Greek heroes and other legends, but this was the first time he would encounter her full-length play in verse, and the companion plays, from whose pages leapt the raw passions of human beings who had been no more than fantasy figures akin to others from his own local lore – Kako oni Kunmo Ekun, Imodoye, Akara-ogun, Agbako and other multiple-being creations of D. O. Fagunwa. The few plays in the school library were school performing editions. There was certainly none by the exotic name Merediti and, apart from Shakespeare, none in verse, and none that dramatised the legendary world of the Greeks; there was none that even suggested the existence of any legendary beings in Mr Kaye's world, apart from the fey creatures of *A Midsummer Night's Dream*.

Mr Kaye looked out of the window and saw the three boys –

Christopher had now joined them on the lawns with their library pile. He invited them into the house, curious to see their selection.

'Ah, I see you picked out the Euripides.'

He was rewarded by blank looks. He relieved Maren of his pile and selected the volume of plays. 'This volume is the one I am referring to. The plays of Euripides.'

'I thought it was Merediti, sir.'

'Merediti, Maren? Surely you mean Meredith.'

Komi and Christopher giggled, and Maren flashed them a warning look which said, just you dare go and repeat this to the class. But Mr Kaye was examining the volume. 'Ah, the termites and cockroaches have eliminated some of the lettering here. But the name is Meredith, Maren, and he is not the author, he is just the translator. The man to whom all the credit goes is Euripides, the great classic tragedian.'

'Tragedian, sir?'

'Tragedian, yes, from tragedy. You will remember that we have spoken of *Macbeth* as a tragedy, right?'

A chorus of comprehension as Kaye continued. 'Shakespeare was our great tragedian, but the Greeks invented the mode, Euripides was one of a formidable trio, the other two being Aeschylus and Sophocles. But you did not come for a lesson but to augment your private libraries. So, let's see what else you have got. Aha, William Blake, that is hardly surprising, I would say. Let's see . . .'

He flicked open the pages. 'That is a disappointment. I had hoped that it contained my favourite, *Jerusalem*. Have you come across that great patriotic poem, by any chance?'

Christopher eagerly said, 'Yes.'

'Ah, what a surprise. It is not a poem one would expect to find widely disseminated outside our shores. Do you happen to know it by heart?'

'Well, only partially, sir. Our church choir sometimes performs it, like an anthem.'

'Really? How amazing. Would you remember to what tune it is sung? Good. Then perhaps you will oblige me. I am most, most curious.' His eyes twinkled. 'Fortunately it is not Maren whose voice we would be compelled to tax unfairly, not to mention the limits of our own auditory tolerance.'

He smiled and the three boys broke into giggles. Christopher cleared his throat and began in his piping soprano voice which had made him the obvious successor to Maren as the soloist during the chapel services. The event had distressed Maren at the time, not the fact of his rejection, for which he was grateful since it freed him from demanding rehearsals with Mr Long, the Geography master, and – for a pianist – tone-deaf. Long's efforts at teaching the school new hymns – when he augmented his piano playing with his voice – were a cruel exercise in tonal contradiction. Maren had developed an irrational but intense dislike for him, which made him quite content to be rid of his presence, but the reason for his dismissal bothered him. His voice had broken. It happened suddenly, without warning and without any understanding of what had occurred to him. A loss of a faculty that he had always taken for granted left him wondering what else would disappear from his body's functions – hearing, for instance? Or speech? Kaye, fortunately, was directing a school play at the time, one in which the principal character was also required to sing. Reluctantly, since he had marked down Maren for the part, he began to groom another pupil, explaining patiently to the inconsolable boy what happened to the human voice at a certain age, how the vocal chords provided the sound of the human voice and were subjected to the same changes and capabilities as the rest of the human body. 'Like my hair for instance, Maren, which, you must have observed, has been thinning in the middle though it remains luxuriant at the peripheries . . .'

Christopher had begun singing, and a frown appeared on Kaye's face.

> *Last night I lay a-dreaming*
> *I had a dream so fair*
> *I stood in old Jerusalem . . .*

> *Jerusalem, Jerusalem*
> *Lift up your hearts and sing*
> *Hosanna, in the highest . . .*

It was clear that something was wrong, though the boys had no idea what. At the end, Kaye said, 'Thank you, Christopher,' then walked to the gramophone in the corner of the room and proceeded to crank it. From a stack of records he carefully extracted an extended

78 rpm disc, dusted it carefully, and placed it on the turntable. Holding the head in one hand, he explained: 'It was not quite the poem I had in mind, competently rendered though it was. It was not the poem by Mr Blake. As it happens, Blake's *Jerusalem* has also been set to music, which I shall now proceed to play. It is, as I said, a rather patriotic piece, one might even say chauvinistic – a word which I shall not attempt to explain, since the context is, I hope, only too clear – but it also offers an interesting comment on the social history of England in Victorian times. Perhaps, if you are interested, we can discuss it on my return from leave. I have the volume here which contains the poem, I shall lend it to you – lend, I hope your understand? In fact, I think I shall leave it in the library, where you can then borrow it at your leisure.'

He dropped the needle arm gently. 'The singer is Paul Robeson, Maren. You may console yourself with the thought that he, like the rest of us, would most certainly have undergone the normal experience of hearing his voice break. Now listen to the poem . . .'

> *And did those feet in ancient time*
> *Walk upon England's mountains green?*
> *And was the holy Lamb of God*
> *On England's pleasant pastures seen . . .?*

Paul Robeson's booming voice filled the room, overwhelming the young listeners. But it was not until the second verse began that Maren felt profoundly stirred, feeling an intensity of faith that he could not precisely define, only that it was different from the narrow religious kind, that it embraced the entire human universe, yet contained a personal message for every being. In his mind, it bore an affinity to the words of the illuminated manuscript, '*Four score and twenty years ago . . .*', reinforcing the sensation of a profound universal discovery. The clouds had opened and a rain of combative peroration was streaming down, very different from the sermons and the hymning of St Peter's, Aké, yet close in spirit to the *oguso*** torchlight procession of Ransome-Kuti's 'Grammarians' on Foundation Day, all the way from Igbehin Downs to Aké hills, belting out the march, '*He who would valiant be*', and closing the week-long

*Fibre kindling.

celebrations with the Egba anthem *L'Ori Oke ati Petele* ... Paul Robeson and William Blake – he could imagine them both in step with the white-uniformed boys, their valiant steps in consonance from the downs of Igbehin, against the backdrop of Olumo rocks, winding past the cenotaph of the great warrior Lisabi, and filing into St Peter's Church, transformed at this time of the year into a huge, festal theatre ...

> *Bring me my Bow of burning gold!*
> *Bring me my Arrows of desire!*
> *Bring me my Spear! O clouds, unfold!*
> *Bring me my Chariot of fire.*
> *I will not cease from Mental Fight,*
> *Nor shall my Sword sleep in my hand ...*

Back from leave, English master Kaye held the piece of paper at arm's length, his face a map of anguish; even his ragged moustache appeared to have drooped in despair as he shook his head slowly from side to side, groaning, 'What have I done, Maren, what have I done?' The boy watched him, wondering what could have driven him to despair in the lines he had crafted with such care.

'Read it aloud, Maren,' and he held it out to him on the extreme tips of his fingers, as if he was afraid of catching a terrible disease from the sheet. 'It is good training to read one's poetic effusions aloud. One learns a lot, Maren; one learns a lot by listening carefully to oneself, be it in poetry or prose, just as in answering questions in class. Read it aloud, Master Maren.'

The boy took back the offering he had penned in tribute to William Blake, feeling relieved that he was being made to read it in the staffroom, not in front of his entire class, with Kaye's caustic comments cutting him to the quick.

> *Is Africa a land so base*
> *Are we born into servitude*
> *Have we to bear that yoke always*
> *Of slavery in such magnitude?*
> *Perhaps our acts are not so smart*
> *To those who come our land to spoil*
> *Have they not taken the better part*
> *Of our ancestral, arable soil.*

He paused. For a long moment, teacher and pupil stared at each other. 'The next verse, Maren, the next verse.'

The boy shook his head. 'No, sir, I don't think I want to read it.'

Kaye sighed. 'I should think not, Maren. The effort, of course, is to be applauded, but this is not quite the kind of flattery of which imitation sometimes is held to be. Mr William Blake,' and his voice turned dolorous, 'Mr William Blake must be turning in his grave.'

Deflated, but puzzled, he walked slowly back to the classroom. It was the midday break, and only half the class was present. The last lesson had consisted of a geography test which he had finished on time so as to have the full period of the break to discuss his poem with Kaye. Now that discussion had finished abruptly, and the anguished look on the English teacher's face was still branded on his mind. The boys in the classroom were reading or lounging about. Only one figure was hunched over his desk, and that was Odali. In his dejected state of mind, he would hardly have noticed, but then Christopher was standing in front of him. Clutched to his chest was a batch of exercise books, and Chris was clearly waiting for the last, Odali's.

This was unusual. Mr Long was a stickler for precision. On the dot of the bell he had ordered the cessation of writing, then told Christopher to collect the answer books and bring them to him in the staffroom within five minutes, looking pointedly at his watch as he spoke. It was not unusual for one pupil or the other to plead with the class monitor to go round the others first, collect their papers while he rushed over his final sentences or made some last-minute corrections. Whoever was monitor was usually obliging, but everyone understood when the period of grace ended; there was never any question of one individual still scribbling after all the others had surrendered their books. And Maren knew that he had been away from the classroom at least fifteen minutes.

'Listen, Odali, I simply must leave now,' Chris was insisting. 'I'm sure I've already got into trouble with Mr Long.'

Odali continued to scribble away.

'Look, Long is going to come in any moment, and then I will be in hot water, not you.'

Odali murmured some kind of impatient plea but did not stop

writing. Chris took several steps away, turned and warned, 'I really am leaving now. I am not joking.'

Odali frowned but did not look up. Chris left the classroom. Maren took his place at the desk he now shared with Christopher, buried himself in a novel and tried to forget his débâcle at the hands of Mr Kaye. A few minutes later, he heard a bellow of disbelief.

'He left? Are you telling me he left without my paper?'

Odali dashed to the door. Clearly he had thought that Christopher was bluffing, probably hiding behind the door to force him to surrender his paper. But the class monitor was not merely gone, he was already emerging from the staffroom, his arms empty of exercise books. Other pupils were drifting back into the classroom, skirting the figure of Odali who was waving his exercise book like one demented.

'He left without my paper. He left without my paper, that beast of no nation!'

By now the beast of no nation, a quiet lamb of the Lord if ever there was one, had seen the commotion from a distance. Wisely, he went round the block and entered the classroom by the opposite door while Odali waited to pounce, nearly frothing at the mouth. When he next turned to call the class to witness the great injustice done to him, and the dire punishment he would inflict on his assailant, Christopher was already seated, reading quietly like one who had not a stain on his conscience. The sight reduced Odali to apoplectic stuttering.

'He is reading. He is sitting there reading.' He leapt across the room and pushed the exercise book in the monitor's face. 'If you know what's good for you, you will take this at once to Mr Long.'

Christopher looked up. 'I can't. Long already told me off for being nearly fifteen minutes late.'

'What do I care about that? You want me to fail? How dare you leave my answer book behind? Deliberately. You did it deliberately so I will fail.'

'Odali, all you have to do is to take your book there yourself. At the most he will penalise you by two or three marks. But I simply cannot take it.'

'He cannot take it. He cannot take it. But you could take your own, and the rest. You have suddenly lost the use of your arms and legs? Are you not Mr Long's monitor?'

Christopher sighed and resumed reading. Sitting beside him, Maren tensed, knowing from experience what would follow. A gesture that had the effect, intended or not, of signalling to Odali that he was ignored, that one had no further interest in his existence, was a starting pistol for the commencement of hostilities. Maren felt his bones jar with the blow that actually landed on Christopher's face. Two or three more followed, packed with all the rage and terror of having earned himself a zero in a class test that would reflect on his term's report. Most of the violence came, however, from the very thought that a smaller boy had dared him, had refused to succumb to his will, and this, in the presence of more than half the class. In the few moments left before the bell sounded for the end of break, Odali was determined to reduce Chris to a pulp. After the first clutch of softening-up blows, he snatched up Christopher's book and flung it across the classroom, leapt backwards into his favourite Randolph Turpin crouch, though he knew full well that Christopher never, never struck back, no matter the provocation. Weaving from side to side, feinting against non-existent punches, he jabbed the seated boy once more and Maren underwent yet again that experience of disembodiment, of standing outside himself, helplessly under the control of another being, and he found that he was on his feet, racked by rage, barely succeeding in remaining upright because every particle of his body was trembling. His lips were also quivering and there appeared to be a vice around his throat, choking him, but still he heard his voice emerge with a tense calm, demanding: 'Just when is all this . . . this . . . nonsense going to stop?' Odali froze at half-crouch, then straightened out slowly. There was no feigning the amazement on his face. He looked round the class, but especially in the direction of his fellow bullies. His normally bulging eyes impossibly distended, he turned with a slow swagger to confront his interrogator.

'You . . . like to provoke me, 'Kínkòyí. If you have something against me, say it now. Don't think I haven't noticed. You have something against me, so have the courage to say it to my face.'

Something was wrong. Something did not sound quite right. This language, coming from Odali, sounded strange in his ears. 'You interfering ANT!' . . . 'You invisible speck at the end of a microscope' . . . 'You mouthy midget' . . . 'You miserable atom in a molecular theory' . . . all of that, and more, would have been more in character, since there was a full audience, which always guaranteed that Odali would dig into his most repetitious reserves, mostly shamelessly pirated variants of Maren's own verbal armoury. The class knew it, but it would not stop them cheering lustily as each barb was launched. 'Mouthy midget' was Odali's riposte to the smaller boy's 'Mouldy mastodon'. It had taken him weeks to find out what the word was, then a whole term's trial and error to produce a response that not only earned the spontaneous applause of his audience, but was adopted for use by others. It never ceased to rankle in the boy's mind that Odali had succeeded so well in converting his own insult to a more wounding version, regretting the day that he ran into a coloured picture of some extinct species in the one-volume encyclopaedia.

But that day, there was to be none of such exchanges. There was this fancy pugilist, actually talking to his inferior adversary like an equal: 'If you have something against me . . . !' The two personae fused back into one, baffled, all rage abated and the trembling stopped. Maren watched closely but no, he had been in far too many scraps with the bully not to know when he was faking. There was no tension in his bandy legs, ready to spring when his opponent's guard was down, no sly drawing back of his leading right for a swing. He did step forward, yes, to stare him in the eye, as if to prove that he, Odali, was not afraid of him – which had the opposite effect of reducing his potential aggression. It was the smaller boy who normally needed such gestures of bravado, not the likes of Odali. The very question of him, Maren, *not* having everything against the ruffian was, of course, so preposterous that the boy nearly burst out laughing.

He remained watchful, however, and thoughtful. Of the few explanations that he could think of in the few moments of silent confrontation, he fastened on one as the likeliest. Odali was so incensed by the episode of the class test that he had decided to adopt Christopher as the next target of his spasmodic urges for mayhem. Maren's intervention had perhaps indicated to his bellicose mind that this rather awkward enemy would, despite the switch of attention, refuse to go away; this it was that made him suddenly battle-weary. He would have seen it as a case of a victim being promoted to the status of a pliant spectator, yet the ingrate remaining dissatisfied. How else explain this gladiator's temperate, peer-acknowledging whine of complaint?

And at that moment, without any prior consideration given to it, Maren knew exactly what he should do, what he ought to have done more than two years before, maybe. Much calmer now, very sure of himself, he nodded.

'Oh yes, I have something against you.'

Again, the astonishment, as if the answer was unexpected. 'You have something against me?' He turned to the rest of the class. 'You see? I was right. I have always suspected it. Go on, tell me. What have I ever done to you?'

Maren felt more and more certain of his suspicions. Odali was asking for a truce, no less. The belligerence was still in the background, but the tone was definitely 'let's talk it over', and he was calling the class to witness what a peaceful nature he had, compared to his opponent's. Maren resumed his seat.

'Later.'

'When? I want to know now. Say it where everyone can hear you.'

'No. Later, I said.'

'When? Pick a time.'

'All right. Tomorrow morning then. Before classes.'

Odali shook his shoulders, as if discharging them of the burden of alert, for the moment anyway. He nodded, and strutted to his seat.

'I'll be waiting behind the library. We'll talk face to face.'

The boy hardly absorbed a word during the next class, the calm he had felt moments before dissolving into anxiety. The plan made sense, it was such an obvious solution to the arbitrary terror but, would the others agree? If they did not, then he was well and truly on his own, and he did not envy himself the days ahead. He began to think up contingency plans; he could simply tell Odali that he had 'sent home', that he should expect a visitation of the kind one does not see or hear, but whose parting gift would become painfully evident in a day or two – unless he swore to lay off the smaller boys of the class. Or grind some charcoal and blow it in his face, muttering incantations – no, there would be the evidence on his white shirt when he reported him to the class master or even the Principal. Knowing Odali's lust for centre stage, expanding any area of conflict, he might insist that his own parents be sent for and informed, or worse, that Maren's parents be summoned. If his demands were not met, he would be obliged to write to the chief of his village, and then the District Officer, because he might wake up a cripple or develop brain fatigue and fail his examinations, so it was much better to let the whole world know now, even if it meant writing to the *Daily Times* or the *West African Pilot* and involving Zik of Africa himself . . . No, there would be no stopping Odali, who lost no opportunity of dropping heavy hints that he was in correspondence with all the great nationalists, Tony Enahoro, Mbonu Ojike and company, and, but for the white European staff, would have brought them to lecture any time and deal with all the colonial brainwashing to which the students were being subjected and so on.

No, actually providing evidence of a *juju* attack was too big a risk. A much better idea would be to fabricate some kind of *juju*-type object, maybe wrap a stone in rags and leather, obtain some chicken feathers and have them sticking out. He would point the *juju* at the villain the moment he arrived and begin his incantations. Yes, that would be more like it. Odali loved to boast that he was not superstitious but he, Maren, knew that this was a lie. The thug would take to his heels and head straight for the Principal's office. By then he would have thrown the amulet into the bush, dashed to the chapel for the morning assembly. Confidently he would subject himself to a search when they came for him, declare Odali a liar who had had it in for him since he intervened to stop him murdering Christopher; oh yes, let him try and get out of that. All the facts would come out and no one would care about any *juju* or amulet when Mr Long learnt about what had been done to his monitor. After that, all he needed was to keep up muttering under his breath and staring at the bully whenever their paths crossed, which would not be often. Something along those lines, but he hoped such a desperate course would not be necessary. He would just have to wait and see.

After school, he asked Christopher and Shida, who was third smallest in the class, to meet him secretly in Unter den Linden.

There they put their conspiratorial heads together; he was relieved that they did not need much persuasion The following morning, when Odali arrived at the meeting place, he found not just Maren but all of the Tiny Trio. He stopped short as he rounded the corner of the building, then approached warily.

'What are the others doing here?'

'I hope you know your history, Odali.'

'History? What history? You haven't told me why the others are here. You and I agreed to meet face to face.'

'Remember the Tripartite Agreement? Do you recall that part of your history class?'

'Yes. What about it?'

'Good. That is what this is about. We have formed a Tripartite Agreement. If you attack one of us, we all attack you. Any time. Anywhere.'

Odali looked dumbfounded. 'I see. I know this is your idea, Maren. I am going to deal first with you.'

'From now on, we are always going to be together. But if you succeed in catching one of us by himself, then be sure that we will attack you at the very next chance. Anywhere. We won't even discuss anything with you, we will simply pounce on you and deal with you. We will find you no matter where you hide. You'll be sleeping in your dormitory and we will descend on you before you know it.'

Odali laughed in disbelief. 'Are you saying all this to me? Me! Me! You are in trouble 'Kínkòyí. For the rest of your stay in the school, you will wish you had never been born. You are in serious trouble. You have forgotten that you score for the cricket team. When we go on tour . . .'

'We thought of that,' Shida assured him. 'You're very proud of your batting, you think you are a good athlete, it all makes you conceited. When we finish with you, you won't be able to raise a bat, much less run the eight-eighty yards. Even if it is only one finger, we'll make sure we break something. All that popularity with the girls – finished.'

Odali was shaken. He looked the three desperadoes over, one at a time. He could not believe that this was truly happening to him. He, Odali? The effrontery. But they were not yet finished.

'By the way, Yanju is included in this,' Christopher added. 'From now on, you must leave him alone.'

This time, Odali's laughter, ridiculing the idea, was genuine. 'Yanju! He wouldn't dare. Why isn't he here with you?'

'Because we never bothered to ask him,' Maren replied. 'It would be a waste of time. Everyone knows he's sickly, including you, and that is why you keep tormenting him. From now on, you touch him, we deal with you. Now, have you got all that into your head? Three of us here, plus one.'

Then Odali had the great idea. 'And what makes you think I cannot get others to join me in giving all three of you the beating of your life?'

'You think we haven't thought of that? We won't worry about those other thugs,' Maren patiently explained. 'You see, the others don't pretend like you do. You are so vain, Odali, very vain. The others are just ruffians – Major Kakiika, Ashie and company. They don't go around pretending to be Lagos society boys and all of that. But you, we shall let the girls in St Teresa know that you were thoroughly beaten up, and there will be a scar to show for it – on your face. As for Ashie, you know we both come from the same area, I am "sending home" for him. You watch and see what happens to him.'

'Oh, so it's *juju* now.'

The ringleader nodded. 'All is fair in love and war. But you, we want to deal with you with our own hands.'

His face registered all the scorn he could muster. 'You think you are The Three Musketeers, but let me tell you, you are nothing but *Juju* Musketeers.'

The assembly bell rang. Christopher was lead singer and he had even begun to replace Mr Long at the piano for some of the simpler hymns, so he was obliged to be in the chapel before the others. He looked at his two companions and all three turned to go.

'Look at them,' Odali screamed at their backs. 'Just look at them. So-called christians threatening to use *juju* on people, and that one will actually sit at the piano and conduct the hymns. Look at the hypocrites. Pagans! Shameless pagans! You are a disgrace to Government College . . .'

His screams followed them into the chapel, but they were past caring. 'Just the same,' Maren warned, 'don't forget what I said. Always have a paint jar in your pocket for emergencies. He's going to keep looking for his chance over the next few days. People like him can't afford to lose face.'

How it all came about, he no longer remembered. He only recalled that the usual notice had gone up for articles for the school magazine, and he had resolved to set down, in continuous form, arguments that he often held with Komi, Chris, and sometimes even the quiet Dipo over what had become the major concern of his private reflections: did God exist? He had not yet come to a definition of his convictions, fluctuating as he did between a feeling that rejected the existence of such an omnipotent being, or at least the need to worship and bow before his unseen presence, and a fear of the deeply ingrained penalties that would attend such a denial, were he to be wrong. His mind dwelt longer and longer over the question, eating into the peace of his refuge in Unter den Linden, inserting itself between his head and the pillow and usurping even the voices of teachers in every subject, with dire consequences for his end-of-term reports. He was aware that he had become insufferable, intolerant of distractions from the wrestling match that he conducted all within himself, with only the occasional relief from inconclusive arguments, with Komi especially. Komi appeared to take it all in his stride, his psychology magazine reassuring him in ways that Maren could not draw upon, since he found the journal every bit as suspect as religious texts. Each attempted to explain and prescribe for human thought and actions, but failed to answer questions that the texts of real life posed in arbitrary ways. It was all one confused mess, fearing damnation on one hand, yet incapable of suppressing the upsurge of doubts, then downright disbelief.

With every reflection on the phenomena around him, causality began to replace all notion of miracle or divine origin. And yet he found that he clung deeply to evidence of mystery, to the mysterious, to the existence of a plane that remained non-physical.

He no longer made a pretence of exploring the religious tracts still dutifully sent by his father; they did not contribute anything to his sense of wellbeing, his moral sense drew nourishment elsewhere, from other books that he read, from his continuing assessment of the lessons imparted from childhood, the continuing experience of boyhood, and the judgement he constantly passed on people, events, and even nature. Every day, the tracts seemed to grow even more pretentious, unctuous and even ludicrous. He could not see how the setting of a weekly homily could affect one's conduct for a week. His interest in the bible waned; there was literature that spoke more pertinently to him, that engaged his moral apprehension in more challenging, more enlarging ways. The chapel services became hollow and meaningless.

Even so, until he began to prepare his article for the school journal, he still fluctuated between doubts and conviction. He could not deny a certain stirring in some vague regions of his being when certain songs were rendered even in the school chapel. At home, on holidays, the church services, which he could not avoid, had moments when a feeling of elevation swept him along, and he felt at one with a concourse of people harmonised with the universe in spaces beyond the immediately physical.

But the sensation always proved ephemeral, never surviving the rounds of greetings after church service; most of the time, it simply was not there. Easter, easily his favourite season, remained his favourite only because he identified a general rebirth after the Harmattan drought. That made ample sense, and the Church, he reasoned, responded to its essence by celebrating the change in its own special way, with its myths, fasts, and ritual. The Church's canticles at Easter found a ready response in his viscera, sad yet triumphant; a lyrical blotter that soaked up nature and reflected her fragility, and self-renewal. Only years afterwards did he attempt to capture, albeit partially, what it was that seemed to place him on the rack during this phase; at the time he could not even begin to move beyond the question: Where then is God? Show me. Up there, I know he is not. So, if he is, show me where!

But it was worship, regimented worship that first lost all conviction. Without any help from him, the Sunday worship simply divorced itself from what he had come to experience as spirituality. As for the sermons, they existed on a plane of smug repetitiousness; he failed to see what new perceptions on life, on mortality or virtues his father, and all those excitable debaters who gathered around him, could really claim to draw from them, yet by common agreement they appeared to assess them in all seriousness. Did they proceed by habit or addiction? The telling was often of greater interest than the substance, that is, when the preacher had a good public presence – this included a good delivery, original, not corny anecdotes, and an avoidance of obvious moralisation. Much as he would have preferred to resume his place in the choir, especially when it rehearsed the great anthems – Haydn's *Creation* exerted a permanent spell on him – he was increasingly repulsed by the ultimate end of most recitals, and he gradually withdrew.

There did exist, he acknowledged, a territory of the ineffable, what, for want of a better term, he conceded to spirituality; it was an awareness of an essence in all things that transcended the mundane, but this he found present, in a more forceful yet unobtrusive way, in the orchard of Unter den Linden, in the voice of Paul Robeson singing the poem of William Blake; it was present in some nights of unusual pulsations, and could overwhelm him in some torrential storm. Try as he would, both from fear and conditioning, he found that he could not truthfully attribute these to a unique presence, except by rote, by a now repudiated habit of tutelage and obedience.

It was the very process of writing the article that ended his doubts, and it branded him for ever in the eyes of not a few, as the much heralded and dreaded anti-christ. He titled it: *Ideals of an Atheist* and, to make matters worse, it won the essay prize. For once, it was not an achievement that he could even dream of advertising at home.

VI Quacks and Quasi-quacks

Once upon a time there was only Yaba Higher College, in Lagos. It was a place of learned mystery from where emerged serious-looking men and a handful of women, who would later populate the teaching profession in choice secondary schools; occupy the few senior positions in the Civil Service that were permitted to non-Europeans, better known as natives; become pharmacists in government hospitals, land surveyors or public engineers; or acquire the preliminary medical training that might later take them to Glasgow, Dublin or London to be transformed into fully-fledged doctors. Their American counterparts were despised! Even from his first visit, as a seven- or eight-year-old, he had somehow obtained a sense of an independent-minded, adult community, locked in studious pursuits, destined for a transformation that would set them apart from their compatriots. White faces flitted in and out of this community, engaged in equally mysterious pursuits, but there was no indication of any condescension or subservience in the contacts he observed between Europeans and Africans, quite a few of the latter appearing even old enough to have fathered the sprinkling of the milk-pale to sunburnt faces. It made quite an impression on him; there was a definite self-assurance among the occupants of this enclave, black or white, a lack of that obsequiousness that he had learnt to remark in government offices, commercial companies such as the UAC or John Holt, thanks to the sharp commentaries that passed between Ransome-Kuti, whom everyone called Daodu, and his wife, or that Daodu himself addressed to him in the most offhand manner, as if he were also a grownup. Daodu was a fanatic. In his own domain, the Abeokuta Grammar School, he would hammer on his favourite theme, even to a total stranger. 'Only serfs say "sir", that is why these Europeans insist on being addressed "Yes, sir". Here we say, "Yes, Principal," "No, Mr So-and-so," but all these white-run schools simply teach our children the slave language of "Yes, sir"!'

Was it perhaps this ethic of self-liberation, or dignity, that drove the combative prelate to fight so hard to ensure that each one of the West African colonies could boast its own University? The colonial Government still insisted, even in the early forties, that a single university could more than cater for all of West Africa, but Daodu had braved the torpedoes, submarines and bombs of Adolf Hitler to lead his commission to the heart of decision-making and returned triumphant, riding into Abeokuta on a white charger in tribute to his courage and doggedness.

For Nigeria, it was this Yaba College that was moved to Ibadan to provide the foundation for the nation's first University College, ending the long dependency of protectorate and colony on Achimota College in Accra. When Maren found himself a few years later on in Ibadan, a boarder in Government College, while his much older cousin, Koye, a son of the same Daodu, was also in Ibadan as one of the pioneer students of the displaced Yaba Higher College, that spot on the outskirts of Ibadan, Eleiyele, where the College was re-installed, became a port of call on those Saturdays when the school let out its students on 'exeat'.

The College's new premises were less glamorous, being the sprawling barracks of the old West African Frontier Force, but Maren's fascination with this tight-knit, monastic community did not lessen. Not even the discovery that these outwardly unworldly adults were every bit as high-spirited and rumbustious as they must have been in the secondary schools of their youth, diminished, for him, the awe-inspiring atmosphere of a fellowship suffused with a near divine mission. During his early years in Government College, he could hardly wait to complete his immediate education and join this sublime order. Neither could his father, who had set his sights on his son becoming the youngest ever entrant into the institution.

In the end, however, he left school the moment he set down his pen on the last paper of the School Certificate examinations, shot through Abeokuta without stopping, and went to Lagos to seek employment. The Principal, Mr Jefferies, did not encourage him to stay for the post-Certificate year, newly introduced to groom a select few for entry into the University College, and he himself could not wait to get away from a place that he had earlier regarded as home of a more congenial kind. During his last two years in school, he had gradually acquired a conviction that he needed first to earn a living, at least for a year; to acquire some money of his own; buy a shaving set; hopefully gain those extra inches that, just like a moustache or beard, obviously awaited only his escape from school repression to enhance his physical appearance. Of that, he was not in doubt. And he would look for an amateur dramatic society to join – there were a few he already knew about in Lagos. He had also given some thought to acquiring a pipe, but no firm decision had been taken on that score – the essential goal was to acquire whatever was necessary to look and act his own man. That was the first step to becoming a man of the world. It was all the preparation he required, and then he would be ready to take on his deferred membership of an order to which he was still drawn, but in a far different way from how his father imagined, and with no sense whatever of any race for time.

For it was not just a question of passing the entrance examination, but also securing a scholarship. The notion of having his father pay his membership fees and maintenance was one that he rejected out of hand; dependence was to end from the moment he stepped out of the gates of Government College, Ibadan.

His goal was journalism but he failed to secure a place on one of the main newspapers – the *Daily Times*. All applicants took a written test. They were required to report an imagined market fight as they would expect to read it on the pages of a newspaper. He proceeded to cover eight foolscap sides of lined paper with an elaborate account that spanned the background lives of the combatants, the histories of their extended families, their business dealings, etc, etc. Others had long finished but he was carried away by a reality that had taken such a hold on his imagination, forgetting the context into which his account was expected to fit. The European invigilator looked at his watch several times with increasing ostentation, and took to walking up and down in front of his desk until finally, without a change of expression, he snatched the reams of paper from him, snarling, 'I need my lunch. You were not asked to write up the entire newspaper, just report an incident!' So he settled down in the Government Medical Department, courtesy of his Uncle Segun in conspiracy with his parents, who must have offered a special thanksgiving prayer for his narrow escape from the reckless and dissolute reputation of the newspaper profession.

In the Medical Stores, as a clerical assistant, he encountered for the first time the hideous, soul-destroying monstrosity of bureaucratic monotony. His sanity was perhaps saved only by a decision to learn to type, an activity which was itself only a lesser order of monotony but one that had the virtue of visible results, a skill slowly acquired and, as he improved, even a curious delight at forcing out some sort of rhythm from the cranky contraption.

A transfer from the offices in Broad Street to the actual Medical Supply Centre at Oshodi was a gift from the watchful, sympathetic gods, who even accompanied the event with a change of his designation from a contemptible Clerical Assistant, ungraded, to the grandiloquent title of Senior Stores Assistant, albeit Grade III. The 'senior' title more than made up for the lowest rung of the designation ladder, one had to start somewhere anyway, and the change considerably broadened his outlook on life.

First, the department was not in the heart of Lagos, but in the suburbs, where the slack moments could be occupied with rambling through the local bush, linking up with his former schoolmate, Komi, who worked in the same semi-bush area in Post and Telegraphs. Komi undertook to teach him the Morse Code; tapping out rhythmic messages to different parts of the nation became increasingly absorbing, far more mysterious than beating out rhythmic print on the typewriter. Tapping out and decoding incoming messages – all on a voluntary basis as he took over the desks of Komi's workmates in spare moments – provided a kind of mystic thrill – his fingertips touched other fingertips across vast distances, conjuring up personalities for the unseen correspondents, invoking a communicant fraternity in pure imagination. He seriously considered changing jobs, but the work at the stores also provided its own brand of fulfilment. He was at the hub of an essential operation that covered the entire expanse of the nation.

And then the head of the section was unexpectedly transferred, and the awesome responsibility devolved on his shoulders – the results of the School Certificate examinations were out, and this made him the most 'educated' employee left in that section. With his new responsibilities, he lost the freedom of roaming the woods, and Morse-metamorphosing at the P&T, being compelled to keep a close watch on movements in and out of the store, and the dubious activities of his staff; but he nonetheless increased the slack moments by devising a new pattern of work, so now the spare time was spent reading. He climbed atop the bales of medical supplies and consumed the books he borrowed regularly from the public library in Yaba and the British Council library in Onikan, conceding a more or less reasonable amount of time to texts that were essential to preparation for the entrance examinations to the University College.

It was a specially constructed nest, very close to the roof, bounded by jute bales and boxes. From that position, he had a sweeping command of all approaches to Section B, and indeed on the motions of his junior staff. Aided by the wide barn-size doors that were needed to enable large trucks to back into the entrance, he could see the approach of any vehicles, visitors or senior official on rounds of inspection, leave his books there out of sight and be down with his ledger pads and notebooks, taking stock, noting down shortages for the next orders, or issuing instructions to one or the other of his four or five assistants, mostly to go and check if the woman who specialised in roast plantains was already in place outside the stores compound and to place orders for delivery after the departure of the various intruders.

It was snug up among the bales: he was very much at home with the stockpile of cotton rolls, crêpe and gauze bandages, rolls of elastoplast dressing, gypsum and plaster of Paris, first-aid kits, each batch of dressing in neat compartments within their dark blue tin boxes, lint, catguts, and so on. They were despatched to every corner of colonial Nigeria, by train, road, and even special trucks from the Medical Department. His table, with a telephone, was marooned in this huge barn that was Section B: and there, dressed in white overalls, he supervised the despatch of several brands of non-specialised supplies, receiving and filling out indents, corresponding with the Crown Agents for the colonies – through the Broad Street office of course, ref. SMSK and copied to file RS stroke 19 stroke xvi of 3/8/51 for attention also of SEO Ports Authority – studying the berthing timetables for the various ships that would bring in the ordered supplies, firing off and receiving frantic tele-grams. Missionary hospitals – Baptist, Ahmadiya, Sudan Interior Mission, Sacred Heart and others – competed with government clinics and hospitals for the attention of the unknown school-leaver, now approaching seventeen. They drove down from their stations sometimes to take physical possession of their orders, astonished to encounter the diminutive distant director of their expectations. He ignored their evident assumptions; he could see on their faces that they expected a much older officer to emerge from behind the neat rows of supplies and affix his authorising signature to their invoices and indents and vouchers but no, his was the final court of appeal: 'Sorry, sir, but those bales of surgical gauze are destined for Kontan-gora, we can only let you have three boxes of gypsum and two of catgut . . . yes, we did receive your telegram, several in fact, but the clinic in Makurdi has been waiting even longer . . .'

It was heady work, he was supposed to act only for a short while until a replacement came, someone far more senior and experienced but the replacement never came and he remained sole boss of this cavernous warehouse; it even despatched quarterly supplies to its branches in Enugu, Kaduna, and elsewhere, manned undoubtedly by grizzled old civil servants who would probably have exploded if they realised that some lesser-than-grandchild-of-theirs was the Yours Sincerely that demanded immediate acknowledgement of the safe arrival of supplies railed to them over one month before!

All too soon, however, it was time to bid goodbye to the Crown Agents and ocean liners, to railway timetables, to the Sudan Interior Mission, the Leprosy Colony at Osisiomo and the Mental Hospital at Aro, abandon the smell of lint and gypsum and the carbon stains from indents in quadruplicate. It was time to revisit 'old Yaba' in its new surroundings, this time as a resident member of the hallowed order, follow its transmigration to the brand-new campus on Oyo Road, and then abandon even that for a while in favour of its forerunners in the colonial homeland. Firmly secured in his mind, however, was that pristine condition of the close-knit, self-regulating order, an image that would be reinforced a few years later by his sojourn in Leeds, and his periodic encounters with other institutions – Hull, Cambridge, Bristol, Edinburgh, Glasgow, London and others – sometimes as part of a visiting debating team, or on his own;

especially during his brief ownership of an antique four-wheeler that passed for a motorcar, for the sum of twenty-five pounds sterling.

Ibadan University was still only a college, affiliated to London University, whose degrees it awarded. With the approach of national Independence, the College, which had now moved into its new elegant campus on Oyo Road, was also well on its way to the attainment of its own independence or – Autonomy. That was the magic word, and that was the hallowed prism of a general 'university' idea through which the university community – staff, students, alumni – and the literate public viewed the elegant structures, the precision lawns and seductive landscaping of an institution that appeared not only to have attained maturity after several metamorphoses, but remained an only child of the long-gestating giantess that was called Nigeria.

The old campus, where he had begun, still sentimentally preferred by those who, like Komi, had passed a year or more among its ramshackle structures, was a former military cantonment. Its huts were partitioned into small rooms by fibre-mat walls, sometimes two, three or four students to a room, allowing little privacy or, indeed, quiet. All too often, he would himself undergo moods when he longed for its air of impermanence, for its vanished disdain of the fresh paint and cloying symmetry of structures that came with Independence, despite its primitive actuality. The dormitories, common rooms, reading rooms and even the library were eternally permeable to the depredations of raised voices, radios, record players and the sports fields. Not surprisingly, no dissenting voice was raised when a number of hours in the afternoon and night time were designated quiet hours. Often, the roof leaked or the rain forced its way through gaps in the wooden walls. The sheltered walkways between the dormitory rows, facilities and lecture rooms, provided protection against the sun but proved irrelevant in a windy rain. The takeover of rooms by swirling mudwaters, in the few hours between breakfast and return from lectures, was not unusual. Snakes and scorpions were regular callers. The snakes were particularly fond of the spaces behind lockers and bookshelves, and most screams that ripped through the air of Eleiyele were merely notices of such sudden encounters. Then the confusion of feet, the scrape of

beds and shelves on the concrete floor, blows, and yet another
intruder was despatched to the Valhalla of reptiles.

The weather was responsible for a close call of an accident that
Maren was never allowed to forget, earning himself a name with
which long-forgotten faces would sometimes hail him, years afterwards, in the midst of nowhere. It was one of those prolonged
visitations of the rain, not just rain but storm in all its malevolent
tyranny. The students all became virtual prisoners. Their will to
challenge the elements yielded results only when the pangs of hunger
became intolerable and they dashed out, arriving in the dining room
wringing wet and returning to their rooms even worse. There were
four to his room, and sometimes they took it in turns to race to the
dining room and bring back a soggy dinner for the other prisoners
of the weather. Every sport was grounded, even the table-tennis
room was abandoned. There was a limit to the consolation of books
and soon, all kinds of hobbies were improvised to while away the
endless stretch of wet, grey days.

Who began it, no one could remember, but only one – and it
earned him the nickname 'Sobe' – continued the sport long after
the rains had stopped. It was only a simple improvisation on darts.
There was a board against the wall on which the usual greeting
cards, sports and lecture timetables, club notices, and personal
messages were pinned – this became the target board, on which the
scoring areas were marked, but quite differently from the segmented
circle of a darts board. Sometimes their neighbours came and joined
in. The projectile was not a dart, however, but a heavy, all-purpose
kitchen-type knife that was used for peeling oranges, slicing yams,
meat and any other items that supplemented the occupants' regulation diet. It was not unusual for a rabbit to be chased and killed
– and even once, a small antelope, that had somehow missed its
way from its likely home along the curve of wooded stream that
hugged the blocks of lecture rooms. Perhaps it had been disturbed
by other hunters from the neighbouring farms, no matter, there it
stood between the dormitory blocks, a clear suicide case. Out rushed
Ogbuna from their room C5 with a heavy engineering textbook in
one hand and the dart-knife in the other. Caught between this
combination of theory and technological efficacy, and the ring
formed by other students who had leapt out of their rooms, some

half-naked, others with buckets, brooms, more books, anything at all that came first to hand, the shivering creature stood no chance whatever, and soon Ogbuna was skinning it with the C5 special, while others lit a fire and chased off all interlopers from non-participating dormitories.

This knife had a remarkable balance, a feature which the main enthusiast had long discovered, making him very proficient in the new sport. His roommates continued to use the overhand throw, just like a dart, but he threw his underhand, from thigh level, hitting the mark without much effort. The rain stopped and the others lost interest. For him, however, it had acquired a compulsion all of its own, and he took to attempting special exhibition throws from other positions, turning his back and throwing the knife over the shoulder, crouching, stooping, lying in bed. It became almost a reflex action. Walking past the board on the way to lectures, he plucked out the knife from its last resting-place, turned on reaching the door and – whoosh – another bullseye or above average score. He would launch the knife on the move, from the corner of the room; he went out and fired from the window. Finally, one day, trying out a new dance step he had picked up while spying on the ballroom dancing class – he refused to pay his own money for enrolment – he snatched up the knife as he did his foxtrot solo past the board, danced into the corridor, then fired the missile as he closed back on his invisible partner from a manoeuvre which he had heard the instructor describe as the 'Open Telemac'.

The knife homed true, and was followed by a horrendous yelp. He stopped, stared, but the knife had vanished. It was incredible, but he appeared to have missed it by nearly the width of the room; the knife had obviously gone through the open window, and someone was lying on the grass outside, probably bleeding to death. He raced to the window, but there was no body in sight.

Then the cry was repeated, a groan of anguish and self-pity followed by words that sent shivers through the homicidal maniac: 'A-a-ah! *Opolo mi tuka!*'*

The cry, he now correctly divined, had come from the adjacent room. Inwardly mystified – there was no way the knife could have

*My brains are shattered!

flown over the partition – he raced to the room to find his friend, Komi, with a hand pressed against his ear. The offensive weapon was itself embedded in a wooden slat on the other side of the victim's room, having passed through the target board, fibre wall, and light wood backing. Hundreds of penetration assaults had weakened the board, and the knife had cut through it like butter, and had flown across the next room, passing – with unbelievable precision – in the slim space between Komi's right ear and head. It had left a thin groove just where the ear joins the head, then carried on to bury itself in the opposite wall.

When the attack came, Komi was hunched over his desk in deep concentration over a knotty mathematical problem. 'Brain fatigue' was at the time a much dreaded phantom hovering over the heads of the excessively studious, brain fatigue or mental disturbance and even plain insanity – to all of which mathematics students most especially were considered vulnerable. On experiencing a sharp pain and touching the spot on the side of his head, Komi was convinced that his turn had come; his brain had burst and was seeping out of the junction of ear and head. It took the would-be assassin minutes to convince him that it was nothing as serious, just an errant knife that could just as easily have penetrated his eye!

The miracle of the narrow escape was Maren's residual feeling, for it only needed another inch the right, and then? It was the kind of untoward event that his grandfather cherished being told about – their secret pact had ended with his schooldays but he loved to include him in all such experiences anyway, if only to enjoy his response. When he narrated the event to him during the next vacation, the old man picked out a game cockerel from his nomadic poultry, slaughtered it and made *saara*, even as he boasted that there was no way the knife could have found any vital spot, since his grandson was under the protection of the one who directed the energy of all metal, Ogun.

'I did not name you Maren for nothing,' he declared, but only after he had demanded, 'Did you hate the boy who was hit?'

He received the answer, 'No.'

'Did you wish him any ill?'

Again, the answer was 'No.'

'Is there any harm he might have done or was planning against you that you can think of?'

The grandson assured him that, on the contrary, Komi had been his dear friend from school.

'There you are,' said the old man. 'Even if you had fired a gun in his direction, it would not have touched him.'

All that was very comforting, the young man decided, but he never threw another knife in his life. Even the darts board in the games room he kept clear of, throughout his stay in 'old Yaba'.

Yes, there was about Eleiyele an arcaneness, a collective eccentricity, a magnetic field for the bizarre married to its impermanence, a daily improvisation, of openness to a real world, a sense of integration into physical surroundings and humanity, all of which appeared to vanish when the campus moved to its new home that was scrupulously geometric and consciously collegiate. The old campus was stamped into the environment of Eleiyele, part wildlife, part civic centre, part college, market place, nightclub and village assemblage of elders and age-grades, arguing noisily, flitting silently through covered passageways and across overgrown lawns to raucous meeting places or solemn, attentive caucuses of mysterious wisdoms.

Five years later, however, back in Ibadan as a Research Fellow in Drama, he found that the new campus to which he now returned had consolidated its own character. It could boast a good measure of the rehabilitation of a genuine sense of community, somewhat more precious, élitist and privileged than Eleiyele, but a community nonetheless, and one that was rapidly coming of age. It already boasted its own Nigerian Principal, the historian Kenneth Dike, and now, a year after National Independence, a new chairman of the Governing Council was to be appointed. That authority belonged to the University Visitor, an office that came with the fiefdom of the Governor-General. It was normal that speculations, bets and plain rumours should begin to scale the turrets of the University ivory towers; there was one name that should not even have aspired to the dubious distinction of rumour, yet this candidate was proving the most persistent in the list of front-runners within academia. And the line of transmission had begun from the political hub that was Lagos.

Anieke had trained in Canada, where he qualified as a medical doctor. He had returned to Nigeria, and taken up a position in the University College medical department some years previously. His diplomas and certificates distinguished him among his colleagues, European and non-European alike. He was already viewed as the likely first African to head the University teaching hospital, then, like the University itself, still in its infancy.

Then it all came crashing down. From Toronto University to Ibadan came Nemesis in the person of a professor of that university's medical department, come to assess how impressively the new jewel of the Commonwealth's university crown was gleaming, in view of its impending severance from London University. Dr Mellanby, a Britisher, who was then principal of the University College, showed his guest round the college, reeling off names of the brilliant scholars that had been recruited to mould the academic future of the soon-to-be-independent nation . . .

'And, of course, we have one of your own products, Dr Anieke. Brilliant fellow. The first Nigerian to obtain a DSc, in medicine, you know.'

The man from Toronto frowned. 'From Toronto? Are you sure?'

'Of course. I made the appointment myself.'

'A Nigerian?'

'Sure, a Nigerian. He is the only DSc in the Faculty.'

The visitor remained thoughtful through the rest of his stay. Once back in Toronto, however, he called for the records, convinced that he was not yet senile. The event of a Nigerian obtaining a Doctor of Science in his own department at that time could not possibly have been erased from his memory a mere three to four years after the acquisition of such a prestigious degree. The records vindicated his concern: there was no Dr Anieke, DSc, on the roll of honour.

An exchange of letters flew between Ibadan and Toronto. The certificate proved to be the authentic material, that is, it *was* a science doctorate parchment, duly embossed with the seal of the University of Toronto, only it was never issued to one Dr Anieke, and the signatures it bore did not belong to those by whom such certificates were signed. Further enquiries revealed that a Dr Anieke had indeed qualified as a normal medical physician, taken the Hippocratic oath and been duly presented with the corresponding certificate; beyond that, the University of Toronto did not know him.

An engaging personality, Anieke had had little problem in over-whelming the tender heart of a secretary in the office of the Vice Chancellor of Toronto. The form that certified Dr Anieke a doctor of science could only have come from that office, and it did not take too long to prise the truth out of the secretary. She confessed to everything and quietly accepted her dismissal. On the Nigerian front, the newspaper screamed out the scandal. Anieke tried to brazen it out but proved no match for public outrage. He had no choice but to resign to avoid dismissal. He did, however, score one curious victory.

A journal, carried away by the excitation of the unprecedented exposure, had referred to him as a 'quack doctor'. Anieke sued, and won. It was an instructive illustration of the perils of 'Nigerian English', to which legal English, at least at the time, was definitely impervious. To that newspaper, and to most Nigerians, 'quack' simply meant phony, false, forged, etc, and would be applied to any object, concept or act that smelt fishy, sounded pretentious or was not totally satisfying. 'Go away, you quack man,' would not, for instance, mean that the man in question was a transvestite, or was impotent, simply that he was putting on airs, or was being boastful, exaggerating his capabilities in one field or another. The judge held, however, that 'quack doctor' had only one specific meaning, legally speaking – a fake doctor of medicine, untrained, and therefore unfit to practice, a menace to public health if he attempted his trade on humanity. Anieke, thus described, had been damaged professionally and was entitled to damages. It certainly had many of Anieke's countrymen baffled – why, they pondered, should a man not be called 'quack doctor of science', which of course is 'quack doctor' – of whatever – for short? It remained a public conundrum, the general feeling being that the judge required a street-English course if he truly meant to administer justice in the new nation called Nigeria.

For Dr Anieke, however, and his supporters, the judgement meant total vindication. He had already set up a private clinic in Lagos and was up and about in social and political circles without an apparent stain on his character. And then, to complete his rehabili-tation, Dr Azikiwe, the Governor-General of Nigeria, appointed him his personal physician. Those who had continued to trouble their

heads with the niceties of English legalese were silenced. The entire
episode had been clearly one of misunderstanding, probably a deliberate scheme to subvert the progress of a fledgling university. Oh
yes, who did not know the unscrupulous schemes of those other
Commonwealth universities? They knew that the giant was awaken-
ing, their glamour was about to be dimmed. None of this would
have happened if Ibadan had been content to remain under the
tutelage of the University of London. It was the demand for independence, for autonomy, that triggered it all. The white establishment wanted to prove that the black man lacked integrity, that he
had no regard for strict academic standards, it was all a cooked-up
plot to discredit any degree that the University, shorn of the supervision of London, would later award. What was a DSc, anyway?
Who cared? The man was already a qualified medical doctor, that
much had been asserted in open court. What more could anyone
demand?

The University's first real scandal died down and was voided from
memory. Now, two years later, to the astonishment of many, this
can of worms was prised open, and with the apparent consent, even
aggressive participation, of the housefly that laid the maggots. The
University woke up to the prospect that its strayed sheep might not
only actually return to the fold, but in a position that could influence
its policies, oversee its curriculum, intervene in appointments, control its budget and generally minister to its intellectual health. The
Governing Council was the broker of the new political order, as yet
untested and capricious, its function to be custodian of the jealous
order conceived simply as – University Autonomy. For the majority
of the community, the proposed return of Anieke as Chairman of
the Council was one of those notions that had the inbuilt defect
of non-necessity; there was simply no need to create a condition
that required its consideration or debate. It was a false proposition,
one that became unravelled by the very act of naming it. No arguments were involved; the notion simply unthought itself into non-
existence.

Or so decided the University, dismissing the rumour as unworthy
of speculation. At the staff club, discussions shifted to more likely
candidates, prominent and uncontroversial scholars and public figures, more than qualified to a position then considered sensitive . . .

until the ivory walls came crashing down and the University Visitor's nominee was announced – Dr Sylvester Anieke!

The itinerant Research Fellow had returned late at night from Black Morocco's, the nightclub at Oke Bola, when he encountered a group of lecturers in the quadrangle in front of Trenchard Hall, a favourite place for informal gatherings both day and night. The debate was so animated, the gesticulations so violent, that he stopped his Land Rover out of curiosity. When he was told the news, he remained for some time with them, simply listening without really absorbing much. It was such a pointless thing to happen. Then he found the shouting and violence of denunciations rather unsettling for the quantity of beer still coursing through his veins, so he left them, entered his truck and drove back to Black Morocco's.

Morocco's raucous voice sometimes made him think of an unsuccessful blend of Louis Armstrong and Leadbelly, but his permanently untuned guitar somehow suited the rough-and-ready, marijuana-coated combination; no matter, it was a return to that sound that he wanted at that moment, not even the silence of his apartment. In any case, he knew that sleep would elude him that night. The shanty club was just as he had left it. Yetunde, the owner of the club, jet black and bosomy, with the largest, whitest eyes in all of Yorubaland, was still ministering to her clientèle, which included a number of expatriates who competed for her attention and provided comic relief in their attempts to dance to the *juju* music of Black Morocco. Buffalo Kid, the seven-foot-three thug with a heart of gold who appeared to have adopted him for a bookish brother, was still wound round his table in a corner of the tiny room. He shouted 'Brother is back!' and shooed off the men at his table to make room for him. A few peppered snails soon cleared his head of cobwebs and he resumed drinking at a steady, controlled pace. Then he returned to the campus and slept till early afternoon.

When he woke up, showered, dressed and strolled out to catch up with the latest news, he was relieved to find that the Principal had held meetings with some senior staff, taken decisions and issued a public statement. The University could not accept Dr Anieke as Chairman of the Governing Council. Well, that was that. It had not been the collapse of his university idea after all, just a scare.

His head still felt a little dulled from the previous night's activities;

even so, the University's stance definitely called for celebration, so he climbed into his Land Rover and drove into town, picking up a member of his theatre group on the way. Dapo Adelugba was a willowy schoolteacher at Ibadan Grammar School, so thin that he had no shadow, making one wonder where he stored the torrent of beer that he downed so effortlessly. His school was conveniently near Risikatu's, yet another night roost of the Morocco brand, except that it had no resident band, and had never been discovered by the expatriates. Sometimes, however, an *agidigbo* group would stop by late at night, perhaps on the way from an engagement. They needed little urging to pick up their simple box-guitar, and the odd talking drum, and commence their pithy, often lugubrious songs that reeked of cobweb-hung soot that clung to dank rafters, the dyes of the *adire** cloth makers and deep clods of earth at its most fertile. Mostly the *agidigbo* players were wandering minstrels, performing through the streets, then stopping, uninvited, at a wedding or funeral, or child-naming. They played outside the main space of the event, serenading the guests as they arrived or departed, and on the open street they remained, moving from car to entrance and back unless they were invited in. The more confident would seize the moment of a general mêlée to enter and insinuate themselves into a corner where they pounced on the rest moments of the official band to commence their often mischievous, but humorous tunes. But the *agidigbo* group at night, playing for themselves and fellow wanderers of the night was a different, timeless sound. Risikatu's den, even to the smoky acoustics, was so suited to their tunes and sparse accompaniment that it seemed it was their constant patronage of the den that moulded the space and made it uniquely theirs.

In daytime, Risikatu's became an eating place, the huge woman who did the cooking rolled off from her mat in a curtained-off recess in the early dawn and began to pluck her *ewedu* and other vegetables, grind the melon seeds, light the hearths just outside, protected by a lean-to, and gather up her pots and pans. As the last notes of the box-guitar were plucked, steam began to rise from the huge pots, and the stirring stick began to turn the *eba*† or *amala*.‡ A pungent

---

*Dyed cloth both of the tie-and-die method, and the waxed style.
†A doughy meal made from cassava grains.
‡Doughy meal from yam or cassava flour.

smell wafted back into the darkened hut, and this was the announce-
ment of breaking dawn; it was time to begin the drift homewards,
or wait for the breakfast that was intended from ancient times to
cater for a different stamina – the farmer setting off for a long walk
to his farm, and an arduous day. Now of course the urban labourer
had taken his place.

They would end up at Risikatu's, but that would be much later
into the night, when the darkened den would have become its
lambent, other self, racked and caressed by the mournful strains of
the *agidigbo*. For now, they took their patronage to Tunde Nightingale's club in Mokola. Tunde had a high-pitched voice that pierced
and purred all at once; it suited the much larger space into which
one descended from street level, even though it was still open to the
skies. His guitar playing was more melodious than Black Morocco's,
more controlled but short on variety. A physical contrast to Black,
who was short and stocky, Tunde was the original *Opelenge* of whom
the song went:

> *Opelenge fell on a plate*
> *The plate did not break*
> *Opelenge fell on the river*
> *The river was ripped apart*

A willowy being like Adelugba, but taller, his gentle face belied the
toughness that appeared to be standard armoury of the *juju* and
high-life nightclub bandmen. The clientèle at his club was also far
more varied than Black Morocco's. Black's was strictly for *aficiona-
dos*, an acquired taste to which one, however, easily became hooked.
You went to Tunde Nightingale's, the poor relation of Paradise
Club, only if you felt sociable; the young man's mood after Dr
Dike's defiant statement was more than sociable, it was expansive.

Tunde Nightingale was mild only in appearance; his voice and
guitar could turn aggressive weapons, as they lashed society's enemies or slack morals, and sometimes, those who had given him some
personal offence – but then he was not the only troubadour of personal vendettas. The history of musical rivalry among *juju*, *sakara*
and *apala* bandleaders had a most lively chapter inscribed in the
lyrics of the social music of the sixties, even as the bands also
contended for the patronage of the *nouveaux riches* that arrived with

Independence, churning out fulsome compositions that placed their
subjects on the pedestal of ancient heroes, sages and demi-gods.
The politicians were generous with their rewards, egging their
praise-singers on to scale the heights of absurdity in inventing virtues
that were bestowed without discrimination – it was possible to listen
to the same virtue-studded lyrics from the same singer on different
nights, but with a change of name from socialite to politician or
millionnaire. Then one looked round and sure enough, there was
the beaming theme of the evening's adoration, indifferent to the fact
that the garment in which the band now dressed him was a cast-off
from the wearer of the previous night.

Tunde Nightingale was in a bitter and vengeful mood that evening, though that did not show on the affable face with which he
acknowledged his favourite patrons as they drifted in and out. But
the song betrayed a recent, resented loss:

> Ah, Apinke, ibadi aran
> Teletele, aya wa lo je
> K'ibadi re to bere su ju firifiri
> To wa di aya gbogbo ilu*

Sour grapes. And poor Apinke! It needed no inside-informant to
guess that Tunde had just been jilted by Apinke: not that she had
become a prostitute. He soon abandoned that theme and moved to
less personal, better-known tunes. The club filled up gradually; so
did their table as the University crowd drifted in and some joined
their table to discuss the latest turn of events. Komi had just
returned from Lagos. He had good contacts within the NCNC, the
junior partner in the Federal Government, and had tried to find out
why their former leader would try to humiliate the University in this
way. He came away with no rational explanation. Only that Azikiwe
appeared determined to go through with it.

'I have written an open letter to the Visitor,' Maren announced.
'That's all I can think of doing for now. I'm sending copies to all
the newspapers tomorrow. He has to retrace his steps before he
defaces his image. This is not what I expect of Zik of Africa, and

---

*Ah, Apinke, buttocks of velvet
 We had thought you were proudly ours
 Before your rear began to toss without control
 And became the property of all

that's what I try to tell him in my letter. As respectfully as I can, of course. I hope it does have the desired effect.'

'Hm-hm-hm, be careful there,' Komi cautioned. 'This might turn out to be a family matter, to be settled the family way. Like a quarrel between husband and wife. If you get in the middle, the wife turns the pestle on you and the husband attacks you with a machete.'

The tribal angle sobered them up at the table. What Komi was saying was plain enough, and it created instant discomfort. Moreover, he had just returned from Lagos where he must have picked up subtleties of the affair that were not felt in Ibadan. The inevitable argument erupted but, in the end, the illogicality of the situation failed to yield any conviction. The Principal, Kenneth Dike, was Igbo, so were Anieke and, indeed, the Visitor himself, so what did that add up to? If Dike had been a foreigner, a colonial imposition or something of that nature, and the Visitor simply wanted to Nigerianise the position by annoying him out of office, Anieke's appointment would have been guaranteed to achieve that end – but at what cost to the University? Such tactics would be unbelievably crude; and, anyway, Dike was not an expatriate, so that ended that line of thinking.

Tunde Nightingale's shrill voice and guitar competed with the table filled with young, rowdy academics; it soothed no one, however, even though it grew mellow as the night wore on and the beer settled in its accustomed pockets.

Risi, the vivacious one of the bar girls, had been biding her time, her instinct had been perfected from practice and she knew just the right moment to come and drag Maren off to dance, gauging his mood precisely. There was no energy in his protestations; in any case, his table, led by Komi, was aiding and abetting her, prising him off the chair. They knew all about the desultory flirtation that went on between them; it had led to his visiting the nightclub less and less as she began to treat him as her very personal property, ignoring him pointedly if he came to the club with a female companion, or, in a different mood, seizing any chance to pass close from behind and either step on his feet or scrape his head or shoulder with an empty tray. Somehow she stopped short of 'accidentally' emptying a loaded tray on him. In any case, she would have had to come from the front to do that, since the bar was just to one side of the entrance, and he never sat with his back to the door. So now, she dragged him off, tossing all inhibition to the wind as she hugged him and loaded him with recriminations – why had he abandoned the joint? He explained that he had been on the road.

'Liar,' she said, 'you were at Black Morocco's last night and in Lagos last weekend, at Bobby Benson's.'

His jaw dropped. 'What is this? Who have you got following me about?'

She giggled. 'Do you think I have no friends in all those other places? They know I am fond of you, so they always pass on news of you: "We saw your 'husband' in Ife the other day; your 'husband' gave us a lift in his Land Rover at Mokola." So, is it true, did you give those witches a lift?'

He admitted that he did – he had recognised them from Paradise Club, despite the absence of their horrendous wigs, make-up and mini-skirts, transformed by a housewifely *ankara* skirt-and-blouse as they came out of the market with their shopping.

'You will get yourself a bad reputation,' she said.

'You are giving me one already,' he retorted, 'the way you are rubbing your breasts against me.'

She turned round and dug her buttocks in his crotch in the sudden *ajoloole*** that the change in rhythm could be held to justify, flicked her face backwards and up at him: 'Is that better?'

'You are incorrigible,' he laughed, stepping slightly back.

'What was that word you used?'

'Incorrigible.'

'What does it mean, that big word?'

'That you are lovely, of course.'

She shrieked with delight, plunged into another *'joloole*, this time facing him. When she rose, she had become tearful, put her hands on his shoulders and leant into him: 'I know I want to look after you, I want to cook you the big *obokun* fish-head you like so much.'

He stopped abruptly in the middle of the floor. 'Who told you that?'

'Why are you so surprised?' she said. 'I know where you and your friends go to eat sometimes – the sharp-corner opposite the turning into Premier Hotel. The mama gives me news of you all the time;

---

*Digging-in to the ground.

I know she saves you the biggest fish-head. But I tell you, you just haven't eaten fish-head until this lady cooks one for you, in her own house. Just tell me when. You can bring your friends if you like. You don't have to sleep with me, I just want to cook for you, that's all, I want to look after you from time to time. Why should the University girls monopolise you?'

'All right,' he promised. 'I have to get on the road again tomorrow, so I'll stop by for a fish-head brunch – you know what that is, don't you?'

She shook her head.

'Neither breakfast nor lunch, but in-between.'

She screeched with delight and only then agreed to return to serving the thirsty tables.

It was the right mood to set off again on the road, heading for some villages around Ihiala in the East, where he had learnt of a ritual of the planting season. The several events would last over a week, and he planned to stay the entire length of time. Then to Okene: altogether, he might be away three weeks. On an impulse, he stopped at the office of the Principal, conscious perhaps of the long absence ahead, during which much might happen. He had woken up in the morning, wishing that Dike could have been present at their table the previous night. He had only to imbibe the mood of those present then and he would feel bolstered by their resolve, which was without question the mood also of the University community. So he decided to do the next best thing – speak to him.

He was admitted to the office of the man who had once briefly been his lecturer in African History. This was in the early days at Ibadan, before his transfer to Leeds. He came straight to the point, once he had offered an apology for failing to make an appointment.

'I just wanted you to know, sir, over the Anieke affair, the University is solidly behind you.'

Dike looked very touched, speaking with his accustomed stutter, quite slight. 'Thank you, thank you. It is very thoughtful of you to come and tell me this.'

'Well, I just thought you should know. Both expatriates and our own people. I have spoken to several lecturers and even non-academic staff. They all believe it would be a disgrace if the Visitor is allowed to get away with it. As an institution, we would never recover from it.'

'My opinion exactly, I could not agree with you more.'

'You realise of course, sir, there will be lots of pressure. It is not just a question of loss of face, it has become a political thing.'

'I know.'

'If it is allowed to happen sir, anything else can happen, any kind of interference. It's the end of University Autonomy.'

He smiled. 'I have thought about it, I assure you. I thought about it before I made my statement.' His smile grew boyishly confidential. 'Look, these are the Council files right here, I have all the papers with me and I have no intention of surrendering them. I have locked up the Chairman's Lodge and given instructions. And if it comes to resignation . . .' his eyes lit up: '. . . ask my secretary as you go out if you wish: I have begun to pack my papers and prepare my handing-over notes.'

The caller nodded in pure happiness. 'You won't be alone, I assure you, sir. Even I, I am not strictly of the University, only attached, but I shall transfer my attachment elsewhere, to the College of Education or whatever. But several of the staff will also resign, they have said so, and I know them.'

The Principal nodded, very solemnly. 'It will be a hard thing,' he said, 'but it is one of those times one has to take a stand. I have decided that I cannot preside over a university if the present circumstances prevail.'

'Thank you, sir. I feel more than light-hearted. I'm going to enjoy my drive to the East.'

'Oh, you're going East?'

'My research project, sir. It's taking me to Ihiala.'

'Oh, good, I hope that is going well.'

'So-so. The trouble is having to share the time with my theatre company. Both are really full-time occupations. Still, I am enjoying it all.'

'Very good, very good. I enjoyed *A Dance of the Forests* very much, though I must confess I didn't understand it all.'

'Well, maybe that was partly the fault of the production, sir. It is a difficult piece to stage – I found that out – and we had a number of problems. We might resurrect it after a decent interval.'

'Good. You must let me know when that is. Maybe the University can help out here and there the next time . . .' He laughed: '. . . if we are still here.'

'Let's hope so, sir. Anyway, good luck. And congratulations again on that statement, and your stand. Please, sir, don't let them wear you down.'

'I won't, I promise. There is always the honourable way out.'

'Goodbye, sir.'

'Have a safe journey. And thanks again for thinking of coming to see me. You have boosted my morale, you know.'

They shook hands, and he left, treading air, his skin tingling in anticipation of a fight whose conclusion, whatever it was, would not be one of dishonour to the University. Risi had described her house in the warren up on Mokola Hill, and there he headed. She was not at home but had left a message with her little sister that she had gone to the fish market and he was to wait. He decided to seek out Doig, the Welsh illustrator in the Medical Department, and share with him his conversation with the Principal. He could trust him to pass the word to his colleagues in the department – if they all stood firm, there would be no actual resignations. The public outcry would be intolerable if the young University was in danger of losing such a large percentage of its staff. But first to head for the offices of the *Nigerian Tribune* and personally deliver his open letter, addressed to the Visitor . . .

And then he hesitated, a belated recollection creeping in to slow down his heedless charge into involvement. The Visitor, Dr Nnamdi Azikiwe! The same Zik whose inaugural concert he had been charged with marring, thanks to the faded operatic star, Madame Evanti? Now, only a few months later, he was about to attack – not attack, the letter was quite respectful, though pained – but attack was how it would be read and then, would these same faceless Praetorian guards not begin to read plain persecution into his position? No, even with the most generous will, this new 'assault' on the person of the nation's Head of State would be regarded as one too many. He had retired from politics, yes, he was now the 'father of the nation', had publicly renounced all political partisanship, but he was until recently the leader of a political party, and his loyalists remained fiercely protective of his person in every respect. It would

only take one fanatic to accuse the letter-writer and failed Master
of Ceremonies as an agent of some other political party, certainly of
the Action Group which was engaged in a life-and-death struggle
with Zik's former party, especially in the West.

A superstitious strain, despite himself, even crept into his
thinking . . . was it some invisible force propelling him towards direct
confrontation with this giant nationalist figure and pan-Africanist?
Something appeared to be out of control, dragging him along, and
he did not like it one little bit. No, he had to find some other line
of action, not make it a one-to-one open confrontation on the
pages of the newspapers. None of that, no thank you. He turned
the Land Rover round to seek out Dapo Adelugba, whose instincts,
once he had slept off a Risikatu night, could usually be trusted.

Adelugba was out to the world; obviously he had stopped at the
dark den after he was dropped off, Maren having left Nightingale's
earlier than usual so as to get an early night before his drive to
Ihiala. On yet another impulse, he decided to let matters be for a
week, so he left the letter by Dapo's bedside with a note which read:
'Distribute to press if Anieke matter not resolved positively in a
week.' If he changed his mind in the meantime, he would get
a message to him. He hesitated again, thinking he should wake him
up to act as chaperon to Risi's place, but decided to leave him in
peace. The worst that could happen was that he would get seduced,
which was a less alarming prospect than the gang rape to which the
University might yet be subjected by the politicians.

He was in Enugu when news came of the University's capitulation;
it had taken just over a week for the final sentence to be written on
the episode. Every day, he listened eagerly to the radio, stopped to
pick up the journals whose editions were sometimes one or two days
behind the Lagos version. There had been to-ings and fro-ings,
interventions by patriots and other 'well-meaning' voices. Dike
appeared to have visited the Governor-General's mansion more than
once, had opened and re-bolted the Chairman's Lodge a few times,
surrendered and retrieved the Council papers over a dozen times.
Cracks within the University body were rumoured; the Visitor's
office was reported to be already inundated with the Curricula Vitae
of those who could not wait to step into the Principal's shoes the

moment he played out the role expected of his high sense of honour. Reporters were summoned for press briefings at the Principal's office only to have the briefings cancelled at the last moment, or postponed.

Penkelemes! Anieke, bold as sin, had taken up residence on campus and only waited that the files be brought to him. He was determined to get to work at once, especially on all matters that dealt with University contracts. There was also the imminent Convocation Ceremony, one that was especially significant, since it would mark the full autonomy of the University, and the commencement of the awards of her own degrees. Dr Sylvester Anieke, Chairman of the University Council, made it known that he intended not only to officiate at the Ceremony, but to deliver the Convocation Address. Heads nodded confidently . . . good, the man was heading for the humiliation of his life. Whatever happened, the Ceremony would be boycotted by the bulk of the University. No, better still, they would probably process, take their seats, then walk out as he began to address the assembly. That sounded a more befitting rebuff for a small-minded man whose sole motivation in returning to the University that had expelled him was to take public revenge by making that institution bow to him, humble itself before his authority. The Principal would never acknowledge that authority; many swore that they had actually seen his resignation letter, others that he had begun to pack his property from the Principal's Lodge.

But the Visitor and his medical sidekick clearly knew their nationals better than most, and those included the roving dramatist. Anieke's arrival on campus signalled the commencement of defections; perhaps they had begun even long before, for the Chairman of the Governing Council had much to offer. He began to receive, first clandestine visits, usually at night, and then, confident visits in broad daylight. As Convocation Day approached, congratulatory telegrams began to arrive at his Lodge, to appear on the pages of newspapers. Petitions on preferments, promotions, pleas for appointments even to political offices – for his presence there, against the University will, was the clearest demonstration of political clout, and it was best to get on the right side of such a powerful influence in national affairs. The media had split into two distinct camps: the *West African Pilot*, the voice of Azikiwe's former party, the NCNC, batted furiously for Anieke's appointment; the *Tribune* was equally strident and unyielding in its opposition; others lined up in varying degrees of political allegiance and objectivity. The University itself had no voice of its own. On Convocation Day, however, there was hardly any face missing from the roll of dons.

Maren was grateful that the Ihiala festival was over, and he dragged his truck back to Ibadan, arriving after dark. The mood called unquestionably for Black Morocco's and there he headed after scrubbing off the accumulated dust of the untarred stretches of the road from eastern parts. Try as he would, he could not persuade himself that this was not his fight, that he was not strictly a member of the University staff, only attached to the institution. It was a purely administrative link, one that did not even provide the satisfaction of a protest resignation. He had nothing to resign from; all he could do, and had decided to do, was to shift the supervision of his research from the University, as well as the administration of the pittance left of the grant, then quit the University premises altogether. He felt tainted, even corrupted, by any continuing association. But first, he had a question for the Principal. It was not a question of rebuking him, of challenging his decision. All he desired was some kind of explanation, something that would make sense of all that had happened, some clue that would clarify why he was feeling this infliction more than it seemed apparent in others.

It was, after all, a new nation, and he acknowledged that he was new to it, compared to others, conscientiously though he had studied, debated, and plotted its desirable direction from afar. He had travelled down to London from Leeds any number of times to make direct contact with those who claimed to be her immediate leaders, just to assess them and their thinking. Because of them, because of the dangers that he knew they posed, he had consciously made the University his base; it was the obvious space, just manageable in dimension and with a mission that imposed a different code of conduct from whatever might be the norm in the larger society. He had long accepted the need for a kind of reference point, a reservoir for whatever virtues society chose to jettison in its heedless competition for power and material acquisitions. Without consciously phrasing it, he had seen the University as a kind of monastery, but one where wine and other fulfilments of the flesh were not forbidden; a monastery of the mind, however, and of the kind whose inmates took their discoveries into the outer world to seminate its grounds where barren, and to be recharged in turn by such immersions in the real world. To fulfil such a role, the monastery must fashion its own rules and live by them, define its virtues and be loyal to them. It seemed now that such an ideal had been repudiated, and for all time, for such a precedent was one that could not but inform and affect all future policies and their operations. The barbarians had tasted blood. Where next would they plant their feeding trough?

This time, he did not bother to apologise for failing to make an appointment. Dike asked him to enter as soon as the secretary took his name into his office. His eyes looked bloodshot as if he had not slept for days, and his stutter was more pronounced.

'Sit down, please, take a seat. I can guess why you have come.'

The Research Fellow sat down and demanded simply: 'Why, sir?'

'I know, I know. It was a most difficult decision. But, you have to understand – these people, they do not care, they don't care if they ruin the University. The Visitor was determined to go through with it – it had become a party thing, and the party just went along, blindly, not thinking of anything but taking control of the University.'

'But how can you stay? How will you be able to exercise any independent control once you have . . . you have . . .'

'Capitulated?' He smiled ruefully. 'I know that is how it seems to you but, it is the very reasons I have stated that convince me that I have a duty to stay. One must prepare to make sacrifices for issues which are larger than the individual. This University must be saved. It is young and it is vulnerable. Only by remaining here – that is what I realised – it is by remaining that I can salvage the institution, that I can rescue its autonomy . . .'

Sacrifices, he thought? Sacrifice the one thing by which a university must sink or swim – principles? Oh no, this is the Evanti syndrome all over again, failing to accept the right moment to quit the stage. But he said nothing, simply feeling sorry for the man, and anxious to be gone.

'I cannot stay, of course,' he said aloud. 'I shall conclude my research somewhere else. Fortunately, my two years are up, I mean, the grant ends this year.'

His voice was filled with sincere concern. 'But where will you go?

I wish you wouldn't, you know, I really wish you wouldn't. You see, we need you here more than ever. I was counting on your staying, joining the Department as soon as you've completed your research. In fact, I can't see why you haven't come in fully by now. You can take your time with the research. Professor Mahood informed me that she planned to . . .'

'She has. I turned it down. It had nothing to do with this, in fact, it was before this happened. I did not like the conditions.'

'Oh, but surely we can do something about that. We can discuss . . .'

'No, sir, I have already begun to make arrangements.'

'But where will you go?'

'Well, sir, I had turned down Ife earlier . . .'

'No, don't go to Ife.' He waved his hand in dismissal of the newly proposed university, still on the drawing boards. 'Ife will take years to catch up with Ibadan, they can't match our standards. They are rushing things there, and that's not healthy.'

Health! Standards! The man was oblivious of the irony of his words. But Maren only said, 'I haven't taken a decision one way or the other. I'll probably just go on another tour while I think things over. It is obviously a time for me to rethink many things I've been taking for granted . . .'

'Oh yes, I do that myself sometimes. It's a very good habit to cultivate.'

'Yes. I had actually allowed myself to think that my homecoming – my induction home I should say – was complete. That was wrong. I am beginning to believe it will never end.'

'Oh come on, you are too young to sound so pessimistic. You are home. This is home. Even what has happened – yes, even that, it's all part of home.'

'Yes, I believe you're right, sir. When one is able to accept that, then one is really home.'

He nodded slowly, muttering, 'Yes . . . yes . . .,' as if suspicious of a hidden meaning in what his caller had just said.

There was little left to say, and the young man rose. 'Well, I'll leave you to catch up with your normal routine. I know the past week must have disrupted that quite a bit.'

The Principal saw him to the door, held out his hand. 'Good

luck. And you know where the Principal's Lodge is. The door is open to you any time.'

'Thank you, sir.'

It was as he gathered up his papers that he realised that there was, indeed, one gesture that he could make. It was not much, but the very thought of it lifted his depression somewhat, even if his spirits did not actually soar. Until then, he had forgotten that the University had accepted his plays for publication, that he had even corrected the galleys and that the volume was in its final stages for printing. He dropped everything and dashed to the press to ascertain just how far work had gone. Not much further than a second set of galleys, he was told. The staff watched him with no particular amazement – they had long classed him among the University loonies – as he did a victory dance among the machines, then dashed into the office of the manager. He was out, so he shouted to the staff not to touch the galleys until the manager had given them new instructions. He drove all over the campus trying to track down the manager, failed, so he left a message for him everywhere, then raced back to his apartment and dragged out the portable typewriter. There and then he typed out the most satisfying, self-relieving letter, till then, of his existence, almost panting with the non-existent physical effort, but of course, it was the excitement and the relief:

5th December, 1961

To the Publications Committee
University College
Ibadan.

Sirs,

A writer should feel honoured when the country's first university offers to publish something of his work. I believe I was, when you offered to issue a selection of my shorter plays. In fact, I had always looked forward to doing most of my work in some kind of association with this University.

However, since work began on this volume of plays, the status of the University has altered immeasurably. The University has been deliberately dishonoured and the occasion has passed without some comment, without even a weak protest or a futile gesture from inside the University itself. For even those who have the most tenuous connection with the College, there is no word for this but cowardice. I have no wish to further, in any way, however indirect, this conspiracy of shameless acquiescence.

I am well aware that the University is 'running smoothly', that things will 'eventually work out', and that quixotic gestures are just that. Just the same, I must ask you to withdraw from being my publishers. As the work is gone pretty far already, I understand it may be necessary to retain the University Press as printers and offer the plays to other publishers. Anyway, some sort of compromise will, I am certain, be reached – the University is rather good at that just now.

I must thank you for offering to publish my plays. I can only wish you better luck when you come to publish Anieke's Foundation Day speech to this University which, as I learnt later, was *not* delivered to an empty hall – contrary to the naïve expectation of a few.

Yours sincerely,

As he scrolled the letter out of the portable, and added his signature at the end, a huge weight lifted from his shoulders and he regretted that it was still daytime, since all he wished to do at that moment was to go straight to the Seven Sisters' whose band spot was being temporarily occupied by I. K. Dairo, then making a detour through Agoji Mayor's lone jazz club on Ijebu Bypass, and ending up, of course, at Risikatu's.

It was all over, and he was glad. He had no constituency home to go to but one could be found, could be built up from nothing, or built around, only this time with no expectations, no baggage of ideals to attempt to impose on such a waystop – which was what it would ever be, no matter how much of a destination it gave the illusion of being. He felt consoled that it had happened so early, before he put down roots in an arbitrary choice of home. Two years had passed since he stepped onto the tarmac at Ikeja Airport, the end of a five-year absence. His Land Rover had taken him through at least two-thirds of the country, probing its ritual tissues for a contemporary theatre vision, or perhaps a mere statement of being. Despite it all, he was left with the strange sensation of being poised on the nation's airspace all over again, floating in a cloud of the uncertain and unknowable, wondering yet again what homecoming promised or would bring.

VII Credos and Visitations

Like a giant with several heads, each with the brain of a child, PARTY (and even tribal) POLITICS proceeded to tear yet another university apart. This time, the victim was the University of Ife, still located in Ibadan, and its aggressor was the Nigerian National Democratic Party, the breakaway party from Chief Awolowo's Action Group. This rebel faction was led by the mercurial Ladoke Akintola, a man of infinite wit that found lacerating expression in a reedy voice. After the defeat of the Action Group in the 1959 eve-of-Independence elections, Awolowo – unlike the NCNC which went into alliance with the victors, the Northern Peoples Congress – had elected to lead his party into opposition in the Federal Parliament, leaving the Action Group stronghold, the Western Region, to the leadership of his lieutenant, S. L. Akintola.

The heavily scarified Chief – 'S.L.A.' to friends and foes alike, and with variations invented to suit either tendency – did not remain content for long to play second fiddle to his leader. From 1962, Akintola and his supporters began to move inexorably towards a split in the party. For nearly three years he had been Head of the regional government, a Premier in his own right, and in all matters that affected the governance of that region his authority was supreme. His party leader, Obafemi Awolowo, thought differently. For him, the Party was supreme. Its policies, and sometimes its collective decisions on ministerial appointments in the region that it controlled, could not be questioned. But Ladoke Akintola controlled both the regional exchequer and the forces of law and order; it required only a shrewd manipulation of both to entice and intimidate his party parliamentarians, and even some of the NCNC – which was the official opposition in the West – to join him in forming a new party and thus consign the Action Group loyalists to, at best, a ragged opposition.

'*Ina l'ori oke! Ina l'ori oke!*'* With this enigmatic cry – for no one knew what fire the words referred to, or on which mountain it was to be decried – one day an obscure parliamentarian vaulted over several of his colleagues all the way from the back benches, ran up the dividing aisle between Government and Opposition, seized the mace of authority and smashed it on the podium. The Speaker fled. As expected, there was total pandemonium. Awolowo's supporters were taken by surprise. Mostly, they fled through the nearest exits, an alert media photographer catching a memorable image of Tony Enahoro, in full traditional regalia, diving through a window. The few who tried to fight back were no match for the contingent of police which surfaced miraculously and proceeded to 'restore order' in favour of Akintola's men. The Western House of Assembly, its floor littered with broken chairs and torn *agbada*† was cleared of human debris, placed under lock and key, and its functions suspended.

In the capital, Lagos, the Prime Minister was waiting for news of the operation. As soon as he was assured of this proof of a successful breakdown of law and order, he used his disputed powers to impose a State of Emergency on the entire Western Region and appointed an Administrator who was already waiting in the wings. Dr Majekodunmi rode into Ibadan, introduced into the city by sirens and a fully-armed police convoy, placed a curfew on Ibadan township and began to dispose the principals of the fracas into scattered detention centres. They included party leaders, officials, and even a sprinkling of noisy opposition intellectuals. The degree of comfort in the various detention centres was determined by the faction to which the detainee belonged. The detention decrees could not be challenged in a court of law.

The turnabout of loyalists of the former ruling party, the Action Group, the traditional rulers especially, was phenomenal. Maren felt that it deserved celebration, and the event found place in *The Republicans* in a sketch that was danced and sung to the tune of

---

*Fire on the mountain!
†Yoruba male gown.

'The Vicar of Bray'. The uneasy partnership of Akintola and his deputy, Fani-Kayode, both suspicious of each other, yet united in grinding all opposition in the West into submission, was portrayed through an image of Siamese twins, joined at the back, dragging each other over the stage as they argued over directions of the compass – what was forwards and what was backwards – as everything disintegrated around them. Variations on Brecht's mordant exhortation to 'retain the government and dissolve the people' sent the audiences into guarded spurts of laughter, as they found themselves compelled to confront the reality of a creeping fascism. Still, there was sufficient matter for unrestrained laughter, such as the bombast of impenitent politicians, attempting to brazen out evidence of financial malfeasance, or plain ignorance of the meaning, much less the responsibilities, of their portfolios, as Wale Ogunyemi, playing the 'man of timber and calibre, of caterpillar and juggernaut' grandly responded to questions in mimic interviews.

Not so universally relished was a depiction of the climbdown and evident impotence of the father of the nation, Nnamdi Azikiwe, in a subsequent tussle with his Prime Minister, Tafawa Balewa. Too close to the bone, winced a handful among academia, as Jimi Solanke, then a fledgeling actor, in a red-feathered cap and wrapper paddled a leaky boat across the stage, with the inscription: 'April Fools' Ship'. The sight of nationalist icons scuttling away from a sinking ship for their lives was too strong a dose for those who suddenly realised that theatre was a medium they had taken too much for granted, regarding it solely as a venue for a cossetting evening. Professor A., of the History department, accosted the playwright, angrily denouncing him for bringing the office of the Governor-General into disrepute – this was a disgraceful proceeding, he protested, and could not be justified or condoned. The playwright shook his head sadly, much baffled, wondering how close to total collapse the sham edifice of establishment intellectualism was, and how blind to their truthful condition the occupants chose to remain, and for how long. Daily, news of the performances filtered through to the power centres; protests were quickly transmitted to close relations who, it was hoped, might influence restraints, but that prospect was always gently but firmly blocked, the haemorrhage of blood ties picking up pace, easing up the constrictions of well-meant but impotent anxieties, love and concern.

Chief Akintola had a morbid fear of socialism, a concept towards which he felt that his leader, Chief Awolowo, had begun to lean. It was a fear as visceral as the fear (or hate) that he felt for the Igbo people. In his piping voice, he punned cruelly with the names of Igbo public figures, politicians and non-politicians alike. Waxing lyrical, he would denounce their alleged propensity for grabbing everything within sight – *Ikiniani, Ikejiani, Iketaani . . . Ikefaani . . . ! S'omo t'iwa na o gbodo ni ni*?* S. G. Ikoku, one of the younger, left-leaning lieutenants of Awolowo, and one of a group for whom Akintola reserved a special place in hell for leading Awolowo into socialist paths, became *Ikoko*, the Hyena, a rather prophetic naming as this turned out, since that 'leftist' would later demonstrate his real nature by seeking out the offal of political carrion wherever abandoned, and feasting on it. Akintola's Yoruba opponents were not spared the re-naming, or re-interpretation exercise either. His compulsive punning was matched by a shrewd psychological offensive, since he knew how sensitive his fellow Yoruba were to any suggestion of a curse, even from an irreverent tongue that was never reputed to be graced with the sacred *ase*.[†]

'*Oredeyin*,' the incorrigible Chief would squeak, '*Ademeyin, Oguntimeyin, Lanlehin* . . . en-hen, is it not clear that this is a bunch of losers, those doomed to come last in all things?' No stopping to think if any of his own stalwarts were also vulnerable in the area of names that could be punned on to such devastating effect. The rhetoric of the moment was all, and it served his purpose well, however temporarily. Often, Maren envied his talent, knowing he would have been an asset to Orisun Theatre or the Nineteen-Sixty Masks.

'This new creed that is being brought into the party, I shall explain it to you all. Socialism means, if you have two *dansiki*,[‡] you must give one away. If you have two machetes, you must give one away. If you have two plots of land, you must give one away. If you have

---

*The first will own . . . the second will own . . . the third . . . the sixth . . . ! Is there any law which says that our own children also should not own?
†The 'force' of a sacred pronouncement.
‡A Yoruba smock-like dress, casual.

two trousers, you must give one away. If you have two wives, you must . . .' Master of perfect timing, he waited for the cries of mock horror to die down, followed by laughter. 'Wait, wait, wait, you haven't heard it all. All of you are wearing shoes, are you not? Well, start making up your mind now whether you want to hand over the left or the right shoe, because you cannot own two . . . In fact, our local guru of socialism, or communism or whatever they call it in Russia, will not be satisfied with that. When he sees you walking about on two feet with only one shoe, the next thing is, he will ask you what you are doing with two legs when there are cripples around with no leg at all. That is the sermon of socialism.'

The University of Ife was the creation of the Government of the West. It had been on the drawing-board as a cardinal part of the education plans of the Action Group. After the Anieke affair, however, consumed by the conviction that Ibadan University had not only been discredited, but was now taken over by the Igbo, Ife took on a totally different complexion: in the minds of Chief Akintola's party, it became a Yoruba response to the party's perception of Igbo hegemony in Ibadan.

That Chief Awolowo and the Action Group should be seen by them to flirt with Igbo radicalism – at least, in respect of the anti-feudalist convictions of Dr Azikiwe's party, the NCNC – was treacherous enough. But that Ife University, founded and funded on the resources of the West, the Yoruba stronghold, should harbour vocal ideologues of the colouring of the Action Group's putative socialists was a nightmare that the NNDP resolved early to exorcise. In the schism between Chief Akintola and Chief Awolowo, there was little question of where the sympathies of easily identifiable individuals like the economist, Sam Aluko, the Agriculture Professor, Oyenuga, and a few others lay. Very few of them were socialists, but they were active supporters of Awolowo and were also intellectuals. In the eyes of Akintola the combination could only mean socialists. Once Akintola had assumed the mantle of Premier, he resolved that this particular cankerworm must be gouged out, its nest cauterised for all time. He summoned the Vice Chancellor, Oladele Ajose, and gave him his marching orders. Ajose had his speech prepared and edited to the satisfaction of Akintola's overseers, summoned an emergency Congregation of the University and fled to Lagos to attend to some urgent matters. His stand-in, Saburi Biobaku, was left behind to address the restless Congregation in the temporary assembly hall of the temporary Ife campus, then situated just round the corner from the discredited University of Ibadan campus.

'The University *Credo* is quite clear on this . . . the University must support the government of the day . . .'

The riot act had been read. No discussion was permitted.

'I do not understand you at all,' chided Modele, the vivacious, intense daughter of Chief Akintola. 'Why do you pretend to be one of those riffraff, people with no background, no family anyone ever heard of? You don't belong to them; you are well brought up. What have you in common with people like Aluko and all the rest of the socialist riffraff?'

'Listen to me for a moment . . .' Maren interrupted.

'No, there is nothing you have to tell me. I know you better than you think. I've known you since I was like that . . .' patting the air below knee-height, 'and I always admired you. When we moved into our new house in Ajasa, just behind your uncle's house, that was when I first came to know my Brother Ajasa – it was my kid brother who started us all calling you by that name. All of our family admired you. Oh, even now you should hear my father talk about you. He knows you are very clever. So what is happening to you? Why should you put yourself in the same rank as all those Oyenuga types?'

'Be quiet and listen to me. I do not belong to the Aluko or any such group . . .'

'Precisely! So what are you doing on their side?'

'You are not listening! When I say I do not belong with them, I am trying to tell you that I am not a party man. Do you understand that? I am not an Action Grouper – have you got that into your head?'

'Then why are you not with Daddy? Why do you write things in the papers against the Government? And those drama sketches, I've heard about them.'

Maren sighed. 'You are so naïve, it hurts.'

'Naïve? Me, naïve? It is you who have become naïve, Brother

Ajasa. They are merely using you, can't you see that? Awolowo is using you, using them to use you.'

'Good. Shall we then say – they are using me, just as your father is using you?'

'My father? Using me?'

'Who asked you to talk to me?'

'Nobody. Nobody forces me to do anything. I care for you. You are my elder brother, my family's Brother Ajasa. My sister and my little brothers look up to you, we all admire you. How can I stand by and watch you destroy yourself?'

He took her hand. 'Aluko has been charged with sedition. I have been called in as an expert witness by the defence. By responding, I have become a communist, an Action Grouper, an anarchist, an enemy of your father bent on destroying himself – is that it?'

'I'm telling you you have nothing in common with them. You know it yourself. Deep down you know it. Just leave the riffraff to themselves and let them learn their lesson.'

'If they are riffraff, Modele, so am I. You understand? And you must stop talking about socialist riffraff because then, you insult me.'

She clapped her hands over her ears. 'Don't say that. Don't ever say that again. I don't want to hear it. You are not a communist . . .'

'I never said I was. And I haven't heard them claim that label either. You see, you do not even know the difference between being a socialist and being a communist.'

'You cannot be a socialist, I'm telling you. I know you! You like to slum, that's all. You're fond of slumming. I told you so before, didn't I, even in England. That was why you liked to go and work in that bar you told me about, full of prostitutes and drunken Irishmen. That's why you go to these low nightclubs in Ibadan and dance with prostitutes and bar girls – I know all about it. Your socialism is the same thing. It's not you at all. It's only this habit you have of trying to be like the common people; but you're not! You come from a decent family and you can't get away from that, no matter how you try.'

He peeled off her hands from her ears and sat her down, then stood over her. 'Leave home.'

'What?'

'Leave home. Leave your parents. Go away. Tell them to send you back to England – wherever. Just go. Get out. What is happening is beyond you. You are taking on all the passion of something you haven't got the slightest inkling about. You are, to put it mildly, ignorant. An ig-no-ra-mus! Got that? A complete ignoramus. You sit in on all their party meetings. They all indulge you; you're full of opinions and advice and they treat you with deference. But that's only because you are Akintola's daughter, the Premier's attractive, aggressive daughter. You do not know what really goes on deep down, where the real dirt is dished out. Real dirt. And blood. If your father really loved you, he would have sent you away, far far away from him. I would never have let a daughter of mine become as involved as you are in such messy politics. You love him, yes, but I do not consider the way he involves you to be love.'

Her eyes were flashing as she leapt up. 'Daddy loves me. We're very close. I am closer to him than my mother is.'

'*To.**' He prepared to leave. 'That's about as far as I can go with you.' Then he stopped thoughtfully and asked, 'You say you have no secrets from him?'

'None. I tell him everything.'

'Good. Then tell him all I've said. Tell him I said he is feeding off you. He is sucking you dry, like a vampire. Tell him I said so. You are young. Go and find love, real love. Don't let him destroy you.'

'Daddy! Destroy me?'

'Repeat everything I've said to you. And one thing more – tell him to keep his hands off Ife University. You've spent years studying abroad. You know what universities are. Tell him I said Ife is not his private property. We all work for our salary and we do not owe anyone personal loyalty. Our loyalty is to the University. At least, mine was.'

'Was? What do you mean?'

'I handed in my resignation yesterday. Immediately after the "*Credo*" speech. Your father can expect other resignations. He wants to tear down the University. Good. I am not staying around to watch this round. I've quit.'

*Enough said.

'But why? What for? That speech was not meant for people like you. It was for Aluko and all those others. Those who are concerned know themselves. Look, I'll speak to Daddy. He will tell the University not to accept your resignation.'

Maren sighed, shaking his head in frustration. 'Oh, you silly girl, you do like to interfere, don't you? I've quit. I have given the mandatory three months' notice. That means I am still with the University. Tell your father that, and tell him to keep his Government's hands off the University while I remain there. That way, I can still remain a family friend – perhaps. If I had the money to pay three months' salary in lieu of notice, I would quit immediately. But I haven't got it, so I have three months to serve and I shall hate every single moment of it. As a personal favour, ask him just to leave things as they are and take them no further. I really would like to continue to come to your home as a member of the family.'

'Nothing will change that, Brother Ajasa. You know you are always welcome.'

He shook his head, feeling downcast. 'I used to feel so much at home, even here, despite its being your father's official residence. I have a feeling all that is coming to an end.' His smile was wistful. 'Another home lost.'

'Why do you talk like that? You can never be a stranger to us.'

He turned on her with sudden fierceness. 'Understand this. All that intra-party squabble between Awolowo and your father doesn't interest me in the slightest – well, it does, but – oh, never mind. All I'm trying to tell you is . . . look, don't get yourself destroyed with the party. And I don't want the party to destroy the University either. That's all. That mindless *Credo* is the first crack, but if your father just lets things be – he's had his fun now, he and his fascist deputy Fani-Kayode. And those vicious clowns and mercenaries he has around him – Olowoofoyeku and company. We know all those whose advice he relies on – including those shameless traditional rulers like Oba Akran who sends Igun psycopaths to Ibadan to reinforce NNDP thugs.'

'It's not true,' she protested.

'Isn't it? You want me to take you to the Government building three minute's drive from here and show you where they are lodged? They don't speak one word of any language except Ajase, and they know no other profession except killing. That's Oba Akran's contribution to the Independence struggle. That is the kind of confidant your father relies on.'

'And what of the other side?' she replied hotly. 'Have they told you they don't recruit thugs? Ex-convicts that are known to everyone, and armed robbers?'

Maren nodded with satisfaction. 'Good. At last you admit we are speaking the same language. And I'm telling you to get your father to send you away. You've become too involved, too irrational. You cannot pretend to me that you don't know how messy this confrontation is going to get.'

'I am remaining by my father's side.'

'All right. It does you credit, but I insist it does your father none. Make sure you tell him I said so. As for the University – and that's the immediate issue on my mind – he's cracked his whip, and I hope he knows now that not everybody will jump. So this is his chance to drop everything, just let go. Let things die down. He doesn't have to withdraw. No one is asking him to publicly swallow his vomit. Just let it rest, that's all I'm asking – let it rest. Let it be forgotten!'

They parted. It was the last time he would see her alive. There was too much tension for such a frail body, far too much passion for her depth of mind – he knew that already, but had observed it with unusual keenness that evening, and with anxiety, even alarm. He was saddened, but not surprised, that something within her finally gave way, snapping the frail thread by which she still held on to life. Her death left him depressed for a while, musing at length on the political feud between the two families, a feud that he somehow held responsible for the death of a firstborn, one from each family. It had a mythical remorselessness about it, a weight of the imponderable. For the first time, he stopped to wonder about the future, how it would all end, if even he, whose role was undertaken neither for one nor the other, would find himself splashed with the bad blood between the two families. He did not attend her funeral, but sent a wreath merely signed, 'Brother Ajasa.'

Maren had taken the precaution of not living on campus. After Ibadan, a need to distance himself – physically at least – from his next university had led him to hijack – ironically – a government building. Its last occupant had been Rick, an expatriate artist in the Ministry of Information. Maren did not deny to himself that he had enjoyed the process of manipulating a loophole in the bureaucracy, aided and abetted by vengeful officials in the Ministry of Housing. They were daily obliged to allocate and furnish government housing to mistresses, relations and thugs of the NNDP Government, even ordered to arrange regular catering for their occupants from government resources. As a co-editor of *Black Orpheus*, the Arts and Culture magazine that was produced by the region's Ministry of Information on the initiative of Ulli Beier, the German Austrian who came to Yorubaland for want of any other idea at the time, and stayed for ever, he felt no qualms about squatting semi-illegally in a Government-owned residence.

The expatriate Rick earned his nickname of 'G-Man' through his regular patronage of Paradise Club and the medical clinic; he had a remarkable propensity for picking up infected prostitutes, over and above the average quota of the expatriate staff or indeed any known patrons of the birds of Paradise. But finally he took up with a red-headed expatriate figure of glamour, a girlfriend from England who came on a trial visit, fell in love with Nigeria and did not bother to return home to pack her bags. Any further delay, she sensed, and G-Man would be totally lost to Paradise, so she stayed to make an honest man of him.

The one-bedroom bungalow in Agodi where G-Man entertained his short-stay guests had become inadequate for a permanent couple, so they moved to more suitable quarters. Maren staked a claim to the bungalow on behalf of *Black Orpheus*, to which non-human persona it was formally allocated. At the University itself, he did not provide an address, stating simply that he lived off-campus.

It had not taken long after moving in to discover the nature of his immediate neighbours whose house was screened off his by a long driveway that was so thickly lined on both sides that it was impossible even to see the kind of vehicles driving in or out. For days that compound would be silent, certainly empty. Then would come a series of vehicles driving in, discharging boisterous passengers, who set about stirring up the compound as if to make up for its long period of neglect. The sounds that came from what must have been the kitchen and catering department suggested that an army had been billeted there, ever-hungry, and ever-thirsty. When the wind blew over the tall trees and penetrated the dense foliage, the aroma of the smoke that wafted through, especially at night, was neither of wood nor of cigarettes; Maren recognised the pungent smell of marijuana from his many nights at Black Morocco's.

A lull in activities, a motor vehicle would come roaring in and they would take off again, not always all of them at once, and sometimes only for short spells. There was no question about it: these were party thugs, and they could only belong to Akintola's Government party, the NNDP. He began to wonder if taking over the G-Man's house had been such a stroke of luck after all. But they seemed totally unaware of his presence, never stepped out of the confines of their compound – probably acting on strict instructions. Soon he felt confident enough to make a series of night reconnaissances on the periphery of the house and eventually to introduce a frequent caller on the cleaning and kitchen staff. The young scout walked in as a bread-seller while the gang was out, then took to passing through even when they were back from 'operations'. Nothing that he picked up ever hinted that they knew that an enemy of the Government was living right next to their barracks.

The NNDP Government was not yet done with Ife University; it ordered the immediate dismissal of those whom it felt were not 'supporting the Government of the day', beginning with those who were clearly identified as members of the Action Group, or the NCNC. The University obliged. Several staff, including some expatriates, resigned in sympathy. Others, spearheaded by a mathematician, whose calculations had turned with ill-disguised passion to the political blackboard, commenced a series of manoeuvres that led eventually to Government House where a 'peace meeting' had been arranged between Government and University officers. These also included expatriate officers. The meeting ended with a majority pledge of allegiance to the new University *Credo*. Confident that it now had the support, or complaisance of the majority of the University, the Government issued fresh orders. All those who had resigned should be paid their three-month salary – there was no need for them to serve out their notices – and ejected from the University at once. Twenty-four hours' grace, no more. If they were on the campus after that, the consequences, it was threatened, would be very grave indeed.

Living off campus, and preoccupied with rehearsing Orisun Theatre for the next series of his political revues, *Before the Blackout*, Maren was not immediately aware of the hotted-up pace of events. Moreover, a quite worrisome dimension had developed on that same theatrical front. He had picked up sufficient warning that the party hierarchy of the NNDP had decided to act against Orisun Theatre. At a meeting, a number of options were considered, which included sending for Maren and attempting to win him over. He had to have his price, all that was needed was to find out what it was. Their 'man on campus', Dr V.O., shook his head; not only was he non-vendable, he was a fanatic and would not be deterred. Another 'academic link', a would-be independent-minded party man known simply as 'F.R.D.', agreed with him. The meeting broke up with a transfer of that little problem to the 'enforcement' department – the show must be disrupted by whatever means, and its participants taught the usual lesson. The same F.R.D., a quite unpredictable personage, took the warning to Maren, adding that before that expedition itself, a high-level group, including a representative from the Public Prosecutor's office, had been selected to go and watch the show. If there was the slightest chance of the author and cast being hauled up for sedition, no time should be lost.

Maren gave the young company an earlier call time than usual. They arrived thinking that he had thought up some variations or additions to the revue that would require some fast rehearsals. Instead, he lined them up on the stage and addressed them.*

'I thought I should let you all know that your sketches appear to have been extremely successful. Now, you are all expecting me to congratulate you.' He shook his head. 'Sorry *o*, nothing doing. Instead I have to tell you that your very success means that you still have a lot to learn. Anyone who thinks our next line of training is not for him or her is free to leave now because this is where reality catches up with art. Do you all understand what I am saying?'

He looked at their blank faces and smiled. 'Of course not. Right. Here we go. There isn't much time, so tonight's exercises are in the nature of emergency coaching. We have a very likely invasion on our hands; it will be tonight, or tomorrow, but it will come any time. What I must teach you now is elementary self-defence, a training you have to take as seriously as the dramatic craft itself. There is not much point rehearsing your plays for several weeks only to find that some thugs can assault the stage at will, beat you up and stop the show. In the town proper, when we transfer to the Mbari Club, the situation will be somewhat easier; we have our own friends in Gbagi, and a few of them will even be in the audience tonight, not many, I'm afraid, just the few I was able to contact since I received the news this afternoon. But you must form the first line of defence. None of you is ignorant of the first principle of theatre: The Show – Must – Go – On! Is that plain enough?'

There was the expected chorus of 'Yes!', full of youthful, devil-may-care, let-them-all-come enthusiasm. As always, however, such spontaneous responses only deepened the mother-hen in his relationship to this young bunch, often pulling him back from limits that he was ready to assume for himself, where they were involved. Pleased, but anxious, he warned: 'I want no false courage. All I ask is that anyone who would rather not be involved in this, leave right now, so I can rehearse someone else in the role. I shall step in myself where necessary, so don't hesitate to step aside. Right now! There is too much to do in the little time we have so, please, let's not waste any time. Believe me, there will be no hard feelings and you can always return for other plays. I'll give you two minutes to think about it.'

Tunji Oyelana looked round. 'Let's get going, sir. You can see that no one is leaving.'

'All right.' He walked to the wing and picked up a fire extinguisher. 'You all know what this is, of course, but you have probably never had to use one. Normally, there is only one way it should be used, and that is to point the nozzle towards the base of the fire and – Press this Knob. Now, you must imagine that the base of the fire is at face level, the eyes in particular . . . go on, pass it round. I've checked it, this one is empty. There are six others backstage, and they are full. Aim . . . that's it . . . and – press . . . Come on, smartly. Aim, press. Then we'll move on to what you do with the body of the cylinder itself after you have temporarily disabled your assailant. It's a heavy cylinder when it's full, so you'll have to practise that crucial follow-up movement with the real thing, get used to the weight and use it to your advantage . . .'

The attack did not come that night, however, and he returned home with a huge sense of relief. Tomorrow they would train all day and be even better prepared. Also there would be more 'friends' among the audience. As he drove towards his driveway, a Mercedes Benz overtook him. It was an off-white colour, very unusual at the time in Ibadan. In fact, he knew only one owner of such a vehicle: it was the Permanent Secretary in the Ministry of Education. What was remarkable about the luxury vehicle, however, apart from the fact that it was driven through the narrow Government reservation roads at breakneck speed, was that it was packed full of some savage types, not quite the kind who would normally ride in such a car. Laughing boisterously, between ten and twelve in number, they had somehow succeeded in packing themselves tightly into a space designed for five at the most. They hung out of windows, drummed on the top and sides of the car, at least two legs swinging out in contempt of any possible amputation.

He slowed down, wondering if his illegal occupation had been discovered at last and an ejection force was on its way to carry out orders. But the vehicle merely screeched into the hidden driveway of the neighbouring house, ripping off a few of the branches as it vanished into the familiar hideout. Later, there was even more than the usual carousing, beer and *ogogoro** flowing freely late into the night. Whatever operation had been carried out that evening had obviously been a successful one, and one also that the stalwarts had immensely enjoyed.

The mystery was made clear when he drove into campus the following morning for his lectures. An urgent message was awaiting him from Joyce Aluko, and he drove there at once. He could not immediately recognise the sitting room where he had sat quite a few times. The doors – not only the doors but the windows and the roof – must have been left open, and a freak tornado had surely ripped through the house, knocking over shelves, scattering books, lifting carpets and ripping out electric wires.

*Local gin, distilled from palm wine.

'This is nothing,' she said, 'come and see the bedroom. Then I shall show you Sam's study.'

'What on earth happened here?'

'There were about nine or ten of them. They came in Mr Somare's Mercedes . . .'

He stopped. 'The white Mercedes? The one belonging to the Permanent Secretary?'

'Yes. Has someone told you already?'

'No. Go on.'

'They smashed down the door and began to take everything apart. They were laughing and abusing everyone. They said, "Haven't you gone yet? You stupid Awolowo people, you mean you're still here? You haven't gone to your mentor in Ijebu?" Maren, you cannot believe the obscenities they hurled at me, the children were so terrified.'

'Sam wasn't home?'

'He travelled. You know he's been going for meetings since this problem started.'

'Oh yes, they know how to pick their time. But . . . who showed them your house?'

'They were led here by an officer from the Registrar's office. I don't know his name but I can recognise him. He drove the official car from the Registry, pointed out the house and left. I saw him through the window. Look . . . just look at all this . . . they said they are using Sam to teach the others a lesson, all those who have resigned. They threatened to come back today and finish their job if we all haven't moved out by then. How do I even begin to pack out from a house we have lived in for years, long before this campus was taken over by Ife University?'

'Pack out?' Maren queried. 'Pack out? What for?'

'What are you saying? We have to pack out. I have these children here.'

'Oh you can move out. You and the children. But you leave your things here. You gave three months' notice and the conditions of service are quite clear on that. No one can eject you before the end of three months.'

'But what's the point staying? What would be the point leaving our things behind?'

He realised suddenly that she was in no condition to be argued with. 'All right,' he conceded, 'Sam isn't here and isn't likely to be back today, so you can start packing if you like. You have to tidy up, anyway.'

'I have asked the University to help us arrange transportation. At least we are entitled to that.'

'What did they say?'

'A lorry will be here this afternoon.'

Maren laughed. 'They know how to be efficient, when they want to be. All right. I'll be back in the afternoon. If Sam returns, tell him to see me at once. I want to discuss this moving out business with him.'

'I'm sure he'll agree with me,' she said. 'He knows he can't be going on these meetings of his and leaving us alone in the house.'

'All right. Tell him to see me anyway.'

'I won't even need to tell him. I know he'll want to get in touch with you as soon as he returns.'

'Oh, by the way, you remember the so-called "peace meeting" held at Government House? I can't remember now who presided over it – Somare, the PermSec, or the Deputy Premier?'

'The PermSec summoned the meeting. He was there. I think either Akintola or his deputy was present, but I'm not sure now. Both the PermSec and Minister for Education were present, of course.'

'And those who went from here. The ones who agreed with the Government, I mean; we already know the ones who stood firm.'

'I know some of them, but Sam will give you the full story. Oh wait, he took notes. I know where to find his notes, just wait while I look in this rubble . . . God, what a mess!'

It was the worst possible moment for a distraction, especially one that dragged in its wake the weight, not merely of a decision but worse, discussion. Returning home directly from the mayhem in Aluko's house, his first thought, as he saw his waiting parents, was that they had learnt of the campus situation, had leapt to the right conclusion about his likely involvement, and had come to urge caution, restraint. He slid into the family-crisis mode: hear them out, tease them as much as they could bear, reassure them as much as he could bear, and send them on their way. He did not know whether to feel relief or yield to a groan of disbelief, when he found that their thoughts were far from the politics of state or of academia.

They were struck by the half-emptiness of the house. After their last visit, and that was nearly a year before, they had left the house enticingly domestic. For the mother especially, it was a phase of vindication. She had acquired a new family, could become a part of the home, as of right, not residing with them – she would never attempt that – but belonging to it, treating it now as an extension of the parsonage at Aké, ignoring her son's existence and stretching her eternal umbilical cord, not just to one newcomer but to two. She was not alone. Suddenly his makeshift home overflowed with motherhood. The woman with whom he lived had recently given birth, and he accepted his exclusion from the household with more than mere gratitude. It was relief, even rapture. It was a fact that he never wearied of conceding; without the vast, festive support system of such extended family care, he would have escaped to the Arctic wastes and lived solely with whales and penguins before he willingly brought a child into the world. He marvelled at other men of his acquaintance who actually *enjoyed* living with and nursing the monstrosities called babies, the 'mewling and puking' tyrants, whose sole mission to the world appeared to be to replace their mothers by killing them off with every conceivable mode of torture, their strangulating vocal chords especially.

But there were friends and acquaintances of his who loved these inflictions. Femi Johnson, his insurance broker friend, would shoo off his wife at nappy-changing time, and tackle the odious task himself with touching sensitivity. It was something Maren saw with his own eyes; until then he had imagined that O.B.J. – as everyone called him – was merely compensating for his numerous *liaisons* – almost at par with his own – but no, when he watched O.B.J. at work, delicately powdering the rash-red bottom of his latest sub-human, folding and safety-pinning the nappy with practised caution instead of yielding to the temptation of taking his revenge on behalf of humanity by jabbing the pin into the underbaked flesh – not viciously, no, just a mild prick to remind the terror that it also had its moments of vulnerability, and it had better watch out for the likes of Uncle Maren – until he actually witnessed the scene, he did not seriously accept that *roué*'s boasts that he loved taking care of babies! Nothing could persuade him that babies were not born with a sinister intelligence, a cold-blooded, calculating knowingness that giggled secretively at the sight of adults panicking at their slightest cry, fussing and rushing about to fulfil their unstated whims. Babies, he held, should be on the reserved list of national budgeting. The crèche should be a priority national institution, operated on local government level, with trained personnel whose salaries should be just slightly below that of the Head of State, governors of maximum security prisons for dangerous criminals, and the personnel of lunatic asylums. The gigantic deception practised on innocent citizens by such promotions as Baby of the Year, Talcum Powder Baby, New Year Baby and so on should be countered with stringent penalties, from crippling fines to loss of citizenship. All in all, the soundest basis for any claim to intellectual superiority that democratic societies had over others was that, as a more than symbolic act of humiliation and self-abasement, they forced their politicians – full-grown men of (probably) balanced minds – to kiss babies. That anyone should suggest to him that he had passed through such a phase himself was pure slander or, at best, a case of mistaken identity.

He had required no urging before he surrendered the main bungalow to the territorial greed of the newcomer and her mother, ensconcing himself in the unoccupied servants' quarters to the rear of the building, with a thick wedge of unkempt foliage as a solid barrier. Aunties, uncles, grandmothers and extended cousins from both sides descended on the house, and objects sprang up from nowhere, vanished into nowhere, swapped forms and positions at will, turning a sparse habitation into a teeming conclave of long separated clans, coming and going in a seemingly endless stream. The wide corridors around the single bedroom effortlessly found them perches, habitable spaces within a self-multiplying welter of sheer objects. When he looked in from time to time, the scene would strike him as a vivid contrast to the constricted parenting of his first child in London, so stark, so shorn of touch and voices that, for one whose childhood had been passed through birthtime swarms of kin, friends and neighbours, he almost felt pity for the newcomer who, it seemed, had come into the world a ready-made orphan.

Still, he did design and build the child a crib, feeling at peace with the world as visitors oohed and aahed at the unusual combination of local palm stalks and plywood. Later, when she grew big enough to attempt to climb its slim rungs at the wrong times – that is after she was safely tucked in bed, he learnt to hypnotise her to sleep. The mother soon became terrified at the child's headlong crash back- wards into the cot, at the sound of 'Sleep', landing straight into the embrace of a deep slumber that lasted all night, never less than the seven to eight hours which is the least deserved period of repose for any nursing mother. But mothers never seemed to appreciate such labour-saving devices, and she gave him no rest until he agreed to desist. So he practised, amazed at how easy it really was, to change the verbal command to a sequence of gestures. It worked just as magically, and he took good care she never saw it, leaving her now morbidly concerned that the baby had become conditioned, since she still appeared to fall asleep with an unnatural suddenness, and never woke up all night. He thought briefly of setting up a child hypnosis workshop for harassed parents, but the idea seemed fraught with danger for those whose infanticidal fantasising might surpass his own.

And so, full of empathy and gratitude for the childbirth invasion, but safely distanced from the tumult, he made his home in the outhouse with his preferred extended family of books perched on improvised shelves and nursed his portable typewriter till late in the night, worked long hours at rehearsals, stayed longer at Mbari argu- ing literature and politics with Christopher Okigbo, Ezekiel Mphah- lele the South African exile, J. P. Clark, Frances Ademola and infiltrators from either Ibadan or Ife campus, or kept Black Morocco and his soulmates of the night company, far from kin care, mother- love and infant caterwauling. The tumult gradually diminished, but the house was transformed for ever, retaining vestigial traits of its new persona even after the mistress of the crib, nursemaid, mother and all related baggage had been evacuated to their new domain in Felele.

'Where is the rest of the family?' he heard his mother ask.

'At Felele. We've moved – at least they have. I divide my time between the two places.'

'Oh. Well, we'll stop there on the way home. But it's about her we've come.'

He waited. They looked at each other – a habit of theirs, at the end of which they had silently agreed on who should speak.

'You have created problems,' the father began. 'You cannot just take a woman into your house as if she were a goat you picked off the street. She has a family, you know. She is not from nowhere.'

Oh. Now he understood their mission. 'But you know I am married,' he replied.

'Yes, we are only too aware of that,' he retorted, grimly. 'Still, this is Yorubaland, and we have our ways of doing things. Especially now that she has a child for you.'

'I know. But that does not unmarry me.'

The mother intervened. 'If you must know, her relations came to see us. Actually, we are related, in some distant way. But what matters is, things can no longer be left as they are. You have to meet with the family.'

'I have met them . . .'

'Not that way, stop joking with a serious matter. You have to meet them properly.'

He drew a rein on his thoughts, which continued to stray towards the unresolved situation on campus. The intrusion seemed unreal, and he found himself tempted towards a brusque termination of the visit.

'Has she complained?' he asked. 'Has she stated that she is unhappy with the situation?'

They looked at him, aghast. 'Does she need to? Her family has come to us. Do you think they came without first talking to her?'

'They could. You know that yourselves. They could feel that their daughter was shaming the family by living "in sin", and decide to do something about it.'

'All we are asking,' the mother pleaded, 'is that you do the traditional asking. That isn't much is it? Then, if you happen to get divorced . . .'

'No, please! We've agreed not to move near that subject.'

Very quickly, the father retreated to a safer position. 'All right, all right, no one is really bothering about a divorce. The family did not mention it, neither did we. But they are very unhappy about this situation of things. You have to understand their feeling, they feel that we are cheating them.'

'Cheating them? How?'

It was not often that he saw his father fidget with embarrassment. 'You see, one has to be very careful not to appear to be using one's . . . er . . . let's put it this way . . . you have to understand, they feel that we despise them, that we do not respect their family or we would not condone the situation. It's a family thing. And a pride thing. They feel we would not dare do this to er . . . a family for whom we have any respect. You see in what an awkward position it places us, don't you?'

It was a pained silence that followed. Yes, Maren felt he understood only too well what was being said, which was what was being left unsaid. He felt rather sad; it was sadness at the attempt by some other, individual or family, to take something out of his hands, something that he was content to live with, to bear responsibility for, even guilt if guilt it was, even crime if it was so deemed. It did not seem to matter how one proceeded, what declarations one made or how explicit one's actions were – at some point or the other, there would always be those with the means to circumvent acceptance of the consequences of one's actions, or position, always the risk of their diversion onto other heads.

'Why that feeling should exist, I do not understand,' the father continued. 'Her father was a teacher, just like myself. As your mother said, there is even some kinship on her side. So why this feeling should arise, that we are looking down on them . . .'

No! That was one trap to be avoided at all costs, he warned himself. 'I have been honest, very honest with her,' he said. 'And I do not just mean about my marriage, but about myself, and what I think about marriage. I mean, I have spelt it out in the most unambiguous terms.' He hesitated a moment, then blurted out: 'There is also the question of how I actually feel about marrying *her*.'

'We are not talking about that kind of marriage. Since we agreed not to talk divorce, we are obviously not talking about certain kinds of marriage . . .'

'But why go through this ceremony at all – oh, sorry, we've been through that.'

Silence filled the room. Their no-longer-insistent plea began to tug at his indifference. This was a claim towards which his own rising fame had contributed, ironically. But was this any different from blackmail? How many faces of blackmail did one fail to recognise? How many guises? Masks? The victims were well chosen for their piety. The biblical dictum was being reversed – the sins of the son were being visited on the father, and backwards into traceable primogenitors? There was something unseemly about the proceeding that had brought them to this state of guilt, and he was suddenly angry, yet surprised and relieved to hear his voice emerge with no trace of impatience, much less of anger.

'Will you also visit Ghana?' For a moment they looked blank, then disconcerted. 'Oh yes,' he pressed on. 'My Independence child, don't forget her. She came first, you know. She was conceived on October 1st, 1960, and in the home of my cousin, a Lijadu – that point has just occurred to me. Neither I, nor the mother thought about what would develop from a natural encounter. But something did develop, and its name is a child. And that child has claims. Or doesn't she? And her mother? Will you also pay a visit to her parents?'

'Well, they did come here . . .' the mother began.

'Of course they did. And they came with a ring on their minds. The mother, a brother, a relation, and of course they sought out the same blood contacts, your Uncle Segun and his incorrigible friend, Dr Daddi. That was after we'd had this meeting in Ikoyi, with Sobo Sowemimo combining all three roles of referee, mutual friend and relation – he seemed quite bemused by the entire business and was as common-sensible as you could ask for, but – what's the point I'm making now? – yes, they came with a variation on the same theme. The mother was quite pleasant, very reasonable. All she wanted was that I provide a ring, she was not insisting on a wedding, just a token, a ring to indicate that I acknowledge something, some kind of understanding. I said to the delegation, look, let me and Lettie withdraw from you lot and remind each other about what did happen on October 1st, when we met. And what we said when she returned nearly two months later with the news that an Independence child was on the way . . .'

'We don't have to go into all that . . .'

'But we must, we must. Because afterwards they went after the family elders. And Uncle Segun felt so helpless that he had to send for you, and I said, Keep out of this. Just keep out of it. Dr Daddi was no hypocrite, thank goodness – we did meet some time afterwards, and he told me what role he had played and what he had said to his visitors. I did acknowledge the child. She is my daughter. She is your family.'

'You certainly take this extended family business to extremes,' the father sighed.

'That family gene appeared to have skipped one generation,' Maren conceded.

'And you are making up for the omission, I suppose.'

'Not deliberately. Oh, let's face it, I didn't plan it. Neither did she. She is the daughter of a High Court Judge, and I haven't heard of that family complaining that you have "disrespected" the family. So what exactly is this business of "cheating', and looking down on, and . . .'

'All right,' the mother interjected. 'Let's face the present situation. What do we do?'

'Marry all of them,' he declared. 'If they're willing.'

The father groaned. 'Do try and be serious.'

'I am dead serious. I've told you this before, and admitted it scores of times to others, she included – the greatest mistake I ever made was in thinking that I could eventually belong to this Pharisaical tribe called monogamists. No, I take that back. It seems to have worked for you – and for a handful of others I do know about, well, claim to know about. Let's just say, the select, exclusive and minority tribe of genuine monogamists – from my vast knowledge of married people so far. So, let's be practical. What is the meaning of this thing you wish to do on my behalf? And can it be done within the context of polygamy?'

'You can count me and your father out for that.' And the mother's voice was pure outrage.

The son nodded; the promptness of the response was expected. 'Too bad. Then why her, rather than Independence? The mother may be Ghanaian, but she came with the birth of a nation. Well, the . . . no, birth it was, for better for worse, a nation was born. And my daughter was seeded on that day, not intentionally, but that did happen! So, beyond this blackmail of "disrespect", what valid claims have sprung up to contest the right of the Ghanaian ring? The fact that one is living with me under the same roof, and the other is not?'

The mother nodded. 'That sounds a good enough claim to me, or don't you think so, dear? If the other one really cared . . .'

'She cared sufficiently to visit here and rouse up all the relations, excepting you, of course.'

'And whose fault was that?' she asked, almost inaudibly.

'Mine. And I prefer to continue leaving you excepted. I accept all its burden.'

'That's easier said than done!' The resolve on the father's face was unambiguous. 'This one is right on our doorstep. Front door and backyard. There is no way we can stay out of it.'

'It is a family-to-family affair,' the mother added. 'And we are being made to look bad. It is as if we have abandoned all family notion, the way they throw hints this way and that.'

'We've said enough.' The father had grown even more impatient. 'We see things differently. It's been that way since you returned. Just as you've refused to have the children baptised, as if they were not born into a christian home.'

Maren laughed. 'Oh, you two. You're saying that because you have it all fixed. You think I don't know about that conspiracy? It leaked from one of her brothers – he and I are together on that, with you and her parents working on her from the other side. I know you finally talked her into it. When is the event? My next travel outside the country?'

She was hotly on the defensive. 'Who said we were doing anything behind your back?'

He laughed. 'Oh yes, you were. You've picked the date, I know all about it. Akande told me. But I don't mind. I've already dedicated her, and the other one, to the forces I believe in. I took both into the grove two days ago, early morning – ask their mother. Your baptismal font is quite free to add its own blessing; I no longer mind.'

She bridled. 'Why are you such a pagan? What turned you into such a pagan?'

The father smiled, knowingly. 'He's merely trying to draw us away from what brought us here – why are you falling for that old trick of his? Now, let's get back to where we were and you, listen for a change. All this argument – a waste of time. We merely came to inform you, not to ask your opinion. We are going to perform what we accept as our duty. That's all there is to say.'

'I know. I just wanted you to know where I stood.'

'We knew that already, even before we decided to come,' the father retorted.

Again, there was silence. Maren walked to the wide tropical window, its shuttered lid propped outwards on a hinged wooden rod. For a while he stood still, looking out. 'What a *penkelemes*!' he sighed.

'What?'

He turned round, a rueful smile on his face. 'She came back, you know. Of her own volition. She had returned to her fiancé, the one her family approved. I was the nomad, the ne'er-do-well, dangerous confrontationist, the womaniser and peril-at-large . . .'

'We-e-ell?' That was the father.

'Conceded. Lots of exaggeration but, we'll let it stand. I'm simply trying to remind you of something. She was engaged to someone else, and I came into her life. Then the fiancé returned from "de abroad", straight into a steady job and solid prospects. You talk family, family. Well, her family also talked to her about family. They said to her, Who is this bum? And eventually she took note and, one day, she moved in with her former fiancé. I was devastated . . .'

'But very soon consoled,' grinned the father.

His protest was vehement. 'Could you let me be serious for just one moment?'

'Go ahead, go ahead,' but he continued laughing. 'No one is stopping you.'

'I *was* devastated,' he persisted. 'De-va-sta-ted! Oh, you're still laughing.'

'Sorry. I'm listening. We're both paying full attention.'

He sighed. 'You don't believe me, of course, because I don't discuss these things with you. Serves me right.'

'Indeed,' said the mother, with vengeful, undisguised satisfaction.

He felt frustrated. 'I am trying to recall your minds to the entire see-saw proceedings. Him, then me, then him, and again, me . . . such things happen. A woman, or man, outgrows one phase, represented by a human being, focussed on a human being, by circumstances, by the specifics of an emotional need, sometimes even a social need – from which, may the good lord protect the man or the woman, but – it happens. Now that is the background of which we are both a part. I never bring it up. I do not discuss it with her. Ask her, I never have. Never! What this means is that we have been trying to make something work, by ourselves, and it works better without outside interference, without arrangements interposed by others. It stands a better chance if left alone. She knows what I am. There was a woman in my bed when she returned, and there have been other women. Don't look shocked now . . .'

'We are both beyond shock,' the father assured him. 'It's a waste of time getting shocked by you. We would just like to know where all this is leading. Why now? Why are you telling us this now?'

'But I've just told you why. This has not been your traditional boy-meets-girl-families-embrace-one-another kind of wedding-bells situation. The two families cannot now begin to act up, and in concert, over a history that is known only to one side.'

'Even where children are involved?'

Back to the beginning, sighed the son, and finally accepted the futility of further discussion. As if not one word of all that went before had been uttered, he asked, as evenly as he could: 'At what level is this being planned? Feasting? Music and dancing?'

'We don't like noise any more than you do.'

'Oh, not you. But suppose they decide to make a big thing of it?'

The father shrugged. 'There is nothing we can do about that. It has to take place in the – in the home of the woman.'

Maren nodded. 'Yes.' He took a deep breath. 'Well, you must do what you have to do. This is very simply a question of two families getting introduced to each other, isn't it?'

There was hesitation. 'Well, ye-e-es.'

'More than that?'

'Not that much more but, yes, a little more,' the father admitted.

'How much more?' He pressed on, anxious to bring the discussion to an end. 'If I said that the ceremony amounts to two families getting married to each other, would that be too far off?'

The father smiled. 'I suppose it's one way of putting it.'

'Good. Now I have a clearer picture of the kind of ceremony it's going to be. It is really a thing between two families, one that does not require my presence at all.'

The mother protested. 'It would be nice if . . .'

'No. I give my approval, and that's it. You'll do it anyway, it's out of my hands, so, since I can't persuade you out of it, I prefer that you do it with my consent. But I shan't be there. I may look in at the very end, when nearly everyone has left. May do. I can have someone come and tip me off when virtually everyone has gone, and there is only her immediate family at home.'

The mother pursed her lips, evidently unhappy. He tried to tease her out of it. 'Oh, look at you both, at your age, getting married again.'

'And whose fault is that?'

'Mine, mine, mine, am I denying it? If I had taken care to remain obscure, this would not be happening. At least, I would be able to handle it the way I choose, the way I really am.' He heard his voice rising in anger at no one in particular. 'I meet a woman, fall in love with her or we simply find we're compatible; she agrees to live with me; a child comes or does not come in the order of things and that, for me, is marriage – by whatever name. Mutual consent. And to be mutually dissolved if it comes to that, with a moslem-type simplicity at its best. To you that's heresy but, that's the code by which I live. For me, it's the genuine bond, not church or court registry, not even the traditional ties or exchange of vows in any idiom. What people call formal marriage has no meaning for me; it never has. When I see a man and a woman contentedly together, I don't ask for their marriage certificate. It's sufficient for me that they consider themselves married to each other, that they're content to be together, that they accept responsibility for anything they bring into the world, and continue to do so even if the union collapses . . .'

He was stopped by the bored expression on their faces. 'All right. You've heard it all before. And they've all heard it from me too, she included, oh yes, dozens of times. All right, it's settled. The ceremony goes ahead whenever you wish. God bless these elastic

traditions, that's all that is left to say. Go and marry their family.'
He injected his voice with a solemn resonance, raised his hands as
if above their heads but kept his distance and intoned: 'You – have
– my – blessing.'

She swung her handbag at his head, but it was only a feeble
attempt at response to his belated effort to dispel the strain of the
afternoon's exchange. Her swing lacked its usual verve, and he
ducked in a desultory fashion, just a token gesture, and he caught
the handbag even more easily than usual. He had restored it to her
before he recalled that he had not bothered to retaliate, as he normally would, by rifling its contents.

He was up early the following morning, eager to make up for the
time lost on the family intrusion. He knew it was hopeless from
the start, hence his decision to identify beyond doubt those who
had participated in the 'peace meeting', what they had said, and
what degree of complicity one could, within – not beyond – reasonable doubt, attribute to them in the present turn of events. But he
made the effort anyway. He spent all morning going from lecturer
to lecturer, cajoling, arguing, pleading and threatening. If it is Aluko
today, it may be you tomorrow. You think your views are moderate
but power is rapacious, especially power in the hands of small men.
Power needs to dominate. When the Hortons and the Oyenuga and
the Aluko are gone, they will turn on the moderates; they will
demand more and more and will never be content until you grovel
before their might. All it takes is for us to organise. We can defend
the campus. We can say to them, Don't ever come into the campus;
if you do, we will down tools. All teaching will stop. We can go to
court, get a restraining order against the Government. The University has to remain a repository of alternative ideas, a sanctuary. I
don't care how it's defended, but we could begin with the courts . . .

He was rewarded with snorts of derision. 'The courts. The courts!
You've seen what the Government has been doing with the courts,
haven't you? You think any court will grant us accelerated hearing?
You think we could ever get them to grant us quick relief?'

'But you have yet to try!'

'It's a hopeless idea. The time would be more usefully spent
resettling the family.'

Confronted with a succession of hung heads and a stubborn pessimism, he sighed. 'You just do not understand, do you? First it was Ibadan, and see what tools they used to destroy the place. Now they've come down to thugs. THUGS! So what will they try next? Flush out dissidents by invading the campus with lepers? Why not?'

The notion was not far-fetched. In 1963, during campaigns towards the Federal elections, one of the favourite tactics of the Northern People's Congress, the Government party and powerful ally of the NNDP, was to seek out the rented homes or offices of opposition leaders, then take rooms, apartments or entire floors in the same building, and install lepers in them. The allies of such opposition leaders were favourite targets for the leprosy ejection treatment. These invaders went to sleep in a reasonably sanitised environment, woke up in the morning and wondered how their allies, whom they had come to assist, could have lodged them in a leprosarium. The lesser-known cadres were simply charged in the Alkali courts on any trumped-up charge, sentenced to lengthy terms and locked away. Lawyers who travelled north to defend such party workers who had fallen foul of the rough-and-ready tactics, failed to locate their clients or were hounded out of their hotels by a series of unpretty stratagems. The women of the North were especially vulnerable. They were loathed! They had not only broken social and religious norms by their public militancy, they had allied themselves with *keferi*, unbelievers from the South, with Kanuri and Tiv pagans, to undermine the feudal complacency of the North. It was an unforgivable crime. Some, like Salawa Gambo, who imbibed her radicalism at the feet of Fumilayo Ransome-Kuti, were declared common prostitutes, tried, gaoled and sexually assaulted into the bargain.

A Native Administration prison in Kano was notorious for a somewhat coprophiliac method of eliminating particularly troublesome political activists. Yon da Kolo, a businessman and politician from Lagos, never wearied of narrating his narrow escape even after he sank into a mire of alcoholism that would eventually lead to his death. He found himself in this prison, after judgement in an impromptu civil charge, all oral, brought against him by a trading partner whom he had, in the first place, travelled up from Lagos to confront. His mission was to recover money that the Alhaji, his partner, had defrauded from his company, Dizengoff.

Such defence tactics were not uncommon throughout the country, but rarely, in other parts of the country, would the accuser find himself in prison after a few minutes' summary trial, without being given a chance to call witnesses or produce documents. It was the Alhaji's word against his, in the former's solid zone of influence, and da Kolo found himself accused, tried and sent to a Native Administration prison until he could produce the money that his trading partner now alleged was owed him. His partner also ensured that he was confined in this particular prison, having informed the judge privately that da Kolo was a southern politician come to campaign for the NCNC, and had tried to enrol him for his campaign against the Emir, counting on the fact that they were friends and business partners.

At night, Yon da Kolo asked to be taken to the toilets to relieve himself. It was the common dug-out toilet, some distance from the cells. A trusty was charged with the task and they had almost reached the spot when the night warder, just come on duty, came running after them, shouting to the trusty in Hausa. They stopped, he caught up with them, and then he led da Kolo to another toilet. At the time, Yon da Kolo imagined that the other toilet was merely a cleaner one, and that the senior warder had thought the first unbefitting a man of his stature. Even so, he remained puzzled by the warder's demeanour; he sweated profusely, his hands could not cease trembling and he kept repeating something that sounded like a prayer, since it was frequently punctuated by the word 'Allah'. And the warder warned him not to go near the first toilet under any circumstances, no matter who tried to urge him to use it. Do it in your cell, he counselled, if matters get desperate; I shall get the trusty to clean it up, the *banza*!

Not until the morning of his discharge, some ten days later, his company having finally located him and come to his rescue, did Yon da Kolo receive an explanation about the two toilets. The warder took him aside, told him to sacrifice a ram for thanksgiving on returning home. The first toilet, he revealed, was the home of a viper, kept specially there for the purpose of despatching certain kinds of public nuisances, mostly those who had become menaces to the feudal order. The victim let down his trousers, squatted to commence business and out of the dark corner, the viper struck. Some *penkelemes*!

The NNDP had not yet resorted to catching a few vipers and throwing them through the windows of dissident lecturers, but perhaps matters might yet come to that. Certainly their thugs had their own refined methods for dealing with opposition. Apart from burning down houses, and inflicting machete, cudgel, crowbar and broken-bottle wounds and deaths, they had recently taken to raping the wives of the opposition, preferably in the presence of the husband himself. A rebellious Assistant Commissioner of Police in Iyaganku, Ojeli, was a disgusted source for details of many such incidents, such as the violation of a legislator's wife, whose husband was not merely held down as she was raped, but was repeatedly struck and slashed to make him chant the refrain 'Fani the Power' to the obscene song with which the rapists accompanied their task. The man, a Western legislator from Ilesha, showed unusual character in his decision to report the assault to the police, but Ojeli's view was that he was simply dazed out of his senses. Confronted with this unimaginable infliction, at least in the circumstances of postcolonial, post inter-tribal, post slave-raid conflicts, he had simply become confused. For this was a kind of family shame that one kept a careful secret, confided to the patient memory of ancestors, or else exorcised in a brutal, vengeful way.

No matter, he drove his wife, not even to a hospital but all the way to the seat of Government, Ibadan, where he was an honourable member of the House of Assembly, led her violated body into the headquarters of law enforcement and made her tell her story. Then they were sat down behind the desk, the Assistant Commissioner said, and made to write their formal statement.

I had thought, Ojeli admitted, that the very effort of putting their humiliation down in writing would do the trick but no, they wrote everything down, to the last detail. It was very strange, he said, here was this respected member of society, someone his electorate looked up to in time of trouble, their final refuge if you like, and he was admitting in writing that this thing had happened to him, to his family. But he did not seem to mind. He just wanted to make the report like any other person – frankly, I think he had lost his mind.

So I had to take them both to my office, I read the statements out and I asked him: Honourable Sir, are you sure? Are you sure you want to make a report? Because if I take this up, it will have to go to court. The media will get hold of it, they will publish it in all its lurid details, and then you, and madam, will still have to live in your community, among your own people. Are you sure you want me to go ahead?

That was the moment that it all sank in. They looked at each other, and it was as if they had found themselves in an alien world, whose rules, or rather, lack of rules, had just begun to dawn on them. But the rules, or at least the usages of the society they knew still held them bound and helpless. They looked at each other, turned their faces to stare at his office carpet, said Ojeli, and then they stood up, thanked him, and left quietly. They did not even remember to ask for the return of their statements; he kept them.

The thugs of the opposition were no better. There was a difference, however: they did not command the protection of the state, neither in Lagos nor in the regions. The East was the one exception, and it was not unusual for the Eastern Premier, Dr Michael Okpara, to send reinforcements to his allies in Awolowo's West in an emergency. Thugs were everywhere, billeted in sumptuous houses, in secret camps, transported in police vehicles and provided full state protection. The nightclubs became their night haunts; each group marked out its own preserves and it was a most unfortunate individual indeed that wandered into the wrong club, one that had become the territory of an opposing party. If he had not really earned enemy prominence in the ratings of the other side, he could easily ransom himself with a round of beer for the stalwarts, even pass the night in a truce of mutual bantering. It was another story if he was on the party's 'Wanted' list.

It was barely a month since a feeling of unease had crept over him, as he headed for Oshogbo one Saturday afternoon, making him twist restlessly on the driving seat, sending his thoughts awry, incapable of focussing in any one direction. Try as he would, he could no longer recover the sense of anticipation with which he had left Ibadan. The prospect of watching a new play at Mbari Mbayo, Duro Ladipo's offshoot of the parent Mbari in Ibadan, was becoming less and less enticing. Palm wine, pounded yam with goat meat or bush meat stew after the show, the resident *juju* band, made up of Duro's own company, Twins Seven-Seven and company, playing till the late hours – he had succeeded in 'saving' an entire weekend to indulge in the pleasures of Oshogbo. Watching Susan Wenger at work on her batiks was a therapy; she was so much at peace that it radiated through the house as she worked, this strange Austrian woman, who had found a home among the Yoruba, found her own goddess and become her priestess. She had strange ideas sometimes and they would argue passionately. Why, he queried once, is the ground floor of your three-storey building always so filthy? Goats were allowed free entrance and their faeces littered the floor in competition with chicken droppings, there was dust of several days' thickness, used plates left unwashed, and a general air of domestic decay or indifference, in such marked contrast to her apartment on the top floor where she lived with her husband, Ulli Beier. Yet this was where she worked, it was her main studio, her reception room where the local women – traders, worshippers, priestesses, house-wives – came to consult, or simply to sit with her, and some men also, including chiefs from Oshogbo, Ede, and Ilobu. And in spite of the filth, especially at dusk, Maren would sit and watch, sipping palm wine, drifting off into his own thoughts and distractedly listening to the life of Oshogbo and neighbouring villages as it filtered through the web of community that she had spun around her being.

But the dirt continued to annoy him. 'Why must you keep this place so filthy?' he would ask.

'Oh yes, you bourgeoisie, everything has to be trim and proper for you; you are so proper, you are losing your soul to artificial order, abandoning spontaneity. If I make this place the way you would like to see it, my women will not feel comfortable in it, I shall alienate them. They will feel it is an *oyinbo* place.'

He flared up. 'That is a slander, and it is so damned patronising.' And he would proceed to lecture her all over again, how the traditional Yoruba compound is so wedded to cleanliness that the sight of a child playing where there is litter or dirt within the compound would earn such a child a clip on the ear or he would be made to skip the next meal as punishment. A child could play around only when there was no more work, visible to the eye of the child, a decision requiring only the child's own initiative. And the first among such visible chores was keeping the home clean. 'So your thinking is warped there,' he would admonish, 'very warped, and the next child that enters this place, place the broom in the hand, however young, and that child will know what to do.'

It remained the sore point between them until he found she had given in and changed the unwholesome principle of her generous, accommodating being. Her huge cement sculptures which littered Osun Grove left him with ambiguous feelings; sometimes, he felt reconciled with their presence; other times, he felt that they lacked *presence*; and other times still, he would feel distinctly hostile to their existence. It is an act of great self-abnegation to surrender a place of collective spirituality to the concrete language of one individual, however talented, and to dominate the fluid essence, the *mystery* of an ancient shrine with mono-structured emplacements, assertive, therefore obtrusive. But the grove remained a place of pilgrimage, and it was like a continuing dialogue on both the artistic and spiritual plane, to leave the home of Susan Wenger and stroll down in the early morning, through the just-awakening markets and down to Osun River, meander through the grove, pausing in places simply to float idle, rid of constraints, or resume the dialogue with Susan's traditional competitors for the mantle of the gods.

And Oshogbo was the hinterland outpost of what they had begun in Mbari. It was casting up new artists of varied talents, experimenting in various media – oils, acrylic, bronze plates and aluminium, bead, sand and seed collages, silk print and explosive fabric designs – each visit was a new revelation . . . It was to these that he looked forward when he set out for a weekend of escape from the violence and betrayals of Ibadan, to get drunk on art and palm wine, not neglecting dalliance with the languid courtesans, who blended the grace of rural discretion with an ardour that contented the most demanding . . .

Until the unease crept all over him, pimples on his skin, instigating a severe itch in his palms and a tingling in his hair-roots. For several miles he sought to play down the feeling but finally he acknowledged defeat, turned his vehicle back in the direction of Ibadan, and at once felt relaxed, but puzzled. He drove straight to his new house in Felele, arriving after dark. He encountered neither illness nor news of death at home, indeed no sad or sinister messages, no outward sign of danger or misadventure anywhere. He made an extra check on all the doors and windows of the house, ensured that they were secure. The nightwatchmen had named him an honorary watchman on account of his prolonged midnight walks in an area that was still partly forested; he went and spoke to them, picking up the day's most recent political gossip; everything was as before. Then he returned home, gave the house a final check, and went to sleep, knowing it would be a light, uneasy slumber.

The knock on the door came just after midnight, only half an hour after his head had touched the pillow. It was a two-storey house, with a balcony overlooking the frontage from the upper floor. He got up cautiously, dressed, went to the front room, and peeped through the curtains. The front door to the ground-floor flat was beneath the hanging balcony, so it was impossible to see whoever was at the door. The knock was repeated.

'Who is it?'

'Na police, sah.'

'Ah.' He felt relieved at last. So this was it. 'Give me one moment; I'm coming down.'

He slammed the door to the upper front room, opened it again, and returned to the window. He scanned the bushes, trees, and strained his neck to see the vehicles parked at a distance from the house. One was a taxi, another a pick-up in what could be the dark blue police colours. A third vehicle was parked even further away, a large-sized saloon car whose make or colour he could not discern. Straining his eyes still further in the poor light, he caught sight of clothing and movement among the shrubs. He waited a little longer, then went back to the bedroom and locked the door on his family. From his study, he picked up the only weapon in the house, a mere air-rifle, retraced his steps and silently opened the door to the balcony.

He waited in the dark corner of the balcony. As he expected, a third round of knocking ensued, more impatiently. In the meantime, he had continued to scan the movements in the bushes, seen other figures glued to the dark sides of the walls of neighbouring houses, mostly uncompleted and unoccupied. All in all, he guessed, there must be twelve to fifteen people in the raiding party. He decided to respond to the knocking.

'You say you are the police?'

'Yes, sir. We've come to talk to you.'

'Step out from under this balcony so I can see you.'

Two men obliged, looking up. They could not see him, however. One of them was in police uniform – the Native Administration police. The other wore mufti. Maren moved to the railing from where he would be visible, raised the air-rifle over the railing. The air-rifle was the kind that was operated on a downward breech lever, with a noisy snap-up. He operated it now, its metallic clack resounding with intimidating effectiveness in the silence of the night. In that same silence, his voice must have carried for miles around.

'Since you are policemen, you will be able to recognise this, and you know what it is capable of. I shall now begin to count from one – to ten. At the count of ten, I shall begin to fire. I intend to shoot at anything standing, moving or surrendering. One!'

'Sir, we are just here to . . .'

'Since when have police begun to harass innocent citizens at night? Two!'

'Sir, please, it is not an arrest. We were instructed to investigate . . .'

'Standing. Running. Even with hands raised in surrender. And I am coming after those who are in hiding. I can see you all clearly from here. THREE!'

They broke, and fled. From all nooks and corners, like a worm-infested firewood when the heat has reached the hollows, they scurried out, calling on God, Allah, Sopona, Sango, fleeing in a hundred directions, falling into ditches, stumbling over cement blocks, over surface pipes, culverts, scrambling over low walls, diving under hedges and crashing their way through like the Gadarene swine in diabolic possession.

Near the junction of the road where the private car was parked, Maren saw a pot-bellied figure wrapped in white emerge from behind a hedge and race towards the car. He was soon overtaken by the far more nimble interlopers. They piled into the car, which took off at full speed, ignoring the fat man who kept waving to them to stop. Fatso then changed direction, heading for the taxi. The taxi driver appeared to have woken up just as the man opened the door. He took off with one leg of his desperate passenger still outside, so there he was, hopping on one leg, trying to keep up with the taxi on the uneven road, clinging to the door, until they turned the corner and were out of Maren's sight. Maren recognised who it was. It made him race out of the balcony, now determined to catch at least one of the raiders so he could use his confession to publicly accuse the mastermind of the raid. He had identified the likeliest fugitive, the figure headed towards the darkest part of that area where he was very much at home with his night walks. He took off after him, shouting to the watchman he knew would be at the end of that track, guarding one of the buildings under construction, to assist in cutting him off.

It was a futile hunt, however, as he realised after nearly an hour in the bush. For a start, all the nightwatches had also vanished when they heard the threat of shots, although he was not to know this until he had given up and begun to drag his frustrated self homewards. They emerged one by one, admitting without a trace of embarrassment that they had simply holed up and refused to budge as soon as the countdown began.

F.R.D. – as he was mostly known – was something of a maverick. In youth, he had been a member of the Zikist Movement, then moved into the camp of Awolowo, whose Private Secretary he eventually became. He became a passionate Action Group partisan, until the split within the party, playing an honourable role of arbitrator until he felt that he had to choose. Then, in his usual forthright manner, he confronted his leader, Chief Obafemi Awolowo, accused him of inflexibility, of placing at risk Yoruba fortunes within the national polity and informed him that, on that account, he was shifting his allegiance to Chief Akintola. Maren admired his principled stand and, despite his own contempt for the politics of the breakaway NNDP, they remained friends, arguing incessantly on the rights and wrongs of every Nigerian party and policy. It was the same F.R.D. who had warned him of the impending raid of Government thugs on *Before the Blackout*.

It was difficult to tell when F.R.D. began to go mad. What before was tolerated as a trait of blunt irreverence crossed over the border into megalomania. The lavish, limitless spending within NNDP circles probably took its toll on him eventually, a real tragedy, since F.R.D. was one of the few followers of Awolowo who were not bought, but quit their leader on principle. Delusions of grandeur followed, an exaggeration of self-importance in the labyrinthine politics of the party, of alliances, of the local politics of his home-town. His counsel, shrewd at times, inane and impractical more often, became unassailable, in his mind, for any projections of the party's fortunes. He moved around with a caseful of files copiously cross-referenced and a retainer following him from car to office, from office to meetings: then not just one retainer but two or three. He demanded audience at will, cursing when the audience was declined. Unable to appreciate his diminishing importance or influ-ence within the party, he persisted in championing causes that were of no interest to his health or that of his party; they were simply causes that gave F.R.D. the powers – he imagined – of intervention. At the very nadir of his influence, he complicated his existence by a sexual malady that called itself love and drained him of the largesse from the NNDP as fast as he succeeded in replenishing it. The object of F.R.D.'s infatuation, an *ingénue*, was blessed with a shrewd, unscrupulous manager – her mother – with whom he had also had an affair. Working together, they plucked him like a well-tuned, dutifully responsive instrument and – probably – exacerbated his as-yet-merely-suspect mental decomposition.

Maren could think of any number of slights – real or imagined – that might have led F.R.D. to the midnight invasion of his home, not least of which could be an attempt to prove himself to the party as one who did not hesitate to deal even with a former associate of increasing irritation to the party. Certainly he had been teased often enough about the strange company he kept, his insistence on keeping his links with dissidents and critics of the Government. As expected, he had tried to intervene in the tussle between the Univer-sity and Government, but neither side paid him any serious atten-tion, least of all Maren. Could that have constituted the unforgivable snub? Then there had been incidents of a personal, near violent nature. Maren, stung by a slander carelessly inaugurated by the interfering maverick, had once gone to his house, invited him to get dressed and join him on his own lawn for a beating. He had entered the house snorting summary justice, crashed into his bedroom, only to find F.R.D. snoring in bed, stark naked, his rotund belly heaving and resettling like a mound of *amala* being moulded onto a serving dish. There was no way he could have inflicted any punishment on him in such a helpless state, so he reeled out his catalogue of crimes, called him every name his mother declined to give him, then assigned him two minutes to get dressed, while he went out, *preux chevalier* of combat rules, and waited for him in the living room. F.R.D., hopelessly short-sighted without his glasses, blinked and blinked, nodded his agreement to the gentlemanly consideration, and watched him leave the bedroom. Then he sensibly locked the connecting door against the rampaging lunatic, made his escape through the bathroom window and was last seen haring down the road, hailing a taxi and heading for the nearest police station.

Some such slight or the other must have become magnified in his mind, or else it was a case of sheer opportunism. Drained and wrung dry by the mother-and-paramour team, F.R.D. must have become desperate for some way of regaining favour with the party. What was certain – it was not difficult to find out the facts – was that he had informed the Premier that Maren and his 'boys' were planning an assault on top personalities close to the Premier. He had uncovered the plot purely by chance and confronted Maren with the facts, urging him to abandon his diabolical mission. Maren had pretended to accede to his plea, bided his time, then marched into his house to attempt to silence him permanently. The distant incident of Maren's punitive intent on his person came in handy – F.R.D's lurid accounts had been formally recorded in the police incident log book, terminating with a *deus ex machina* account of how, but for such an intervention, the NNDP would have lost a valued defector.

The Premier, it was reported, teased him without mercy, repeated yet again that it served him right. Trying to hunt with the hounds and run with the hare had only one result; he hoped he had now learnt his lesson. All the same, he passed him on to his Special Services man who sent a note to the Native Administration Police at Yemetu. Four police were provided to lend legitimacy to the operation while party 'stalwarts' made up the rest of the assault force. Maren was to be taken, his house given the full treatment. No decision had been made regarding what should actually be done with the quarry once he was in the net. Perhaps this was left entirely to the discretion of the complainant himself; the Premier, and indeed his cohorts, had no real interest in the outcome, deriving their pleasure solely from the prospect of watching the party maverick abandon his moral corner and join the mainstream party culture.

For weeks afterwards, F.R.D. went around with two armed police escorts, one by the driver in the front seat of his car, the other next to him in the back. His report to the Premier on the night's misadventure provided weeks of hilarity among the party hierarchy. Their mission, he complained, was a perfectly legitimate one, sanctioned by the Premier's directives to his Hatchet-Man-in-Chief, and the presence of four policemen. Maren had, however, produced a machine-gun against the arm of the law, read the riot act and, not content with the fact that the police had commenced an orderly retreat, pursued and hunted them all night throughout suburban Ibadan. He, who had accompanied the police simply as the eye of the Premier, to keep watch on operations and ensure that they did not get out of hand, had been abandoned in the most cowardly manner by his own driver, or more accurately, by the party stalwarts who piled into his car and left him stranded. Even the hired taxi had dragged him for several yards before he succeeded in extricating his foot from the vehicle – all this because the madman with the machine-gun was at their heels, firing long bursts at any motion in the night. He had dived into the bush and taken cover, then walked all night through the bush, seeking disused tracks, keeping off the main roads because this homicidal maniac was lurking beneath stones and materialising behind electricity poles, determined to finish him off.

'You trekked all the way from Felele to Odo Ona, F.R.D.?' the Premier was reputed to have shrieked in his inimitable falsetto.

'My Premier, that man is a bloodthirsty animal.'

Chief S. L. Akintola was tickled. 'So he is now a bloodthirsty animal? When he began his bloodthirsty dramatic sketches against us, and we decided to take action, weren't you the same person who began preaching at us the sermon of free speech?' He broke into his ready routine of wicked mimicry. ' "If a hair on Maren's head is touched" . . . oh, was I watching you, and despairing of you half-

and-half academics that day! I kept saying to myself, look at this too-know we have been foolish enough to admit into the party.'

'My Premier,' F.R.D. protested. 'This is no laughing matter, sir. The man has gone mad. My life is in danger.'

'All right, all right. Go and see the Commissioner of Police. Arrange with him whatever protection you need.'

VIII Heretics and Return Visitations

Before he chose opposition after the 1959 Federal elections, Obafemi Awolowo had offered Nnamdi Azikiwe power at the centre. The Northern People's Congress had obtained a parliamentary majority over each individual party, but the NCNC and the Action Group could have teamed up to form a majority and place the NPC in opposition. Awolowo declared himself ready to serve under Dr Azikiwe in any capacity. The NCNC, however, chose to become a junior partner in a Government led by the NPC.

That alliance broke down as the parties commenced skirmishes towards the next battle for power at the centre, long before the actual elections of 1964. It was only a matter of time, and the NCNC announced its union with the Action Group under the name UPGA, the United Progressive Grand Alliance. On their part, the NPC and the NNDP formalised their relationship under the umbrella of the Nigerian National Alliance, a name regarded by many in the South as a reluctant concession to disguise the reality of its composition and ambitions, the latter being the domination of the entire nation under the reality of a Nigerian *Northern* Alliance.

Michael Okpara, the NCNC leader and Premier of the Eastern Region, was now in a unique position. Although UPGA, which included allies both in the North and the Middle Belt, had agreed to boycott the 1964 elections, alleging malpractices, terror tactics and pre-determined results in the North, West and Lagos even before the voting, the elections went ahead anyway. North and West were controlled by the Nigerian National Alliance whose main arm, the NPC, controlled the Federal Government. The boycott suited the Government, and it simply ignored every miserable protest.

In the East, however, the NCNC controlled the State Government, and Premier Okpara had effectively prevented any semblance of an election, backed solidly by a rebellious electorate. A stalemate ensued. Zik of Africa, the Governor-General and Commander of the Armed Forces, took his titles seriously for a while, and refused to swear in the 'victorious' party of the NNA with Tafawa Balewa once again as Prime Minister of the nation. The Chief Justice of the Federation, Sir Adetokunbo Ademola, was summoned to interpret the powers of the Governor-General vis-à-vis his Prime Minister. He went accompanied by his fellow Justice Louis Mbanefo, and both told Azikiwe in polite but blunt terms that he had no powers, that his titles were mere window dressing – a confrontation that Orisun Theatre celebrated in *April Fools' Ship*. Azikiwe capitulated, endorsed the NPC-NNDP as the victorious party and swore in Tafawa Balewa. Michael Okpara set a new date for Eastern elections, vengefully suppressing all opposition to the NCNC in his region. The West turned out to be the losers, with their allies, the progressive Northern Elements Progressive Union, NEPU, and a straggle of die-hard Middle-Belt rebels as companions in misery.

The people of the West only waited, however, watched and waited. The regional elections were not far off, and there they were resolved to make a stand. There would be no more boycotts, no more concessions. The breakaway party of S. L. Akintola sensed the aggressive mood; it was equally determined to eliminate all opposition.

Along the way, the NNDP identified the academic sector as the main obstacle to a total control of popular thought – an erroneous conception, but this was the meat it was fed by its own eyes and minds in academia. This dissident sector had to be crushed, and the populace had to be shown that its champions within the ivory tower were not merely silenced, but humiliated.

Right or wrong, Maren thought, as he headed for Oke Ado and Seven Sisters, this is my reading of this reality, this is why a readily available mercenary force of the Government has been brought in to 'teach the acadas a lesson', and with maximum publicity. Seven Sisters was just emptying of its lunchtime clientèle; he looked around but none of his 'friends' was around. Relieved to find that Kodak, his main target, had been seen around the club earlier in the day, he gave the barman's boy sufficient money to track him down wherever he was in Ibadan, ordered some beer and settled down to wait.

Kodak – Maren never bothered to ask him the origination of his name – had joined the circle of 'friends' only six months after he returned from prison. Their contact stemmed from a violent incident that had taken place right on the frontage of Mbari Club almost a year to the date after his homecoming. Gbagi, where Mbari was situated, was, at the best of times, a hive of commercial chaos. During the festive seasons, however, most especially at christmas and the New Year, Gbagi became a venue for every kind of entrepreneur, from genuine agents of dubious Indian and Lebanese bargains to tinsel racketeers and 'Lucky Dip' operators. Kodak belonged to the last group.

Their method was simple. They planted a large packing case in a street corner or any available pedestrian thoroughway, the packing case being filled with beautifully wrapped packages of all shapes and sizes. For a fixed sum, the passer-by picked out a package and – that was his or her luck. Naturally, they had first planted among the crowd members of their own gang who tried their luck, opened their packages and screamed with delight as they pulled out gold watches, jewellery and even wads of banknotes. Mbari kept clear of both conmen and gulls; it was not the business of its members to police public cupidity or gullibility.

Maren had driven in one afternoon for rehearsals, however, parked his car and headed for the entrance to the club. And then he stopped, attracted by the demeanour of an elderly woman, and the especial attention being paid to her by Kodak and one of his henchmen. The woman was obviously in some kind of dilemma, the 'Lucky Dip' operators had become aware of it and were egging her on. Something out of the ordinary was taking place, something of greater lucrative potential than the profits to be made from the casual passer-by staking the odd shilling that would not be missed. The woman appeared frightened, yet fascinated; the relation of her gaze to the box was identical to that of a rat hypnotised by a snake before its sudden lunge. The two men crowded her, bullying and cajoling her all in the same breath. She was a frail, lost-looking creature, clearly a stranger to Ibadan, caught unexpectedly in the wiles and guiles of a strange city which, however, promised something unusual, exciting and profitable.

Maren moved towards her – she reminded him in some way of his paternal grandmother but that was only by the way; he sensed at once that she was about to get into serious trouble. A woman was with him in the car, so he told her to go inside and see who was around, in case he needed help, but he found that she waited beside the car anyway. Suddenly, the hairs rose on his skin and he knew that the old woman, and he, were in very serious danger. He snarled at the companion again to get help from inside Mbari, rushed forward to drag the old lady from danger but, before he could intervene, Kodak had struck the woman hard on the chest. He saw his hand dive inside her *buba* and emerge with a package. The next second, the package had flown over the heads of the crowd to a waiting accomplice. Then the assailant strode casually away from the scene of his crime, very cool and indifferent, as if he was just another passer-by, nothing remotely like the owner of the frenzied salesman's voice that daily deprived the optimistic, or merely curious, of their shillings. When Maren looked briefly away for a moment, to see how the prostrate woman was faring, the thug was gone, and the crowd was milling around like a speeded-up mass of ants whose normal rhythms had been disturbed.

The woman screamed, clutching her breast: '*Owo mi o! Owo mi o! Ah, iba ti e j'owo mi!**

Kodak's assistant pushed a wrapped package into her hands and laughed. '*Iya*, what are you shouting about? This is your package, what more do you want?'

'But I had not decided anything. I did not put my hand in the Lucky Dip. I had not agreed to anything. And it is not my money he took. Did I hand it to him? It is money belonging to our trading group. They collected it and sent me with it to buy goods. Why should I want to spend my cooperative's collection on Lucky Dip? You all saw him – he snatched it from me.'

The partner in crime placed himself squarely in front of her, occupied himself with shouting her down, so Maren grabbed him

*My money! My money! Ah, if only it were my own!

by the shirt and spun him round. 'If you people don't return this woman's money . . .'

The villain turned to the crowd in exaggerated innocence. 'Hey, look *o*, just look this man *o*! What money have I taken? You are all witnesses – did anyone see me take money? Look, search me if you like, search me from top to bottom. I am just an innocent man trying to earn a decent penny for christmas – is that a crime?'

The next moment, a wiry, wild-eyed individual, obviously yet another member of the gang, dashed to the hardware stalls opposite, grabbed a machete and plunged into the crowd. As they scattered, he raced round in a circle, drawing the blade along the ground and raising sparks which threw the crowd into greater panic. He circled Maren twice, then began a war-dance facing all directions at once. Maren braced himself for the assault, looked quickly back to see if help was coming from Mbari but all he saw was his supposed messenger preening herself by the car, brimful of self-confidence and protective presence, posturing and daring the machete-man to do his worst. Sickened to the pit of his stomach, he felt a sudden movement from his captive and the next moment, the man had twisted himself out of his clutch. The rest was confusion in a flurry of motions. Yet another figure had appeared from the self-distancing crowd, scooped up the packing case and, covered by the machete-man, melted into the labyrinths of Gbagi. By then the Mbari crowd had heard the commotion and trooped out, but the air had turned miraculously peaceful, purged of all villainy. There was only the crumpled figure of the old woman on the ground, moaning and asking the world how on earth she was to return to Akure without the goods her guild had contributed their meagre capital to purchase, in their annual effort to make some local profit for the New Year season.

It became an obsession to catch the felons. The sense of loss in the prostrate woman reminded him of the far more quiescent bafflement and despair of his grandmother in Ìsarà, when her women's *esusu*,* entrusted to her for safe-keeping, had vanished from the nook in which she kept it. As a child, he had heard his

*A self-help scheme in which participants take possession of their collective savings in turn.

grandfather complain to his Headmaster son of the torment to which his wife had put him over the missing tin of money, how peace had eluded his household and he had had to flee to the sanctuary of the home of his second wife. The tin had turned up eventually; it had been taken by the *ogboni*, not for the cash it contained, but for certain cultic items which had belonged to her deceased brother. The old men brought back the tin one evening, and asked her to check the money she had left in it. Not a penny of it was missing and they had left, repeating that they had only taken what was theirs.

Something in the violation of this woman struck a chord deeply within his being; it was of an order with the violation that was all around him, the erosion of all that he held sacred. The blow that was delivered against the breast of the woman reverberated continuously inside him, making him lose concentration in the afternoon's rehearsals, indeed, depriving him of all his immediate capacity for judgement, be it of the artistic or unrelated kind. The woman was resting on a couch in the library while a collection was taken, most of the money coming from proceeds from previous performances. Then they put her in a public transport to return to Akure, advising her to have some other member return to Ibadan to make the purchases. The only promise that Maren extracted from her was that she would return to Ibadan after the New Year, to help identify her assailants.

He went to the local police station at Iyanganku, asked to see the most senior officer on duty. Tracking down the Lucky Dip gang was as easy as walking down any crowded street: sooner or later one was bound to catch up with them; the sign was a crowd, any crowd of any size surrounding the usually invisible object of attraction, and a sales voice that combined oiliness with hysteria. The Inspector of Police agreed that the gang had become a nuisance. The Lucky Dip was only a cover for the more lucrative asides of the business – pickpocketing especially, and the occasional violent robbery. It was agreed that Maren would send out his scouts from Mbari; as soon as the new location was identified, the Inspector would be contacted and a raid would follow.

Three times a raid was attempted, and each time, just before the arrival of the police, the gang melted away and regrouped at a new location. It was too uncanny a coincidence and the scouts, who waited to watch the raids, reported that the gang's movements had not been hurried, that they had not panicked, that they simply picked up their box of fake goodies and walked away as if to a schedule of itinerancy that had been prearranged. Moments later, the police trucks would arrive, disgorging fire-breathing officers who proceeded to strike terror into everyone in the vicinity, then pile back into their conveyance, grinning all the way back to their station.

On the third occasion, Maren selected a convenient shop from whose doorway he could watch the action. He focussed his attention on the ringleader, Kodak. Sure enough, a well-dressed figure approached the packing case, just like any other would-be gambler, dropped a coin into the hand of Kodak's assistant and picked up a package. And then he saw it – just a casual movement of the lips as he brushed past Kodak. Kodak did not react. The man went through the crowd and, once outside the ring of turned backs, flicked his package into the gutter without even bothering to examine it. Kodak gave a slight nod to his assistant and melted through his captive audience. The assistant picked up the box and moved in another direction while the man he recognised as the machete-man followed Kodak at a casual distance.

Five minutes later the police truck arrived, stampeded the rem-nants of the crowd and other christmas shoppers, charged in every direction, questioned innocent food- and cigarette-hawkers and some shopkeepers who sat outside their shops, then charged back into their truck at the end of a charade of an operation that had lasted no more than three or four minutes. It was so obvious to everyone within the neighbourhood, a familiar display of police *penkelemes*!

So he went higher, to the Assistant Commissioner, whose con-scientious logging of the decadent career of the NNDP, including the gang-raping of the legislator's wife, poured tirelessly into the indifferent ears of his superiors, had finally worn him down. He had requested a transfer from the Criminal Division, and it had been granted with record alacrity. He was no longer in charge of the Criminal Division, but was being groomed for the newly created 'E' branch, a section that would deal with internal security, subversion and allied threats to national stability. Then came the surprise, a fact of which the older man had been aware all the time: Ojeli, the Assistant Commissioner, was Maren's former Senior from Government College, Ibadan.

They would meet again soon, in slightly different circumstances, but he was not yet to know that. All he wanted was the head of Kodak on a potsherd, preferably at the crossroads where sacrifices to Esu are left, and if it was an 'old boy' that would bring it about, it was all the more credit to 'Up School'. All the household gods of the old woman from Akure were awake on that day, for Ojeli had also been assigned the duty of training a special squad, to be known as the Mobile Police, which would act independently of the regular police divisions. He would do the donkey work, train the 'specials', but he knew himself that he would not be placed in charge of them after their training; no, they would be transferred to other commands, to senior officers 'with fire in their eyes' and a pocket that was ever open to the thrust of the obliging party fists.

Ojeli listened to him dispassionately, smiled, nodded with understanding, and promised help. The next time that the Lucky Dip gang was located, Maren was to send to him directly. In the meantime he would place on alert a small squad of his trainees from the Mobile Police.

Mbari did not need to look far for Kodak and company the next time round. Emboldened by his control of information from the police, Kodak returned to the parking lot in front of the club. That confluence of roads, of passageways that were shortcuts to and from Dugbe market, and roadside stalls, was simply far too lucrative to be abandoned. The need to assert his authority over such territory, to tweak the noses of the *akowe** crowd who had served him notice that his presence at the gates of the house of culture was unsavoury, appealed to his bandit personality, so back he came, with four packing cases this time, and special inducements such as a free balloon or a plastic comb for any three or four dips at a time.

When the raid came, he was, for the first time, taken unawares. Maren had situated himself in his Land Rover at the top of the road before the left turn towards Adamasingba, at the corner where it could not be seen, determined not to miss any of the action. It was

*The literate or privileged class.

simply unfortunate that Kodak should choose that as his escape route, his muscle-bound body rippling through his chiefly *agbada*. Maren's heart skipped several beats. Of all the members of the gang that he would choose to tackle alone, the very last would be Kodak. The man was not only built like a tank; he had a mean personality – well, that did not take much arguing; anyone who could thump an old woman on the chest the way he did . . .

As the fugitive rounded the corner at the crossroads, heading towards the Baptist Church, Maren realised that he had still not seen the Land Rover, so he ducked to avoid being recognised through the windscreen, leaving the door off the latch. All he had to do now was listen for the heavy thump of the man's feet. As he heard the heavy panting almost by the door, he kicked it open with both feet, bracing himself against the steering wheel. Kodak staggered, dazed by the impact, then Maren found himself leaping out of the vehicle, twisting the man's *agbada* around his head, a motion which fortunately also imprisoned his gorilla-strength arms, and so wrestled him to the ground, trussed up like a mummy. By then the nearby shopkeepers had recognised him and come to his aid, soon followed by two of Ojeli's men at the run. They yanked him up and frog-marched him off to meet his companions. After the truck had left, Maren went behind the bar at Mbari to serve drinks all round, found that his hands were trembling so much that he could not continue, and had to call on Smith Eyo, the all-purpose assistant, to pour out the drinks.

Nine months later it was with a similar sense of clamminess and tremor in his hands that he found himself alone, that is, with only a sprinkling of strangers, on an afternoon at the Seven Sisters Club, when in walked Kodak. He had earned a year in prison, much of which had been remitted for good conduct. If anything, Kodak, filling in the bamboo frame that marked the entrance into the court-yard, looked ten times bigger than when he had last seen him. Their eyes met and held. Maren then turned away to his beer and emptied the remaining contents of the bottle into his glass. His hand went down to test the metallic leg of his chair, felt reassured. It was the kind that folded flat; it could serve as a defence long enough for him to back out through the entrance and seek the safety of the busy Oke Ado street.

The bandit, however, picked another table, far from where Maren was sweating, wondering how nice it would be if Buffalo Kid or Yellow were to walk in just then and provide the necessary deterrent. But Kodak merely ordered his usual stout and some fried bush meat, which he ate with a fussless deliberation that somehow managed to exude violence – but that, Maren thought, could have been just his own state of mind. Whatever it was, there was something in the way Kodak ate his bush meat that gave off a suggestion of just how the thug proposed to masticate his own body when he finally got round to that vengeful proceeding. It was surely time to leave but, explain it how he would, Maren could not bring himself to do so. Something held him back, sipping his beer and covertly watching this threat to his immediate health, or indeed existence. And then suddenly, without being aware of any conscious decision for such a move, he watched his other self get up, pick up his glass and walk over to join Kodak.

Nor did he experience any particular surprise that Kodak stood up as soon as he reached his table, his mouth agape, half the thigh of a grasscutter sticking out of his mouth. His manner was by no means aggressive, it evinced only some kind of dis- belief and a watchfulness that was part of his nature. Maren watched this stranger companion pull out a chair and beckon the waiter.

'Sit down, sit down,' Maren urged. 'I didn't mean to interrupt your meal. I was leaving, so I thought I should at least say hallo. I mean, you saw me after all when you came in, but you never acknowledged my existence. That was quite unnecessary.'

Kodak sat down slowly, masticating wordlessly. He did not take his eyes off Maren's face.

The waiter arrived. 'Bring another stout.' Maren smiled at the ex-convict. 'I know they don't serve that much stout where you were. When did you come out?'

Kodak appeared to find his voice at last. 'Last week. I have been in Akure since my discharge.'

'Akure? Is that your hometown?'

He shook his head. 'I went to look for the old lady.'

'Oh, your mother lives in Akure?' It was a strange expression for someone of Kodak's class to use, he thought, but perhaps he had picked up that expression in prison, among some *tiroro** convicts.

'No, I said I don't come from Akure. It was that old lady I went to look for . . . that one, you know . . . the trader.'

Maren's face hardened, his mind having turned in only one possible direction. 'I see. You left prison, and the first thing you did was go and look for the old woman. And then?'

'I went to beg her.' And his eyes dropped to the floor, away from his plate and the table, as if he wanted his eyes to encounter nothing but the lowest level of his existence. 'I went to beg her to forgive me, to forgive what we did to her.'

Slack-jawed, Maren could only stare at him, and wonder at the feeling of shame that overcame him. When he had heard Kodak's words his mind had gone in only one direction – the thug wanted to be revenged on the easiest target on which his little mind had conveniently focussed as the cause of his imprisonment. But the man had actually gone to apologise, to plead for forgiveness!

'You know, *oga†*, you were also to blame. No, don't think I am blaming you, I am not doing that.' His face worked desperately to find the right expression. 'What I want to say, sir, for next time, is – I will say it in Yoruba – *Owo ti e gbe fun wa yen, o le ju. Enh? E o mo wipe, bi baba l'e je fun wa. Nt'iwa o, omo yin la je.‡* You should have called us, admonished us . . .'

'Wait a minute. We did. When your accomplices began to pick pockets while you distracted the public, we called you and told you to cut it out.'

'And we did, sir, we did. I called my boys and told them, look, *Oga* Maren and the Mbari people, Mr Beier, Mrs Hendrickse, Mr Nwoko and the rest, they don't want that sort of business in front of their premises. Anyone whom I catch, I will give him a message that will make his own mother not recognise him. Believe me, we never picked another pocket in front of Mbari ever since you warned us.'

'And then you proceeded to do something worse. You beat up an

---

*Affected. Westernised.
†Boss.
‡The hand that you stretched out to us, it was too heavy. You are like a father to us, don't you know that? As far as we are concerned, we are your children.

old woman and stole her money. You remember what you were first charged with? Robbery with violence. You are lucky the prosecution decided to reduce it to a lesser charge of stealing. Or – was it altogether luck?'

His face puckered with the mischief of a child. 'Ah, there you see what I am saying, *oga*, others were not so hard on us. You were too hard, very hard. If the matter had been left to you, we would still have been in prison for a much longer time. You see, when it happened, you should have called me inside and said, "Look, I saw what happened, you must give that woman back her money." *Oga*, you know me, would I have argued with you? *Walahi*! We would have given it back, not one penny missing. I would only have begged you to make the woman give us something for all the trouble.'

'You would what?'

'Ah, *oga*, you were not there when it all began. That woman gave us trouble. She would not make up her mind. We could see that she had this money, and so one of my boys pulled her aside and told her that he would help her pull out the real lucky dip, the one that contained the real jackpot, but that it would cost her a lot of money. He asked her how much she was prepared to afford, and she actually told him how much she had on her. Sir, we suspended so much side business – not pickpocketing *o*, I swear we never did that in front of Mbari any more, but there were other things, and we suspended all that just to work on her . . .'

Maren interrupted. 'Kodak, all that is *awawi*.* What you did was vile. You pounded that woman's breast so hard, the ground shook beneath my feet . . .'

'I know, sir. I know. You said it at the station, and I could not forget it. *Oga*, when you said to me, "*B'o ti e n'iya nle, se b'omu iya e lo mu d'agba*,"† believe me, sir, you finished me that day. I just told my lawyer to leave me alone. I said I would plead guilty, if he could just get me a charge that did not carry ten years.'

'You are a lucky man.'

'And I just knew that as soon as I was discharged, I could not rest until I found the woman and begged her. You see, it was that

*Special pleading.
†Even if you have no mother at home, wasn't it at a woman's teats you were suckled?

thing you said. That is why I say that the hand you took with us, it was too heavy. Instead of bringing the police to chase us all over Ibadan, you could have called me, and shamed me as you did after we were caught.'

Maren ordered himself another beer, studying the man intently. Finally: 'I tend to believe you. But then you see, one never really knows with people. You will admit that there are others, even within your own gang, who would simply have laughed in my face. Any of them could have said to me, "Sorry sir, if you don't know about me, Mister Dokita, I was not raised on my mother's milk. I bit my way out of her womb and then I called for *ogogoro*, and that is what I have been drinking all my life. Not water, not even oyinbo tea." Yes, that is probably the kind of retort I would draw. Some of you would strangle your own mothers just to get at their life's savings.'

He laughed. '*Oga*, I can't say you don't talk true when I know that it is true you talk. That is why we are all different. *Howu*! Even you acada people are not all the same. We know those of you who say one thing during the day, then they sneak into the homes of politicians at night to say something different. They ask for favours and betray their own people. It's bad. We see them all the time, you know, we talk among ourselves. At least we know what we are. I have been a thug since I ran away from secondary school. I was too strong. Even the teachers were afraid of me. They were afraid to report me at home because they knew I would wait for them on the way home. So, I am a thug. I know what I am. And people are right to call us thugs, everyone calls us thugs but we're not all the same kind of thugs. There are some of us who will thug for any politician, as long as the pay is good. Some of them you will see on this side today, then they are fighting their former comrades tomorrow. For some of us, that is very bad. It is shameful. Some politicians, in fact, when they get broke, some of these ones who have become jobless because of the dirty work of NNDP and its NPC, believe it or not, sir, we not only thug for them, we give them money. We give it to their wives, or children, so they don't feel ashamed to be taking money from us. So we are all different, that's all I am trying to say . . .'

Kodak's massive figure now broke through Maren's recollections of their earlier encounters. He was panting slightly, beaming, he guessed, with anticipation. If Maren took the trouble to track him through Ibadan, 'dead or alive', something really exciting must be brewing.

'*Oga*, I came as fast as I could.'

Maren shook hands with him, invited him to sit down. 'Have a stout. You look very thirsty.'

He nodded, clapping the bar boy on the back. 'How this boy traced me to Adamasingba, I just don't know.'

'It's an urgent matter. I have a visit to pay tonight, and I need company.'

'In town or outside town?' was all that interested him.

'Right here in Ibadan. On Ife campus.' He saw Kodak's eyes open wide. 'It's a family affair and it needs to be handled delicately. I don't want any ruffians. It's a social visit, that's all, just to pass on a message. There will not be any violence.'

'How many of us?'

'Not more than four. At most six. Our own people will make up all the number we need.'

He snorted. 'You mean University people like your kind, *oga*?'

'I've told you, it's a talking matter. And it is our kind of talk. We will do the talking, and all you will do is – nothing. You will simply sit down, and listen. And you will leave with us when we are ready to leave.'

He shrugged. 'Acada people! Anyway, what time?'

'Bring your boys to Mbari at seven o'clock. I shall pick you up myself. That way, I can send back anyone with alcohol on his breath, or reeking of the slightest trace of marijuana.'

Kodak sighed. 'As you wish it, *oga*. I can see it's a real family affair.'

Of the group who had attended the so-called 'peace meeting', summoned by the Permanent Secretary for Education, Maren had marked down three, one of them the expatriate Mr Price, whom he considered the most vulnerable. Mr Price had also been reported as the most loquacious at the meeting, and he could not help wondering why such a man could not at least stay neutral in a crisis of this kind, among strangers to whom he evidently felt no commitment but regarded quite simply as the source of a comfortable living. Instead, he had given such an unctuous, fawning performance that it astonished even the Nigerian supporters of the NNDP *Credo*. The Permanent Secretary had made a point of asking him, and a handful of others, to stay behind for further discussions.

The volunteers from Orisun Theatre were waiting outside the Price home when he arrived with his group. He nodded to them, and knocked on the door. Price, a red-headed, plump figure, was just emerging from his bathroom and had only a bath towel round his waist. He peeped through the window, recognised Maren and opened the door. When he saw that his visitor also had company, he became embarrassed and offered to go and change into something more comfortable. Maren decided that his unexpected half-nudity was actually a psychological bonus, so he insisted that he remain as he was. They would not take long, he assured him, it was hardly worth his while changing into something different; moreover, he and his companions were in a hurry, as they had several more calls to make before the evening was out.

Outside, the Orisun boys deployed themselves, with conspicuous furtiveness, along the windows, looking on the inside from the dark. Wherever Price turned to look, there was a face staring at him, saying and doing nothing, just staring. From time to time there would be a raised voice outside the house, a kind of angry motion, then other voices that appeared to quieten the impatient one. At such moments the faces would disappear from the windows, trail off into the distance, then return quietly to their stations to continue their watch. Inside, Kodak and his four companions sat stolidly, sharing their interest between the half-nude figure of Mr Price and the furnishing and general interior decoration of the bungalow. There had only been the driving time between Mbari and campus for any form of instructions, but they were playing their role very conscientiously.

'You heard what happened to the Aluko . . .,' Maren began.

'Disgraceful,' Price barked. 'Very disgraceful. It's unfortunate that the Vice Chancellor was away at the time. We expect a strong statement, yes, action, from him when he returns.'

'Yes, I heard that was what was agreed at the meeting with the PermSec.'

'Ah, good. You know all about the meeting. We had some very frank talk with the Government. The Vice Premier was there.'

'Do you happen to know when Professor Ajose will return?'

'Quite soon, I'm sure, very soon. The moment he learns of what has occurred here . . .'

'But you don't know exactly when that is, do you? It may be next week, and of course it may even be tonight.'

'True, true, that's true. But the Registrar has sent him an urgent message.'

'You have not considered the possibility that he left campus so the Government can have a free hand. I mean, giving the *Credo* to his deputy to read and all that . . .'

Price looked profoundly shocked, his blushes cascaded from the roots of his hair to the exposed region of his navel. 'Our Vice Chancellor? Oh no, he would never do a thing like that. No, no, don't even give it a thought.'

'All right, I won't. But while he's away, while you and others agree to do nothing in the meantime, thugs are free to roam the campus and harass your own colleagues. Is that the idea?'

Price was now truly frightened. His scared eyes darted from window to window, tried very hard not to notice the very obvious presence of the very obvious counterparts of those who had unleashed mayhem on the Aluko family. He began to stutter badly.

'Look, Maren, I mean, in the absence of the Vice Chancellor . . .'

'. . . and of his political overseer, who also discovered he had urgent business outside Ibadan after inflicting his *Credo* on the community – he hasn't been seen since then, has he? So who is really in charge at the moment?'

He clutched eagerly at the perceived safety line. 'Yes, yes, isn't that really the point? We have no one in charge, no one around is competent to take any decisions. We can hardly afford to take any action that the Vice Chancellor may be compelled to repudiate . . .'

Maren swept his hands around the living room. 'But look at all this, Price. Look at this cosy place of yours. And there is your study, with all your books. You are strictly in Administration so you won't have any lecture notes, research notes, so you have no idea how it feels to see thugs come in your home and destroy all your work.

Still, you have things you value, especially your peace of mind, your right to security. Am I right?'

'Oh yes indeed. I know exactly how Aluko must be feeling right now.'

'Do you? I'll tell you what I am sure you do know. You know that the Mercedes that brought the thugs to destroy Aluko's house belonged to the same Permanent Secretary of Education with whom you held a "peace meeting". Now, if you really know how Aluko must have felt, you would be bound to ask how that came about, wouldn't you? Did you?'

Price changed tack and decided to bluster. 'Look here, Maren, there's a limit to just how far one can go asking questions that are based on only a one-sided report. Nobody has proved conclusively that it was the PermSec's car. We only have Joyce's word for it.'

'Did you try to make it a two-sided report? Did you tell Mr PermSec what the victim had to say about his car, and obtain his view on the subject? Look, you people went there as – representatives of the University. When are we going to receive a report on how you represented us?'

'Any time from now,' he added hastily. 'Anytime. We scheduled another meeting for tomorrow in the Vice Premier's office. That's where the final decisions will be taken . . .'

'I know. That's exactly what this little visit is about. I have a message for you to take back to your meeting.'

Price blanched. His eyes darted to the men in the room. Message? That was what the men of the Permanent Secretary said as they destroyed Aluko's home – 'We have a message for you . . . take that message to the rest of those making trouble for the Government.' He was jolted into relief when Maren, as if reading his mind, went on to elaborate.

'If you like, you can write it down,' he said. 'I don't want there to be any mistake. I would prefer that you use my own words as closely as possible.'

'Sure.' His voice was pathetically eager. 'I'm sure the Government will be glad to listen to all shades of opinion. I'll be very glad to repeat anything you have to say.' He fumbled in a drawer for a pen, found one, and located a pad. 'Go ahead, I'll take it all down.'

'Right. Tell Mr Somare, and any others you meet from the

Government, that we know we cannot compete with them in thug-gery. Neither do we wish to. We do not have the resources which the Government obviously has, and we don't relish the very idea, anyway. To me, thugs are human beings, dehumanised by others. If we are compelled to defend ourselves with violence, we won't hire thugs, but we won't hesitate to call on people called thugs who happen to be our friends. And we won't *send* them, we'll be right alongside them. Are you writing all that down?'

'Sure, sure. I've got it all.'

'Tell them that even if we had all the thugs we could afford, we know we couldn't even begin to take on people like Mr PermSec, who can use the resources of the Ministry as he pleases, plus the security votes of the Premier and his deputy. At least, not for now, not until we are able to mobilise the region. So, here is our position. And listen carefully. All the nine people who have resigned from the University, and any others who may yet resign, must be allowed their full entitlements, and that includes remaining in their residence until their notice expires. Do you think that is a fair enough demand, Mr Price?'

'Oh absolutely. Absolutely.'

'Good. In that case I know you will support it at your meeting.'

'You can count on me.'

'Good. One thing more, you can tell the PermSec that, if the Government does not abide by those conditions, if they send one more thug into campus, we will also, in turn, harass those whom we are convinced have collaborated in the assault. And if they succeed in evicting one of those who have resigned, we shall equally evict those whom, we are convinced, supported the eviction. The Government can send in any amount of protection it wishes. We shall simply bide our time, and evict them.'

Swallowing hard, Price nodded vigorously, and scribbled away.

Maren continued. 'We are, after all, only speaking of a period of three months. The Government can spend that time expending its mindless violence elsewhere. Just three months, but the principle is important. You are in Administration, so you know damned well that these lecturers are entitled to remain in their residence. They resigned, they were not dismissed. Even Government officials who have accumulated their leave before retirement or resignation are permitted to spend that leave in their residence. I think that's a fair analogy, don't you think?'

'Oh yes, I agree you with you entirely,' Price assured him.

'Thank you.' He nodded to his companions. 'In that case, I'll leave everything in your hands. I know you'll make an effective negotiator.'

'I'll do my best, I promise. I'll speak to our colleagues before the meeting. It's the very least we can do.' He scribbled away furiously, laid down his pen with a flourish of resolve. 'Look, stay and have a drink, I haven't even had time to offer your friends anything. I really would like us to discuss this whole crisis in more detail. I am sure there are other things the University could do . . .'

Maren shook his head. 'Sorry, I'm afraid we haven't the time. I told you, we have quite a few other calls to make tonight. Some other time, maybe when things have settled down . . .'

'Sure, sure. Any time. And thank you so much for trusting me with your confidence.'

He saw them to the door, shook hands vigorously with every one. The Orisun boys were already melting away into the dark, heading for the next rendezvous.

Two days later, Maren encountered an old lover. M.O. had taken up with a lecturer with whom she now partly lived. He had gone to the lecturer's house on the University of Ibadan campus to borrow some West Indian music for his production of Barry Reckord's *You In Your Small Corner*. He was not aware that she now lived there until she opened the door to him. She flew straight for his jugular, eyes flashing, lips wet with the saliva of contempt.

'I knew you had sunk low, but I never guessed that there were still depths to which you could sink. What are you looking for? Who wants you here?'

He thought at first that she was accusing him of pursuing her, of following her into her new situation, maybe to embarrass her, sour up things for her by revealing their former relationship. Bewildered, he tried to assure her that he had not known that she was now living with this lecturer, and had no interest whatever in her affair. A lazy drawl came from some other part of the house, demanding to know what the noise was all about.

'It's this . . . this thug. This common street, nightclub brawler.'
And then, aware that she now had an audience, her voice lost its
immediate shrillness of spontaneity, coated its venom with a veneer
of *tiroro* BBC superstructure, even though she had never been
beyond the shores of Lagos. 'You really make one embarrassed to
be associated with you,' she continued. 'You are supposed to be an
intellectual, a member of this academic community, but you spend
your time hiring thugs and parading them through Ife campus,
terrorising your colleagues. It's so disgusting, one doesn't even know
what to say to you, or how to begin.'

Her lover now emerged, his nose entangled somewhere up in the
ceiling frame. 'Ooh, it's you. Are you alone? We hear you don't
go anywhere without your thugs, just like any of these third-rate
politicians. I must say you are full of surprises, and not very pleasant
ones. Come in, what can we do for you?'

Maren stood still, turning his attention from one to the other.
Finally he found his voice. 'You said you had some calypso
records . . .'

'Oh yes, I'd forgotten all about that.' He waved his hand in the
general direction of a stack of books and records. 'Maybe you'll find
something in there to suit your needs.'

'Thank you,' Maren said. 'I just wanted to be sure that I was in
the right place. Wanted to reassure myself that you did suggest that
I come here this afternoon, have a drink together while I tried out
some of your records.'

'Oh yes, I remember, do go ahead. Darling, can you find him a
drink?'

'I said I just wanted to be sure. Now I am. Good morning to
both of you.'

Lover-boy snapped himself back to earth. 'Hey, what's the matter?
Just because I . . .'

But Maren had left, leaping into the driving seat through the
doorless truck. Within, he felt sick, wondering what it was that
made the University a place towards which he leant despite its
treacheries, clowns and phonies.

Then he took solace as he recalled that, earlier that morning, the
'peace group' had reported back that the Government had assured
the quitting lecturers that their terms of employment would be

respected. No one was obliged to leave his quarters before the expiration of the three months' notice. Then, just as suddenly, he felt that he did not even give a damn whether or not the Government kept its side of the bargain. He turned the Land Rover in the direction of Oke Ado, headed towards the jazz club of Agoji Mayor. There at least he would find a substitute record for the music he wanted, drink a beer in the noonday peace and quiet of the deserted club or, at worst, be pestered only by those who earned or cadged a livelihood in the real world.

Agoji Mayor's was not quite empty. Basking in the pre-lunch hour quiet was the genial figure of J. M. Johnson, the Minister of Labour whom he had held in great esteem until the General Strike that had followed fast on the disputed Federal elections. Would the unrest ever end, he began to wonder? This was proving very different from what he had envisaged as he grew neurotic in his haste to return home and . . . yes, do what, exactly? One crisis followed another until he sometimes felt that he was trapped in a time-warp, tossed into a centrifuge that spun him endlessly within a fourth dimension of existence, a diabolical *penkelemes* whirligig. One stream of heady days, weeks, into yet another current – only the tempo appeared to vary. Did the Strike really achieve anything? Small gains, yes, but ultimately? Salaries were increased, but would the system ever permit controls that gave value to such increases – rent, food, health? The rapacious landlords held the reins of government. Hardly had the wage increases been granted than their wives and the market women multiplied the cost of staple goods. Still, he felt that on their side they had done their bit, given battle where they could . . . the Strike Solidarity Committee centred on Ife and Ibadan campuses: Tayo Akpata, Dapo Fatogun, Lawyer Omotoso the self-sacrificing, passionate marxist. From their meagre earnings they raised funds, solicited more, passing the fugitive Labour man, the gun-toting Emmanuel Ijeh, from one hiding place to another, dodging the 'E' Branch men on their tail when necessary, but sometimes affably inviting them to their table at the night club near Omotoso's home, which the 'E' men patronised, feigning an interest in the prostitutes. They stuck out a mile, and Maren would beckon them over, saying, 'Let's talk. We know who you are, let's talk. Why are you against this strike? It is, after all, in your own interest, don't you know? And anyway, what makes you think we will not do our duty by the workers?'

It was a bitter moment to discover that the Nigerian Workers' and Farmers' Union, strategically situated in the teeming working population of Idi-Oro, had shut down totally, without reason and without explanation; all its printing machines, freshly donated from communist China, idle, the leader himself away on a prolonged visit to China. There had been meetings at the Green Springs Hotel outside Ibadan, where the leader, Otegbeye, had led them all to expect much from that movement. Thereafter, only silence and inertia. And so their stream of tracts and newsletters lost that facility and organisation, and Dapo Fatogun's primitive, nomadic set-up came to the rescue, but it was mostly the neutral, commercial prin-ters such as Abiodun Printing Press in Ibadan that furtively set and proofread the strike literature that issued from the committee, most of the work being done at night to avoid police attention. Revolution was within sniffing distance, a worker's revolution, and Maren sur-rendered himself to the torrent of anticipation. A definitive blow would be delivered to the increasingly corrupt and complacent class of rulers, whose concept of leadership had now manifested itself roundly in action just as he had feared, observing its beginnings as a student in England. They existed solely to wallow in the abandoned privileges of the departing colonial masters; their relationship to the masses was simply that of leeches and parasites.

The hard-line Marxists were willing to bide their time and Maren lost patience with them. Volunteers of his line of thinking moved around the country meeting the labour leaders, returning to hold strategy meetings with others in Gogo Nzeribe's Lagos apartment. Mokogwu Okoye would maintain that the bourgeoisie had not attained the level of economic transformation that made the takeover by the proletariat inevitable. You are text-bound, Maren protested, you ignore the special conditions of our post-colonial society; this is one revolution that will skip the bourgeois phase, and the moment is now, while the post-colonial order is not firmly entrenched, the power structure feeble, and mass discontent at its highest since Independence. Back and forth it all went, back and forth, just like the various agents moving from Lagos to Enugu to Kaduna, Kano and Ibadan, stiffening up labour resolve; Michael

Imoudu's flaming rhetoric lighting up the labour rallies at Mushin, Yaba, at Onikan racecourse, Kano and Enugu, confidently predicting the downfall of the Balewa Government unless it yielded to workers' demands, while the Government of Tafawa Balewa infiltrated their ranks with money and tribal suspicions, shrewdly reminding its adherents that this labour action was not without its political motivation – recent election results had, after all, been fiercely contested, and the nation had teetered on the verge of a violent power tussle. Nor did its propaganda machine neglect to accuse the sympathy of the 'progressives' for Awolowo and his radical lieutenants who were languishing in prison cells all over the country, convicted of treasonable felony. Radicalism was a disease of the South, and the strike was only another attempt by the South to spread its poison and achieve what Awolowo had failed to do – snatch political power from the North through non-democratic means . . . it was only a matter of time, and cracks would begin within the ranks of labour.

Then, at the height of the virtual collapse of all the nation's public services, with the strike already eroding even the functioning of the private sector, the Prime Minister summoned an emergency cabinet meeting. The outrageous aspect of the meeting, however, was that the most essential member of the cabinet was absent, the one who held the Labour portfolio! The media carried photographs of him in full regalia at the Lagos *eyo** festival, participating with zest, seemingly without a care in the world.

So Maren, never one to miss a chance, cornered him at the jazz club and took him to task. J.M.J. smiled, bought him a beer and settled himself more comfortably on a bar stool.

'I was not needed at the meeting,' he explained, 'because we had met the previous day and taken all the decisions that mattered. The meeting that was reported was no meeting at all. Oh, it was attended by some of the Ministers, but the key ministry there was not mine, no, it was not the Ministry of Labour at all, but the Ministry of Finance. Good old Festus was in charge. The cabinet met in one room, the Labour leaders waited in another. Then there was a third room where Okotie-Eboh held court. In went the Labour

*A masquerade celebrated especially in Lagos.

leaders one by one, the key ones who had been carefully selected, and they received a handout from the Minister.' He read the shock on the younger man's face, patted him on the back, and consoled him. 'I know how you feel; I felt the same way. Remember I came up through Labour myself, and things were different then. We fought colonial power with the might of our unions; the white man would never even have dared to offer us money, he would have been publicly denounced!' J.M.J. finished his beer, took his hand. 'Don't be too surprised if you hear that I've resigned from the cabinet. Well, maybe I shan't be so precipitate but, I assure you, I will not accept to serve a second term. I have a comfortable home in the heart of my constituency. I think I'll prefer to serve them from there, at a different level.'

It was meagre consolation to remind himself that the strike had held out longest in the West, and to be able to assess, objectively, and take some satisfaction in the contribution of the Strike Committee to that struggle. He had long accepted that, most especially in its long-term objectives, the strike could only be accounted a negligible success. He had extracted from the exercise one sole achievement – that it could be counted a full dress rehearsal for a final confrontation that now seemed unavoidable. The nation was under the arrogant alliance of a feudal oligarchy and a venal political class, an alliance that found great favour in the eyes of the displaced but still active colonial master. The Labour movement was a force that appeared suited to the task of overturning this structure and restoring society to a progressive agenda. It all seemed so obvious, so necessary, a sacred trust even . . .

IX Of Ideologues and Geniuses

The exterior world did periodically provide a respite, seldom sought but always welcome, never a real refuge, indeed often exacerbating his discontent through its own seeming order, its apparent sense of direction, its values or search for values, a structure of self-examination that was habitual, certainly through the prominent placement of its humanity in the order of concerns by its leadership. That world provided interludes of sane detachment, or at least, of a different order of encounters, non-lethal, mostly on the plane of genuine exchanges, discoveries; at the worst, one could withdraw from confrontations, or place them out of immediate view on the shelf of ideas for sorting in less acrimonious circumstances. Most often, and for varying reasons, from the domestic to the political, it was sheer bliss simply to 'get away from it all', far, far from the madding crowd . . .

What does a young theatre manager-playwright-director-impresario do when an ambitious three-company repertory season ends in deficit, and sundry creditors – carpenters, cloth sellers, printers, petrol stations, *wosi-wosi* traders (the backbone of theatre props supply) – exhaust their legendary patience, abandon their favourite-son understanding, and begin to clamour for payment? Maren found himself faced with the only answer: leave town!

A small grant from a foundation had speeded up the long nurtured project, and the three-months' salary 'in lieu of notice' from the renegade University joined in to boost the financial grounding for the realisation of the idea. Agodi's 'squatters lodge' was available both for camping and rehearsals. Geoff Axworthy of the Drama Department had agreed that, during the long vacation, the Arts Theatre of the University of Ibadan should make its facilities

available for the experiment, even making over the use of the depart-
mental bus. A general theatrical resurgence in the 'catchment area'
of the South appeared to guarantee, at the very least, that the venture
would break even. Kola Ogunmola, the Yoruba actor manager and
playwright, was at the pinnacle of his histrionic gifts – an incredibly
mobile face and fluid body, matched by visual wit; while Duro
Ladipo, his rival, was quarrying deeper and deeper in the tragic
mode, and with a spectacular sense of history and epic. The youthful
Orisun Theatre was growing more and more intrepid, complement-
ing Ogunmola's broad social comedy and moralities with direct,
topical satires and the occasional comic pieces. It was time for the
three differing genres – in language, form and orientation – to
interact and perform in tandem. The financial risk – if it was ever
considered – was easily dismissed.

Artistically, it was an acknowledged success, especially for the two
representatives of the Yoruba theatre – Kola Ogunmola and Duro
Ladipo. Orisun Theatre, being the host company, handled the logis-
tics, looking after the welfare of the guest companies – Duro Ladipo
proved especially difficult and demanding. They acted as drivers,
food scavengers, paramedics, inter-group rivalry counsellors,
woman *palava* adjudicators; took care of publicity – in short, undertook all the drudgery and found themselves under-rehearsed for *The
Lion and the Jewel*. But they ripped hilariously through the various
editions of *Before the Blackout*. Duro attained new tragic heights in
his solidly evolving *Oba Koso* and Kola grew ever more innovatory
with his musical adaptation of Amos Tutuola's *Palm Wine Drunkard*,
later to attain its justly celebrated visual and dramatic pinnacle at
the 1966 Dakar Black Arts Festival two years later, with the artist-
designer, Demas Nwoko's collaboration. In the end, however, came
financial reckoning. Maren divided up what loose change was left
among the guest companies and placed Orisun on temporary suspension, retaining Tunji Oyelana as a one-man force. The rest were
found part-time jobs in Mbari and other culture-friendly establishments. Then he took out his File 20 – *Lectures, Conferences, Etc.* and
examined the two or three invitations that had been neglected during
the hectic season of *penkelemes*. The most promising and exciting of
these was a month-long Theatre Festival and Conference in post-

liberation Cuba. Cuba was also furthest from the abode of his creditors.

One did not go to Cuba – not from Nigeria! One did not travel to the Soviet Union or any of the Eastern European nations. Nothing on the passport pages of most ex-colonial countries on the African continent would ever suggest that such nationals ever visited a communist country. The immigration officers of such countries would actually ask if they could stamp the visitor's passports, and if the answer was, 'Not on my life,' that was it. They waved the comrade in without any further question. Ghana was, of course, prominent among the exceptions.

The gathering of so many writers in one place, from all corners of the globe, was a first for the playwright, quite different in mood from an earlier – all-African – conference in Makerere, Uganda. Here, Latin American, European, Asian and African voices clashed over the dialectics of a revolution that was actually resulting in a unique creative ferment. Cuba had had a revolution – yes – but was it a marxist revolution? Even within the ruling junta, this was a touchy issue. There was an attraction towards the mainstream revolutionary theory-praxis, which was disinclined to divorce marxist ideology from both the impetus and the actuality of this revolution, but this was purely wishful thinking. Maren found that his insistence on the separation – that the marxist conviction came later – did not make him very popular, but he stuck to his guns. It was a popular revolution that succeeded without the marxist 'weapon of theory'. He had read Fidel Castro's *History Will Absolve Me*, he reminded them. As a student, he had followed media interviews with Fidel Castro when he was holed up in the mountains, and was presented as some idealist loony who did not stand a chance against Batista's forces and the covert gringo support. Nowhere had there been the slightest invocation of the marxist god. That there was a marxist or two within Castro's band was not to be denied, but why was it necessary, he demanded, to genuflect to an absent deity when the human revolutionary will proved itself capable, without this divine aid, of toppling a degenerate régime and reinstating the humanity and the primacy of the people? They looked at him askance, shook their heads at his 'naïvety', determined to revise the history of that revolution before the fumes had dispersed from the flames of combat.

Something about the symmetry of a simultaneous act of theoretic transformation and physical liberation held them spellbound, and they were prepared to lie in defence of what the text had preordained. It would take years before this trend was reversed – officially.

The marvel of it all, however, was that in the domain of the arts, Cuba remained vibrantly open, and was determined to remain so. This was what made the debates at the Casas de las Americas sometimes a strange, perverse, proceeding. The European marxists were far more *proletkult*, at least in their pronouncements, than the Cuban art which was on show – theatre, painting, dance, sculpture, poetry and music. There was a cloying regurgitation of the Stalinist-Zhdanovian line – not by all, admittedly, but quite stridently by the self-appointed *apparatchiks* and custodians of the wedlock of social realism with proletarian aesthetics. Maren's problem was mainly that, to him, they did not sound *sincere*. They sounded very much as if they merely wanted to please their hosts. He looked at them, comfortable products and beneficiaries of European liberalism, who would not last one day in one of Stalin's camps. Yet here they were, mouthing the need for state control of artistic directions and the essential nobility of *utilitarian* art over artistic inspiration, over the 'artist's art'; reducing all arguments to a simple-minded contestation between art that served the people and the hoary bugbear of 'art for art's sake'. He longed for the company of Okigbo-in-Makarere, Okigbo, who had simply confounded the utilitarians at the Makarere conference with the blunt declaration: 'I write my poetry for poets only!'

You could only upbraid, insult or ignore an extreme position such as that; you could fulminate against it and assign it to petit-bourgeois-decadent-liberal crucifixion, but you could not *argue* with it because it was sublimely arrogant, replete, and hermetic. You bounced off its skin and floundered in your own revolutionary spittle. You are reduced to only one course of action: to abandon all discourse and go all out to make your revolution so you can guillotine Christopher Okigbo, except of course that that mischief-laden leprechaun would still cheat you of triumph by improvising and declaiming an appropriate last-minute eclogue even as the blade fell. God! those mouthers of artistic duty from within the lush hospitality of conference halls and academic symposia!

Irritated beyond measure, his mind constantly on the *penkelemes* on his home front, from which these few weeks were supposed to be a respite, he found himself falling into needless traps in his intemperate denunciation of the more incorrigible of such ideological *poseurs*, frequently backed into positions which he then hotly denied holding. The Cuban participants appeared to listen more than contribute; at least he obtained the feeling that the intellectuals and formulators of a Cuban cultural policy were exploring the ideological terrain at a careful remove, through the multiple minds that had been brought together.

The eclectic, creative ferment was, of course, the unanswerable argument for his position. Indifferent to the slanging matches that went on in the Casas de las Americas, the Cuban Government was adopting an all-comer, open-door policy to the Arts. The golf-courses and club houses of Batista's élite society, the resorts of affluent American invaders, had all been turned over to artistic movements for dance, music, painting. The canvases were overwhelming in their chromatic *joie de vivre* – as if there was a concerted effort to capture and disseminate the explosive spirit of liberation for all time. Very little was to be seen here of socialist realism, excepting the murals, and even those parted company with the postured monotony of the Stalinist proletarian mural.

Cuba was indeed overwhelming, yet irritating. The euphoria that followed the failed invasion of Cuba by US-supported Cuban dissidents at the Bay of Pigs still pervaded all conversation, attitudes, and instilled a sense of both national and individual worth and pride that probably excelled even the triumph over the repressive forces of Batista. Fidel Castro dominated *everything* – it was all Fidel, Fidel! It was impossible, even unnatural not to recognise the reality of an extraordinary *event* in the person of the charismatic giant – he *looked* gigantesque in his fatigues, his standard combat boots, holstered pistol and, of course, the combined extrusions of a huge beard and Habana cigar. The personality cult was not contrived, it was not a phenomenon that was carefully nurtured. Cuba's personality cult was very simply the force of Fidel Castro – his history, personality, will-power and oratorical intensity. Quite simply, Fidel was a manifest embodiment of that cliché – 'larger than life'!

The irritation came mostly from three directions: one was the creeping regimentation of life for the ordinary Cuban; the next was the inevitable side-effects of a personality cult – the growth of sycophancy; and finally, alas, evidence of racial discrimination. The blacks were most definitely at the bottom of the social ladder – but then, this revolution was hardly three years old, and Batista's social structure had been entrenched in the island for decades. The regimentation of social life was already developing into a regimentation of thought, as the 'second' revolution – the marxist one – fastened its hold on the society. It was remarkable that the situation was very different in the Oriente province, within Santiago de Cuba for example, where the people walked and talked like thinking, not programmed, beings. The daily sociology of Oriente was loose-limbed, spontaneous, and independent, a marked contrast to Habana. The people of Oriente struck him as liberated in every way; in Habana, the liberation often sounded rhetorical. And the women of Oriente had a winning carriage, skin tone and beauty that made him decide on the spot that, if ever it came to a choice of exile, it was Santiago de Cuba, or nowhere else on earth!

In Habana once, a middle-aged man looked at him with disapproval, the cause of offence being the miserable tuft on his chin. Why, he demanded, was he wearing a beard? Did he see anyone in Cuba with a beard except Fidel? In deference to the leader, and to stamp him with distinction everywhere, the revolution had decided that only Fidel was permitted to exercise the privilege of a beard.

Maren was flabbergasted. What are you going to do, he asked him? Place a barber at the immigration posts and insist that your visitors shave before they are granted entry? Do you really feel that this straggle of hair on my chin constitutes the slightest threat to the hirsute triumph in which your leader's face is camouflaged? But the man remained unimpressed by any arguments. As a young, and seemingly intelligent fellow, Maren should not be seen with a beard on the streets of Habana. At the Casas de las Americas, where he recounted the experience, the man was dismissed as a crank, but Maren did observe, for the first time, that no one he encountered in Habana did wear a beard.

Castro delivered a four-hour address one day to the Union of Architects. Armed with the smattering of Spanish that he still retained from his studies in Leeds, Maren attended. He was instantly struck by the capacity attendance, and by the spruce line-up of the *comandantes* on stage. One of them was of striking appearance, and not merely because he was black. He had a most impressive bearing, handsome, at once as detached and arrogant as he was observant and alert. When the orgy of standing ovations commenced, engulfing the line-up on the podium, he stood out as the only one who refused to be swept, literally, onto his feet. He applauded, rose with the others on one or two occasions, but remained in his seat for most of the speech, listening intently, and perhaps even critically. Maren made a note to find out who this was, but somehow, until his departure, never did receive a satisfactory answer. He learnt his name, and the Ministry under his control, but never did receive any detailed information about his *history*. He felt strangely dissatisfied.

The initiation of standing ovations was keenly competitive, and it passed the hours for him, since Castro spoke so fast that Maren's rudimentary Spanish was of no use to him. A woman seated two rows in front of him, to the left, was clearly determined to emerge the victor. She leapt up like a jack-in-the-box at the slightest provocation, and the assembly rose with her. This went on for the first two hours, and then enthusiasm began to wane. Her supporters diminished gradually until, at last, she was the sole *applaudisseur*, springing up with a suddenness that suggested that a rocket had exploded beneath her, clapping to the bitter end with unflagging energy even after everyone, including her husband seated next to her, had deserted her. She continued to throw her glances all round the hall, as if attempting to exert her will on the audience, looked down on her husband, but he stared straight ahead, unblinking. It all looked very strange, in the middle of a serious and, from what little he could follow, well-argued summons to Cuban architects to transform the Cuban landscape with buildings that catered for the masses without losing their aesthetic appeal, and reverse the trend of servicing the affluent few. To this woman, however, it would not have mattered in the slightest if Fidel Castro had been addressing the sugarcane cutters on the virtues of improving the quality of rum.

It was a relief when the scandal of the French communist youths broke out. According to the complainants, and as taken up with outrage by *L'Humanité*, whose correspondent had travelled with the group, the youths were divided into two groups as soon as they arrived. One was sent off to the fields to join in cutting sugarcane while the other remained in Habana. The division was, however, along sexual lines; it was the boys who were despatched to the fields, while the women spent their evenings on the beaches in moonlight parties with the *comandantes*. Maren found it very odd that the correspondent – a very outgoing, warm personality – should be so outraged by what he, Maren, considered a fair division of labour. Indeed, the *comandantes* – stern, immobile units on the podium, seemingly implacable forces as they strode through crowds and corridors around their leader – rose sharply in his estimate – they were human, thank goodness. And what of Fidel himself, Maren enquired, did he also partake in these moonlit beach parties? He did go for moonlight swims, he was told, but had not been accused by *L'Humanité* of participating in the 'uncomradely' activities of his lieutenants.

This had Maren a little worried until his own affair with a journalist, also French. She had tried for a long while to capture an exclusive with the bearded *guerrillero*, unsuccessfully. Then one day, after one of his general press conferences, Castro's aide called her aside and informed her that her request had been granted, and that a car would pick her up at the hotel at eleven at night. Thrilled at the prospect, she prepared her list of questions, and was taken to a chalet, where the interview lasted all night.

'And was it *all* interview, *all* night?' Maren asked.

'Of course not,' she smiled roguishly. 'Fidel,' she added, 'is an *ardent* man!'

Hoping that he did not compare too badly, Maren felt that he could leave Cuba, confident that the revolution was in the hands of a rounded human being.

He left Cuba for Prague, filled with regrets; then Berlin, where he attended a conference organised by Dennis Duerden's Transcription Centre and an American foundation, trying to tap any handy foundations for funds for his drama company, without much success. *En route*, both going and returning, the creaky Cubana propeller plane often made him wonder, as it hopped from island to island, if his underlying concerns about the future were not purely academic, as he, in company with some other delegates, laid bets on whether or not the plane would end up as their coffin in a watery grave, so

unsafe did it sound and so violently did it shudder at the slightest
air turbulence or indeed just from its own motions. But the Cuban
pilots and engineers evidently knew their war-horse, and time and
time again delivered them safe and sound.

A message was awaiting him when he returned to Ibadan: there was
a theatre director who had travelled all the way from London to see
him. She was staying at the apartment of Frank Speed, and appeared
determined to remain there until he showed up.

He found her in the kitchen, washing some vegetables at the sink.
His immediate impression was that of a dumpy little woman, with
funny eyes and a total lack of inhibition. For she was not in the
least put out by the fact that he had stumbled on her wearing a
brief shirt that covered only half her buttocks, nothing more. If she
noticed his embarrassment, she did not show it, so he quickly
shrugged off her appearance and introduced himself. She offered
the limp wrist that attached her wet hand to the arm, and announced
that she was Joan Littlewood.

A week later and he was heading once again for the exterior world.
Joan Littlewood had come to Nigeria to discuss the filming of *The
Lion and the Jewel*, a play which appealed, he discovered, not only
to her sense of the theatric, but to her search for the raw pulse of
life and impatience with the humbug of her own establishment. It
appeared to be a continuation of her 'Mother Courage' epic of
survival through British and European cities, covered wagon and
all, albeit of the motorised, travelling theatre version. It was this
same urge that she attempted to domesticate and stabilise – the
largest accommodation she was then capable of – in making her
theatre home in Theatre Royal, Stratford, in the East End of
London, as far from Establishment theatreland as she could go. But
of course the Establishment critics found her there, as did the
Establishment following, and hailed her various triumphs – *A Taste
of Honey*, *The Quare Fellow*, *Fings Ain't Wot They Used t' Be*, and so
on – one success after another which ended up in transfers to
mainstream theatres and the thinning out of her repertory core of
professional artistes.

As usual, he was at first unexcited. Some years earlier, while he
was still a student in Leeds, Sam Wanamaker, then opening his new

theatre in Liverpool, had also been taken with the play, had even invited him to arrange a reading with potential foreign actors in his theatre; but had stopped short of providing train fares for the assortment of European, Indian and African actors that he had assembled in Leeds. It was a puzzle to him how he was supposed to raise fares for a volunteer group to travel to Liverpool and feed them there. Nothing would have pleased him more at the time than to have his commercial theatre début while still a student, but equally nothing would tempt him to get into debt for an unsecured enterprise. It was also the same play – it had to be, he had nothing that he could consider a finished play beside the one-act *Swamp Dwellers* – that had attracted George Devine at the Royal Court Theatre, and earned him a place among his circle of young protégés. Still, this was to be a new medium – film – and he had to admit that the prospect did interest him. Until then, he had only been involved in documentaries, including one with the Canadian Broadcasting Corporation, categorised as a 'dramatised documentary'. He tended to recall that, because the final editing had ended up in a Soho studio. It was the first time he had failed to see sunlight for one straight week – give or take a slight dose of poetic licence – as the director, Alan King, himself, and the Isle-of-Ibiza cameraman tried to edit eighteen hours of footage down to a one-hour programme in time to beat the deadline for transmission in Canada. What the experience did for the Ibizan exile, a forsworn Englisher, he did not care to find out; before the ordeal was ended, he had himself forsworn the film medium for the rest of his life.

Would this be any different? He had seen her productions at the Theatre Royal, Stratford East, and had admitted instant empathy. Nigeria, or Yorubaland, was, however, a far cry from the East End of London and the concerns of her authors of the Theatre Workshop. So, to his mind came the cautious question: what did she want? Another one of *them* seeking replacements for a jaded environment, attempting to rejuvenate her creative drive with an injection of the exotic? Her indescribable eyes – pop-out, asymmetrical, almost suggestive of the mongoloid – danced with pure anticipation whenever she discussed the character of Baroka, the 'dirty old man' of this Yoruba village, whose cunning and sexuality bested the village schoolteacher for the hand of the village belle.

'Where shall we find him, you smart black Irish, that's going to be the problem? This cunning old lecher with such persuasive cant. That's the part that's going to be difficult to cast. I've seen them, mind you. Since I arrived I've been looking at everyone and, you know – not on this campus, mind you, they're all dead, dead up there and I bet down there, too. They've all been fucked up by the British. What are they still doing here, anyway? Get rid of them! Throw every fucking one of them in the sea where they belong! Mind you, I must say some of them are nice, real nice. Everybody has been kind to me here and some of them can actually think. I thought they sent out only those who can't tell their arse from their adam's apple, dead from there downwards, as I'm sure you've noticed. But they're all fucked up. You should have thrown them all out a long time ago: as a matter of fact I thought you had. They're messing up your own people, you know; I've met some of your own. We've had chats in the staff club – oh what a mini-Riviera you've got there! Why can't they go into town and do their own boozing there? Christ! You should listen to some of the talk I pick up in that place – is that what they do all the time? They don't talk like human beings, you know; they talk like their fucking white colleagues! Why do these people allow the British to do that to them? Don't they know we're all fucked up in that country? Surely they must know what's going on outside; when you visit the markets and walk the streets a little, you see the real people. That's when you know there's still hope. Anyway, the moment I read the play I knew that the British hadn't got away with everything. Thank God there are still fucking young poets like you, you're not a bad poet, you know. All our poets are dead up there, most of them are fucking pouffes anyway: their brains are all fucked up. They need to come and see these, your Yoruba people, see some real life and learn how to bloody well think like human beings again.'

The emotionless tone, only mildly querulous, was an unsettling contrast to the Gatling-gun, unpunctuated, breathless style of delivery that failed to break the rhythm of whatever she was doing – rinsing her hands, lighting her cigarettes, pouring a drink, pulling out a chair or opening windows. He wondered whether this was the way she really talked, or something that came over her in alien lands.

London, and the round of Joan Littlewood's backers began. There was Harry Saltzman and Cubby Broccoli. They were just wrapping up their secret weapon – *James Bond 007*, first of the series, and never had he met a team so certain of a commercial killing. The 'sweet smell of success' pervaded their Mayfair offices, wreathed the rubicund figure of Harry Saltzman especially. Broccoli was a little less ebullient – but it was evident in all their motions. Even their staff, flunkeys and business consultants appeared to exude its fragrance as Joan and he waited for a meeting to be concluded so they could all go for lunch or visit some studios where interiors of the projected film might be shot. Everything was on offer to Joan Littlewood whom the pair considered, quite straightforwardly, a genius. She moved about like a child in a sweet shop, indulged, pampered and confused by a veritable *embarras de richesses*.

Then there was 'the Orchid', another worshipper of the East End director, with apparently less resources than the James Bond pair but no, that was no problem. He had spoken to backers, the magic name of Joan Littlewood had opened vaults, and all she had to do was say the word. Was it an American crew she wanted? Or should they travel to Australia to see what the Antipodes had to offer in state-of-the-art equipment? Over drinks and meals, Joan, and her manager-companion, Gerry Raffles, dissected other prospective producers, one face or name merging into the next consortium. There was something about Gerry Raffles that put Maren off for a while – on the tactiturn side, looking up from down-lidded eyes and somehow giving the impression that his head was full of calculations. Later, Maren would thaw considerably towards him but, right then, he told himself that Joan was the one with whom he had any business and to whom he could relate in any way. In the evenings he visited theatres, ended up in the bar at the Theatre Royal, and once he accompanied them to a party at a pub where they appeared to be favourite guests – it was the East End pub owned and run by the Kray brothers. Maren was introduced to them.

'Ah, you're from Nigeria,' they said. And he sensed a spotty rise in the level of attention among those within hearing. He knew it was not a trick of the imagination; knowing looks were exchanged, and a few glances definitely came his way, with notable interest. Ron, or the other twin – in the smoke and noise did not really try too hard to tell them apart – beckoned to one of the clientèle to come over. 'Tell him about Nigeria,' he said.

It was uncanny. Here he was in the East End of London, minding his own business, and not just Nigeria, but his own Western part of it, had pursued him there. The Kray brothers' man had been invited to Nigeria by a highly placed member of the Western Government, someone right within the cabinet. The man who was speaking to him appeared to hesitate over the actual presence of the Kray twins in Nigeria itself, and Maren felt he should not display too much curiosity. He detected some form of embarrassment, perhaps, about the man having to admit that the East End crime lords had been bested in a crooked deal by their prospective Nigerian partners. But he admitted quite readily that he had himself been part of the delegation to Lagos and Ibadan, and had taken part in the negotiations.

They had been approached by someone through the Western Nigeria office, then in Portland Street. The scheme sounded too good to be true. Anyway, there was this newly independent country. As far as they were concerned, it was full of opportunities of the kind anyone could beg for and the marmalade on the bread was that the people who brought them in were in government. I mean, what more could anyone hope for? As far as they were concerned, this was a no-lose position. The enterprise involved banking, land speculation, and a sugar factory then under construction. The deal had become unravelled, or the would-be partners from London had taken fright after being 'conned' – his own expression – by the Government side. So they cut their losses and ran, spreading the word around the London underworld that it had nothing to teach the Nigerians. They were masters at the game, and if anyone was in any doubt and was still determined to have a go, the only advice they could offer them was that they had better keep their hats on during talks or they would find they had been scalped before the first greetings were exchanged.

It was no ordinary night at the pub; indeed, a section of the pub was closed to the general public that night, and that was where the party was taking place. He was pleased to meet the parliamentarian Tom Driberg again; he had not seen him since his efforts on behalf of Anthony Enahoro. Maren was not particularly curious about the party, but he did observe that a smallish individual appeared to be the toast of the crowd. He received frequent pats on the back and had glasses clinked with his more than anyone else. Was that the celebrant, Maren wanted to know? Joan Littlewood revealed in a strangely conspiratorial whisper that he was indeed; an auntie of his had just died and had left him a fortune.

Pointless to query whether it was the death of the aunt that the centre of attraction was celebrating, or the welcome inheritance, or both. Maren expressed himself content with the fact that the East Enders appeared to celebrate death like most Africans. Judging by the quantity of champagne that was going down, not to mention oysters, caviar and canapés, he remarked that the lady must have passed on at a very ripe old age, since that would be the yardstick by which his own people would lavish such extravagance on death festivities. Joan corrected him in an amused whisper: no one had really died – well, in a sense, the man had made a killing but there was no corpse. He had pulled off a job – a jewellers' shop – and the haul had been substantial. The gang was celebrating his success.

Well, well, here was a 'slumming' tendency that was decisively one up on his own. He was acquainted with crooks, associated with them, but could not conceive of knowingly celebrating a robbery with them. It seemed to be a trait within the vocation of artists, intellectuals and priests, each with differing motivations and degrees of genuine identification – but he found he could endorse only the Jean Genet model – the man himself as thief, gaolbird and writer, in whatever proportions. Outside of that, he read only voyeurism, or perhaps it would be more accurate to describe it as the vicarious drive. Even in the case of Genet, he remained unconvinced by Jean-Paul Sartre's attempt to convert Jean Genet into some kind of saint – the arguments belonged in the familiar territory of self-indulgent academic preciosity. Eyeing the gaggle of guests who, he was convinced, did not lead the lives of the habitués of such haunts but longed to be associated with some of the perverse glamour of the underworld, he fell to wondering if his own association with the Kodaks and Buffalo Bills was really any different. True, none of them would dream of confiding in him about their crimes or inviting him to partake of or celebrate their proceeds, but was the difference not merely in kind? Until that night at the Krays' club, he had taken such contacts for granted; now he began to wonder. There was an innate contradiction somewhere and he remained uncomfortable with his presence there all evening. Still, it was champagne all round, of the best and on the house. He only hoped that his would-be collaborators would not end up trying to interest the celebrant in the possibility of investing in *The Lion and the Jewel*.

Harry Saltzman placed an office in Soho at their disposal, with a secretary-typist, where they would begin the labour of turning the play into a film script. 'No strings attached, Joan darling,' he insisted. 'I just want you to take your time, see this thing the way you want to film it, then decide what kind of film this is going to be. You want to go to Paris? Fine. The States? Just let us know. There are some new breakthroughs with the camera, you know, my company, in fact, is taking an interest in its manufacture. Maybe that's the sort of equipment you need in Africa: why don't you fly over and see what they've got? . . .'

And so on and on it went. The project became drawn out, diffuse, certainly it was taking up more time than he had bargained for. At the most, the visit to London should have taken a week; now they were in their third week, nothing had been achieved. Only talk and more talk and meetings and introductions and suggestions and coyness and blandishments and ego massages. Maren sat in the Soho office, churning out page after page of a film version, having first waded through several models of feature-film scripts. Joan moved in and out, one idea cancelling out another. Then flashes of inspiration, the sudden imagic clarity and originality, and into the waste basket would go several pages and a new concept would gain definition. The next moment she was chattering non-stop to herself and anyone around, setting out the drawbacks of one producer after another, contrasting French film techniques with the British – the latter always primitive, although there were exceptions such as . . . well, actually, maybe the best solution would be a British film crew and a French principal cameraman . . . Harry Saltzman never did go on his knees or pick up a chair to crown her, but there would be the sudden break in his voice, the sign of desperation and then: 'Do you *want* to go to France, Joan? I have to leave for the States today: we're doing a sneak preview of the Bond film for distributors over there. Do you want to come with us, you and your Nigerian friend? Or shall I have my secretary make arrangements for France?'

Impresarios, Maren held, must be beings of infinite patience, but perhaps they merely feigned such patience until they got what they wanted and then, heaven help even the genius who had led them a merry dance, played hard to get, or merely acted the *prima donna*. Since he was not an impresario, did not have a penny of his own to his name nor available millions at the end of a telephone line to other 'angels', backers or lenders, he found his patience, even his affection, for this unusual woman wearing thin.

There was also his increasing guilt towards the *penkelemes* from which he had taken a leave of absence that was extending into an indefinite AWOL, as the weeks stretched out. Not to mention the fact that he had hoped to return with some funds to pump into both his own domestic needs and the needs of the group gathered around him. He was jobless, had no immediate prospects beyond what his writing might bring, yet here was this brilliant but disorganised mind, part theatre genius, part bag lady, talking and thinking in broken streams of consciousness even when confronted with precise questions that required precise answers. From her sudden fascination with the documentaries of the French anthropologist, Jean Rouch, whose work she had not actually seen, only heard about, she leapt to the Irish Question, the drink problems of Brendan Behan, and what the hell did the fucking Americans think they were doing in Vietnam; and anyway weren't the Irish the Yoruba of the Western world? And if Maren didn't know it, he was a black Irishman and that was what the fucking Britishers needed at that moment; but in any case, were the British even capable of appreciating anything decent when they had no idea of how to have fun. 'You've seen it, haven't you: the Brits just haven't been brought up to know how to enjoy themselves. It's all the protestant ethic, fun is sin, now that's what's got to be corrected. I've been thinking of this Fun Palace . . .'

'A what, Joan?'

'A Fun Palace. Don't you think it's what this bloody country needs?'

'And what is a Fun Palace, Joan?'

'What does it sound like, Fuck-face? A place where people can actually go and enjoy themselves. Use their brains to enjoy themselves. I've been looking at some of this equipment, you know; Gerry and his friend, with all their schoolboy masturbation with gadgets, they are on to some really interesting things. If one approaches a Fun Palace with all that in mind, I mean, technology is not all bad when you think of it . . .'

This woman, Maren said to himself, is bad for your health. Desperate, overcoming his chronic unease with discussing money, he finally attempted to crash through her barrier of floating ideas with a warning that he was heading home without delay.

'Do you want to take an option on the play?' he asked.

'What I'm thinking is maybe we go to Paris and . . .'

'Joan. I have to leave. I received very bad news from home yesterday. Some of my friends have been arrested.'

That did get her attention. 'Damn it! The poor sods. You know all this is the work of the British bastards, don't you? They've really got your people all fucked up . . .'

'I've got to get back to them. Has any of these interested people – Saltzman or the Orchid or whoever – have they so much as suggested taking an option on the work?'

'I'm trying to be careful, Maren. We don't want to get ourselves tied up with those conservative types, you know. Have you heard of Jacques Tati? He's doing some fantastic things in his new Paris studios . . .'

'I know of Jacques Tati. I saw his *Jour de Fête* as a student and I loved it.'

'He's on the set for his new film right now. Maybe we should take old Harry up on that and go to France? No, it's better to go with the Orchid. It won't do to put oneself in the hands of any of these people, you know. No use letting Harry Fuck-face think he's got it in the bag.'

'You want us to go to Paris on the Orchid ticket, is that it?'

'We-ell, I've been thinking, why not? At least he's not chasing James Bond all over the place. He wants to come with us. Might be not such a bad idea after all.'

'I'd take a trip to Paris any day, but we should have done that before now, instead of blowing the time away in Soho and swanning with the Kray brothers . . .'

'Oh don't be such a po-faced Britisher. Yes, I could see the disapproval on your face the night we went in there. You know, the British have really done a number on you people. You're just a fucking *petit-bourgeois*, you know. If you weren't such a fucking Yoruba genius, you'd be ending up taking tea with the Queen Mother.'

'Joan, I must get back home.'

'All right, all right. Let's decide tonight over dinner. Gerry's American friend is coming – he's another Gerry, the one I've been talking about – he's into this and that you know, all those technical gimmicks. You should see them both get together over all those gadgets, just like fucking schoolboys. When they get together all they ever talk about is electrodes and wavelengths and cathodes and things like that. But Feil is a fucking good cameraman; he worked with that shit-face – what's his name now – Peter Brook – on *Lord of the Flies* . . .'

'Now, who is Feil?'

'Feil? The other Gerry I was telling you about. Very different from all those bloody Americans. Gerry – that's my Gerry – he says he's a bloody genius with the camera.'

'Is that decided then? Are you working with him?'

'No, nothing is decided yet – we don't want to rush into anything, but he sounds just the kind of person one could go to Africa with. Well at least we can try him out, for fuck's sake. Get him to take some location shots, do screen tests . . . we don't even know yet if he'll be interested.'

'Does that mean we are all heading back home?'

'That's what I've been trying to explain to you. We can't really do anything until you take us round some villages and we take some shots of those lecherous old types in their natural habitat, so to speak. It's all very well me and you going round like a tourist taking in some peep-show; if we don't get the camera to do some peeping, all these people won't know what we're talking about.'

'That suits me. That means I can leave any time. You follow at your own pace.'

'No, no, don't do that. Don't be such a spoilsport. You *have* to see Tati's studios with us, it's all arranged.'

'Since when?'

'And Jean Rouch. From what I've heard, he may be the kind of cameraman we're looking for. He's done some fantastic things in African villages.'

'Joan! Jean Rouch is not a feature-film maker. He is an anthropologist who uses the cinema. He is not a cameraman you hire; he does his own thing from start to finish.'

'But he's made a film. Harry's sent for it. We'll go and watch it tomorrow.'

'Jean Rouch is an academic. He's a scholar, a field researcher in anthropology. He has not made any feature film.'

'Another fucking academic. Anyway, he was just somebody to consider. You see, the French do these things better than most, I mean, the kind of film I want from your fucking play. It's poetry you know, we've got to get the poetry on that bloody celluloid otherwise we miss the point. That's why I want to see this other man, Cartier-Bresson.'

'Who?'

'Cartier-Bresson. Ever heard of him? You have to see some of the work he's done. The photos, they're sheer poetry.'

'Are there two of them, Joan? Because the only one I know is a still photographer. Is there a film director or whatever called Cartier-Bresson?'

'Oh, you're just locked up in this British thing, that's your problem. The French have a different approach to film . . .'

'Joan. Cartier-Bresson takes stills, still photos. He is reputedly brilliant at it but that it what he does. He takes – still photos, Joan. What use would he be to you on a cinema set, and what makes you think you can hire him as a film cameraman?'

Saltzman; the Orchid; the architect, Cedric Price, Joan's special friend whose flat she often used in London, where many of the exchanges took place; and the two Gerrys, all tried to clear her mind of this new entry of Cartier-Bresson into the creeping project of *The Lion and the Jewel*. Tom Driberg no longer took part in the discussions, having long given up Joan as an adorable but directionless *enfant terrible*. For Tom the Fun Palace was the last straw. The film gang soon found that nothing could expunge either Jean Rouch or Cartier-Bresson, or any other outlandish notion, once a personage, object or vision had entered the listing in Joan's exotic catalogue for a project that, for her, also occupied the regions of exotica, much as she endeavoured to embrace it as a surrogate for a craved reality. Still, Jacques Tati's studio made sense. The Orchid had seen it, it appeared worth a visit and, perhaps, once she had been thrust into the midst of actual filming, on a working set, and talking shop with the irrepressible Jacques Tati – Maren had formed a very clear picture of the man's personality – their problem genius might actually return raring to embark on her own film project. And so the caravan took off for Paris and Jacques Tati, Maren flatly refusing to participate in any motion that involved tracking down Jean Rouch or Cartier-Bresson.

For the film project, the visit was a disaster. Jacques Tati's set appeared to have acted as the final catalyst to Joan's mental projections for the Fun Palace, which now came to dominate everything in her mind, theatre included. What London needed was not theatre, or films, but a Fun Palace. What exactly was a Fun Palace – animal, mineral or vegetable? Maren still could not tell. All he now learnt was that her architect friend, Cedric Price, had been drawn into it and was providing some kind of designs – Maren could never gauge how persuaded Cedric was of the new obsession, but he certainly wished to please. The Arts Council of Great Britain and other institutions regained their rightful places in her demonology because they did not jump to finance it. Various local government councils became corrupt, conservative shitbags because they would not provide land where she wanted it – Battersea? Bermondsey? East Stratford? The prospective sites changed at every conversation. How did the Fun Palace differ from the circus? From the seaside promenades and fairgrounds?

No one knew exactly, least of all Tom Driberg who, in his lazy drawl, would plead: 'But Jowwhn, it would help if I only knew what this new thing is all about. I can't simply go to the Prime Minister and ask him to sign over Parliament Square for your pet project. He'll point out – and quite rightly I must say – that the nation already has a Fun Palace called the Houses of Parliament.'

Still, the designs multiplied, filled her promiscuous bag, where they jostled for place with a dozen playscripts which she attempted to doctor from time to time, and the few sheets of paper that contained all the cinematic conversion she had achieved on *The Lion and the Jewel*.

Jacques Tati proved, however, to be worth a visit to Paris on his own, from any corner of the world. He was working on the set of *Mon Oncle*, an open-air, spatially ingenious construct that deserved to be preserved as a fairground and flexible film- or multi-media-theatre space – it was not difficult to see how it came to capture Joan's imagination and reinforce her Fun Palace ideas. Jacques Tati was the same loose-limbed personality in real life as he was on the screen, full of mischief, as Maren was to find out in his short stay. After an all-day shooting on the set, he hosted them in an authentic, not touristic, bistro, run by a family of husband, wife, sons and daughters, the patron himself moving solicitously among his restricted guests, watching their reactions to his kitchen skills, ready to snatch the plate off the table if the diner so much as looked dubious as he ate. Only after dislodging the plate would he even ask what the diner had found wrong with the food, as Maren discovered when the man mistook an expression on his face for one of disapproval. It took a lot of persuasion to reassure the man that he was merely savouring the unusual flavour – that it was his own Yoruba 'po-faced' version of approval – and he called Joan to witness. The plate, already back in the kitchen, was restored while the patron stood over him, watching his treatment of the next few forkfuls. Maren grinned like mad, nodding with every fibre of his body to the percolation of the truly delicious juices of the best duckling he had tasted in his life. He was rewarded by the sight of his host visibly relaxing, beaming with satisfaction and a new-found love for his Nigerian guest.

It was only as they drank coffee afterwards that Jacques Tati revealed that he had organised that little drama. The proprietor did indeed have a reputation for such occasional interventions – a frown of doubt or disapproval, and the guest's plate would vanish from under his nose; then a courteous but determined interrogation – underdone? overcooked? too salty? too tough or too tender? not enough cream? There would be no going back. If the complaint was one that touched, or was suspected to touch the essence of the dish itself, then that was it for that item. No matter how passionately the client pleaded his satisfaction with the dish as it was; he was presented with the menu all over again and had no choice but to make a new selection. And so the cinema comedian had primed the proprietor in advance, determined that his guests should have a real-life taste of the Gallic perfectionism lodged in the bistro temperament.

It was glorious to be back in Paris, even though he had neither time nor inclination to visit his old haunts, the encounter with Jacques Tati more than compensating for that deprivation. The niggling problems on the home front persisted. Maren returned to London before the others, resumed work in the Soho offices while he awaited Joan's return. The verbal whirlwind blew into the offices a few days later, in its deceptively gentle but disorganised fashion, and announced that she had to leave immediately for Ireland where Brendan Behan had been taken seriously ill. He needed someone to stay with him, to see that he took his medications regularly, and stayed away from alcohol, and generally to nursemaid him.

Maren felt stymied. He had shared quite a few boisterous (one-sided) glasses with Brendan in the bar of Joan's Theatre Royal in Stratford East, where Brendan's play was running, but he had his own 'sick' situation at home, and the sickness was not from alcoholism. And just what, he asked, was he supposed to be doing in the meantime? And how long would Joan be away? And was there any hard commitment coming forth from the direction of the Saltzmans, the Orchids, Petunias, Chrysanthemums, or whatever? She waved her hands airily – Saltzman's accountants had instructions to continue to pay a weekly allowance as long as Maren was kept in London on the project. Commitment, Maren spat between gritted teeth, commitment! Was any of them taking an option on the damned work? And did they understand that he had to get back home as fast as possible? That he was needed at home even more desperately than Brendan Behan needed Littlewood? All the improvisation and casualness and camaraderie were all very well, very charming and even, in parts, stimulating, but he was embroiled in a real-life situation, not one of this theatrical make-believe, of 'darling' this one moment and 'fucking' that the next, and anti-Establishment imprecations that flirted with Establishment finance in return for nothing but indecisions, distractions and airy non-commitments and self-release in iconoclastic non-sequiturs. When, if ever, were they really getting down to work? To a timetable? A decision on producers, crew, and so on? When, to get down to the most critical consideration right then, when would one see the colour of a contract?

But she was gone anyway, and Maren was left in possession of an entire floor of offices in Soho, a secretary-typist, and sheets and sheets of paper. Strolling through the empty space, he realised suddenly that Joan would never make the film. He had a suspicion that she was afraid. Her magic lay in other directions, on the stage boards of Theatre Royal, Stratford, where she took Brecht into the divergent theatrical current of the British, and especially of the deeply regional music-hall tradition, or music theatre. She had tapped into this neglected source, bringing to it her experience of itinerant street theatre. Mistress of improvisation, sometimes even to a fault, where it relied more on faith than technique, she could remain constantly inventive, coaxing unsuspected levels of performance even from amateurs. Her domain was the Theatre Workshop, with all the flexibility and creative freedom that the term expressed, but she was ill at ease with the screen, where images were frozen for all time. To make matters worse, this was a different culture, a text also that was not only outside her normal cultural certitudes or dictates, but was already 'set' – a plain story, with a beginning, middle and end. Joan Littlewood's genius lay in manipulating the 'unfinished' work, breathing visual life into it. With *The Lion*, she was confronted, in addition, with a society that held for her – its theatrical potential conceded – mainly a voyeuristic fascination.

Maren became more and more persuaded of this as he went over in his mind what now seemed to be nothing but a series of demands, conditions, distractions, consultations . . . all of which now struck him as escapist ploys, albeit unconscious, but most certainly contrived to talk and argue and research the project to death. Some time, probably when work began on translating the play into film language, she had taken fright. Then, Cartier-Bresson! Fun Palace! Jean Rouch! Brendan Behan! It was time he returned home. But first, there was the little problem of money. He had been away nearly six weeks and he dared not return empty-handed. Far too much depended on his bringing something back after being out of action for so long.

He mused on the problem, tossed up the choices between the three main prospective producers. He decided that the situation called for contrary reasoning – which of the three was least likely, both from his own observations, and Joan's forceful opinions, to get the film rolling before the expiration of a year's option? It was a curious switch of which he only slowly became aware – he did not, after all, want the film made, at least not just then. Somehow, he had gone off the idea. One section of his mind attributed the cause to Joan's flip-flopping, another to developments on the home front – it was true that he now wished to avoid any serious commitment for another year; he had gradually developed the feeling that he must not be tied down, must leave his hands and feet free for whatever demands events at home were likely to make on him. So, it became a case of inverse qualification – which of them appeared least capable of realising the project within a year? He decided that, despite his flamboyant confidence, it was the Orchid.

And so, it was the Orchid he called, and they met for lunch. Was he interested in taking a year's option on the play? The Orchid was only too delighted. Anxious, however, to insure his plans, Maren proceeded to lay down one condition: Joan Littlewood would either direct the film herself, or be given the chance of first refusal. She would also have a free hand in deciding her own crew. Even Cartier-Bresson, laughed the Orchid? Even Pablo Picasso, Maren insisted. The Orchid shrugged. All right, he said, the clause would be inserted in the agreement. He promised to have the cheque, and the papers ready for signature, the following day. No, Maren insisted, only whenever Joan was back. He was not backing away from his decision, but he wanted to tell Joan himself, and the two Gerrys, the two Gerrys especially. He had already thought out a way for ensuring that Joan did make the film – if she wanted to – just in case the Orchid did upset his assessment and Maren was confronted by the sight of a ready-to-roll Orchid in the substitute village of Ilujinle. And he had the certain feeling that, left to the Orchid, Joan would not be allowed within a thousand miles of the filming, once he got his hands on a year's option.

And he also remembered to insist: 'Make that cheque directly cashable, because I'm leaving for home the very day that agreement is signed.'

X Squatters and Other Awkward Guests

He took to spending less and less time at the bungalow in Agodi, using Mbari for most of his rehearsals and surrendering the bungalow to guest companies, including amateur groups. He had indeed become accustomed to the new environment in Felele, a new area under development, still so much part of the bush that grasscutter pawmarks littered the backyard some mornings. Agodi, which he shared with the NNDP thugs, was not that much removed from nature either, or else he had succeeded so well in persuading the other homeless denizens of Agodi that he had left the place for good, that it did not take long for one of them – so it appeared at the time – to seek permanent shelter near the building, leaving home in the morning to forage for food and returning in the evening. The bungalow had served its turn, nurturing both indigenous and English-language theatre. It did double service for the production of J. P. Clark's *Song of a Goat*, for it was in the open air of its premises that the nightly rites of the sacrificial goat were concluded. That piece of – for some tastes – grisly realism was a feature of the performance that Maren had insisted upon, if only to exorcise the playwright's sudden proneness to motor accidents. Even when driven by others, Maren included, John Pepper's Karmann-Ghia went remorselessly for the nearest obstacle, trees and all, even within the University campus. The goat was decapitated in full view of the audience. There was a night of near possession. Maren, playing Zifa, with hours of practice on plantain stems behind him, decapitated the goat that night with a single stroke. Segun Olusola, playing the younger brother, discerned a weird look in his eyes, fled and did not stop running until he had reached the safety of Agodi. The Mother, Francesca Pereira, danced like a demented witch, her cry of 'A brave stroke, my son' sending unaccustomed shivers through the audience, as several conceded afterwards.

It was Anthony, the general caretaker, cook and washerman, who first observed the squatter, a sleek python, emerging from the direction of the house in the morning. The bungalow was one of the old colonial wooden structures raised on concrete stilts, one large, sprawling bedroom surrounded by huge swathes of verandah space, where the company camped down on mats and mattresses during workshops and performances. For a long time Maren had even toyed with the notion of converting the space beneath the wooden floor – its concrete stilts were nearly six foot high – into some kind of garden of rare plants, of the kind that did not require much sunshine – culled from the botanical gardens nearby – but he was never sufficiently settled to embark on such a project. And then, of course, the period of his precarious tenancy put paid to any such ideas. The ground beneath the bungalow therefore remained arid, dusty, the underspace of the wooden floor itself clogged with filthy cobwebs and a thousand wasps' nests. Beyond wasps, spiders and jiggers, therefore, not one square inch beneath the bungalow was congenial to any living creature, not even the common rat. Yet the python was seen regularly emerging from beneath the building in the morning, and returning at set times at dusk, with clockwork precision.

Finally, Maren kept watch and, sure enough, the sleek coil emerged in the morning somewhere from, it seemed, the floorboards, slithered its way through the sparse foliage that grew around the house, vanished into the bush. In the evening, it returned the same way. The ring of foliage was meticulously searched; it revealed no trace of the snake's habitation. Then the floorboard of the house was examined from within, inch by inch. No hole by which the snake could enter was discovered, no niche or crevice that could serve it as a resting place. As if the unusual tenant – or simply visitor – recognised the zone that spelt danger, it always moved with lightning speed across the open ground before disappearing into the bushes. All attempts to ambush and dispose of it once and for all therefore remained abortive; the snake was gone before the first missile could be launched.

And then, of course, several of the attempts were merely half-hearted. There was something about the regularity of movements of this snake that instilled apprehension. A lively debate about its presence had indeed split the theatre groups into several warring camps. Duro Ladipo's group was persuaded that it was Kola Ogunmola who had introduced the snake, with the purpose of terrorising Duro's group and possibly even killing off the great tragedian himself. Kola Ogunmola was just as certain that the snake was Duro's *alter ego*, out to do mischief to him; why else had the snake proved so elusive? Moreover, was it not significant that Duro was never around whenever the reptile appeared? The conclusion was obvious – Duro Ladipo could not be in two places at the same time, so he had to be either within the snake's body or else within his own human body.

Orisun, for its part, was convinced that the snake was an NNDP agent, out to get their man. Their thugs had been expected at performances but had obviously been scared off by news of preparations which had somehow leaked to them. The more concerned believers in this theory despaired of getting Maren to a *babalawo*, not merely on account of the dangerous intruder, but to be fortified against other psychic assaults that might be in preparation against him. Anyone would be a fool to think that the snake would be acting alone; there would clearly be back-up forces, maybe in the shape of one of the thousand wasps which had made their home beneath the bungalow. And come to think of it, whoever saw so many wasps together underneath one building? Perhaps it was not just one wasp but the entire colony of wasps that the NNDP had programmed, and was ready to unleash, *à la* Alfred Hitchcock, when the signal was given. They tried to get him to abandon the bungalow completely, but gave up when he reminded them that the wasps had been tenants beneath the house even before G-Man came to live in it. One only had to take a look at the mud hives to see that they could not be much younger than the colonial structure itself.

If the reptile was indeed an NNDP dacoit, it got a well-merited comeuppance one afternoon when it broke its usual routine. Maren was in the house with Wale Ogunyemi, working with him on some new part, when he noticed a gleam in the sunlight beside a pile of mown grass on the lawn outside. It was fat, long, and unquestionably sluggish, quite unlike the greased lightning that dashed out across the front of the house in the mornings and evenings. Keeping his eye on the monster, he asked Wale to get a stick. Then his voice took on an urgency as he watched the snake drag itself into the pile of grass. Wale had just sufficient time to grab the bronze *ogboni** staff, one from Maren's most prized collection, and then he was out of the house, leaping like a madman, ignoring Maren's protestations that he might do damage to the ancient *ogboni* staff. Wale had also caught a vanishing glimpse of the reptile and knew that, once inside the mound of grass, it would prove nearly impossible to flush it out. And it could slide off into the nearby bush across the large perimeter of the mound.

Maren dashed out after him, grabbing the nearest weapon to hand. Once arrived there, however, the question then became: how to go about it? The quarry could be anywhere within the mound. Perhaps it even had its home within the pile of grass which had lain there for months awaiting the dry season when it would be burnt. It was then that Maren recollected how sluggishly the snake had moved; no, it would not be too far from its point of entry. Quickly, he began to scoop out the grass while Wale stood guard with the upraised *ogboni* staff. They could feel the movement as the trapped reptile crept deeper and deeper into the centre of the humus. It must have decided to change direction because, suddenly, with a desperate burst of energy, it turned to use the now much lightened route from which the grass had been lifted. Wale thwacked it neatly amidship and a rain of blows fell from both Orisun hunters. The massive coil thrashed futilely, then lay still.

In no time, Wale was preparing a fire to roast it but Maren stopped him. 'I want it skinned. I intend to make a pair of slippers out of it. When I wear those slippers,' he laughed, 'their psychic force will be turned against the snake's masters. Skin it carefully and we'll peg it out.'

After its stomach was split, two fair-sized *emo†* popped out of its

*An enclave of elders, lawgivers.
†Tiny rodents.

gut, freshly swallowed and dead. The mound of grass had proved its undoing. Clearly the rodents had made their home in the pile and it had found this an easier feeding ground than its normal forage in the woods. The company fed off its delicate meat during rehearsal break that same night. Not all of them, however, since some were still convinced that it was no ordinary snake; its flesh might turn into something else – a tortoise or snail, with its shell intact, and then what a hell of a stomach ache that would prove! They looked askance of Maren, at Wale and others, convinced that one or the other must have been possessed of a stronger charm than the unknown enemy; only such a superior force could have succeeded in putting the snake to death. Maren's complaint that Wale had bent the top of his *ogboni* staff with his blows only confirmed it – of course! Everything finally made sense. It was the *edan** force within the *ogboni* that vanquished the deadly envoy deployed against Maren by his mortal enemies. It all went to confirm what they had always known, that Maren had a strong head; how else could it be that he was at home at the snake's most vulnerable moment, that is, when it had just dined? And how came it that the *ogboni* staff was conveniently at hand to settle the score once for all? What instinct made him buy the staff in the first place, collector of antiques or not? There was, undoubtedly, a protective shield around Maren that the enemy could not penetrate!

Whether the snake was a secret weapon of the aggrieved party or not, its Government still had its own plans for the former lecturer of Ife. Perhaps the snake was indeed an agent, and had at least succeeded not merely in locating the hideout of the wanted man, but in transmitting the information back to its headquarters before its sudden demise. Certainly, a few weeks after its disappearance, irked perhaps at its failure to bring the latest reports of doings in the enemy camp, officials of the Ministry of Works and Housing appeared in Agodi accompanied by a large lorry, and a policeman from the station that was attached to the House of Assembly. Ordering the straggle of squatters out, they piled an assortment of stage props, books, scripts, costumes, a refrigerator, mats and mattresses into the lorry, and took away what keys they could find. In the midst

*A figurine endowed with sacred powers.

of the operation, the policeman was heard to give a cry of alarm. When the others rushed inside the building, they found him holding a revolver, grinning in triumph. A revolver! And where, he was asked, had he found it? In an empty chest of drawers, he claimed. He was simply making a routine final check to ensure that nothing had been left behind. The three or four inmates of the compound were immediately placed under arrest, all except one who had succeeded in slipping off to look for Maren and warn him of the development.

Leaving an official of the Ministry of Works in charge, the policeman dashed off to his police station to report the sinister find. His boss sent him back with two more policemen, both senior, to sweep through the premises with a fine broom, turn out every cranny and turn up any more lethal material. The escaped actor had found Maren in the meantime and he returned while the search was on. Feigning astonishment, then righteous indignation at the invasion of his premises, he demanded that they either vacate the compound immediately or produce a search warrant. They confronted him in turn with the gun, whose presence they asked him to explain.

'A gun? Where did you find it?'

'In this very place,' the officer replied, pulling out an empty drawer.

'That's strange. I've never seen such an item in there. But then I don't really live here that much. As you see, I have turned the place over to three acting companies. They come and go and bring all sorts of things in here. Let me take a look at that.'

Before his partners could stop him, the man had thrust the gun in his hand, snarling, 'Are you trying to say that you have never seen this gun before?'

Maren quickly pawed the gun, turning it over in his hand. 'I haven't said anything yet. I know we staged a sketch not so long ago where a gun featured. You know, a stage gun – we call them props. I am trying to see if this was the prop we used.'

He pretended not to hear one of the officers whispering tensely to the discoverer, 'You should not have let him touch it. Now we can't use the evidence of fingerprints.' Loudly he said, 'Our *oga* says we have to bring you back to the police station.'

'Which police station?' Maren demanded to know.

'We're from the House of Assembly post.'

'I see. You still haven't shown me your search warrant, or whatever.'

The man from the Ministry of Works and Housing spoke up. 'We had instructions to come and clear the house. Actually, we had been looking for your residence for quite some time; a letter came that you were no longer an employee of the University, and that you were occupying a government house. We tried to trace which house it was and we only succeeded yesterday. So the PermSec sent us instructions to go and clear you out immediately. We had to have a policeman with us to witness the evacuation and sign the inventory with us.'

'Were you there when he found this er . . . this so-called gun?'

'Don't answer him,' the discoverer screamed. 'You are not to answer any question from him.'

The official, however, ignored him. 'No, sir. We were busy clearing up in the kitchen when we heard his shout.'

'Good,' Maren nodded. 'I just wanted to know.'

'Let's go, let's go.' And the policeman began to shoo them out. 'We have finished searching and he is wanted at the station. Anyway, I don't want to stay in this *juju* place.'

'What *juju* place?' Maren was now ready to lose his temper with the man. 'Look here, you. You were sent here to perform some dirty job, which you have done. What I won't stand from you is this kind of scandalmongering. Where have you seen any *juju* in this house?'

The cop threw back his head and roared with laughter. 'Look at this one *o*. He is trying to look so innocent. These acada people, they try to pretend that they are better than illiterates. A University man, he calls himself, but he keeps *juju* inside his wardrobe.'

Maren looked from one officer to the other. 'Is this man mad? Or are there other things you people have been planting in this house?'

'But sir,' said the third officer, who had said nothing till now, 'it is nothing to be ashamed of. He showed it to us – it's in here.' And he walked over to the wardrobe and flung it open. 'There, sir.'

Had all these people gone mad? Or was this the opening gambit for a diabolical game the Government wished to play with him? Charge him with illegal possession of a gun, then reveal to the press that they had found his house festooned with the most evil kind of *juju*. The doors of the wardrobe, thrown open, merely yawned empty. He turned round to the policeman, frowning.

'Underneath, sir,' the man said, pointing to the partition about four inches from the base of the wardrobe, with an electric lead just visible from his standing position. It was the section in which a light bulb was affixed and usually kept alight in order to protect the wardrobe from damp. This small compartment was screened off from the rest of the wardrobe, the connecting piece of wood being perforated to enable the warm air from the bulb to seep through gently into the main body of the cupboard.

'This anti-humidity thing,' Maren laughed, 'is that your idea of *juju*?'

'But it's there, sir. If you bend down you will see it.'

And at that moment, Maren wondered who on earth could have installed charms beneath his wardrobe, and on behalf of whom. That they were intended to harm, he had no doubt, but such things simply didn't bother him. As he bent down to take a look, and to fish out whatever was there, his mind ran through a handful of members of the group who might have had the opportunity to enter the bedroom and leave the presumably injurious stuff hidden there. Then he saw . . .

'I need a stick.'

The Ministry of Works man dashed outside and brought back a stick. He observed that the policemen had retreated, seeing that he was intent on bringing out whatever was inside the compartment. The stick arrived, and he began to scoop out stuff . . . out came the skeleton of a rodent, then dried leaves, dried grass, more skeletons, feathers, miniature skulls that could belong equally to small rodents or birds, other indecipherable objects that could have been veg-etal, or hairy tegument . . . and suddenly the light dawned!

He now lay flat on his side, and applied the stick to a different purpose, poking the sides, then the floor of the compartment. He found what he was looking for at the corner – a round hole, about one and a half times the size of a golf ball. He got up smiling, dusted himself, then told the watchers to follow him. 'One of you should remain behind,' he said, 'and watch if anything comes through that bottom compartment.'

They trooped obediently after him down the steps. He turned at the bottom of the steps, passed through a break in the foliage and ducked underneath the base of the bungalow. He made for the spot above where the wardrobe would roughly be. There it was, the hole which led through the floor into the wardrobe, right in the corner of the beams across which the floorboards had been laid. The officers craned their necks to watch him poke through the same hole with the stick, pushing it all the way through until it disappeared completely. A shout from the bedroom indicated that the lookout had seen the stick.

The quiet officer spoke. 'So you think someone planted it there, sir? You think someone pushed the *juju* through that hole?'

Maren laughed. 'What *juju*? You've just solved a long-standing mystery for me and my company. I've been living in this house with a python for heaven knows how long. It's been actually bedding down in my wardrobe.'

'You mean a snake, sir!'

'In my bloody wardrobe. We killed it only three weeks ago. We had seen it come and go but never found out where it hid itself.' He shook his head and laughed. 'In my wardrobe. That was the nest you saw me scoop out. All that debris, the leaves and twigs are at least a year old.'

They ducked under the beams again and emerged from under the bungalow. The policemen – all except the discoverer who kept stolid guard on him – insisted on going in to take another look at the python's nest, their faces filled with amazement. When they emerged, they gave him the most peculiar looks, shaking their heads in wonder.

'And you have been living here for more than two years, sir?'

Maren nodded.

'I think that snake has been living there just as long,' the quiet officer continued. 'I know about snakes. My father is quite famous in my town for treating snakebites and he keeps snakes about the house. He is well known, sir; people come to him for all kinds of treatment.'

'Well, that snake is now just a pair of slippers.'

'Oh, you shouldn't have bothered about him, sir. That snake could never have harmed you. They are quite domestic, you know, pythons and a number of other kinds. He must have got used to you by now; he would know your smell and recognise your own sounds. He really must have liked being with you or he would never have stayed so long.'

Maren gave him a peculiar look, as if to suggest he was mad. 'Well, he should have introduced himself. I don't like the idea of a non-paying tenant in my wardrobe.'

That was one policeman with a sense of humour. He chuckled for the first time and pointed to the loaded lorry from the Ministry of Works. 'Neither does the Government, sir.'

At the police station, there developed a lengthy delay during which telephone calls were made, plain-clothes, but quite obvious, police officers came and went. He was left alone, noting only that the activities became quite frenzied as the time wore on. His lawyers had been contacted, but they were not allowed access to him; nonetheless they succeeded in sending him instructions to say nothing and admit to nothing. Eventually, the investigators thinned out, and he was left alone with no more than three officers in uniform – one of them was the witty one – and one plain-clothes officer. Bail, he was informed, had been agreed, but he must first make a statement. The regulation lined paper was produced, and a ballpoint pen, and the felon was invited to state his side of the story. Maren observed that the witty officer, who, it appeared, was now in charge of the station, had made various efforts to establish sympathetic eye contact with him, even when the legislators' police post was inundated with officers from different branches, mostly in mufti. As the force thinned out, however, and he handed him the statement paper, he spoke out.

'Don't forget what your lawyers told you. Don't write down anything more than you have to.'

Maren made no reply. He preferred to begin with a distrustfulness of any officer, no matter how friendly or witty he seemed.

'My name is Ojo – your lawyer will tell you more about me. I was the one who smuggled in their note,' the man said. 'They want you in "E" Branch in Iyaganku. You have to be very careful,' he warned. 'There's a South African called Ceulman who's been put in charge of organising that division. We've just learnt that he is in

Ibadan; what for, I don't know. Be careful of him. I'm just telling you so you should know.'

Maren finally looked up, giving up the pretence that no one was talking to him. The officer continued, 'You should know also that Corporal Adekori – the man who found the gun – has made a statement. He claims he found the gun hidden under your mattress . . .'

'That's a bloody lie!' Maren exploded. 'He . . .'

The man smiled. 'I know. I was there. Even when he came to the station to report the find, he said it was in a drawer. And he repeated the same thing in Agodi. I'm telling you so you would know, that's all. One more thing you should know,' and he cast a quick look around. 'He's stated that you attempted to bribe him – control yourself, sir,' he admonished, as Maren rose from his seat. 'I'm just telling you so you would know.'

'But bribe him to do what?'

'To pretend he never found the gun.'

'Is the man mad? The find had already been reported here. You people had already been despatched to turn the whole place upside down to look for other incriminating items.'

The man gave a lopsided grin. 'I am only telling you so you should know.'

Maren flapped his arms about. 'But surely, when you make your own statement – I mean, how will they reconcile that? When? When was this bribery attempt? I was never even alone with the man for a moment. He must surely know that you can expose him.'

'He says it was when we left you with him. You remember, we went back into the house to look at the python's nest.'

Maren threw down his pen in disgust. 'This doesn't make sense. Wait just a minute, let's go back a little. Your man Adekori finds a gun, he rushes to the station and announces this find, leaving the gun in the "position of find" to quote the man himself, "so as not to destroy any evidence of actual location thereof." Whereupon you and your colleague are sent to check the place more thoroughly, take possession of the gun and so on. You see the gun, yet I am supposed to have attempted to bribe the most junior among you to make him deny ever finding such an item. Am I right so far?'

'In the main, yes.'

'Which means that if I attempted to bribe him, I must first think of bribing you and your colleague. Have you also made a statement to that effect?'

'We were not asked to make a statement,' the man replied.

'I don't get this,' said Maren, shaking his head to clear it. 'This is a miserable little corporal, well below you. He says I tried to bribe him, he does not report the incident to you when you emerge from the house; he does not suggest that I also tried to bribe you . . .'

The quiet officer laughed. 'In his statement, he says that he saw us two closeted with you, and that he heard us telling you off, though he does not know what it was all about. You see, that was our bait. Or lifeline. It's being left for us to decide whether or not we choose to grab it.'

'And what are you going to say?'

The officer sighed and shook his head. 'You University people, you are so remote from what goes on. The Deputy Commissioner did not bother to ask for our statement because he does not really need it. If we choose to corroborate Adekori's statement, fine. If not, we are simply ignored. They want an additional charge of attempted bribery, maybe just to embarrass you. The DC was on the phone to Government House for quite some time. That's where he takes his orders from – I'm only telling you so you should know. If we want a special thank-you handshake from Government House, of course we'll confirm that you also tried to bribe us.' He stabbed at the still-empty statement sheets. 'Please, write your statement, then you will go for your interview at the "E" Branch. I know the man there, a complete gentleman. He won't keep you long.'

'Who is he?' Maren asked. 'This corporal of yours, just who is he?'

'He came in through the party. He was recruited here, trained on the job and posted to the House of Assembly. We call him Special Assignments Officer.'

'A thug, in short.'

'No,' said the quiet officer. 'Some poor relation of the Premier himself.'

He had totally forgotten that Ojeli was the man in charge of the new 'E' Branch. Maren was ushered in with meticulous courtesy and offered a seat. Ojeli leafed through some files before him, asking to be excused for just a few moments.

'I am anxious to get home as early as possible myself, so I'll just rush through these and we can have our little chat.' He chuckled. 'I wasn't expecting us to get together again so soon since the little affair of the Lucky Dippers.'

Maren said, 'We have a performance at Mbari tonight. If I could get there in time to start them off...'

'We won't be long, I promise. I don't really see why this case should be referred to us. As far as I can make out, it's a straight-forward case of illegal possession. Anyway, just a few more moments with these files and we'll be done.'

A white man came in through the curtains from the next room. He looked slightly hunchbacked and did not strike Maren as having any special business to discuss. He had come to look him over, that much was plain. Maren ignored him, gnawing his nails mentally as the moments slipped by. With all the commotion that had taken place over the afternoon, he was afraid that some disorientation would have taken its toll among the company. He kept his outward calm, however, and waited. At last, the 'E' Branch man was done. He pushed aside his files, and brought out a slim file, his case file, Maren imagined.

'So what have you been up to, Maren? What is all this about a gun?'

Maren shrugged. 'A stage prop, I guess. I know I have seen it around, maybe a year ago, probably less. I have three theatre com-panies moving in and out of that place, not to mention mushroom groups and starving artists.'

He smiled. 'Well, to tell you the truth, that is not really my business. I am not investigating that case at all, you understand. But some people seem to think that we should take an interest in your activities, so, we receive instructions from high up, and we follow them. Now let me come straight to the point: do you believe in violent revolutions?'

Maren stared at him in bewilderment. 'Do I believe in violent revolutions?'

'That was my question, sir. Do you believe in violent revolutions?'

Maren shrugged. 'That depends.'

'On what?'

'On which country we are talking about. And what period of its history.'

'Well, suppose we say Nigeria, and now. Do you believe that what Nigeria needs right now is a violent revolution?'

'No. I do not believe that a violent revolution will solve our present problems. There will be sporadic insurrections as a result of these fraudulent elections, but I don't think we need a violent revolution.'

Ojeli pulled out a drawer in the right side of his desk, pulled out a file bulging with newspaper clippings, documents and notes. He leafed through the pages with slow deliberation, arrived at a news clipping which he teased out.

'In 1962, you attended an Afro-Asian Writers Conference in Cairo. There you called for a violent revolution in all former colonies, including Nigeria. The full text of your statement is reported in this Egyptian newspaper.'

'That is not possible,' asserted Maren.

Ojeli passed the clipping to him. 'Take a look. There is your picture, and that is the text of your address. Your name is splashed all over the page.'

Maren took a long look at the clipping. 'This is clearly a forgery,' he said. 'I never attended that meeting.'

Ojeli looked disappointed. 'Look, Maren, you are not being accused of anything, so there is no need to be on the defensive. I've told you, I'm not even in charge of the criminal case against you. But I have been instructed to establish some things about you.'

Maren sighed. 'You know, this is about the third time I've been accused of lying, all within the past three hours, and all of those accusations – pure concoctions. I am telling you, I never did attend that conference in Cairo.'

'But you went with Tayo Akpata, Femi Okunnu, Elizabeth Brown and some self-styled comrades.'

'Yes, I did travel with them. I did arrive at Cairo airport, but I never attended the conference. I did not even enter Cairo.'

He shook his head. 'I don't understand. Even in the final report of the conference, your contribution is there, just as the contributions of other members of the Nigerian delegation.'

'I did not attend the Afro-Asian Writers Conference. I have never been to Cairo in all my life – except of course the airport.'

'You really want me to believe that?'

'It happens to be the truth.'

'How come? I mean, what is all this about? What are you trying to tell me?'

'It is a long story. Look, you promised I would be in time for curtain up at Mbari, and I really should be there at least a good half hour before; I know there will be emergencies – some of the costumes and props were carted away by the Works and Housing people . . . and so on. We may have to do some desperate improvising. For all I know we might even have an actor or two missing – some of them are recent recruits, easily frightened by this sort of thing. I've been away for nearly six hours now, and they may think it's their turn to be rounded up.'

The officer thought for a moment, said, 'Just a moment,' and disappeared into the adjoining room into which the hunchbacked white had also retreated. There was some evident consultation and when he emerged he began to tidy up the desk.

'I tell you what we'll do. It's a long time since I've been to that Mbari of yours, so why don't I go with you? Then, once you've got the play started, we can sit down at the bar and have our chat. But that means you'll have to return here tomorrow, because everything has to be formally concluded. Police work apart, I am really dying with curiosity. I mean, what you are saying is, one mustn't believe everything one reads in the newspaper? Well, even a child knows that already, but this is a different dimension altogether. This is an international conference, hosted by a government . . .'

Maren smiled inwardly, admiring the ploy of the decision. The policeman was about to gain a useful *entrée* into the Arts Centre, with its suspect breed of artists and intellectuals, and interrogate him at the same time. Still, it was a reasonable bargain, and there was nothing he could do about it, anyway. He was really worried about the effects of his uncertain fate on the company, and on the night's performance.

From the very first moment, he had resented the procedure of the Cairo conference. Invitations had arrived through the Nigerian Trade Union and the Nigerian Youth Movement, and he could not help wondering what these had to do with a writers' union, or association, or whatever. The two groups had somehow acquired the authority to decide who should be at the conference and who should not. The delegation itself, nearly fifteen strong, included only three writers. He accepted the invitation, and the statement that he had in mind when he arrived in Cairo had little to do with revolutions, violent or peaceful. As soon as he became aware of the composition of the delegation, and the poor-relation status to which writers had been assigned beside the trade unions, his resentment had grown inordinately. He quietly determined to give battle in the conference hall in Cairo.

The invitations had also come late, almost as an afterthought. They arrived so late that there was no time to obtain the necessary health injections. So he contacted the Embassy: would there be any problems? None whatever, said the Ambassador. The organisers also contacted the Embassy to let them know that a handful of the delegates would have no time to obtain the necessary innoculations. Again the Ambassador assured them that the Minister of Health had been contacted, and would personally meet the delegation at the airport. They were cleared to travel for the all-important encounter of ex-colonial nations, organised – but he only learnt this long after the conference – by the Eastern Bloc. Maren did make a mental note, however, that all the non-writers had obtained their invitations well ahead of time; they were not rushed and had all their health papers in order. One other writer had the same problem as he did, that was Elizabeth Browne, a poet from Uyo.

Elizabeth was so heavily pregnant that it was a marvel that she was allowed to travel. When she walked, her motion did not appear to be born out of her own volition; she seemed to be carried forward by the sheer weight of her stomach. She had published some poetry on the pages of newspapers and she brought with her a slim volume of some privately-published poems. A combative, radical personality, she had had running battles with conservative politicians both in her riverine areas of the East and in Lagos. It was not long before they found a common ground of complaint: what were all these non-writers doing at a writers' conference, and where were the more important writers of the Nigerian nation?

The problem began immediately on arrival at Cairo Airport. It was a Friday night. There was no Minister to meet them, only a junior officer from the Foreign Ministry. By then, the Health officers had taken possession of Maren's and Browne's passports. They would have to stay the night at the special Airport Hotel which served for quarantine cases. There was evident embarrassment on the part of the Trade Unionists and Youth Movement delegates that a part of their delegation, indeed a full two-thirds of the writer composition of the delegates, had to be abandoned at the airport, but Maren put them at their ease. They would stay at the Airport Hotel and join the others whenever the Health Minister could be contacted.

The two groups parted company. The Airport Hotel was on the other side of the tarmac, and it was still that period of aviation when humans could actually walk safely across runways, so they were led off at a leisurely walk in the balmy Egyptian evening air, looking forward to visiting the pyramids during conference slack times and tracking down the trysting spots of Cleopatra and her many lovers. The porter trundled their luggage ahead and finally, waving his arm in a grand flourish, announced that they had reached their destination.

'Destination?'

'Just where are we, in the name of Africa?' Elizabeth Browne demanded.

Maren turned to the porter. 'Listen, there is some mistake. We were to be taken to the Airport Hotel.'

'Yes,' the man confirmed. 'This is the Hotel. For quarantine cases.'

Four low-slung wooden huts made up the 'Airport Hotel'. Each was divided into about six rooms, all opening directly onto an unswept corridor. Each room contained beds for between four and five inmates, some of them double-bunks. The interiors were as filthy as the outside, and the two travellers looked into several of them to see if one at least might be an exception. There was none. Window curtains were ragged strips, fly-blown; the sheets and pillowcases had obviously been used by other victims of the quarantine laws and had not been washed. One look at the rooms, and at some of the occupants they contained, and it was apparent that all the diseases of the world were lurking in those rooms, and that it was a place to collect such souvenirs, not be protected from them.

They did not need to exchange words; one look at each other and they turned round and began the walk back to the Airport.

A young white man had been watching them; they had noticed him as they peeked into the rooms but he seemed preoccupied with the book in his hand, and they had quickly excused themselves for the intrusion and moved on. As they passed by on their return, he stepped out of his room, with a mischievous look on his face.

'Where are you from?'

'Nigeria.'

'I am from Poland,' he said. 'A journalist. Did they also tell you you were being taken to the Airport Hotel?'

'Oh. You too?'

'I've been here ten days now. The food is as bad as the rooms. They promised me the Minister would soon release me but this is my tenth day.'

'You seem very cheerful about it.'

'I'm a journalist,' he repeated, as if it explained everything.

'So am I,' said Elizabeth. 'But I am also a poetest' – she always pronounced the word that way – 'poetest'. 'But I am not staying in this pigsty. No way. I did not come over from Nigeria to catch diseases in a foreign land.'

'We're going back to the airport,' Maren said. 'We'll sleep on the benches there and then see what happens tomorrow.'

'I'll walk with you to the gates,' the cheerful Pole offered. 'Most of the inmates here don't speak any language I understand, so I haven't really had any company the whole time I've been here. What have you come to Egypt for?'

They answered him as they walked back the distance to the gates. 'Look at the barbed wire,' the man said. 'The place is like a prison camp, yet they call it a hotel. I have never seen a place like this since I saw films of concentration camps. I don't know how long they intend to keep me here; I think if I had brought some diseases with me, it would be apparent by now.' He prattled on and on, clearly starved of articulate company, delayed them a while at the gate, then reluctantly let them go.

At the airport, the Health Officer received their return with aston-ishment. 'But that is the hotel where we put everyone. It is only for a short while.'

'Too long for us,' Maren retorted. 'And most of all for a woman who is nearly eight months' pregnant. She should be in a clean environment, not in that garbage dump. Look, we are both here as guests of the Egyptian Government. We don't treat guests like that in our own country.'

'Maren is Nigeria's greatest dramatist,' Elizabeth announced, 'And I am a poetest. And a journalist. And I intend to write an account of the kind of treatment you have given the real creative people in our delegation. It is a disgrace.'

The officer tried to pacify her, offered her an armchair in his office. 'I am very sorry, but my office is right here. The Hotel is run by a different department.'

'Please,' Maren pleaded. 'Don't call that place a hotel ever again. Don't so much as use that word.'

'All right, all right. Please settle down. But – b-b-b-but – Madam!' He was staring in horror at Elizabeth Browne, who had taken down the cushions from the chairs, laid them together on the floor and was gently lowering herself onto the makeshift bed. 'Madam, this is an office. I cannot have it turned into a bedroom.'

His eyes were riveted on Elizabeth's incredible protrusion of a stomach. She lay on her back and her stomach rose from the office carpet like a beached whale, pulsating gently with her breathing. The poor man had clearly never had such a ponderous invasion of his office floor in all his life. He turned to Maren for help.

'But my dear sir, she cannot sleep here. It is not a sight for an office, definitely no. She cannot sleep in my office.'

She let out a stifled scream. 'The luggage. The porter has taken it to that place. And I have my medicines there. I must take them before going to bed.'

'I'd better get them,' Maren offered. 'I don't like the idea of leaving even my luggage overnight in that place. No knowing what sort of germs it might pick up.'

The Health Officer tried to hold him back, his face a mask of misery. 'But please, sir, you must do something. She cannot stay here, not like *that*! It is not dignified for my office.'

Maren shrugged. 'Do you want me to lift her up? Because I don't see how else we can resolve it.'

For the third time that night he traversed the tarmac, so ill-lit that he could see the stars clearly. His mind drifted to the varied mythologies and actual histories that involved Egypt, from the bible and the Pharaohs and the famed Exodus to the labours of Champollion and his assiduous tribe of European Egyptologists, and the new breed of Africans that contested their findings, the Senegalese Cheik Anta Diop, implacable and irreverent; Basil Davidson; Chancellor Williams, and others. Now that he was in Cairo, he would see for himself something of Diop's iconographic evidence which, even more than the linguistic, he had found unanswerable. The Egyptians of the Pharaonic dynasties were negroid, if Diop's arguments held, but he had always wondered whether they were largely negro slaves or if they indeed constituted the priesthood, and were part of the Pharaonic dynasties. Arrived back at the 'hotel', he found the bags in the first unoccupied room, obviously the one assigned to them, picked them up and began his walk back, his eyes still beamed on the Egyptian skies and his expectations aglow with the touristic part of the conference. And, oh yes, the confrontation for which he had prepared himself on the flight – who the hell were these strange bodies, Trade Unions and Youth Movements – to interpose themselves between Nigerian writers and their counterparts from the rich cultures of India, Japan, China and so on, whom he was dying to encounter? His studies had made him a distant acquaintance of Rabindranath Tagore. Foraging outside the Leeds curriculum, he had become fascinated with Japanese *No* theatre – now he was to meet the heirs of Tagore and the contemporary practitioners of Japanese theatre. Chinese theatre, which he knew for the opera only, did not, come to think of it, hold much attraction for him . . .

'Stop there!'

The gratingly sharp order came from somewhere in the dark. He turned his head only out of a mild curiosity, never imagining that the order could be directed at him, as he continued walking.

'I say, stop there!'

A figure emerged from the direction of the voice, its face partly swathed in a loose scarf, trailing a long coat, military style of the 1914 War vintage. He held a long, thick stick in his hand, probably five feet long. Maren stopped. The figure approached.

'Go back,' he ordered.

It was a foolish question, since the answer was plain, but he asked it for want of anything else to say in the circumstances. 'Are you talking to me?'

'I say go back!' He stood squarely in front of him, just a yard away, thrusting his featureless head truculently forward.

'I am going to the airport!' Maren explained. 'I am staying the night at the airport.'

The man pointed a long arm in the direction of the hut he had just quitted. 'Back!'

Very patiently, oozing all the goodwill he could muster, Maren explained, picking his words carefully. 'I have just come from the airport. I came from there just now, a few moments ago, simply to pick up these bags. My companion is over there, waiting for me . . .'

'Go back. Quarantine. You not going anywhere. Go back.'

They were quite close to the gate. Maren cast a glance at the gates, looked at the man, and suddenly realised that this man appeared to think that he was a prisoner and that he, the guard, was his gaoler. It was a surreal moment: a strange land and a darkness that was pockmarked by a faint bulb hanging from the last of the tarred, makeshift huts, the distant, suddenly immeasurably distant lights of the airport, and the occasional sweep of headlights from a vehicle cruising on the tarmac; he, somewhat unbalanced by his light travelling bag in one hand and Elizabeth's heavy suitcase in the other, confronted by a stranger in a trailing First World War coat, his face mostly swathed in a scarf, for all the world like an exhumed Egyptian mummy – in the dark, he appeared to have no face at all, was monosyllabic to boot, and finally the stiff, outstretched sleeve, ending in a long staff, its meaning umistakable. No other being was in sight, just the two of them in a vast expanse of menace barely relieved by shifty pools of light. At that moment, the traveller felt that he would give anything to be home.

'I am not going back in there,' he said, stepping forward to move round the man.

The man stepped swiftly back to block his path, shifted his stick so that he held the ends in both hands, placed it against his chest and pushed him back.

Maren put down the bags, his mind already racing through all possible explanations for this strange confrontation. 'All right. Maybe you think I am stealing these bags.' He made stabbing gestures at the downed cases. 'I am leaving them here and will return later for them. Or if you prefer, we'll both go together to the airport, leaving the bags behind.' And he stepped back to avoid the pressure of the stick, stepped aside again and took a step forward.

Instantly a piercing whistle tore away all the surreal pretensions of the night, and turned it physical. For almost at once, he felt a heavy blow on his back which catapulted him forward into his interlocutor. He had only a brief moment to wonder by what magic the man, whose motions at least he could see clearly, right in front of him, could have hit him on the back with his stick, then stopped his forward stagger with his body at the same instant, when several more blows descended on him from all directions. Futile thoughts, for suddenly they were all pouring out of every crevice in the diseased burrow. He glimpsed what looked like a thousand raised sticks charging at him from every direction, for all the world like an inkwash frontispiece of a charge of lancers in a colonial history book, and he was, in that utterly meaningless moment, truly afraid that this was the moment of his death, an anonymous death in a strange land, and for an unknown cause.

His interlocutor had not hit him; perhaps he was the head guard and such menial duties were left to his subordinates. No matter, this figure, with his stick loosely held, was the only clear object Maren could see beneath the flailing sticks. He lunged for his weapon, snatched it and began to defend his life. All pain disappeared, there was only a blood lust which consumed him, and he went for their heads, jabbing and slamming with every ounce of his strength, only occasionally going for the knees, and always with maximum ferocity. Each blow, he intuitively felt, was his last, and he was repeatedly amazed to find himself still left with another, and to sense that his strength, rather than waning, appeared, if anything, to increase with every blow, given or taken. How long the fight lasted, he had no idea, only that his death was taking much longer than he had imagined at the beginning, and that he had begun to stumble over the prone forms of some of his erstwhile assailants.

It was the Polish journalist who saved his life. He heard the commotion, looked out and recognised the Nigerian with whom he had spoken earlier, raced to the sole telephone in the corridor which connected each block in the quarantine directly with the Health Office. What he screamed into the phone was: 'They are killing the Nigerian!' repeating it over and over again. Elizabeth overheard it even as the Health Officer began to inform her that something serious was going on in the 'Hotel'. She went into a fit, raised herself at a speed which astonished the officer and literally pushed him out of his office with her stomach and into the jeep. No way were they going to stop her getting in; she was in the front seat beside the driver as the cavalry rode in just in the nick of time, as happens in the best movies. The scene caught in the jeep's headlamps, as Elizabeth herself would describe it gleefully afterwards, was: three of the guards prone on the ground, two doubled up on their backs clutching their knees and stomachs, and a clearly crazed figure still flailing away at the remaining three or four, one of whom made the mistake of looking at the approaching headlamps and receiving the last blow of the fight to the side of the head, which sent him to join the sleepers.

Three officers, including the Health man, leapt out of the jeep shouting and waving their arms, but Elizabeth was already catching up with them, now very much like an armoured vehicle in her own right.

'Murderers! Murderers!' she continued to scream. 'This is an international incident. You have killed the Nigerian playwright. This is an international incident. This is murder. Premeditated murder.'

'Madam,' the officer tried to calm her. 'It seems to me it is your Nigerian writer who has done all the killing.'

'It is still an international incident,' she retorted. 'It is murder. Attempted murder. You have tried to kill a member of the Nigerian delegation; it is an international . . .'

Maren still did not feel a thing on his body, not since the first half-dozen blows that had commenced the hostilities. But he felt a weariness within him, a formless but definitely spiritual weariness, and there was nothing that he longed for at that moment except to be home or, at least, as far away from the arena of violence as was possible. And speedily. Declining to answer any questions, he dragged himself into the rear seat of the jeep, indifferent to the babble of voices among the guards and the officers, and waited to be driven back to the airport. He was not surprised to find that he had taken swift refuge in total detachment, in a familiar state of disembodiment where he watched, or felt himself as a separate entity. It was from that distant state that he watched the cases lifted into the car, heard Elizabeth's incessant protestations and the solicitous questions from the Health Officer, all sensations coming from a totally different clime of sensibilities which his body longed to join.

At the airport, there was near equal commotion. The Nigerians had been telephoned in their hotel and two of the trade unionists had come rushing back to the airport even before they had unpacked. The Protocol Officer from the Ministry accompanied them, trailed by an assistant. Maren listened to assurances that the Minister for Political Affairs was being contacted at that very moment and would be at the airport first thing in the morning. He listened to apologies, explanations, watched the various levels of agitation, submitted himself to First Aid for his multiple bruises and only then began to feel real physical pain at the spots where they belonged. In the background somewhere he could hear Elizabeth recounting the scene she had witnessed, demanding that the Nigerian Government be telexed immediately, and anyway wasn't there a Nigerian Ambassador and if so, why was he not at the airport when a prominent Nigerian writer was being murdered and what did he intend to do about it? He lost restraint only when the official began to explain that the Health Minister was away and would be away till Monday, having gone to his home town for the weekend where it was impossible to contact him and it was unfortunate that this was Friday night but the Minister for Political or was it Foreign Affairs would himself come to the airport the following morning and would personally escort them to join their comrades in the heart of Cairo . . . Maren snapped.

'I don't care if Nasser himself comes here, at this very moment, to take me into Cairo. I do not care for the Conference and I just wish to get out of here.'

'No, no, please don't do that. Tomorrow morning, you'll see, everything will be all right.'

More calmly, he requested that they check the next available flights for him. The Nigerian trade unionist groaned. There were no available flights to Nigeria for another three days, and the tickets would be invalid on other airlines.

Maren turned to the Protocol Officer. 'Do you mind if your assistant simply checks out all the night flights for me?'

The government official threw up his arms but nodded to the assistant to comply. He continued to press his plea, however, on the recalcitrant guest. 'Please, my friend, be reasonable. In fact, I am imploring you to go beyond being reasonable, and to help us. We have problems also with her, you know. And I am sure that if you stay, she will also agree to stay.'

'Oh, is she also threatening to leave?'

'Can't you hear her screaming in the next room? She wants to leave on the same flight as you.'

'Oh. I wasn't listening.' He now paid attention to the shouts emerging from the next room where Elizabeth had been taken in a futile attempt to calm her. 'I see. Are you sure there will be someone here to effect the releases in the morning?'

Eagerly, the man said, 'I give you my word of honour, sir.'

'There is a Polish journalist in that place. He's been there ten days, he said. He was the one who telephoned this office; I owe him my life.'

The Protocol Officer waved his hand in dismissal. 'Oh please, my friend. What happened was unfortunate, very unfortunate. But I don't want you to believe that the guards were trying to kill you. We don't kill our visitors, *please!* It was all a misunderstanding.'

'I owe him my life,' Maren insisted. 'I never said that the guards were trying to kill me, whatever I believed at the time. But I would have got myself killed. There's a difference there, you see. I know I was on the way to getting myself killed. And that journalist saved my life.'

'All right, all right. You want us to do something for him?'

'Will you try and get him released tomorrow also?'

'Anything for you, my friend. I promise. In any case, if he has been there ten days . . .'

'Yes, ten days. And of course, you will get the appropriate Ministry to do something about that so-called hotel. I think your Minister should simply pay a visit there, that's all that's needed. Pay a visit there himself. So, as for Elizabeth . . .'

'You will talk to her?'

'She will stay. It wouldn't surprise me if she decides to drop her baby right here in Egypt, after all this agitation. But I shall speak to her, and I guarantee she'll stay. The genuine writers are under-represented as it is – that is something else for your organisers to look into, but Elizabeth will bring it up anyway. That's going to be the main topic of our conversation until I catch my flight.'

'But I thought we had agreed you were no longer leaving!'

'Me? No. I never said any such thing.' They both laughed. 'Don't you try to trap me. Where is your assistant with the information, anyway? Any available flight from here will suit me. Fortunately I have some money on me; I can purchase my own tickets.'

'Is there nothing we can do to make you change your mind?'

'Nothing at all.' He felt very sorry for the protocol official who was actually proving more and more likeable. 'I wish there were some way in which I could explain why I am leaving. Believe me, I have taken no offence, none whatever. I merely wish to forget what happened and I can't do that here. Sorry, I'm putting it too simply. Let's just say, I feel an overwhelming need to take myself out of here, go away somewhere, preferably home. Something happened to me there, you see, and it was something rather scary. The most scary part is that it was familiar . . .'

His assistant returned from Information. 'There is only one flight from here before morning – it leaves for London – 2.30 a.m.'

'I'll take it,' Maren said.

Ojeli, the 'E' Branch man, into his third beer, a pile of denuded *suya* sticks between the two of them, shook his head in total bewilderment, rubbed the back of his hand against the stubble of his chin and belched gently. 'Excuse me. And you never did enter Cairo?'

'No.'

'Well, was there another conference in that same Cairo which you attended before? Or after?'

'I have never been to Cairo.'

'All right. Another Afro-Asian writers' conference then. Anywhere at all.'

'I have never yet succeeded in attending an Afro-Asian writers' conference. I was once headed towards yet another, in Bandung, but I got stuck halfway. I have to confess that I am not a very lucky traveller. It would be simpler to claim all the fault and just call myself an inefficient traveller. Sometimes, yes, it's true I forget the odd visa, or my innoculation certificate has run out. But most of the time, believe me, it simply is not my fault . . . No, don't laugh. I am being objective and it's true. Absolutely true. The organisers tell me, you don't need this or that document, and it turns out they're wrong. Or: we'll be waiting for you at this transit point, and they're not. Or a Prepaid Ticket Advice does not arrive on time or something happens to make me lose my temper – racism is one frequent cause, and especially in those unexpected, 'solidarity' places, like Asia! Or Eastern Europe. That always gets me. Once in Paris I nearly got shot by nervous immigration men who had taken me for an Algerian – another long story. Sometimes it's some petty, pea-brained, cross-eyed official with that almighty power of admitting or denying you entry and I tell him to stuff his entry stamp and I return home. I love returning home – hm, maybe I should qualify that – I love turning homewards, yes, that's more like it.'

Ojeli chuckled. 'What's the difference?'

Maren shook his head. 'Too complicated. Next time, we'll chat about that. I have this feeling that your Department and I will be seeing quite a bit of each other – just a feeling I've been having lately. Unfortunately, I doubt that it will always be this civilised. This sort of – er . . . well, approach you've taken . . . you know, your coming here to do your job, sampling the congenial atmosphere of Mbari while still getting on with your investigation.' He laughed. 'Oh yes, I know you and your white colleague must have decided you could kill several birds with one stone by acceding to my request – in your own way. No, don't deny it, Senior, I know it. Why not? Anyway, to get back to the main thing: it's all going to become far more vicious; in fact, it's already becoming very vicious. Take today alone, what have I just undergone? First, a miserable corporal claims

I tried to bribe him, then something turns up in my files, something I never said, in a place I've never been – it's all very ominous!'

'But have you ever said anything of that nature, at any conference? Maybe they had expected some such statement from you and when you didn't participate, they simply lifted that and gave it a new time and place.'

Maren remained silent for a while, and the policeman pressed on. 'You think you can now recall something along those lines?'

'So you can amend my files accordingly?' Maren mocked. 'No, I wasn't trying to recollect any like statement at all, for the simple reason that I never made it. It is not in my nature to make it you see, because I am constantly terrified of my own violence.'

'Oh, so you think you are a violent person?'

Maren wagged his finger in admonishment. 'Oh, Senior, Senior, here am I trying to talk to you like an "old boy", and you want to put me on record as admitting to being a violent person! It's so true what they say: once a policeman . . .'

'No, no, I was just trying to understand what you said.'

'And I am trying to explain why I never join those who call for a violent revolution, in spite of the fact that I accept violence as a sometimes necessary component of positive change. Yes, a sometimes necessary component, and one that I am always ready to endorse, instigate and even partake of, where circumstances leave one no option. You can put that down in my files when you get to the office. It is important that the "other side" – whichever it happens to be – is made to know it ahead of events, so, I repeat, feel free to put it down. But remember to let them know that I am not unique in that respect. The difference is that I will not deny such a fundamental truth of myself, even in a court of law. But the rhetoric of violence only disgusts me. And that is what is so ironic about that statement put into my mouth at a conference that I never attended – I say ironic, because the reason I jettisoned the conference was that very one – my personal unease with violence. The fight at the airport reminded me of something in myself that I recognised a long while ago, something that I accepted as a fact of my being, but it is something with which I have never become, nor ever wish to be, reconciled.'

'And that is why you decided not to attend the Conference?'

'No! Not "not to attend the Conference" but to "get away" from a place which unleashed the violence in me. I don't know if a policeman is allowed to believe in possession but if there is indeed such a thing, I was – *possessed*!'

Ojeli burst into a loud guffaw. 'And now, you are caught – *in possession*.' Again he roared with laughter. 'Oh, I think that's a good one. If I may be immodest, it is a very good one. At least you won't be able to tell me that a policeman has no sense of humour.'

'Yes, yes, and you are the second policeman I've met today with a sense of humour, so I suppose that balances out the police lies I've also had to put up with today. And by the way, shouldn't the accurate expression be – not caught, but *accused* of being in possession?'

Ojeli's demeanour changed quite suddenly. 'You know the truth, and this is speaking very honestly – "Up School" and all that. I really don't know what the fuss is all about. I have inspected the bloody gun. If it has been fired during the past three years, I deserve to lose my commission.'

Maren shrugged. 'I told them: it's a stage prop.'

'Sorry, I shouldn't even have brought it up. As I said, it's not in my Department at all. It's just that this Cairo thing in your file was brought in . . . all the way from Lagos. I think a hot line from the House of Assembly police post must have blistered the ears of someone high up, who contacted Lagos . . . well, that's the lot of a policeman. Always expect the unexpected. And it's turned out to be quite an evening after all. I really wish I could meet this Elizabeth Browne.'

Maren could only wonder how much tougher the session would have been if Lagos had known that he had been to Cuba.

The three-year-old Lagos University, a federal university like Ibadan, soon joined both Ibadan and Ife by sliding into the now seemingly mandatory rites of passage – the academic *penkelemes*. It had been widely expected that the incumbent Vice Chancellor, Professor Eni Njoku, an Igbo, would obtain a well-deserved, though not guaranteed extension of his tenure in office. Enter Professor Saburi Biobaku of Ife *Credo* fame, sponsored quite openly by a powerful Yoruba lobby, spearheaded by the now rabidly anti-Igbo NNDP.

Maren gloated inwardly, maintained a serene distance from the media war that was being waged on clearly partisan lines – the Yoruba-owned press for Biobaku, the Igbo for Eni Njoku. The *Post* newspapers, owned by the NPC-NNDP Federal Government, campaigned furiously for the appointment of Dr Biobaku.

Since his departure from Ife, Maren had been urged by Lagos to join its English department, but he continued to postpone a decision, unwilling to undergo at close quarters yet another tarnishing of the university idea. Cutting through the tribal rhetoric of the ongoing contest in Lagos, however, he perceived only two qualified candidates manipulating both political and tribal influence to secure a prestigious position. The only sinister element was the choice of Biobaku, of all unwelcome candidates, as the Yoruba challenger. Was this intended to be a replay of the *Credo* theme, this time on a national level?

A freak incident very nearly persuaded many, Maren included, that the issues involved in this instance were far more profound than they really were. The nation was galvanised by an attempt on the life of Professor Biobaku by an irate student. As with every turn of events in this Lagosian foray into 'varsity *penkelemes*, however, it proved to be the merest farce. Biobaku's assailant had been armed with nothing more lethal than a schoolboy penknife which succeeded in inflicting a pathetic scratch on the intended victim. There and then Maren decided that the University, as a national institution, had finally signalled its destiny, which was to be an arena of perverse theatricality. With equal perversity, he signalled his intention to take up the standing offer from Lagos.

An Igbo colleague from Lagos University, contemplating his own resignation, rushed to him in Ibadan to express consternation at his decision: 'a contradiction of all you are known to stand for; it will demoralise the de-tribalised, progressive elements within academia . . .' and so on and on, with patriotic anguish.

Maren listened to him with ill-concealed boredom, his soul-searching before his decision having proved to be one of the shortest duration he had ever undergone on any such issue. Finally he asked his visitor, 'Has any University regulation or statute been breached? You know, regarding appointments of Vice Chancellors and so on?'

His visitor was taken aback but admitted, 'No. But we're talking here of the principle of . . .'

'Oh yes, the principle. And ethics, et cetera, et cetera. What university principle, or ethics, have been flouted? I am not a Biobaku fan, so this is not a personal thing with me. I hope you will also concede that I am not a Yoruba jingoist.'

'Sure, sure. Why else would I come all this way to appeal to you?'

'Good. Now listen to me. You Igbo singlehandedly subverted the University of Ibadan. The Yoruba followed suit: unaided, they inflicted a near mortal wound on Ife University. Now the two incorrigible groups have shifted the battleground to Lagos, mauling each other, and the University, over a position that could rightly go to anyone, incumbent or not. And you seriously expect me to take sides? A plague on both your houses!'

'You won't last,' Komi warned him.

'I don't expect to,' he replied. 'But I can't help relishing the notion that some kind of poetic justice has been done. Njoku is the unfortunate scapegoat but, even there, I don't recall him uttering a word of condemnation when his fellow Igbo, Anieke, was foisted on Ibadan by Azikiwe.'

'But Biobaku!' Komi persisted. 'How are you going to deal with that? Or with him for that matter, when he resumes his antics in Lagos? You expect him to have changed? He is going to act obliged to those who put him there!'

Maren chuckled. 'I admit Biobaku appears to have got off lightly, but, there is no better teacher than a good scare. He is actually a prisoner, you know. Daren't move a step anywhere without that hefty bodyguard of his, who reminds me of Kodak. Look, it's all a gamble. I have a feeling he'll bear in mind what we did in Ife and realise that he is entering a prison that is run by more than one set of gaolers. No one is expecting a Saul to Paul conversion but, we'll see what can be done before I get thrown out.'

'On your head be it,' Komi warned.

'I won't be giving up my house in Ibadan, you can take that for granted. The family stays here while I commute between here and Lagos, at least for the first year.'

'If you last that long.'

Maren shrugged. 'We'll see. I suspect there is also a bit of political opportunism lurking around my decision. The final showdown is just around the corner, for the West I mean. Operating from a Lagos base does offer certain advantages.'

'You're crazy. Lagos won't be simply the NNDP, as Ife was. This is the entire works – NPC, NNDP, Yoruba revanchists, anti-Igbo minorities in the Rivers areas. They do have legitimate grouses, you know – I know that, I'm one of them. The resentment against the Igbo is high; it isn't just hot air, believe me.'

'Maybe. But it doesn't change a thing.'

Komi grew desperate. 'This is the Federal Government itself, run by a party that is so contemptuous of its allies that it actually flaunts a regional name – Northern Alliance, not even a neutral name, to suggest a National grouping. Yet it claims support in the West, East, and Rivers areas. You think it's only the Yoruba rooting for Biobaku? Are you sure you've kept up with the *Post* and the Northern newspapers?'

'More or less, more or less,' Maren admitted.

'I'm not so sure,' Komo persisted. 'The feudal alliance has definitely marked down Lagos for its own; Biobaku may prove to be only a holding device. They probably have their real candidate waiting on the sidelines.'

'I am only mortal,' Maren sighed. 'I cannot resist the irony of the enemy welcoming me into its camp.'

XI Wasting the West

Finally, 1965 and reckoning time. The people of the Western Region had borne their humiliations patiently; they had even undergone privations that were unnecessary, being merely petty and vindictive. Chief Akintola's party, nettled by an artificial victory in the 1964 Federal Election, a victory that was won by default, since the rival party had boycotted a clearly loaded contest, declared war on the people. It was a strange situation; here was the electorate, robbed, yet passive in conduct, content to wait for the next opportunity to redress their fortunes, and still the Government went to war against them, unleashing a violence that the robbed had eschewed. The resentment had become palpable. It was expressed in various ways, from the cold reception of Government officials to the quiet ostracism of party bigwigs, and these included traditional rulers, some of whom were chased from their thrones and took refuge in the policed safety of the capital, Ibadan. Some, like the Zaki of Arigidi, or the Olowo of Owo, would not return for decades; others died in forced exile. The media captured the mood of the people, even the media controlled by the Government, since these were simply boycotted and ceased to communicate with anyone, except incestuously within the insulated circle of party and Government. And that Government turned violent. Its most pacific weapon of control was the withdrawal of resources from hostile sectors – local governments, schools, hospitals. Traditional rulers who like the Odemo of Ìsarà refused to take the oath of loyalty, covertly or overtly, had their salaries reduced to the derisory level of one penny a year precisely.

The West was wealthy; its cocoa resources had been well managed – at least, before the arrival of the NNDP. The region was the envy of its neighbours: successful, free and compulsory primary education had set a standard and a goal for the others. Its health programme was efficient and spread wide to benefit the rural areas, not just the urban. Then it all began to dwindle away, and the paucity of resources was visited most viciously on communities that showed no overt love for their rulers – which embraced nearly the entire people of the West.

Their discontent, therefore, transcended the mere choice of their rulers. Only the restricted coterie of party leaders, their legislators, their agents, fawners, enforcers and a handful of cooperative traditional rulers, enjoyed the resources of the West. The farmers grew resentful; the cooperatives that guaranteed fair returns of their products had been encouraged to slither into states of impotence, making it easy for their funds to be diverted by a desperate Government. Finally, they showed their teeth. Armed with ancient Dane guns, exhuming their traditional battledresses from decades of gathered soot, cobwebs and neglect, they stormed the cities, freed hundreds of their colleagues from Ondo, Ilesha, and other provincial prisons, overran police stations and seized their weapons, menaced Ibadan and threatened the fragile pretensions of Government in the West. The revolt ceased only after days of dialogue; the Army had refused to accede to requests, even by the Federal Government, that they engage the rebellious population in combat. Sections of the Army did, however, begin to train and arm NNDP thugs, politicians and even Ministers. The latter took to wearing guns under billowing gowns and waved them about at the slightest excuse. When the radical faction within the Army came to make its move in the *coup d'état* of 15 January 1966, Premier Akintola was enabled to die like a true *Aare Ona Kakanfo*,* engaging the arresting detachment of soldiers in a last stand shootout, his submachine-gun blazing to the end, taking a few souls with him.

Meanwhile, the police laid siege to the West. They shot up schools and markets, rounded up the wives and children of the insurgents and took them away as hostages. Villages were torched and bull-dozed; crops were destroyed and normal trade paralysed outside the main cities. The *Baale* and other village and community heads learnt to live each day in preparation for several weeks in police cells and

*Generalissimo.

prisons, hostages for the good conduct of their people. Curfew followed curfew; restrictions of movement became a way of life, arbitrarily imposed by any invading truckful of police, far from the watchful eyes of the city-bound media. These performed as best they could, but they were front-line targets for the suspicious eyes of the resentful police. Inevitably, each new atrocity could take days to break through the physical barriers of censorship, and many were left unreported. The rebellion persisted. The Government of Akintola tried what it did best: dispensing huge bribes among the leaders to break their ranks. There would be no more defections, however, and the period of vacillation was over. The West had attained its definitive state of polarisation.

The proceeds of robbery were flaunted before an increasingly impoverished populace: American cars of ever-increasing lengths and vulgar opulence, with kaleidoscopic fins and wings – wings on which the masses declared that their wealth had taken off. They watched the social exhibitionism of the politicians, their wives and families; saw mansions of extravagant dimensions spring up in the midst of hovels, often forcibly demolished, the land acquired by fiat; marvelled at the patterns of insatiable, public consumption among the privileged few. The West watched its wealth, its basic resources, even its means of productivity mortgaged to Indian merchants, Greek and Lebanese. And orgies became a way of life at the top, social parties at the slightest excuse, parties that had no beginning and no end, simply flowing into one another in seas of champagne. Oh yes, the champagne-status craze began much earlier than many Nigerians recall – spilling over across the seas on 'official' tours that lacked purpose or result, except that they accelerated the process of malformation of a special class of youth, the privileged scions of the *nouveaux riches*, for whom the Nigerian schools were not good enough: they must be sent to Eton, Harrow and other élite establishments in the colonial homestead, returning for holidays to fanfares and rounds of orgiastic socialising. The International Schools, begun at this time, served those who could not quite afford the fees of overseas schools; there at least the children could pick up alien manners and conduct, and vie in airs of superiority with the vacationing half of colonial aristocrats. It was no different in the East, or indeed among the Northern feudal and new-sprung élite, or of course the Centre, with its flamboyant and blatantly corrupt Ministers, especially in the crucial Ministry of Finance. The difference was that the West was discontented and its mood was foul.

New words entered the Western, and thus the national, vocabulary, capturing the mood of the period. *Onilegogoro** celebrated the arrival of miniature skyscrapers, not as public buildings but as the privately owned property of one individual; and to entrench their domination as a symbol of public desire, the women introduced a new fashion in headgear, similarly named. These had the obvious distinction of obscuring the view of anyone who sat behind any woman thus attired, unless of course such an individual was eight feet tall or more. Victor Olaiya, the High Life king, provided the phrase with its final guarantee of immortality by composing and making popular the song with the title – what other could it be – '*Onilegogoro o!*'

The head of the entire débâcle, Ladoke Akintola, found that his facility with words, his inveterate punning, was a double-edged blade. His initials, S.L.A., received a tonal conversion to *Ese-Ole*,[†] and the people conferred upon him the unpalatable chieftaincy title, *Baba Lamilami*.[‡] In a desperate effort to reverse the trend of popular feeling, to counter the charge that the cocoa-based wealth of the West had not been frittered away by the Government, he speeded up the formal opening of the first publicly owned *ile gogoro* of the West, which he christened 'Cocoa House'.

It was to have been a sumptuous affair, but such was the state of security that many of the guests – at least those of his party – arrived in disguised vehicles – ambulances, fire trucks, goods vans. The tape was no sooner cut and the speeches ended than all the guests headed home, leaving untouched the sumptuous collation that had been prepared for over a thousand guests but for which less than a hundred had turned up. The security forces far outnumbered the guests, and it was they who set to, and demolished the board of unaccustomed delicacies.

It did not matter that the Premier, in a passionate and bitter

*Owner of the house of heights (*ile gogoro*).
[†]Feet of a robber.
[‡]King of Dragonflies (a reference to the dragonfly's motion of skimming the surface of the water and darting down to lick the source dry).

speech that would be mocked by amateur performers all over the West, presented the elegant building as the property of the toiling farmers: the minds of his widely dispersed audience in the West were only focused on the personal *ile gogoro* that they firmly believed he had built in Lagos, and the question of how such outlandish structures could have been raised, except with their money. It was that period when rumour had become unassailable, and the embattled Premier had no more recourse to the justice of truth, of fair hearing and the benefit of doubt. He was driven to more and more repressive and insensitive acts, relying solely on legitimation by the state machinery of the Centre, of his allies in the North, and the thug-and-police alliance of his home region.

The West nursed another wound that would not be healed, or, to be more accurate, a wound that could have healed with time was violently reopened. The region's acknowledged leader, Obafemi Awolowo, and his main lieutenants, were still in prison – the mis-government of Akintola's party now conferred upon them, but upon Awolowo especially, a near-mythical salvationist stature. In any case, the long-drawn-out legal fight to repatriate Tony Enahoro, one of his right-hand men, from England, where he had taken refuge, had succeeded in keeping the issue alive, especially after his eventual return by the British in 1964.

Tried on a charge of treasonable felony, Awolowo's men had received lengthy gaol sentences. It was a curious trial, and Awolowo's guilt was made quite plausible by the prosecution's por-trayal of an obsessively ambitious man, who had become frustrated by his electoral failure at the Centre, believed himself to have been cheated, and took to violent preparations to seize power. Party cadres from Awolowo's Action Group had unquestionably been sent to Nkrumah's radicalised, anti-colonial Ghana for training, but was it armed training or was it, as claimed by the defendants, purely ideological training at the Winneba School of Political Science, to which many political cadres flocked from all over the Continent, especially from those countries that were still engaged in liberation struggles?

The trial had several unsatisfactory aspects. That some of the accused should turn State Evidence was normal proceeding in any trial, but the evidence of torture to extract confessions, bribery, intimidations and family blackmail – the threat to harm families of the accused by the use of state muscle – was not easily dismissed. Ceulman, the South African policeman, became a demonic invocation, accused of being the principal torturer. The Government strenuously denied the South African origin of this shadowy figure, but no one conceded the slightest credence to such denials. There was at least one instance of emotional blackmail that was known to Maren. It involved a lawyer, a prominent member of the Action Group and one of the accused. He was taken from his prison cell in Lagos at night, and taken to the Italian restaurant, Quo Vadis, on Broad Street. There, he was astonished to find his young wife of barely two years waiting at a table. His escorts sat at a discreet distance, leaving the couple to a dinner of their selection, paid for by the state. Pleas, tears, cajoling, threats . . . whatever it was that transpired between them, by the following morning, the lawyer had agreed to turn State Evidence, and charges against him were reduced. Later, however, overcome by remorse, he recanted.

Some had been able to escape across the border when the rounding-up had begun. The most prominent was Anthony Enahoro, a former Zikist, and subsequently, staunch follower of Chief Obafemi Awolowo. He had been gaoled under the colonial administration for his fiery anti-colonial denunciations, under circumstances that were especially painful to him and his colleagues: when they were brought to trial, their idol, Nnamdi Azikiwe, not only dissociated himself from their pronouncements; he repudiated and denounced them as 'hotheads'. They went to gaol defiantly, acquiring in the process, however, an unexpected kind of political education that would inform their future choices – both negatively and positively.

Tony Enahoro's escape to Ghana was facilitated by a mathematics don at the University of Ibadan, the uninhibited Dr Chike Obi, himself an unorthodox political animal. He once proposed dictatorship, even some form of fascism as the solution of Nigerian problems. Chike Obi was disdainful of wealth or material possessions; unlike most of his colleagues, he was content with a modest Volkswagen. So certain was his feel for the political mood of his people that he took on Nnamdi Azikiwe's former party, the NCNC, on the platform of a party he had barely formed, the Dynamic Party, and routed the NCNC candidate in Azikiwe's own former Onitsha constituency, despite the undisguised endorsement of Azikiwe himself. A fiery rhetorician, Chike Obi was every bit an instinctive populist, the Igbo *alter ego*, in many ways, of the people's politician of the West, the Ibadan stormy petrel called Adelabu, another giant-killer who humbled Obafemi Awolowo's candidates in the West for the NCNC, and deprived the political arena of a truly colourful presence through his mysterious death in a motor accident between Lagos and Ibadan.

As usual, there were many theories about that accident, which also involved a Lebanese business partner. The most widely accepted certainty had some semblance of plausibility. For once, Adelabu had made a miscalculation. Never one to fail to back a conviction by action, he had ordered bales and bales of cloth with a special victory motif for a forthcoming election. If his predictions had been right, Adelabu stood to make a fortune. Nothing gladdens the heart of the average Yoruba, man or woman, than the overt symbol of belonging, solidarity, common purpose or simple, downright *ote* – intrigue – than the *aso ebi*,* in which tens, hundreds, or thousands of bodies would swarm the streets, singing, and dancing or demonstrating in one single cloth motif, individuality being expressed only in the variations of tailoring styles, and sometimes not even that. If the results had come as predicted, both the Lebanese and Adelabu would have been made for life. Then came the unexpected reversal. Returning from Lagos after a meeting that merely looked into the stark face of financial ruin, the Lebanese, who blamed Adelabu for his situation, suddenly seized the steering-wheel from the driver as they drove towards a bridge, twisted it and crashed the vehicle into the gully. That was the most widely accepted version of his death. The reality was, however, far more banal: no Lebabese was even present with Adelabu in the car, his driver had simply had an accident.

Such was the emotional hold he exercised on his followers that several days of riots in Ibadan followed his death. But Adelabu, who had introduced the famous phrase *penkelemes* into Nigerial coinage to denounce any situation of a 'peculiar mess', was gone, permanently, and the political drama of the West was sadly impoverished.

*Communal attire.

Chike Obi, his intellectual soulmate, was seized at the border between Nigeria and the then Dahomey, but his mission had been accomplished and Tony Enahoro was safely over the border. There was never any concrete suggestion that Chike Obi was part of the 'treasonable' team, but every attempt would be made to rope in one who had not only declared himself an admirer of Chief Awolowo, but was a political ally of the Action Group. His greatest crime, however, was that he had clearly assisted Tony Enahoro in escaping over the border, although legally this constituted no crime, since Enahoro was yet to be declared a wanted man.

Maren decided to visit Chike Obi in Kirikiri during his confinement, both to congratulate him for his action and to lend moral support. There was, however, also a practical, opportunistic side to his visit.

For quite some time now, it had become apparent to him, as well as to many others who were more than rhetorically involved in anticipating the many possible directions of the struggle for power, that a catalogue of emergency responses to a variety of possible developments must be prepared and constantly updated. Maren did not forget how he had been turned back at the border shortly after his resignation from the University of Ife. After the betrayals, and the state rehearsals for violence, he had sought a weekend's recuperation in Cotonou in the former Republic of Dahomey, this being the nearest temporary escape he could afford. It was certainly the most convenient. At the border, he had his first taste of the arbitrary restriction of movements by the secret police.

It was a strange, unsettling feeling. This was his own country, the space of earth in which he was spawned, and now he was learning, at the very late age of twenty-eight, that it was his prison. On the surface of it, he felt that it ought to be a small thing. Others had been dispossessed of all they had, violently deprived of all means of earning, pursued and persecuted, as they tried other means of providing for family; some had been eliminated by the goons of the NNDP and their NPC allies, tortured, raped and dehumanised. Yet there he was, merely deprived of a peaceful weekend by the sea and some cheap wine, stopped from crossing an artificial border between the two still colonised spaces – never mind the so-called Independence – and yet he had this feeling that the world had come apart

and all the debris fallen on his head. He argued that he had not
been charged with or convicted of any crimes; he had had his taxes
deducted at source to pay for these very agents of his restriction;
no prior information had been sent to him that his passport would
be withdrawn; but, just like that, at the whim of some unknown
persons who had obviously entered his name in a Restriction dossier,
he found himself unable to cross his national boundary.

The matter was worse. Before he was even informed that he could
not travel, his arrival had triggered off a frenzy of activities among
the Immigration and Customs officials. They swarmed into his car;
took out the seats; pulled up the carpets; prodded the panelling and
the door padding; opened up and emptied the glove compartment;
then turned their attention to the boot and the chassis. The toolbox
was meticulously examined; the bonnet was raised and they poked
among the parts; looked beneath the chassis; for a moment he
thought they might deflate the spare tyre and take out the inner
tube for inspection. Finally, his luggage – mostly papers, lecture
notes and manuscripts – was rifled. He had hoped to put in a few
hours' work on a new play in between wine and seabathing – so
there were these sheets with scribbles all over them, and of course
names of characters. Who is this Eman then? Who is Danlola?
And . . . oh . . . something far more intriguing had come up. One of
them had pulled out a volume of Alexander Pope. It was one of the
special editions of which he was rather fond, and it contained a
folded facsimile of some pages of Pope's original manuscript from
The Dunciad. The secret service man looked up at Maren, smiled,
and spread out the folded script decorated with the calligraphy of the
European Enlightenment period. It was all over his face, suddenly
cunning, triumphant: the sleuth had uncovered a coded message
cleverly stuck between pages of so-called academic stuff!

'What is this one, *oga*?'

'Poetry.'

'Poetry? What kind is that, sir?'

'Satirical poetry.'

'What I am asking, sir, is, what does it mean?'

'I don't give free lectures. If you want a course in poetry, it
shouldn't be too difficult for your Department to track me down.
We can then discuss terms.'

The book was detained. So was a record that happened to be in the car; perhaps it was suspected to be yet another conveyor of secret messages. Only then was he informed that he could not travel anyway.

'Where do such orders come from?' he demanded.

'From Headquarters.'

'In Obalende?'

'Yes.'

'Can I speak to someone there? Can I use your phone?'

'Telephone? There are no telephone lines to this place.'

'No telephone? Surely you must have some way of contacting Lagos.'

He was met with shrugs and blank faces, but he also spotted discomfort on the faces of some of them.

'Do you mean the only way I can contest this order is to travel to Lagos?'

'Hn-hm,' said the Alexander Pope *aficionado*, tossing his words casually over his shoulder. 'That's the way we do it here.'

He recognised it was a lie. The tall masts and criss-crossing wires around the building were not there for nothing. He moved close to the face he had easily identified as sympathetic, someone who acted as if he was carrying out a distasteful duty.

'Who do you suggest I ask for when I get there?'

'Ask for M. D. Yusuf.'

Turning his car round, he sped to Lagos, raced up the stairs of the building – it was near closing time – and encountered a man descending the stairs. He was a light-complexioned man, with a rather gentle, intelligent-looking face. For no reason that he had time to work out, he panted: 'You must be Mr M. D. Yusuf.'

The man's eyebrows rose in some surprise. 'You got here very fast,' he said.

'Oh, so they did succeed in getting in touch with you.'

Again, his face betrayed surprise. 'Oh yes. That's normal.' Then a slight frown appeared on his face, quickly erased. 'I know who you are; I ought to know. But how did you know who I was?'

Maren shrugged. 'Guesswork. I had heard something about you.'

He smiled. 'I think the real problem is that you had your Western Travel Certificate in addition to your passport. You should have given that up when you obtained a passport.'

It was not true. He knew of hundreds of Nigerians who retained their Travel Certificate for the West African coast and used their passports only for overseas travels. The wily cop was simply not yet ready to concede that Maren was now a subject of Security interest, a subject of constant surveillance and arbitrary restrictions. He kept silent about the search to which he had been subjected, said nothing also of the fact that he had requested that the border officials get in touch with their headquarters to confirm directly that he was not free to travel. He concentrated instead on studying the man about whom he had heard a few things, a self-effacing personality it was said, but very efficient, intelligent, and even with progressive ideas. He had not yet attained his later prominence, and no one knew exactly what position he held in the Special Branch then in forma-tion. He seemed pleasant enough, however, and was an obvious believer in what Maren had come to term the Ojeli School of Sleuthery – suave, civil but slithery.

'I left instructions,' he said. 'Just see the officer in room B1 – along that corridor. Do enjoy your weekend in Dahomey.'

In Dahomey he was at least ninety-five per cent certain that an agent had been detailed to follow and report on him, and that he had identified the individual. On his return, his car was subjected to an even more rigorous search than before, a thing he had believed was virtually impossible. Through a window of one of the offices, he caught a glimpse of the man whom he had identified as his tail. There and then he made up his mind that there had to be easier ways to spend a weekend in Dahomey, without border hassle and without any prurient interest being taken in his methods of unwind-ing. More seriously, however, together with the small group that had begun to coalesce from the *Credo* experience, it had become a straightforward matter of their personal security: opening up lines of unmonitored entries and exits, and not simply through the obvious Badagry border town but up-country, west of Saki, Igboho, and so on. The smugglers' routes were the most obvious, and of these they had already mapped out a half dozen or so. But it made sense to have these constantly augmented, and Maren's solidarity visit to Chike Obi had the secondary purpose of 'debriefing' him for details of Enahoro's escape route.

Tony Enahoro committed the tactical error when he made his

escape of leaving the safety of Ghana and moving to the United Kingdom. He had been fooled by the historic image of that former colonial power as a political sanctuary, forgetting that the Britishers still regarded their former colonies – and especially their puppet governments – as their privileged wards, to be indulged even at the expense of their own concepts of justice and fair play. Enahoro fought a prolonged battle all the way through the various tiers of the British legal system and even the Houses of Parliament.

Maren had joined the fray very early. Now the contacts he had made during his apprenticeship at the Royal Court came in useful. He travelled to London and spoke to the parliamentarian Wayland Young, later Lord Kennet, whose family had befriended him in his London days. Then there was Tom Driberg, whom he had met through the director Joan Littlewood, and whose politics were very radical. Tom Driberg also knew West Africa, was an admirer of Kwame Nkrumah and despised the calibre and tendencies of politicians the likes of Nigerian rulers. Tom Driberg had a bluff, cant-detesting personality. He had a razor intelligence, and Maren was flattered by his attentiveness to the cause that had brought him to London. Only several years later, as he got to know about his sexual tendencies, did Maren wonder if there was any testing intent in the choice of the restaurant to which he had taken him for dinner – *The Gay Hussar*. Perhaps there were signals that evening that totally passed over his head, but Maren recalled nothing that could be remotely interpreted as importuning. He recalled the meeting entirely as one of an exhilarating discussion of the politics of West African decolonisation, with the subject of Kwame Nkrumah clearly dominating his projections for the Continent – and the quantities of the Hungarian wine, Egri Bikavér, that they both downed in the course of the evening. Driberg rallied stoutly to Enahoro's cause, both behind the scenes and on the floor of Parliament, as did Wayland Young in his own quieter, but no less effective, manner.

Ralph Schoenemann, Maren's old colleague of the Aldermaston March days, now secretary to the philosopher Bertrand Russell, was also coopted and student groups mobilised to campaign and lobby against the threatened repatriation of Tony Enahoro. The 'fugitive offender', as he would later describe himself in his biographical account of that period, lost the battle eventually. It was a shameful event in the British decolonisation process, but only those were surprised who had not really understood in what terror Chief Awolowo and his politics were held by the British Government, both under the Conservatives and Labour. Very few people at the time would have believed, for instance, that the colonial Government, in addition to sowing the seeds of discontent in revenue sharing and lopsided development, through its imposition of false census figures on the new nation, also cold-bloodedly laid the foundation of electoral rigging in its former colony.*

There were unforgivable crimes – from the British point of view – that had been committed by Chief Awolowo. First, his party had accelerated the pace of Independence beyond what the British desired or found convenient. Next, he had attempted, and nearly succeeded in, upsetting the balance of power that the British had carefully nurtured for their former colony, one that would ensure the continuation of British interests and policies in Nigeria. There was also his 'betrayal' of the secret defence pact between Nigerian leaders and the Colonial Office, a pact that was made a condition for the fulfilment of the demands for Self Rule during the crucial Lancaster House conference in London. Finally, Obafemi Awolowo had flirted with socialism, aligning his policies and ideologies with radical leaders like Kwame Nkrumah and Sekou Touré. There was simply no way that Tony Enahoro, his articulate and radical lieutenant, would be let loose to continue his activities towards the undermining of the Government of their docile pupil Sir Tafawa Balewa, any more than they would hand over the reins of government to Obafemi Awolowo himself. It was the British who taught electoral rigging to Nigerians, but very few Nigerians, not even the astute Obafemi Awolowo himself, was aware of this at the time.

The Nigerian people as a whole, and certainly the bereaved section of the West, were not then especially concerned with the manipulations of the British. The enemy remained localised and was unambiguously identified as the Government of the NNDP, and its aggressive, power-complacent ally of the Northern People's

---

*A full account of this conspiracy is given in the unpublished memoirs of a civil servant in the colonial office. It is the first time that a British civil servant has confirmed the allegations made by some Nigerian scholars and radical politicians against the colonial Government in this crucial period.

Congress. The Regional Elections of 1965 were seen as a last chance in their battle for self-liberation.

Unimpressive in appearance, certainly without charisma or oratorical conviction, devoid of vision and without any sense of strategic planning, Awolowo's deputy, Alhaji Adegbenro, was nevertheless accepted as the new leader of the Action Group and the people rallied round him. The rump leadership was without resources – at least not any resources that were comparable to those of the Government in power – and the West had virtually been turned into a police state. They relied, therefore, on the sole weapon in their possession – the popular will. Faced with the daily expression and overwhelming evidence of such popular strength, the NNDP simply abandoned any serious campaigning and concentrated on planting its party cadres in electoral offices; giving marching orders to the police to ensure maximum intimidation, and coercion and browbeating to the electorate. 'Whatever you do, however you vote, no matter the resistance, this Government,' they declared, 'will remain in power.' Even before voting began a large proportion of the contested seats had been declared won by unopposed Government candidates.

An unprecedented level of hubris and contempt was attained when the Deputy Premier, Chief Fani-Kayode, appeared on a television and radio programme and declared: 'Who needs the people to vote for us? The angels in heaven have already cast their votes for our party!'

The people heard and responded. Soon, it became clear, as the voting began, that every single ploy of the 'angels' was being successfully checkmated by advocates of the devil. The desperation of the incumbent party became palpable. Returning officers at polling stations were instructed not to announce the results at the polling stations but to forward them to Ibadan, where they would be collated and announced. It was the most blatant declaration yet of the Government's rigging resolve. Until then, each candidate would receive the certificate of the result, signed by him, counter-signed by the opponent and certified by the returning officer at the counting station. And of course, the monopoly of both media of radio and television was firmly in the hands of the Government, while its allies at the Centre and in the North utilised their media also to publicise whatever results were declared by the NNDP Government.

The Action Group had the *Nigerian Tribune* for its ally, a newspaper owned by Chief Awolowo but constantly crippled by banning, shutdowns, arrests and detentions of its editors and journalists. Yet even when that newspaper could only produce its clandestine editions of four pages daily, it continued to be bought at the exorbitant prices its production methods required, and its opportunist vendors demanded. The official voice of the Western Government, the *Daily Sketch*, persisted in rolling out its thousands of copies, which ended in free distribution and were used for food wrapping by vendors. Eventually even this use grew to be seen as a mark of collaboration or contamination, and was often rejected.

But the people were well ahead of their political leaders who were clearly in disarray, devoid of ideas, trapped in a legalism that was regarded with amusement and contempt by the Federal Government, and in a pietism that was as alien to its opponents as the notion of fair play. The Action Group had become dominated by eggheads, lawyers, rosary- and prayer-bead fondlers. Not even the cynical, last-minute rejection in 1963 of a recourse to the Privy Council of Great Britain as the Highest Court of Appeal, as set out in the Constitution, served them as a pointer to their current predicament. Both sides in that crucial dispute – one that involved the legitimacy of power in the West – had agreed to arbitration by the Privy Council. Immediately on receiving judgement, however, a decision that annulled the NNDP Government and restored legitimacy to the Action Group, the Government at the Centre hurriedly passed a law that ousted the jurisdiction of the Privy Council. Alhaji Adegbenro enjoyed the briefest non-tenure of regional Premiership in the history of Nigeria: the doors of the legislative house were simply locked against his party. This jettisoning of an embarrassing colonial hangover was not universally lamented, however, but it did serve as a useful pointer to the neutrality or otherwise of the Federal Government in a regional dispute.

Emboldened by one act of illegality and state terror after the other, the NNDP Government no longer bothered to wait for results to come in from the different polling stations but began to award victories at breakneck speed. Individual Government candidates took over, awarded themselves whatever share of the votes they pleased, and brought them to Ibadan, where they were dutifully broadcast by the Government media. The result of this was that in some cases, the party had already looked after the interests of some candidates, awarded them votes and had the results broadcast, only to have one such candidate arrive posthaste at the Broadcasting House, having failed to listen to the radio. He presented his results and, as long as he was of the NNDP, they were also broadcast. It did not matter in the least: the figures might differ but they agreed in the main thing – the NNDP man was the winner.

It was to this scene that Maren returned after the Commonwealth Arts Festival where his play *The Road* had received critical acclaim. That welcome respite donated by the exterior world was over; once again, it was *penkelemes* time.

Hardly pausing to register his presence at his new base, Lagos University, he drove round Ibadan and adjoining towns, marvelling at the chaos within a once disciplined party, its leadership improvising, running blindly against one obstacle after another like a beheaded fowl, totally oblivious of the mass of discontented followers that only awaited a direction for them to follow. The NCNC Government of Dr Michael Okpara in the East had done its best. It not only sent to Ibadan a powerful transmitter, it provided a small team of reporters armed with portable recorders, who proceeded, at enormous risk to themselves, to go round some polling stations, interview candidates and voters, obtain direct results from returning officers, then radio their headquarters in the East, from where the actual results were transmitted to the whole country. In the West, needless to say, most radio receivers were tuned permanently to the Eastern Nigeria Broadcasting Corporation. Before long, a few Action Group candidates had made some form of indirect contact of their own with agents of the ENBC. Through bribery or by coercion, they obtained certificates of their elections, passed the information to the staff of the ENBC and obtained, at least, the satisfaction of hearing their names broadcast as winners. The frustrated journalists of the *Tribune* also took the results they had obtained to the operators of the secret transmitter.

Only within his small, virtually ad-hoc group did Maren find any measure of solace. It had developed from Ife University's confrontation with the Government, and was very cautiously enlarged, mostly by himself. They maintained a loose structure, and their strength lay mainly in their habit of spending discussion time principally in leapfrogging the thinking of the NNDP, and then seeing what, if anything, could be done to thwart or counter its plans. What they could execute themselves, they then carried out. Other measures they passed on to other groups within the political structure of UPGA, the United Progressive Grand Alliance.

They had this other advantage, a strong collaboration from among the police. Maren found that dissidents among them sought him out without any effort on his part. Suspicious and wary as he was, often going to great lengths to check and test the sincerity of those who approached him, he found only two or three instances of deliberate plants or disinformation from that source. Even when the information was of concern to others – politicians or simply other activists and suspected dissidents – the policemen, he found, generally preferred to talk to him. Of course, there were others who found themselves in the same position of enjoying the trust and confidence of such rebels within the force, but he never quite worked out what yardsticks of judgement they used. It was a phenomenon to which he eventually became accustomed, often spotting, before they opened up or attempted to contact him, the very individuals who would prove an asset in specific political situations.

The telephone operators at Oniyanrin remained, by contrast, faceless. His bungalow in Agodi enjoyed the benefit of a telephone and, at odd hours of the day and night, the phone would ring, and a voice would ask, 'Is this Mr Maren?'

On receiving confirmation, the voice continued, 'I think you might be interested in this conversation.' A click followed, and the voices of some party officials, commissioners of police, ministers, judges, the Premier himself and his deputy, would follow. Most frequent of such conversations were those of the Premier attempting to put pressure on a judge in connection with a case – such as the sedition trial of Sam Aluko.

Maren had no telephone at his house in Felele, but still the faceless operators sent him a message, asking him to provide them with a number, preferably one that was residential and would therefore guarantee a twenty-four-hour listening post. The Agodi experience came in useful. There were always empty Government houses in the Reservation if one looked hard enough, and they mostly had telephones. The group commandeered one of these, set up a roster and took turns to camp down in the shuttered building, obtaining a stream of the most varied conversations: operational orders, clearly illegal, issued to the police from party leaders; tirades against the Commissioner for failing to display sufficient severity during an operation; demands for midnight arrests and arbitrary detentions; demands for the immediate release of apprehended thugs who belonged to the NNDP; search-and-destroy orders; bribery attempts; curses; even long, pointlessly malevolent discussions that centred on the imprisoned person of the party leader, Chief Obafemi Awolowo, and some of his lieutenants. The Premier's Lodge appeared never to sleep, but it was not he that was the only author of the many discussions. Party meetings, tactical sessions would go on till early hours of the morning and, from time to time, someone would pick up the phone, dial a number and relate what progress was being made at the meeting.

Maren's extensive travelling around the country during his research project also yielded unprojected dividends. He had made personal contacts of all kinds and in all kinds of places, normal, natural contacts with no thought of any political complications, but with an unsuspected harvest of trust. To a lesser extent, since they had a less prominent public profile, this also applied to others in the group. What they all shared equally in common was a distrust of the politicians in their individual persons, and of the kind of structures of compromise that they were obliged to erect. And so, none of them was, or had the slightest inclination to become, a party member, but there was no question, during this period, where their sympathies lay. Indeed, they were more against, than for. Akintola's NNDP had proved a reprobate organisation; even its NPC allies now began to pronounce it a liability.

In the domain of ideology, neither Dr Okpara's 'pragmatic socialism' nor Awolowo's sometime 'Fabian socialism' cut much ice with the group. In any case, there was a very real, urgent battle to be fought, and that was against what was probably best described as the enthronement of feudal fascism and its guarantee of a fatal, lingering death for progressive society. The collaboration of the Federal Government with the retrogressive régime of the NNDP was the clearest warning signal of a drift towards a repressive, one-party state; indeed, the notion was already being mooted and discussed with increasing self-assurance among the reactionary allies. Even the NCNC in the East had become apprehensive of such a development: it had its own venal share of membership, who had proved that they would jump on the bandwagon of one-partyism rather than be left out of the sharing of what the NNDP had christened the 'National Cake'.

The Deputy Premier of the West, a brilliant legal scholar in his own right, had epitomised this phase of national political decadence by an increasing degeneration into the cynical language of purely consumption politics, devoid of pretence of service and commitment: 'They call us the Chop-chop Party. So? Who doesn't want to chop? I want to chop. Don't you want to chop? Let those who don't want to chop stay in opposition. Those who want to chop, come over to our side. Ah, me, I want to chop *o*!' Again, it was a philosophy that was propagated on radio and television. At the time, the nation still had the grace to be shocked.

The grand design to seize power at all Regional centres, and by all means – money and terror especially – was no longer a project for speculation. The manifesto of the power-seekers, and their design for self-perpetuity, was also no longer a hidden agenda.

Since they were devoid of any confidence in the integrity of the political class, which they therefore refused to join, Maren mentally referred to this group simply as the *Credo* group, permitting himself the perverse pleasure of crediting its activities, nominally at least, to the declaration that had formally annulled the autonomy of the University, launched the violence of the state on its staff and employed state funds to corrupt its leadership. Moreover, half the number of the small group belonged to both Ife and Ibadan, the rest being civil servants and schoolteachers. *Credo* was an easy word to pronounce; it appealed to the religious among them; and, even in a secular order, carried a positivist conviction. It was also a useful password, easy to remember.

Kaye Whiteman, then a columnist of the enduring, London-based

West Africa, remained unaware of the fact, but he was responsible for a certain number of minor events that followed, or failed to follow, the NNDP's now blatant rejection of the democratic mandate of the West. Certainly he did, unwittingly, prevent the home of the Government newspaper in Ibadan from going up in flames. By the time that event was again considered for attention, other factors had intervened, and the rationale for the destruction of that media house had been vitiated. At least, a mood, not exactly of optimism, but of the end of despondency, had replaced that of apparent helplessness and surrender. And that made the *Sketch* even more irrelevant than ever; indeed, it became a joke. In tandem with the Federal Government's *Post* newspapers, they had become the *alawada*,* the *saka jojo*† of the Nigerian media. The people were entitled to their light relief.

The premises of the *Sketch* were situated in Oke Bola in Ibadan, a terrain, at the time, of sharp rises and declivities. It occupied a position in one of the latter, in relation to Kingsway Stores. The derelict space to the right of the store, facing the store itself, not then converted into Kingsway's extended parking space, overlooked the premises of the newspaper, separated from it by a sheer drop of some eight feet. The entire compound of the newspaper was cemented from one end to the other.

Maren had agreed with his associates that this bastion of state propaganda was both a legitimate and a feasible target. The hour when the staff was at its thinnest on the premises had been noted – it was usually between four and five in the morning, after the last of the delivery vans had left. That was when whatever staff was left would be forcibly evacuated, at gunpoint if necessary. Warning by a hand-delivered note, or by telephone, might produce an unpredictable reaction. By then, a hijacked petrol tanker would have been driven to the derelict space and backed to the edge of the drop, its tank cover removed. Then it would be pushed over the ledge to crash and disgorge its contents all over the grounds of the newspaper house, its spread facilitated by the smooth layer of cement. A lit torch would be flung from the overhang into the grounds, and that

*Jesters.
†Cardboard puppet play with comic motions. Silent film.

would be it. This, it was agreed, would provide the signal for an uprising against the despotism.

Maren met Kaye Whiteman, whom he had known from his London days, in front of Trenchard Hall at the University of Ibadan campus. Kaye had just returned from Obafemi Awolowo's house in Oke Ado that morning, where the Action Group leadership had been holding an all-night meeting to discuss the crisis. The Governor of the West, Sir Odeleye Fadahunsi, was under pressure to swear in S.L.A. for another term as Premier, following the NNDP claim of overwhelming victory at the polls. Alhaji Adegbenro, the Acting Leader of the Action Group, had transferred to Awolowo's house which had become the party headquarters. All the bigwigs of the party were present, including their think-tank – Professor Hezekiah Oluwasanmi, Akin Mabogunje, Sam Aluko, Oyenuga and others. They had been meeting for over twelve hours and then, at dawn, Loremikan's police had charged into the compound, tear-gassed the occupants, arrested a handful of the household staff on the grounds that they were thugs, and moved out again. The caucus resumed their debate after wiping their tears, allowing the tear-gas to disperse, and having breakfast.

Maren was unmoved. 'It serves them right,' he said. 'And they ought to be ashamed of themselves. That is the home of their imprisoned leader but they leave it undefended. A bunch of police thugs can invade what is a private home, tear-gas all its occupants including the family of their leader, and what do they do?'

'What could they have done?' Whiteman asked.

'I've told them,' Maren said. 'I've warned them, at least those of them I can bear to speak to. But they'll never learn. Not until Loremikan's men pick them off one by one.'

And then Kaye Whiteman quite casually let drop an information that Maren had not been aware of. 'You know, it's a miracle that they didn't find the transmitter.'

'What transmitter?'

'The ENBC transmitter. The one they've been using to broadcast the results.'

Maren was stunned into a prolonged silence. 'The transmitter? In Awolowo's house?'

Kaye nodded. 'That's where it's been installed. For the past week. You know Okpara sent a team to cover the elections . . .'

'I know that. But you're saying to me that it is actually in Awolowo's residence?'

'That's right.'

It sounded incredible. Loremikan's men had been hunting the transmitter since it had invaded the West and the election results, despite the Government's control of the entire proceedings, turned sour for them, and the Eastern unit had begun to provide a different version of events. Akintola had personally screeched his orders for its destruction over the telephone and summoned the Commissioner to his residence to scorch his ears some more for his tardiness and inefficiency: 'What a performance, Mr Commissioner! What a detective service, when you cannot even find a simple, conspicuous equipment, a whole radio station the size of Bower Tower that even a child could spot from a hundred miles! Or are you now telling me that something which is broadcasting to a whole area like the West, even reaching the East and North, is something you can hide in your pocket? Is it a pocket knife or is it just a kola nut that a farmer hides under his *ikori**? Do you want me to leave my job as Premier and come and lend you a hand? What sort of training do your people receive, Mr Commissioner? *Abi*, is it not the same training as the *oyinbo* experts dispense to all colonial police? Every year we send your people on all these courses; you go to London, you go to America, you go to India, you go to Indonesia, and – *Upon ne nko? Abo e da? Ere wo la ri je nbe*?'[†]

'Were they armed?' Maren wished to know.

'No. Just tear-gas. They came to disrupt the meeting, that's all. A show of brute force, nothing more. Except for the officer who led them. He had a pistol in his belt, but he never took it out. It was more a symbolic invasion, that's what I felt, to destroy the sanctity of Awolowo's house.'

Maren had been made to believe that there were professionals in charge of this one solitary link between the West and the outside world; that its location was a well-protected secret; that the

*Yoruba cap with a side flap, sometimes used as a pouch.
†And at the end of it all? Where are the returns? What do we get to eat from it all?

protectors knew their job. It was an all-Eastern operation, a present from Dr Okpara to the embattled West, to the Action Group, insisting on the rights of news coverage by any state agency in any part of the country. Busy with their own designs, the *Credo* group had not bothered their heads with a responsibility that appeared to be in capable hands. This, however, was the one source of truthful communication with the rest of the nation and even within the West's own political body. The ENBC, for instance, did not merely broadcast the results handed it by the Action Group, it re-broadcast also what the Government party claimed for itself, then left it to listeners to make up their minds. It recorded, then broadcast messages, interviews; it had become the single most effective resistance communication system in the West. Yet it was lodged in the most hated edifice of the Government's psychopathy. Someone, somewhere, needed to have his thinking unwarped.

If the police missed it the first time, they would not the second. Perhaps even now, as he drove towards town . . . Schooling himself not to panic, Maren raced to Seven Sisters, which had become the group's informal meeting place. The short-term plan was that Kodak would round up sufficient hands to rush to Oke Ado. They would deploy themselves casually in the grounds opposite Awolowo's house, among the machine sheds, the food stalls and some hostel buildings run by a Roman Catholic or Baptist mission, a favourite hunting ground for the romantically inclined. Kodak's men would not even need to take the risk of carrying anything under their *agbada* or whatever loose clothing that they adopted to hide their accustomed weapons. The machine sheds and the wooded portions of that area would provide all they required to fend off any further assault.

From the agreed position, they would command a good view, not only of Awolowo's house, but also of all the approaches that the police might use. It was unnecessary to remind Kodak that Loremikan would be armed, as usual, but he did so. Everyone knew of his sadism, his psychopathic compulsion, which required no excuse to shoot at any unarmed target, and without warning. There was hardly any village that did not consider Loremikan a personal mission, a score to be settled whenever opportunity offered itself. Already Loremikan could boast a number of narrow escapes, including the latest near Omida, where a log of wood thrown through his windscreen as he rounded a corner along a rough track caved in the head of his driver, but missed him. The car plunged into the bush and the villagers went after him, but a truckload of his men arrived in the nick of time. The knowledge that he was the most wanted man in the West had turned Loremikan into a rampaging beast, Maren reminded Kodak. He hid his terror under bluster and a lengthening catalogue of atrocities. Kodak nodded grimly, mumbling his hope that it might fall to him to complete that unfinished task.

Only then, towards noon, was he able to address the gnawing need to utilise his channel to their police allies to find out what exactly had happened at the house of Obafemi Awolowo. Was it, as Kaye Whiteman believed, just psychological warfare, designed to keep the opposition on the hop? Or were they after specific individuals? And, by the way, he knew that the police had been searching high and low for the rogue transmitter. Had they found it yet? Ojo had become his principal contact since the Agodi evacuation saga. His position was unique, since he was a senior officer at the House of Assembly police post, which the Premier and his deputy considered their own private police force, while he also remained part of the deployable personnel of the headquarters at Iyaganku. What it meant, in effect, was that the function of the small unit at Agodi was a kind of liaison between the NNDP thug militia, and the regular forces of the Commissioner in Iyaganku. Ojo promised to contact Loremikan directly and find out what he had been up to.

The answers came a short while later. The signature tune had become a part of him – 'I just thought you should know,' . . . and then followed the disclosures. The Action Group think-tank was indeed the target; the raid had been designed to demoralise them. It was, in fact, a decision taken from the top – even Loremikan, ever eager to please his paymaster, was feeling upset. He had confided in Ojo that he would not dare assault the home of the imprisoned leader on his own, only under compulsion. Even so, it was one task for which he had not displayed much enthusiasm. Whatever else he was, he was still a Yoruba, wasn't he? The culture in which he was raised simply did not permit the desecration of the home of a man who had been to the top, and then crashed down, whose heir, his very first son, had died in a motor accident while he was in prison

– no, Loremikan protested vigorously, snapping his fingers round his head to ward off the consequences of the act of desecration – he would never do a thing like that on his own. That would be daring one's head to take on the curse that had befallen the man whose arrogance had invited one disaster after another on himself. Oh no, not him! He had taken care not to enter the house itself, had ordered his men to throw their canisters through the windows, arrest the two or three house servants wandering around the place, smash a few glass panes and bulbs to teach everyone a lesson, and quit the premises as quickly as possible. He had taken care not even to touch the walls of the house or penetrate its doors – look, everyone knows that Awolowo is an Ijebu man and you know what kind of medicines they produce in that place. He was not afraid of any man face to face, he was no coward, the Western people had learnt that the hard way, and he was no pushover when it came to self-fortification – they know about those things in my village, believe me – but your fortifications can desert you if you break some kind of taboo, and what greater taboo could there be than that, defecating on a man's doorstep when the elephant trap has landed him in the pit! It was all very well to try and break the will of his followers, to confront them with their impotence. But they were doing that already, they were producing results. No good could come out of this latest action, he sighed, no good would come from it . . .

An hour later, the tone of the news had changed. 'I just thought you should know . . .' The arrested staff, who were in fact 'casuals' – a driver of one of the people at the meeting, another a bodyguard – had been subjected to some routine interrogation by Loremikan's staff. In responding to questions such as: How many people were at the meeting? Who were they? Were there any thugs billeted there?, they had revealed that the only strangers they had noticed were some Igbo people who seemed to stay there all the time. They appeared to be treated as rather special; food was taken to them in the room they occupied and sometimes people went in to see them. Loremikan had received the news with excitement and had promptly contacted Ojo in Agodi. Could these be the broadcasting unit they had been searching for all over the West? Ojo had promptly offered to lend him some of his surveillance men. They were now about to set off – he hoped that Maren knew what that meant. Maren understood. All Ojo could do was provide them with a warning. He was too much of a policeman to tamper with facts, especially facts that were the result of a formal investigation.

'If . . . ,' Maren picked his words carefully, 'if they happen to be there, how much time would they have before . . .'

'Oh, it has to be a round-the-clock surveillance. For an effective raid, we would have to await a twenty-four-hour report. The personnel might be there but not their equipment, or vice versa. So we have to be patient. I told him to be ready in twenty-four hours, after our report. Thoroughness is the name of the game, you realise.'

'A-ha. We appreciate your thoroughness.'

'We try to be efficient,' Ojo laughed.

For the first time, Maren visited the home of the Action Group leader.

On reflection, he had to admit to a sneaking admiration for the gentlemen of the party caucus. No sooner had they finished breakfast than they resumed their deliberations, the insolence of the assault brushed aside. As he came through the gates, he looked up and saw them gathered in the upstairs room, locked in earnest debate. He learnt that they telephoned the Governor from time to time, trying to obtain some glimmering of the Governor's position, so as to plan their own strategy. They were plain sitting ducks, the premises did not boast one defender. The only staff he encountered were the gateman, and a few domestic staff who had been indoors at the time of the raid and had therefore escaped arrest.

These people were compulsive candidates for martyrdom, he felt. Apart from a handful who had quit, declaring that they had tasted enough of Loremikan's tear-gas, the rest were obviously determined to continue. In some way it was an act of defiance, he supposed; to continue, they probably felt, was the only way to uphold the honour of their imprisoned leader, and redeem the violation of his home. They would not be satisfied until Akintola could arrange for the squeamish Loremikan to be replaced, and a riot police unit deployed from outside the West who would smash the place to bits, and baton-charge the gurus for daring to gather and meditate within privately owned premises. Well, he only hoped that they would feel all the nobler for it.

For his own tastes, as he drove in he had glanced across the road and was more than reassured by the lolling, joking, but alert presences that he recognised as Kodak's men. By nightfall, they would be joined by those members of *Credo* whose faith in the methods of the opposing side was circumscribed by the arms they were carrying, and their fussless acceptance of the right of self-defence. His exchange with Ojo had guaranteed that nothing would happen for twenty-four hours, but that was from the police side only. There was nothing to stop the NNDP from mounting its own raid any time in the night, determined to profit from the softening-up assault mounted that morning by Loremikan's side. Such thinking, or 'leapfrogging', as he preferred to describe it, had become ingrained in his assessment of every development; to assume the most improbable worst of any such association of power-driven men that the NNDP had come to represent!

A car pulled up close to the wall of the house on the outside: vehicles were not allowed to drive in, and he gave silent thanks for such small security mercies. Thinking it was another party adviser come to join the deliberations, he moved quickly inside, only to have his name called by a familiar voice. It was Soji Odunjo, a young party candidate, and son of one of the founders of the party, Chief S. O. Odunjo. On his face was a broad, triumphant grin, and in his hand he waved a piece of paper. He nodded his head in the direction of the upstairs room as he moved towards him.

'Are they still meeting?'

'Oh, yes.' They embraced.

'They've lost touch,' he moaned. 'They do not understand the kind of animals they're dealing with, and they are out of touch with the mood of the people.'

'I'm afraid you're right,' Maren agreed.

'I was here yesterday. I came to report what was happening in my Egbado constituency. I wanted to know what they had decided. They are the party executive, plus the think-tank. They are supposed to provide leadership. I warned them that we were being raped, all over the Region, raped. I asked them to take a decision one way or the other. Whatever we choose to do, we simply cannot continue to play the game by their own rules. Do we fight or not? I wanted an answer.'

'Well?'

'They told me they were still trying to get in touch with Sir Odeleye Fadahunsi, the Governor. Can you imagine that? Half the results were already announced, even from places where counting had not begun, from places where the electoral officers had disappeared, taking the ballot boxes with them, or simply never showed up! More results were pouring in every moment. From the half-hourly or hourly announcements, they were beginning to emerge in batches. The pace was accelerating so wildly it was clear that Akintola would declare himself victor by dawn. So I left them to their meeting and dashed back to my constituency. Here, take a look. That's my winner's certificate.' And he thrust the piece of paper at Maren. 'Duly stamped, witnessed, and certified by the Electoral Officer.'

'Congratulations. How did you do it?'

'How else? After I left here I stopped by my house and picked up my shotgun. When I got to the Officer, I put the muzzle to his head and gave him one minute to produce the results.'

Maren chuckled. 'I suppose that is one way to do it.'

'It's the only language they understand. It's the language in which they've been cursing us all this while. Even before I dashed here yesterday, I warned him that if he disappeared like some others of his colleagues, I would hunt him down to the ends of the earth. Not just him, but his entire family. He knew I wasn't joking.'

'So now, what next?'

'I'm going upstairs to wave this at them, and I'll tell them how it is done. And it's not by waiting for an appointee of Government to make up his mind whether or not he will take power away from a Government that placed him there. Imagine. As if the Governor has any choice but to endorse Akintola's victory claims.'

Maren watched him take the steps nearly three at a time, wished that the party had a few more like him, because then he would not be in that place at that time, minding a business that was really not his own, at least was not a situation of his own making. He moved inside the house, walking instinctively towards the area of the house that seemed likely to contain such contraband as the broadcasting team and their transmitter. He found them in the vast study of the imprisoned leader, and they were packing up their equipment, rolling up wires and boxing up their tapes and micro-phones. For several moments, he watched them, unseen.

Finally, the boisterous, non-stop talkative comedian, Ukonu, the leader of the group, turned, and saw him. They were meeting for the first time, but Maren recognised who it was at once. He had seen him on Eastern television programmes, and in any case, he would have recognised anywhere the voice of the stocky man with the close-cropped hair and slight American accent who rushed to embrace him.

'It is Chief Baroka in person, don't tell me different.'

Ukonu was taken aback by his cool response. 'Why are you people packing up?'

'Hey? You haven't heard? Nobody has told you what happened here this morning? Man, we ain't pushing our luck any further.' He turned abruptly on his colleagues who had stopped working. 'Boys, you're wasting time. Stop staring at the man as if you haven't met Fame in all your life. What about me? You see me all the time and you don't stare at me like that. So come and shake the man's hand and get on with the packing. Move, my people, move.'

Maren shook hands with the team one by one, managing a smile for all. He waited for them to return to their chores.

'You mean you're leaving for Enugu?'

'You've said it. We're crossing the regional border fast, before that goon changes his mind and comes back. They don't like us here, man, and we know it. But we thought we were safe here. We never thought the goons would dare attack Awolowo's house. That's it for us.'

'Oh, if that's all you're worried about . . .'

'You want us to find something else to worry about when we've got this one that's more than enough? No, seriously though; we've really finished our job. Only a few more results to go, and in any case, the Chief Electoral Officer, who also happens to be the Chief Candidate, has already declared the results.' And he broke into his infectious wide-mouthed laughter, cut it off as if on a secret cue and composed his face to take on a serious aspect. 'We've got to go, man. The police have been looking for us everywhere. This morning was too close a shave. Hey, look at it, man, take a look.'

He thrust out his chin. 'See where the blade nicked me?' And he went into yet another round of laughter.

Maren pulled him by the shoulder. 'Come. There are some things you have to know. Let's go somewhere quiet.'

'Sure. As a matter of fact I was dying for a pee when you came in. I'll just take that leak and then we'll talk.'

'That's okay,' Maren said. 'I need to use the toilet myself. After you.'

'No, come on. It's one of those roomy ones with five *pissoirs*, where you can line up and do business five at a time. They are quite right about that man, you know. He doesn't like to waste one moment. So if he is having a meeting with his men and they want to pee, they don't have to queue up. And they can carry on discussing serious politics while they pee. They're right about him; he thought of everything!' His irrepressible laughter accompanied them from the study, followed them through the deserted, forlorn corridor that once echoed with passionate politics, and into the Gents'.

Once in the toilet, Maren felt an overwhelming sense of the ridiculous at what he knew he was about to do. There was, however, no time to waste. On no account could the transmitter be permitted to leave Ibadan; indeed, to leave that house, since looking for a new location, then setting it up and renewing contacts, would consume valuable time. He had come there to record a number of messages, and to have others record several more. Those messages must be transmitted directly to the ENBC, to minimise the risk of the tapes falling into wrong hands. The focus of the struggle had to shift; control of it had to be taken away from the caucus who were deliberating impotently upstairs. If they chose also to participate – and he intended to attempt to persuade them – all the better. They were the recognised party leaders; he and others like him were mere volunteers. However, the state of inertia, of virtual surrender, had to be broken, and the communication facility of the Eastern unit was crucial to it.

Maren slipped into his other skin, watching from the sidelines. It was the only way he could redeem himself from the sense of the ludicrous that overwhelmed him at such moments.

'Ukonu, I'm afraid we can't let you go just yet.'

'Hey man, don't make me feel bad. Or worse, 'cause I feel bad already. We've wound up. We've told them at home we're on our way and they told us we should have been on our way longest time. In short, my boss ordered me to get out immediately.'

'That's too bad,' Maren heard himself say. 'But you still can't go anywhere. I shall take you outside in a moment and show you some of our people in front. They are guarding this place. No one comes in that we don't want, and no one goes out. I'm sorry.'

Ukonu looked bewildered. 'Man, what's going on here? What are you trying to tell me?'

'I promise you you're safe for the next twenty-four hours. I shall tell you when to leave and we'll escort you to safety. I shall remain with you throughout. But right now, you remain.'

'I still don't get you,' he protested. 'We're already packed, man. What do you expect me to say to Enugu?'

'Tell them you were forcibly detained.'

'But how? Who is going to believe that story unless we actually got arrested, and I'm not planning on doing that.'

'But you have been arrested, Ukonu. You are under arrest until you've broadcast every last result of this election. The complete list of the authentic results will get here before curfew. You'll have the entire list and help us transmit everything to Enugu, ward by ward and seat by seat. When you get to Enugu, just continue broadcasting it over and over again, as often as you can. And then there will be several interviews and statements you'll take with you, including the most crucial one. That, most especially: it's a call for a general uprising in the West.'

'Hey man, don't tell me the party has finally got round to that. Is it Alhaji . . .'

'No, the party will never get to that point. I am making the broadcast.'

'You, man?'

'Yes. I have to do it. But we won't even be able to decide when we want you to broadcast that message until later. That's a decision we'll be taking tonight. So, we have a busy day ahead. Go and tell your boys to start unpacking.'

'Hey, wait a minute. You know which side we are on. But our time is up here. We have to go. I no longer have a choice in the matter.'

So Maren watched impassively, separated from himself, as he finished urinating, zipped up his trousers and stepped back from the urinal. From inside his shirt he pulled out a gun and pointed it loosely at the floor. 'I'm sorry, but I wasn't joking when I said you were under arrest. You have a choice. We can either use this to protect you – and we have quite a few more around – or we use it to detain you forcibly. Now which of the two do you prefer?'

Ukonu stared, his broad face frozen in disbelief. He backed slowly away, not lifting his eye from the gun. 'Hey,' he blurted out finally, his finger pointing at the weapon. 'That's a real gun!'

'It's a real fight, Ukonu, at least now, or very soon. We need you and your equipment for another twenty-four hours, even less. If we can't make you stay, then you simply must leave the equipment – and that means you may never see it again. Naturally, I would prefer that you stayed, but that's up to you.'

Ukonu's face broke wide open in two halves, split by a wide grin. 'Brother, am I with you! I am under voluntary arrest!'

Maren watched him dash from the toilet, heard him shouting orders to his team. Then he turned and stared at his reflection in the mirror for a long time. He saw his arm hanging down, the gun at the end of it. He replaced it thoughtfully, then went out and into the study that had been turned into the transmission room. He sat behind the mammoth desk in the study, thinking the man must have planned most of his political strategies behind this very desk. He pulled out some sheets of paper and tried to concentrate. He began writing brief statements, beginning with the unlikeliest – the ones he was already convinced that none of the recognised party leaders would ever agree to record, but he wrote them all out anyway. Once that reluctant duty was out of the way, he began scripting his own statements, pacing them mentally as he felt that the course of the struggle was likely to develop. The first would follow the conflagration planned for the Government media house called the *Sketch*.

Then he noted that this other Maren was no longer admiring the huge working desk of his absent host for its craftsmanship and shape, or the smoothness of its polished timber. When he stretched his legs, he found that there appeared to be lots of space beneath.

He pushed the chair back and looked: indeed, the space was capable of accommodating two or three grown men, fully stretched out. So he decided there and then that that would be his sleeping quarters for the night, if there was any sleep to be had. It was a good place from which to spring an effective surprise if the place was raided. He had already allocated positions to each member of the incoming team; they would come in just before curfew. He discovered that that someone he had recognised in the toilet mirror was wishing fervently that the other side would make the mistake of raiding the place again, thinking it was undefended. Yes, even Loremikan, who had earned death twenty times over, he and his uniformed thugs; he wished they would come charging in. He glanced up at the door, projecting the figure of the Police Commissioner at the head of his men . . . It was a sight that filled his stranger companion with vengeful anticipation.

It was a busy afternoon, and it grew busier towards evening, tailing off towards midnight. The caucus upstairs had finished their meeting and dispersed. As he had expected, the party would not make the crucial call for resistance. Others, however, came in, recorded messages of solidarity, called on the illegitimate Government to quit and urged the people to stand firm.

They took turns to stand watch, but it was a quiet night, and he slept soundly under the commodious desk of the imprisoned leader. About an hour before dawn, he woke up Ukonu, told him it was time to start packing his equipment. Ukonu looked distinctly unhappy; he had hoped that his 'arrest' might be prolonged indefinitely but that was not to be. At the first break of light and the end of curfew, he saw off the team. It was the signal also for the *Credo* team to leave, having stowed their shotguns, two rifles – one a mere .22 – and two pistols away in the vehicle that was parked at the corner of the house. Kodak and company would hang around a while, if only to amuse themselves with the sight of Loremikan's stormtroopers; then they also would disperse.

The domestic staff brought in breakfast for the broadcasting unit as usual, and were astonished to find them gone, only Maren in their place, using the telephone. Normally, he did not eat breakfast, just had coffee, but that morning he felt a need to do the unusual, and so he asked the staff to leave him a tray. He completed his call to Ojo, who informed him of the precise time that Loremikan's squad would raid the place, convinced that they had the Eastern team and their equipment in their grasp. It gave him just over an hour, so he sat and ate a leisurely breakfast in the book-lined room, wondering whether its owner was having breakfast at that very moment in his Calabar prison, over six hundred miles away. Did he often think of his eldest son, Segun, he wondered, or would it be like him to blot out that loss, allowing nothing to weaken his morale in the loneliness of prison life? Segun had lost his life in a motor accident, at the very ebb of the party leader's political fortunes. The news had come to him in Kirikiri prison where he awaited trial with others, charged with attempting to forcibly overthrow the Government of Tafawa Balewa. Knowing something of his stoicism, he would probably have said at the time, perhaps it is as well I am in prison, since tradition forbids that I witness the funeral of my offspring.

Maren recalled now, with a feeling of guilt, how he had once dismissed the young man as one of the spoilt scions of the new political families – which he was, to some degree, while a student in the United Kingdom. But he had returned with a clarified sense of mission, shedding the image of the young, pampered playboy. An unexpected visitor had one day called on him in Agodi, and it was Segun, seeking him out on his own, anxious to know what his 'elder brother' actually thought of the politics of the country, pressing on him earnest, searching questions; as if he wanted to cut a clear path of his own, unfettered by his father's own determined course and his overwhelming personality.

It had turned out to be a long afternoon. From an initial suspicion of this stranger's motives – unlike the Akintola family, Maren had not been anywhere close to Awolowo's – he quickly came to recognise a kindred spirit. It seemed just the kind of thing he knew he would do, making an uninhibited intrusion into a source that might hold possibilities for clarifying one's ideas, directions. And then, suddenly, after so brief an interval that, for a while, he retained the feeling that he had seen the younger man only the day before, Segun was dead, and that was the end of that hope, that promise of transformation. And Maren would sometimes wonder whether this youth had somehow known what he, Maren, had thought of him, had sensed his impending death, and called on him to erase that mental epitaph and bear witness to what might have been if . . .

It was a soundproofed room – polished wood panelling, heavy drapes, and a solid barrier of burdened shelves: law, politics, religions of every kind, history and biographical tomes. With Ukonu's busy team gone, an eerie quiet had descended over the chamber, augmenting even further that state of disembodiment in which he had passed the last fifteen hours. It was time to stop daydreaming.

He took a last look round, and left. At the entrance to the house he met Kaye Whiteman again, come to gather news of any decision reached by the caucus. 'You seem to enjoy being tear-gassed,' Maren said.

'Oh? What's happening?'

'Nothing yet, but if you remain here another fifteen minutes, you will either get a scoop or end up gassed. You might even be placed under arrest – I hear your name is surfacing as being pro-opposition.'

'Really?'

Maren nodded. 'Oh yes. Mind you, it wouldn't be totally undeserved. You may not have intended it, but you did us a very useful turn yesterday.'

His trained journalist's mind moved rapidly. 'Oh, the transmitter? The Eastern boys? I was wondering what you were doing here so early.'

Maren nodded. 'I've just seen them off. Loremikan thinks he's coming to net them in fifteen minutes. He's using a narrow mesh to make sure no one escapes – any kind of stranger is to be rounded up and brought back to the station and – you look very much like a stranger to me.'

XII 'The Smell of Roast Yam'

The following Saturday afternoon was set for a bout of gastronomic self-indulgence; he had participated in a half dozen or so before then, always on a Saturday afternoon when the host, Femi Johnson, would fill the table as if food were the sole purpose of humanity on earth, and dare his family and a few close friends to match his voracious appetite. Saturday afternoon was an all-Nigerian cuisine, nothing foreign was permitted at the table, and a skimpy, or merely sampling, approach only earned Femi's endless derision.

When Maren first witnessed the collective performance – wife, children, a neighbouring couple and another friend – he felt himself outclassed even by the smallest member of the family. So he took to fasting twenty-four hours beforehand, then thirty-six, but it only made matters worse. Still, the feast remained a high point of anticipation, and whenever he could set a Saturday aside, it was sure to find him at Onireke, having not only starved ahead of time but exercised – mostly with press-ups – in some vague hope that this distended the stomach muscles and left more room within to come close to, at the very least, a respectable consumption level with the youngest of the family.

For bringing one down to earth, there is nothing like contending with a half dozen adults and a clutch of juveniles, trying to justify the favourite saying of the national sybarite: *safe for food to waste, na belle go burs.** Maren repaired to Onireke with even less a part of himself than usual, determined to become whole before the late afternoon dispersal of his competitors-in-gluttony. It would be, he knew now, his last day of participation in such a rite for . . . he no

*Sooner than be defeated by food, let the stomach burst!

longer attempted to guess for how long. What had become clear to him, however, was that his pattern of living had changed for ever – at least for as long as the repressive order remained. And that order did threaten to persist for quite a while.

A staunch member of the circle arrived late; this was Michael Olumide, who was the Controller of the Western arm of the Nigerian Broadcasting Service. He had received an urgent summons to report at the Premier's Lodge with a recording team. The Premier, Akintola, would make a broadcast that evening and he wanted it recorded. There was a possibility that he might even make the broadcast live, but he wanted to tape his speech in advance, just in case. Femi Johnson, ever insatiable for the inside scoops of politics and intrigues, pressed and pressed for a hint of what Akintola had recorded, but the stolid Controller of the media would reveal nothing, only that the Premier would broadcast, and that it would be at the usual news hour in the evening.

The previous night, Maren had found himself doing a curious thing, something that he could not explain. He had gone to the Premier's house. Those days, the beleaguered Premier hardly ever slept there, preferring both the company and safety of a mistress that he kept in Bodija. Maren had gone to his official lodge, for the first time in several months, in a state of mind that he could not fully explain. Perhaps he had indeed gone there in the hope that he would find Premier Akintola at home, so that they could talk in the peace of the night. He slowed down as he approached the gates, ready to drive straight through if there were cars or signs of the presence of party stalwarts and sycophants.

The compound was deserted: that had become the pattern in recent times. He entered the house, hallooed but received no response. A steward came out, recognised him and reported that only the mother was home, that she was already upstairs in bed. Should he summon her? For a moment, he hesitated, then told him not to bother.

In the immediate passageway before the private lounge, towards which he headed, there were two mammoth refrigerators – he was familiar with both. One stored beer and soft drinks, the other wines and champagnes. He opened the first, intending to take out a beer, sit in the lounge and drink while he waited in the hope that the man would return home before dawn.

And then, probably from habit, he also looked in the other refrigerator. He had never seen it so full; clearly a party was in the offing. From top to bottom, crammed into every cranny and the door shelves as well were dozens and dozens of bottles of champagne; pink, white, *brut, sec, demi-sec, doux.*

Slowly, he opened the other cooler, returned the beer, then gathered armfuls of champagne bottles and carried them to his car, quite openly, indifferent to the possibility that someone might appear to challenge him. Then he went back to the first cooler, retrieved his beer, sat in the lounge and drank. He was there for over an hour, but there were no movements in the house. He left, drove to the University campus and, selecting randomly, distributed all the champagne, down to the last bottle, to the astonished staff. He gave no explanations, simply dropped a bottle in each hand or left it at the door. If he paused that evening to ask the reason for his actions, he could not recall; only that it was something that he did on the spur of the moment, and that he went home afterwards, not even stopping at Risikatu which lay, conveniently, on his way home. He recalled, however, that he slept soundly, his deepest sleep perhaps in many weeks.

Femi continued to pester Michael for any titbits, any scrap at all from what the Premier intended to inflict on his people, but Maren found himself indifferent. What could it be beyond more threats, more arrogance of power, a desperate man's rhetoric to sanctify infamy by defiling the airwaves yet again with claims of victory? Every Intelligence report that came through to them confirmed the party's resolve to cling to power. And so, even the fraction of himself that he had brought to the feast took off abruptly, without warning; but he rescued it quickly, snatched it down to earth and anchored it deep into the bowl of pounded yam and the *apon** stew, studded with cow's 'internal affairs', giant snails, venison and dried fish. No one noticed that he had been away. Still the light-headedness persisted and he knew why.

It was due to an unexpected sense of relief, and he wished that it

*Ground kernel from the orombeje fruit.

were possible to invite Kaye Whiteman to the feast, a gesture of
gratitude that would only have mystified the journalist. But for their
chance encounter near Trenchard Hall, and the distraction of the
transmitter that had resulted from his disclosure, the *Daily Sketch*
building would by now have gone up in flames. Maren was by no
means averse to the idea, only uncomfortable at the unpredictable
effect of an entire tank of petrol engulfing the building, and the
likelihood of its spreading to other buildings. However, the group
had decided that it was a risk worth taking, and the *Daily Sketch*
was nearly as physically isolated from its surroundings as it was
alienated from the people. However, Michael Olumide had now
unknowingly provided an alternative, one that, he was certain,
would be welcomed by the others as eagerly as the ram substitute
was by Abraham for his trussed-up son. In any case, this was one
decision that he had taken instantly; what was more, the other
Maren had silently excused himself from the company and commenced a fussless planning.

He ate as casually as he could, anxious to be off, then took his
leave, conceding early defeat in the competitive feasting. Nothing
had been planned for that Saturday – it was, by agreement, their
day off, once the Eastern team had left. The problem of rounding
up any members of the *Credo* group was near insurmountable –
most of them had also gone on their own version of Saturday
unwinding. In the end, there were only three available. Now he
wished that he had kept at least one of the tapes that Ukonu had
taken back to Enugu, especially the one that called for an uprising
throughout the West.

No longer surprised at the phenomenon, he watched his companion self move like a programmed automaton, homing in on
resources that were recalled from dormant hideouts of the mind,
recalling the shape and layout of the Broadcasting House, the reception room, the stairs, corridors, the side entrance that opened into
the road across which stood Obisesan Cinema Hall, the Cooperative
Building, while on the same side was the Insurance Building with
its attractive mural that had been executed by – the G-man. Once
more, he went over the transmission studios as he last saw them,
several weeks before, when he had been looking for Femi, and was
told that he was across the road, in Michael's office . . . stopping to

say hallo to the pioneer writer, Amos Tutuola, who worked in a
poky little office on the ground floor – but no longer as a storekeeper
– up the stairs again and through the corridors once more . . . mentally recalled where the split-level began and the corridor sheered
sharply away from the rear wall, made of decorative blocks that
exposed the corridor to any curious eyes from outside, from the
Kingsway Stores; then fell to wondering who might be on duty on
that fateful evening, only hours away.

It was already late afternoon, and there could only be feverish
improvisation. He had already marked down a young American
research student who owned a tape recorder, a professional brand,
that used just the kind of spool that was needed. Tracked down, he
was given no option but to make his equipment available. Since
he was accustomed to his own tools and a good technical quality
was essential, he also had to supervise the recording of the new
message, quickly scripted by Maren. The apartment of the medical
photographer, Frank Speed, was commandeered – he was away
from the country at the time. By five o'clock that afternoon, the
message was on a spool, and they had made a spare copy that would
be sent on to Enugu, just in case. All that was left was to pick up
the trio, drive casually through the vicinity of the Broadcasting
House and select positions for the woefully inadequate band, school
them on what would be required of them if things went wrong, or
right.

And then it had to happen, the worst imaginable affliction that
could attack a body tuning up for a mission that required precision,
and was limited by time – a running stomach. The combination of
the peppery stews and the beer at Femi Johnson's maybe, exacerbated by the to-ing and fro-ing on the pot-holed roads and the
rutted tracks between the lumberyard shacks at Oke Foko, looking
for Kodak, appeared to be working havoc in his stomach. Or perhaps
it was the possibility that he might actually end up shooting the
Premier, if he did show up, and there was no other way to stop him.
Gaining entrance into the building early required hiding in the
record library, which he alone knew well. He kept up his telephone
calls to the very last possible moment, making casual enquiries
about Akintola's intentions. By then the six tablets of Thalazole that
he had swallowed all at once – instead of two, three times a day –

had stoppered the subversive tap that was threatening his evening out.

There were two scenarios, and both were straightforward. One was if the Premier decided to come in person, the other if he stuck to the recorded message. The first had to be played by ear, everything was left to the on-the-spot decision of the first of the three men who would be deployed around the Cooperative Building, the Kingsway Stores, and the Insurance Building opposite the Broadcasting House. They could take on the motorcade, concentrating on his own vehicle, using the advantage of the night and of surprise. They tried to guess which route the motorcade might take, but it made no difference anyway. The first man along the route held the decision: if he chose to act, the other two must follow. If not, they would simply melt into the night. One barrage would trigger off a panic, the motorcade would accelerate into the next, and then into the third. At night, beyond a token response in the general direction of attack, the escorts would not stop to instigate further enquiries or go in pursuit of the attackers. That would be suicidal, since they would have no idea how many were involved in the ambush; also their first duty was to take their charge out of the danger zone. In any case, the loyalty of the guards was already a source of suspicion and complaint for the isolated Premier. The logical response of the party, whichever way one looked at it, would be to speed off as fast as they could gun their motorcars. Maren squelched all argument about who would actually enter the studios and insert the new tape. He knew the interior better than the others and that was that. Moreover, the inside person had the responsibility of creating a violent diversion that would disrupt all activity, if the Premier did come in person to do a live broadcast, successfully braved the ambush and entered the building. This was best done by starting a fire in the record library and he had planned exactly how it would be done. Whatever it took, the broadcast must be prevented.

Normally, there should have been someone to drive the car, wait for the one who would enter and whisk him away at the end. However, there was no one to spare. Three one-man ambushes, even of the hit-and-run kind, against a three- to five-strong motorcade was bad enough; two would be too ludicrous for effectiveness. There was only one answer; recruit a willing outsider who would know just enough to obey instructions but would not be exposed to risk. Maren's walking image did not need to think for long; within Orisun, there were three whom he knew he could always count upon for such limited chores; he chose Jimi Solanke. Jimi did not even have a driver's licence but he could move a car, put it in reverse and take a corner with safety. In any case, Maren would take the wheel as long as he was in the vehicle. To make driving easier for Jimi, in case he had to drive, he swapped his car for a friend's Volkswagen, explaining that he had a tryst to keep, and did not wish to be spotted by the girl's protective parents.

It meant parking the car somewhat further away from the Broadcasting House than he had planned, placing it on the slope on Lebanon Street after the short link between Lebanon and Kingsway Streets. The police were stationed in the lobby and on the frontage of the building itself. If there was a hue and cry, it made sense to assume that they would all rush in, by which time he would be through the corridors on the top floor, waiting at the foot of the stairs to the side, until the police had quit the front to investigate the commotion. Then he would walk briskly to the waiting car, while the others dispersed as they had arrived – individually.

When he stepped out of the car, he told Jimi to take the driving seat; if he was not out in fifteen minutes, he should simply drive off and return the car to its owner. In the darkness, he could not see Jimi's face to see how he reacted, but he knew he would do as he was told.

So he watched himself walk through the short link road, saw the third man in the presumed route move slightly in the shadows, watched himself raise his hand casually to acknowledge that he had noted his presence and that nothing had changed in the arrangements. This stranger ducked into the entrance to the side stairs, arrived at the corridor, walked past Michael Olumide's office, onto the split-level corridor and then into the studios. The tape was being readied for broadcast. And then there was this voice, which he had last heard in the guest lavatory of Obafemi Awolowo's house, and using the same alien language, all within one week. He watched them hesitate, saw on their faces the look of disbelief, the momentary wonder if it was all a joke, and then, of course, almost at once they knew it was not. So there was no need at all for him to fulfil his threat and shoot an idle console to remove all doubt that the gun was real, and that he meant business. He had a distanced notion that he ought to be amused by the eager response of Oshin, the Shift Leader, as he stammered, 'No, sir, no need at all,' scrambling to off-load the Premier's spool, but he was not.

Instead, he reached for the discarded spool, saying briefly, 'No, I'll take that.' He stuffed it beneath the loose *agbada* he had selected for entombing the gun and spare magazines. The Shift Leader's hands were trembling and the intruder became nervous that he might not succeed in threading the tape on time, since the Premier's voice must not be kept waiting but must resound to the people on the second after the Announcer's introduction, but Oshin got it right in the end. The recording had been carefully made with the main message at the beginning, since he had no intention of remaining in the studio once the tape was up and running. Still, he wanted it to run as long as possible, so he heard a cold voice issuing from his head, warning them not to touch the tape, that there were others with guns trained on them, right inside the building, and that not one of them would reach home alive if the tape was turned off. It appeared to have worked. It was some other duty officer who rushed into the studio after the seditious message began, tearing off the tape. But by then the 'Premier's message' had gone out to his people: 'This is the voice of the people, the true people of this nation. And they are telling you, Akintola, get out! Get out, and take with you your renegades who have lost all sense of shame . . .'

It had all taken twelve minutes from the moment that he stepped out of the car. Jimi was still in the driver's seat, the engine running. He slid over to the passenger seat and Maren entered the car, nodding to him. 'I'm glad I made it in time. It would have been a long walk home.'

'I had no intention of leaving, sir,' Jimi replied, 'however long it took you – whatever it was.'

Five a.m. saw him off, heading East and towards a reunion with Sam Aluko, who had settled with his family in the Nsukka campus of the University of Nigeria, far from Somare's Ministry thugs. He was moved from place to place as the WANTED notices began to appear – with increasing rage and stridency – in both Federal and

Western Government media. In the evening, the police would knock on the door of his latest refuge, enter and shake hands with everyone, the Wanted Man included. Headquarters in Lagos had sent a signal that the fugitive was in Enugu, and they merely called – all this with a deadpan face – to make a preliminary check. In the morning, they, or their colleagues, would be back for a formal search, and they hoped someone would be home to let them in. Well, good night, and, declining even a drink, they again shook hands all round, leaving out no unknown guests.

The contacts continued, the police in Ibadan proving so efficient that they traced all the phone calls, and pulled in Femi Johnson, Michael Olumide and others for questioning. That exercise was futile but a tiny handful of the teaching staff at Ibadan and Ife remained true to themselves, providing information, solicited and unsolicited, about real and imagined sightings of the Wanted Man on the day of the crime, sightings which made him a likely suspect, and they declared themselves more than willing to appear in court. Others, the expatriates especially, were threatened with expulsion from the country unless they gave such evidence as the police wanted, as they slowly built up their case.

The past, he easily accepted, was dead – at least for now. When he met the Eastern Premier, Dr Michael Okpara, in his office, he presented him with a shopping list. 'I am returning home shortly,' he told him, 'but not the way I came. These,' he listed, 'are what we have; the following, we are in dire need of – where can you assist?'

Dr Okpara was an impressive figure at any time; behind his desk during the *tête-à-tête*, his eyes danced with the sheer prospect of battle. 'Do you need men?' he asked.

'No,' Maren told him, 'we are only a few for now, but we have a huge pool of reserves.' It remained only a question of how to deliver the requests in batches, one at a time, in designated spots. Okpara summoned his political aide, ushered them out to discuss the details.

And then, out of nowhere, Komi appeared. He was not a member of the group but knew of them, and was trusted. He had volunteered to seek out Maren in the East, find out what, if anything, he wanted them to do. As a Warri man, he knew his way around the East, despite his long stay in Lagos and the West, and was anxious to contribute something besides long, futile discussions in staff clubs or nightclubs. They had all put their heads together, reviewed the situation, and decided on a shift in strategy: the fugitive should return and stand trial.

He found himself instantly hostile to the idea. Stand trial in Akintola's courts? But they had all repudiated his legality, so what was this but a contradiction? All night they argued. The road Maren wanted to tread was a different one, the road that had been mapped, for which the various calls to action had been taped and stored, had not envisaged any submission to legal authority. The burning down of the *Daily Sketch* was to have been the signal for that new phase, but the raid on the Broadcasting House had served just as well. Nothing that he could observe had changed – so why? Komi pressed on him the arguments of the discussion in which he had taken part. A political trial was what the West – and indeed much of the nation – needed at such a time. There was an even chance that he would be found guilty; there was, however, the greater risk that he would be caught and dragged to court in chains. If he went voluntarily, the trial, whichever way it went, would only hasten the destruction of the Government. It would galvanise the people and there would also, needless to say, be massive international interest.

'You must see the trial as a potent weapon,' Komi argued, 'even more deadly than what can be achieved with Okpara's "supplies".' Komi had spoken to others, even outside the group, and they had all expressed the same view. He had been to see his lawyer-politician friend, Bola Ige, and he had asked him to convey the same message; so had Dapo Fatogun, a consistent collaborator from the National Strike of 1964.

Maren shook his head, stubbornly. 'I agree my return should be part of an overall strategy, but something is missing from this one. You see, the people you spoke to are limited in what they can do, even the *Credo* lot. When everything is in place, I'll be on my way.'

Komi sighed. 'I warned them. Well, I'm staying till tomorrow, anyway. When you've slept over it, maybe you'll change your mind. Oh, I nearly forgot, that thug, Kodak . . .'

'He's not a thug, but go on.'

'I ran into him in Mbari. He's been there almost every day since you left.'

'Did he say anything?' Maren tried not to sound too eager.

'Oh, just that we should greet you if we ran into you. But he wasn't all that keen on your returning.'

'What did he say, exactly? Do you remember?'

'Oh yes. Something like: tell *oga* no need to hurry back because he will smell the roast yam wherever he is.'

Maren's expression changed abruptly. 'That is the message you should have given me to start with. We leave tomorrow.'

'But . . . he said there was no need to return.'

'Hn-hm, he's right there. But now I accept it's time to get back.'

'So, what is all that supposed to mean?'

'The fire *this* time,' was all Maren would say.

They sat down to plan his return in detail. It was agreed that he should first make the round of newspapers in Ibadan and Lagos, announce publicly that he was on his way to give himself up and stand trial. The police would not be allowed to claim that they caught him, especially as he was set to deny that he was ever a fugitive from justice. His trip to Enugu was a normal one, taken in the course of his profession. He had been, he could truthfully claim, mostly on Nsukka campus, engaged in academic pursuits. It was there that news came to him that he had been declared a Wanted Man. He spent some days making enquiries about this strange development, then decided, of his own volition, to return to Ibadan.

With Komi following in his own car to keep an eye on his progress, Maren returned to the West and Lagos in a car loaned him by the Eastern Premier, with a driver. He left with a promise that the first consignment of weapons would be assembled, waiting only for him to give the word – when and where they should be delivered.

Dapo Fatogun, his ancient collaborator from the previous year's General Strike, black as the inside of an ancient clay pot, was not home when they arrived but the Alhaja looked in his 'message box' from practice, and knew where he would be at any hour of the day. She quickly despatched her househelp to find him. Dapo arrived soon after, took him in tow into Lagos and drove him round to the media houses.

'Did you hear of the gaolbreak?' he asked.

'Agodi prisons?'

'Yes. Over thirty got out.'

Maren nodded. 'Kodak hasn't been idle.'

'They've set fire to electoral offices in Ilesha.'

'It's only the beginning,' Maren said.

His disguise was a light one, just an *agbada* and cap, and a few faces did a double-take as the car drove by. A few hands waved discreetly and a few eyes winked, indulging in a few moments of conspiratorial alliance. When they returned to Dapo's house, operating a security routine that Dapo had maintained since the earliest days of the *penkelemes*, the landlady in the upstairs flat was alerted. It was a signal Dapo had not been obliged to use for a long time. She turned to her businessman husband, Bode Akindele, and whispered, 'That rebel is back at his game, and the other one is with him. He came this afternoon.'

'Which other one?' he asked, not really curious.

'The Wanted one.'

That made him sit up. 'In this Lagos?'

'They're downstairs in the apartment. They drove into the garage in the dark, then pulled the door behind them.'

Bode Akindele waved his arms across his face. 'I don't want to know. I don't want to see them. You are the rebel in this household, and the day they take you away, I won't even say I know you. Just take them their food and leave me alone. See if there is anything they need, just don't bring me into it.'

The Alhaja smiled at his familiar blustering, gave him a quick embrace, and went to prepare food and rifle the refrigerator for cold beer.

Dapo drove him to Ibadan the following day. They found Femi Johnson rehearsing a play with his amateur group, Players of the Dawn, at the British Council Hall, and whisked him out. Maren stayed the night with Femi while his lawyers sent word that he would be available to be picked up at his Felele house the following morning. But he was driven instead to the police station where the press were waiting. His lawyers had insisted on the ruse, in case he was arrested in his house, then taken to some unknown destination.

In the office that was converted into a detention cell, he was able to receive visitors in between light interrogations, identification parades and discreet observations by Secret Service men, some of whom came in as 'suspects' and were left, with apologies, in the same room with him, while they tried to strike up some form of conversation. The most constant visitor was Femi Johnson, invariably on his way from work, toting a cool-bag containing drinks, and a lunch basket. He stayed long hours, mostly musing on how his friend was coping in such confinement. A wild man from the German radio named Gerd Meuer, braving the xenophobic reaction to foreign pressmen, baffled, irritated and entertained the officers all at the same time; and they finally learnt to live with his unpredictable irruptions. Once he crashed through their latest 'restraining orders' with a picnic basket, laden with an eight-course Indonesian meal, prepared by his wife. Both prisoner and gaolers had their fill of the exotic treat while the Investigation Department continued to seek witnesses, take statements, look for missing bodies. The American researcher had been whisked out of the country for his own good, having begun to go to pieces at the thought that the trail of the recording might lead to him.

Maren braced himself for the visit from his parents, searching well in advance for words that would make them recall every attempt he had made to prepare them for any such circumstances, understand the finality of his decisions, and accept. They came, as he expected, with solemn faces, ushered in by the Inspector, who treated them with the utmost delicacy and respect. They took their seats on the bench, facing him across the wide table. He watched as the mother folded her shawl neatly and placed it beside her handbag. They enquired after his health, then all three fell silent, eyes averted from one another. Maren decided to break the silence with the now familiar routine.

'Who is dead?' he enquired.

But the father threw him off track by responding, 'You have never answered this question I kept asking you. Why did you return the way you did, sneaking in like a thief in the night?'

Maren thought for a moment that he caught a wisp of a smile flit across his face, but this was so unlikely that he dismissed it as a trick of his eyes. He shrugged and repeated his non-question: 'Who is dead?'

'Have you killed anyone?' the father retorted, as if he had now decided to play along.

'Well, you are both wearing such long faces.'

'Is this the sort of place where people smile?' observed the mother.

'Oh yes,' he assured her. 'People smile here quite a lot. All my visitors bring a smile with them, or I tell the police not to let them in.'

'Well, some people are easily satisfied,' the father scoffed, and, yes, Maren was certain that he had seen that ghost of a smile again, quickly suppressed. 'Me, I ought to come here with drummers and dance all the way in. Since I cannot, what is there to smile about?' And the once familiar grin split his face, a huge slice of melon. The father leant across the table and gripped his hands. '*To!*' – and his sigh was one of acceptance – 'Welcome home.' He looked at the mother and she was dabbing her eyes with the corners of the shawl. Then she began to chant his lineage names, moving from paternal line to the maternal and back again in a seamless weave . . . *omo roba, omo 'Laren, omo afotamodi, omo 'Lubiyo* . . . and his head ballooned until it filled the room and began to press against the walls, and he had to beg her to stop.

Christopher Okigbo's visits took on a strange aspect that he could not understand at the time. At the start, there was nothing to remark about them, just a resumption of old discussions, and bawdy reminders of the impromptu use the prisoner would sometimes make of his wall-to-wall white rug, when he came in company late at night. How, he asked, was he coping in this desertland, where there was just a camp-bed that was unfolded only at night, and prying eyes that watched every move and trained ears that would catch any unusual sounds. He brought wine and poems, his latest, which they read aloud, Okigbo mostly, since he loved to *listen* to what his poems said to him, to see if they still were as he had heard them when written – it was that kind of listening when Okigbo read the poems aloud. And the mood then was still the same as when, in his living room at Onireke, not far from Femi Johnson's, or in his study, he grew distant from a point of discussion, fished out sheets covered in his close scrawl, and plaintively asked, almost childlike, 'Please can I just read a few lines of this to you? I want you to tell me – no, honestly – really tell me how it sounds to you.' Now in police detention, towards the end of his stay, and especially just before judgement, Christopher grew remote, concentrating on some source of detachment, yet he continued visiting. Sometimes he would be on the verge of asking, or saying something, and then he would drift off again, his mind in distant concentration . . .

Weeks upon weeks, with the chill and dust of an early Harmattan beginning to penetrate light defences; the police in charge of his case became increasingly desultory, evincing no real indication of a time that he might be brought to court. Admittedly the force was heavily stretched. The fires no longer erupted in ones and twos but had become a pattern, leaping from one town to the next but always restricted to a category of structures. First it was the electoral offices; then the tax offices that the Government had used as agents of intimidation, levying arbitrary rates and taxes, sometimes collective, and carting defaulters into prison in droves. Despite the crispness in the air and the hot Harmattan winds, however, the fires were never out of control. The attack groups conducted their mission with a technical precision. They doused the target area with restraint, and in most cases, waited and ensured that it burnt to ashes without affecting even neighbouring floors or rooms. Even when the attacks shifted to the homes of officials and collaborators, they ordered out the occupants, sprayed the apartment with a cold efficiency, and set it on fire. Adjoining rooms were never affected.

The season of *Weti e** had begun and Maren could indeed smell the roast yam from his place of confinement. What was more important, however, was that the Government could smell it too, and its agents and collaborators were compelled to choose their own prisons. When they could not avoid movement, they dared not utilise official vehicles, and they adopted all forms of disguises. The wind of *Weti e* was also blowing on the streets. Inevitably, it also began to consume human fodder.

Maren instructed *Credo* to commence agitation in the media for his trial or immediate release, then went on hunger strike, and demanded to be transferred to a regular prison cell for criminals. 'You think this comparative comfort substitutes for my rights to a trial?' The Inspector in charge of his confinement pleaded with him, so did the investigating officer, Ugowe. But now he had grown adamant. 'I want an end to this special treatment,' he insisted, 'or

*Spray and ignite.

the commencement of a legal trial.' Reluctantly, they let him pack his books, and he was escorted to the police cells.

On his second night in the cell, already mildly weakened by the hunger strike, he heard a clatter of boots and a hectoring voice demanding, 'Where is he? In which cell is he kept?' He could not hear the desk-sergeant's response, but another shout by the visitor led to the sound of the heavy cell keys being taken down, then the desk-sergeant marching towards his cell, followed by a figure he recognised only too well, attended by six other uniformed officers. The night visitor was none other than Mr Deputy Commissioner, Loremikan.

'Open his door,' he ordered.

The desk-sergeant obeyed. The door was flung open and the huge, hulking figure of menace filled the entrance. He was armed, as usual, with a holstered pistol, and his belt dripped with tear-gas grenades, making him look less dangerous than he might have been because the belt was askew, as was his hat, and his holster was halfway round to the small of his back.

Swinging a heavy truncheon, the riot control brand – certainly one he had taken from one of the lesser officers, or from the desk, since it was not the swagger-stick that belonged to his rank – he glowered for several moments without speaking, appeared in fact to be looking for words, as if, now that he was there, he did not quite remember why he had come. Somehow, it never did occur to the prisoner that his visitor might be drunk, so he merely thought, Now what?, bracing himself for the worst.

'So you are the one making trouble,' he slobbered at last. 'You think you can cause trouble for the Government, and you even make trouble for the police by going on hunger strike, not so? Hunger strike, enh?' And he lunged forward with the truncheon at a speed that belied his seeming lack of coordination, catching Maren squarely in the chest, just beside the left ribcage. He followed it quickly with another jab and stood poised for further assault. The prisoner reeled backwards, winded; his fleeting thought as he slid down the wall was: Oh, they've sent him to kill me.

Loremikan plunged into a stream of obscenities, restrained only by the desk-sergeant who looked shocked and scared. Somehow, the sergeant succeeded in making him retreat without striking any more blows, or perhaps it was the sight of the prisoner gasping for breath, helpless on his haunches, but he appeared to content himself with issuing threats of future visits of the same nature if the prisoner failed to behave himself and cooperate with the police. He left with his squad, the cell door clanged shut, and Maren stood up slowly, listening to the boastful promises and threats trailing away beneath the stomp of boots. It was not such a lethal blow after all, though it hurt quite a lot and left him winded, but not for as long as he had feigned. A split second before the impact, he had somehow succeeded in caving in his stomach, and the impact of the blow was somewhat muted.

The report of the attack had reached his lawyers by morning and, one after the other, they showed up – Onalaja, Olatawura, Ige, Somolu – all young barristers who had offered their services free. They arranged for him to be taken to hospital and X-rayed. The lesions that showed up on the plates were sufficient for them, and for the judge, before whom they took their complaint. Summoning the officer before him, he read him the riot act, then gave orders that the prisoner was to return to the office of the police station, assigning his security specifically to the Inspector who had brought him to court. He would be held responsible for any further acts of assault.

The brief hearing was comic relief, with Loremikan acting the role of a buffoon caught in a moment of indecent exposure. Its sinister side was that he admitted that, on the night of the assault, he was coming straight from the home of Premier Akintola. It was nothing that he could deny, as his movements had been traced backwards for several hours before the assault. No dimension of the ominous could, however, overcome the malicious pleasure the courtroom obtained in watching the all-powerful, all-terrorising demon of the West reduced to a quivering jelly before the implacable presence of the judge, who, determined to extract from him some kind of motivation, or link, repeated over and over again the question: 'But what were you doing there? That was not your station. What business took you there?'

To all of which Loremikan had no answer except to blubber, 'I am sorry, your Lordship. I am very sorry, your Lordship. I apologise very humbly, your Lordship. I promise your Lordship . . .'

Loremikan's evening of violence soon paled, however, becoming nothing but a salutary memory beside the violence that Maren was shortly after compelled to watch, in broad daylight, inflicted on his second daughter, his first by the mother, at Iyaganku police station. A foretaste of that morning had been accorded him the previous afternoon, but that was violence of a verbal kind, and he was not to know of the worse to come, nor remotely suspect the vulnerable vehicle that would be used. The child was not yet three.

The mother had visited him that afternoon, and he had thought it was a visit of the usual kind, routine but friendly. The welcome smile soon froze on his face, however, when she launched into what was either a carefully prepared peroration, or a genuine spill-over of long bottled-up complaints. Nothing was new; he had heard it all before. The assault thus consisted not so much in the content, as in the place and timing. These were, he could hardly help feeling, not quite the right circumstances for complaint about the inadequacy of housekeeping money, especially since the complaint was couched in a language that demanded instant redress, then turned abusive when the prisoner pointed out that the offending cheque, sent her the previous day, contained the entire balance in his account, bar the minimum required to keep the account current. Incredulous, he listened to her fulminate against his lack of consideration, his indifference to the privations endured by his family. He learnt anew the cost of commodities on the market, of children's clothing; was reprimanded on his spendthrift habits, such as his waste of money on the antiquities he was so fond of, at the expense of his children's welfare.

'Come to think of it, who has any interest in those useless things anyway, like the stupid stones you bring me when you travel, your so-called antique jewellery? Your colleagues take their wives to shop for gold jewellery at Boulos, but all I ever get from you are these things you call valuable antiques! If you don't know it, all my friends are embarrassed for me when they see what I have to show for all your junketing all over the world.'

She leapt from one crest of neglect to the next of status dues and personal belittlement; curiously, he waited in vain for charges of philandering, night desertions, real and imaginary affairs . . . no, it was all material indictment. Meanness at home, but prodigality when it came to his own relations. 'You paid for your baby sister to go to the UK when my own children had yet to own a change of shoes, and it's the same for your friends – and what kind of friends are they anyway, those types you call friends, bums, spongers and ne'er-do-wells? – they come to the house and soak themselves in your beer and expect me to feed them. Feed them! From the paltry housekeeping allowance you leave me every month? When do we ever see anything of the royalties you collect on your books? It all goes on such friends, and your own family. Mine has to suffer neglect!'

She reminded him of her generosity in taking his child by first marriage to her bosom, treating him just like any of hers, not making him feel unwanted, never discriminated against, indeed playing a role in repatriating him from England at great risk, yet his gratitude was certainly notable in his gross neglect of her and hers, and so on. But now she had had her fill and would tolerate it no longer. She did not come from a pauper's home, would not accept to be treated like a pauper and if he thought she would remain content with this measly allowance . . . she flung the cheque at him, took off with high heels clattering, entering the Simca that he had bought her the previous year – admittedly second-hand – and drove off in a fit of sophisticate fury.

It was all declaimed in a loud piercing voice that carried down the corridor, but it was afternoon, and only a few officers were present. The nearest was his guardian Inspector next door, who did not have to listen to overhear every word. After the car was driven off, he waited several moments, then came in, stood silently watching the prisoner as he tried to return to his reading.

Finally, he asked, 'Was that your wife?'

The prisoner nodded, attempting a smile. The Inspector waited some moments longer, sighed, and returned to his office.

The following morning, she returned, on the way to her full-time employment as Medical Librarian in the University Hospital, a 'Senior Service' position. Her car circled the driveway roundabout, then a door opened, and she shooed out all the children. The eldest made his way to the entrance, the youngest was piggy-backed by a maid. The victim, however, clung to the top of the wound-down window, crying her lungs out. And then, from mere distress, a scene of terror developed, thanks to a fortuitous, but not unusual occurrence. The distress turned to fear and desperation as the girl clung to the edge of the door and was compelled to trot after the car while her mother peeled off her hands and edged the vehicle forward. She had only one free hand and the girl clung to the door with both, so that as soon as the mother peeled off one hand and moved to remove the other, the girl replaced the first, with the car moving forward all the time. The struggle – it had to be called that – had moved in fits and jerks to the junction where the roundabout opened into the straight driveway, when there came a roar from the improvised landing pad, a lawn hidden from the frontage by the row of offices – it would normally be used for identification and other parades. The girl looked back, frightened by the noise, then her eyes grew big with terror as a helicopter rose over the row of offices, then banked in the direction of the driveway, its propellers whipping up the dust of an early November Harmattan. She screamed. Then she plunged her short arms over the door and tried to climb the smooth side of the door, her feet scrabbling and slipping against metal.

Her screams were heard above the helicopter's roar by officers and their clients alike, as they all rushed to windows and the main porch, then remained frozen in place by the sight of a woman at the wheel of her car, now flinging off the arms of a young child who was clinging to the car and attempting to climb in. With a final effort the woman succeeded, the car plunged forward, as if also propelled by the menace of the helicopter. As if the spell was suddenly broken, all rushed towards the fallen child. Ugowe, the investigator, was in the lead. He snatched her up even before the prisoner moved, his heels glued to the floor by sheer disbelief, a total block against the reality of the action as it developed, or perhaps a conviction that the game must terminate in the next micro-moment, that it could not last one eyeblink longer – no, it's a bluff, it is not happening, it cannot be happening, she cannot possibly . . . But she was already tearing down the driveway, indifferent to the shouts that rang out from the windows, the threats, pleas, and orders that she should return. So at last Maren succeeded in prising his feet off the floor, rushed out to take the screaming, struggling girl from Ugowe's hands, and attempt to calm her down from her hysteria.

Ugowe was trembling from rage. All he could do was stutter, 'I'm issuing a warrant for her arrest. I am going to arrest her and have her locked up. She dared . . . dared abandon a child . . . like that? In this station? I swear she will sleep in a cell tonight!'

The crowd was unbearable, police officers, complainants, suspects and court cases, pouring out sympathy, voicing outrage . . . He pleaded with them to leave him alone, just for now, please, just for now. 'I need a little time just to calm the child down. I'll be better on my own, believe me. She'll be OK, just give me some moments with her.'

The Inspector was very understanding, ushered out even those who were normally accommodated in the prisoner's office-cell from the overflow of other offices, during working hours. A few moments later, the door opened gently and he slipped in bottles of soft drinks which he must have commandeered from the upstairs refrigerator in his superior's office.

Gradually, the child regained some calm, though she still sniffed from time to time as she sucked her Fanta orange through a straw. Maren's gaze embraced all three children, began planning immediately for their temporary resettlement. It would be temporary, too temporary he regretted, and might not even take place at all. It was all too likely that they would be back in their home in Felele any moment, certainly before he could take the measures he had swiftly decided upon for their welfare. He braced himself once more for the ties and claims of blood, and this time there was no escape; for the first time since his arrest, he truly and bitterly felt himself a prisoner. He did not need to be told that very soon there would be a flock of relations, too embarrassed for words, pleading, imploring, chanting his lineage names, reminding him of his given names, reciting his accolades. He knew that her mother would be among the very first, that she would not walk in but would take the headgear off her head, wear it like a sash around her waist and wail as one in mourning. Nothing would suffice her, he feared, but to roll on the floor, side to side, or drag herself on her knees until she reached him, as if a great tragedy had befallen the family, as indeed it had. An abomination, would be the family pronouncement, no less. And then, of course, his own family, and his parents would follow, and it would amount to more than a foot in the doorway. Unlike the

events that had made him a prisoner, this affair was one in which
even he could not deny them their duty, as one family wedded to
another. And they would accept their portion with good grace,
which was to do the noble thing, to act with generosity.

But it was the visitation of the mother-in-law that he dreaded
most, knowing he could never survive her assumption of a dishonour
that was not hers; he could never let her subject herself to any
abasement at his feet. So he sat by the window, waiting to catch the
first glimpse of her descending from a taxi or the car of a commandeered relation, probably flanked by sisters and cousins, or her
parish priest and counsellors, or members of her guild, brought
along to ease, by sharing, the burden that she had fully assumed.
He began to rehearse his lines, keeping his body at the ready to leap
out, and meet her before she even arrived at the porch, reassure her
that it was nothing, it was all settled, just a moment's aberration,
and nothing that touched his love for the family, his affection for
her, nothing that could divorce the two families, and please you
must go home and not worry your head one moment longer . . .

But it was over. He knew in his heart it was over. And the
Harmattan drift, as usual, tossed around a burnt wisp of grass from
nowhere and yes, he thought, there goes that relationship that tried
to be a marriage. It will hang on, as with many others he had seen,
for a while longer, while the currents swirl around and lend it a
semblance of life, and then it will come down nowhere, disintegrate,
finis.

XIII Pro-epilogue

On the eve of the November verdict, Femi Johnson arrived with a full basket of food, wines and beer, and a flask of coffee, with every appearance of staying all evening, indeed all night if he was allowed.

'What is this?' Maren smiled. 'A wake?'

'You are devious,' he said.

'We've been through all that,' Maren protested.

'No, no, no, I still can't get over it, and it has taught me my lesson. I refuse to trust you from here to there, or from now till daybreak.'

'Now, what's all this about? That is, why all this all over again?'

He applied the corkscrew to the bottle, shaking his head. 'I still can't get over it. Until my dying day – Mike and I talk about it all the time. I mean, we were all there. When Michael mentioned the broadcast, you said nothing, no reaction, nothing whatever. Me, I was dying for the inside gist, as usual. But that mind of yours was already ticking. We sat there eating and drinking, while you had gone into overdrive . . .'

'Look, pour the wine and leave that ancient history alone.'

'Ancient history!' he nearly screamed. 'The verdict is tomorrow, that's future history, not ancient. And knowing you, or rather, not knowing you, I won't even bother to ask what surprise you and your gang may be springing. Because, don't bother to tell me – I won't believe it. Don't even try to persuade me that you'll go to gaol quietly if the verdict goes against you. I tell you in advance – you're lying!'

'I haven't said anything.'

'Nobody's asking you. You'll only lie. And my driver agrees with me – that's him outside, go and ask him if you don't believe me.

And he's been making my life a hell. Every day, the same story. "You are his friend," he says, "What are you doing to help him?" He's a fanatic!'

'You've done everything I asked of you. Tell him to stop bothering you.'

'I've tried. There's no stopping him!'

They clinked glasses and Femi got up, looked through the window, then said, 'In fact, why don't I call him so you can tell him yourself to stop preaching at me?'

Maren watched him leave the office, but he never reappeared at the window and did not approach the car. Instead, he heard his soft walk along the corridor. Femi re-crossed the entrance to the office, walking casually past the Inspector's office, turned at the end, and returned into the room. Regaining his seat quickly, he leant towards him and spoke tensely.

'I just wanted to make sure there were no snoopers around. Now, let me be quick. I'm only guessing, but if you do need a car, I've told Yekini it's all yours. You can take it anywhere you want; it doesn't matter whether or not I ever see it again. Or Yekini for that matter. Both of them are yours. He'll be parked just behind Court No. 3. You know the tree where the women sell cigarettes, kola nuts and things – that's where he'll be.'

'Look, Femi . . .'

'I know you have your own organisation, and I know you have your plans. I'm only letting you know that you have a spare car and driver, and there'll be two jerry cans of fuel, and a cooler loaded with food and drinks. When I leave, I'll tell him to come in and pick up the basket; then you give him whatever instructions you want. I don't have to know anything unless you want me to. Whether it's to take off at top speed anywhere, or create an obstruction or diversion or whatever, or simply meet you somewhere else – he *wants* to do something. Anything, for you. That's all. I don't have the stomach for this kind of thing, but there are thousands who are prepared to lay down their lives for this cause – I'm not telling you anything you don't know already – Yekini is only one of them.'

Maren stared at him, astonished and deeply moved. They had had long discussions all through his visits; he knew how strongly Femi felt, but never, not for one moment did he suspect that he would actually go beyond lending morale to the cause. He looked through the window at the figure of Yekini, calmly seated at the wheel of the car.

'All right,' he said at last. 'But not tomorrow. There'll be no need for anything tomorrow, except to listen to the verdict, and make my statement in the open court, if I'm to be sentenced.'

'You know of course that you are being held responsible for the *Weti e*.'

'They have to blame someone.'

He grunted. 'Hm. You're not involved, I suppose.'

Maren laughed. 'But Femi, you know I've been in detention all this while. The police themselves are my alibi.'

'Alibi or not, it's made the Government determined to see that you get a life sentence. That's why the charge is armed robbery. And there are rumours of pressure being put on the judge.'

'We know. Our friends at Oniyanrin linked us up with a few phone calls to the judge from Akintola & Co. He told them to get their Attorney to do his own duty because he intended to do nothing but his. Even if he finds me guilty, that's all right with us.'

'But how do you think it will go?'

'I do not think. I only know that the judge will administer justice, that's all. That's all we ask for. My lawyers have finished their task. All we can do now is wait.'

'And if you're found guilty? Do you realise what that means? Life!'

'Femi, I assure you, there is no Life Resident among any gaol titles I am likely to acquire in the immediate future. Even if I leave the court for prison tomorrow, wait and see what happens. Beyond Ibadan, do you see any signs of Government control anywhere in the West?'

'Well, even in Ibadan . . . where's the authority?'

'Good, I'm glad you've noticed. Just set my place at your usual end-of-year splurge, because I'll be there in person. The *penkelemes* is about to end – at least for now.'

'You think that? Only for now?'

'I am convinced of it. And it's nothing new. I've carried it on my head since I first met these people – the Independence leaders – as a student. At the beginning, mind you, I did believe that our battle front was Southern Africa. That was what I began to prepare towards – enrolling in the University Officer Corps and all that, just to get the training. In Infantry. You know, I was threatened with court-martial once, during the Suez war.'

Femi's mouth opened wide. In Infantry. 'You were involved in that? You really are a secretive bastard!'

'No. I was *not* involved. I refused to be involved. I received my call-up papers and I said, "Sorry, no, the Suez is the wrong stop. If you're heading further south, I'm with you, but I didn't join your University Corps for some halfway stop where I have no business. I was lucky. If I had been from the Colony, I would have been court-martialled: you know there was that difference at the time, Lagos being Colony and the rest mere Protectorate. I packed my kit-bag – it's probably still where I left it in the attic of my digs in Ash Grove – and I moved out. It would be interesting to stop there one of these days, see if it's still there . . .'

'I need another drink,' Femi said, and filled their glasses. 'And this food is getting cold. All I can say is that you are – yes, I've said it already – devious and secretive. And I feel sorry for those two poor people at Aké.'

'I was not alone there, you know. Quite a few of us felt that way, and not just from Nigeria. It was South Africa, South Africa all the way: you can't imagine the idealism. The first-generation National-ists would take care of the simple business of running a government while we marched south. It was the glory idyll of a kind of *Internationale* all over again, only, this time, on the African Continent. And then, of course, one stumbled into the huge emptiness of mind of those first-come politicians, a bottomless pit filled with nothing but *penkelemes* . . . Then you knew that the task would have to begin here; the trouble is, who knows when it will have an end?'

The mood turned sombre, as the moment approached for Femi to take his leave. Maren opened the newspaper that he used as a file for his jottings, took out a foolscap sheet of paper which was already neatly folded in four, and ran his eye quickly over its con-tents, as if making a final check.

'What is it?'

'Did you follow the press conference of the Government, after the massacre in Ijero? The market, the school . . .'

'Oh yes: the "No blood flows" insult upon injury. I wish I could have . . . !' Femi ground his teeth.

Maren handed over the folded sheet. 'A christmas card.'

His visitor was alarmed. 'What's this? You never send out christmas . . . Ugh!'

Maren nodded. 'The people took it out on that wretched chief, who they decided was a collaborator, tied him to a tree and drove a six-inch nail through his head. I thought I'd use it as a theme. Doig Simmonds designed it for me. The poem is inside.'

'You want me to return it to him?'

'That's your copy. Reproduce it and send it to all your clients. And anyone else you can think of. The Government people will get theirs – courtesy of CWIL.'

'CWIL?'

'The Committee of Writers for Individual Liberty. It's the front for *Credo*. I'll tell you all about it after the verdict. Read it aloud: I want to hear how it sounds, as Okigbo would say.'

Femi Johnson took his time, first going through the lines silently. Then he cleared his throat and his baritone voice purred softly in the improvised cell:

> *Playing Christ is a historic art and elevating:*
> *A six-inch nail through frontal lobes*
> *Lifts a man to heavenly glory and, for a miracle –*
>
> *No blood flows. Only a clam-lipped path*
> *Through grey tissues. Even thus spake*
> *Naaman the captain, precise in thrust of words –*
>
> *NO BLOOD FLOWS! All but he (Saviour Self-Elect)*
> *Can hear the broken bells about his neck, loud*
> *In warning of the approach of an abomination.*
>
> *Only he – lord of all necropolis – reigns blind*
> *To the floating wraith, to the banner of blood*
> *Jubilant before his cain-branded brow . . .*
>
> *A thousand dead is the death of all, bleed we*
> *However little. Since history's retrogress*
> *Has touched us, our minds adjust to a brief heritage*

When mothers die, who would not stoop to kiss
A leper's feet, die of suckling lead. Peace.
To the dead of Ijero; silence will not immure you.

greetings

"Oba found tied to   NEWS ITEM
tree, with a nail
through his head"

                    "No blood flows"
                    - NAAMAN the captain.